In Search of Clusters

The Coming Battle in
Lowly Parallel Computing

Gregory F. Pfister

For book and bookstore information

http://www.prenhall.com

Prentice Hall PTR
Upper Saddle River, New Jersey 07458

Library of Congress Cataloging-in-Publication Data

```
Pfister, Gregory F.
    In search of clusters / Gregory F. Pfister.
      p. cm.
    Includes bibliographical references and index.
    ISBN 0-13-437625-0
    1. Parallel computers. 2. Client/server computing.  I. Title
QA76.58.P49  1995
004'.35--dc20                              95-11238
                                           CIP
```

Editorial/production supervision: *Ann Sullivan*
Interior design and composition: *Phyllis Eve Bregman*
Manufacturing manager: *Alexis R. Heydt*
Acquisitions editor: *Gregory G. Doench*
Editorial assistant: *Meg Cowen*
Cover design:

© 1995 by Prentice Hall PTR
Prentice-Hall, Inc.
A Simon & Schuster Company
Upper Saddle River, New Jersey 07458

The publisher offers discounts on this book when ordered in bulk quantities.
For more information, contact:

Corporate Sales Department
PTR Prentice Hall
One Lake Street
Upper Saddle River, NJ 07458

Phone: 800-382-3419, Fax: 201-236-7141
E-mail: corpsales@prenhall.com

Printed in the United States of America
10 9 8 7 6 5 4 3 2

ISBN: 0-13-437625-0

Prentice-Hall International (UK) Limited, *London*
Prentice-Hall of Australia Pty. Limited, *Sydney*
Prentice-Hall Canada Inc., *Toronto*
Prentice-Hall Hispanoamericana, S.A., *Mexico*
Prentice-Hall of India Private Limited, *New Delhi*
Prentice-Hall of Japan, Inc., *Tokyo*
Simon & Schuster Asia Pte. Ltd., *Singapore*
Editora Prentice-Hall do Brasil, Ltda., *Rio de Janeiro*

Trademarks

My esteemed colleagues in IBM Austin Intellectual Property Law have informed me that since IBM expects other people to respect our trademarks, IBM employees must respect theirs, too. That sounds reasonable. But more to the point, their approval is required for external publication of this work, and they won't give it unless all trademarks used are flagged as trademarks when they're first used. They also told me that a section like this, appearing before the text (and in this case, necessarily before the table of contents) satisfies requirements: It's the first use, and it's flagged. So, here's the fine print:

CXT 1000 is a trademark of Ancor Inc. Chorus is a trademark of Chorus Software Systems, Inc. Convex and ConvexNQS are trademarks of Convex Computer Corp. Cray and Y-MP are trademarks of Cray Research, Inc. Data General High Availability is a trademark of Data General, Inc. Alpha AXP, DEC, DECsafe, PDP, Star Coupler, VAX, VAXCluster, VAXen, VMS, and microVAX are trademarks of Digital Equipment Corp. Encore is a trademark of Encore Computers, Inc. Load Balancer is a trademark of Freedman Sharp and Associates Inc. Fusion High Availability is a trademark of Fusion Systems, Inc. Gould and Reflective Memory are trademarks of Gould Computer Systems, Inc. Apollo, Domain, HP, HP Series 700, NCS, Network Computing Services, and Switchover UX are trademarks of the Hewlett-Packard Company. INGRES is a trademark of INGRES Corp. IDS and ISIS are trademarks of ISIS Development Systems, Inc. Informix is a trademark of Informix Software, Inc. iPSC, Paragon, and Intel Scientific Supercomputers are trademarks of Intel, Inc. AIX, CICS, CICS/6000, DATABASE 2, DB2, DB2/6000, ES/9000, ESCON, ESSL, EUI, HACMP/6000, IBM System/370, IBM, JES3, LoadLeveller, MVS/ESA, NETBIOS, NetView, OS/2, POWER/4, PowerPC, PowerServer, PS/2, RACF, RISC System/6000, RMF, S/370, S/390, SP2, Sysplex Timer, System/370, System/390, TCF, Transparent Computing Facility, and VTAM are trademarks of International Business Machines Corp. Locus Cluster is a trademark of Locus Computer Corp. FUSION is a trademark of Locus Computer Corp. and International Business Machines Corp. Lotus and Lotus Notes are trademarks of Lotus Development Corp. X Window System is a trademark of Massachusetts Institute of Technology. NCube is a trademark of NCube, Inc. Lifekeeper, NCR, NCR3400, NCR 3600 and Teradata are trademarks of National Cash Register, and therefore probably of AT&T. Novelle, NetWare, and Machine-Independent NetWare are trademarks of Novell Inc. DME, Distributed Management Environment, OSF/1, OSF/1 AD DCE, Distributed Computing Environment, DFS, and Distributed File system are trademarks of the Open Software Foundation, Inc. Oracle, Oracle Parallel Server and Oracle Version 7 are trademarks of Oracle Corp. Express is a trademark of Parasoft Corp. Utopia Load Sharing Facility is a trademark of Platform Computing Corp. Pyramid and Pyramid Reliant are trademarks of Pyramid Computer Corp. Network Linda is a trademark of Scientific Computing Associates Inc. HiAv Symmetry, Sequent, Symmetry 2000/990 are trademarks of Sequent Computer Systems, Inc. SGI is a trademark of Silicon Graphics, Inc. SPECint92 and SPECfp92 are trademarks of the Standard Performance Evaluation Council. NFS, Network File System, ONC, Open Network Computing, Open*V High Availability, and Sun are trademarks of Sun Microsystems, Inc. All SPARC trademarks are trademarks or registered trademarks of SPARC International, Inc. SPARCcluster, SPARCcluster 1, SPARCcluster 1000, SPARCcluster 2000, and SPARCstation are licensed exclusively to Sun Microsystems, Inc. Products bearing SPARC trademarks are based on an architecture developed by Sun Microsystems, Inc. SSI is a trademark of Supercomputing Systems, Inc, R.I.P., but the abbreviation "SSI" is not used in that sense in this document. Navigation Server and Sybase are trademarks of Sybase, Inc. Integrity, CLX, and Cyclone are trademarks of Tandem Computers Inc. NCADMIN, NCLOGIN, and NQS/Exec are trademarks of The Cummings Group, Inc. Encina is a trademark of Transarc Inc. UNIX and SVR5 are registered trademarks of X/Open Company, Ltd. Ethernet is a trademark of Xerox Corp. (I never knew that!) Xerox is a trademark of Xerox Corp.

AIX is used as a short form for AIX operating system. AIX/6000 V3 is used as a short form of AIX Version 3 for RISC System/6000. UNIX is used as a short form for UNIX operating system.

All other product names mentioned herein may be trademarks or registered trademarks of other manufacturers. We respectfully acknowledge any such that have not been included above. The preceding two sentences are believed to be a registered legal incantation warding off malign influences. Sort of like garlic.

Table of Contents

In Search of Clusters ✳

List of Figures

List of Tables

Preface

Anyone having anything to do with computers that are to be servers or multiuser systems should buy and read this book. That includes purchasers, sellers, planners, programmers, administrators, hardware designers, software architects, and any other roles or job titles I've left out of that list.

Key needs of those systems—high performance, an ability to grow, high availability, appropriate cost, and so on—imply the use of parallel processing: multiple computing elements used together as a single entity. Parallel processing, with a bit of distributed processing, is what this book is about; it will give you the background needed to understand where the real issues lie in that realm. However, this doesn't mean that this book discusses "highly" or "massively" parallel computers. Those are flamboyant enough to have already attracted a multitude of variably successful explanations and are really of direct interest only in a vanishingly small fraction of the computer market.

Instead, this book uniquely discusses both the hardware and the software of "lowly" parallel computers, the everyday, practical work gangs of computing: symmetric multiprocessors and, in particular, *clusters* of computers. Every major manufacturer of computers, both open systems and proprietary, offers both of those. Really. Right now. Even though you may never have heard of clusters, and if you have, you quite possibly associate them with the bad old days of proprietary glass-house mainframes or plexiglass-house minicomputers.

You do not have to be a died-in-the-denim "techie" to enjoy and profit from this book. Its form and content reflect the author's experience in explaining these issues quite literally hundreds of times to people with at best a semi-technical background. This has included customers who have better things to do with their time than become computer technophiles; marketing reps, both the technically oriented and the Jag-driving backslappers; and development managers, who too often think they have better things to do with their time than understand the technological base of their business.

You do need familiarity with the current computing milieu. An ability to (mostly) understand the thick, monthly computer magazines demonstrates a background adequate to get a lot out of this book. In some areas this may even be overkill. If you've understood this preface so far, you're in good shape.

But that this book has been written to be accessible does not mean that it is *Ye Compleate Moron's Guide to a Child's Garden of Stupid Tiny BASIC Tricks,* either. Its content is definitely not technically trivial. Because it approaches both parallel and distributed systems from a nonstandard viewpoint, that of clusters (which, as is explained, don't really exist) (yet), it offers a fresh perspective that can potentially enrich both. As discussed below in "History," technically sophisticated readers have profited from previous versions that weren't publicly published. Of particular interest have been the analysis of single system image and the characterization of the programming models used in commercial computing.

One result of this unusual perspective is that while many different groups of people will find many items of interest herein, many are also going to find something to be annoyed about:

> ➤ Promoters of distributed systems will be annoyed when the book points out that their already diametrically challenged systems have ignored a significant area, one whose support will of course add even more expense. Also, they may not have realized they were in league with the next category.

> ➤ Vendors and designers of heroically large symmetric multiprocessors will be annoyed when the book points to those systems' inevitable decline, and therefore warns readers to avoid addiction to their products—a new form of being "locked in," just like the bad old days, but this time "locked in" to a declining architecture, not necessarily a specific manufacturer.

- Cluster proponents will be annoyed where the book airs of the real meaning of the industry-standard benchmarks for clusters.

- Highly massive parallelizers are already annoyed. "Flamboyant"? "A vanishingly small fraction of the computer market"? For that matter, "highly massive"?

- All traditional proponents of parallelism will be vexed because, unlike other books talking about parallelism, this one does not try to say that parallel programming can be easy or will be if only enough funding were applied to the problem. Rather, it demonstrates that parallel programming is hard; and therefore mainstream software cannot directly use it, since any increase in the difficulty of writing software simply cannot be absorbed by the industry. There is a way around this conundrum, an already commonly used but formally ignored technique that is often deprecated by parallelizers; that technique forms a major theme of this book.

- Purchasers of server systems will, I sincerely hope, be happy to be given a straight, comprehensible story for once. It is really for them that this book is being written. But they may well be annoyed, too, since this book also points out that there's currently little real support available for the direction the industry will very likely take within the time-frame of large projects just now beginning. I wish I had better news, but contained in the conclusions are suggestions indicating how the process can be accelerated.

The humor- and irony-impaired will also have a spot of trouble here and there.

Finally, this book will also annoy those uncomfortable unless information is presented using the puritanical parody of "the" scientific method taught to my middle- and high-school children: Just the dry facts, ma'am, boring is fine, it means we're not contaminating ourselves with preconceived notions. All that practice serves to do is to hide the actual prejudices of the presenter, be they conscious or unconscious. That situation is far from true here.

The only reason this book exists is that I am convinced that clusters of machines are good for us, the members of the computer industry; clusters will happen whether or not we like the idea; and many of us are proceeding to make the inevitable transition almost maximally painful. Its purpose is to convince you, too. Whether or not you end up agreeing with me, this book will explain an awful lot about lowly parallel computer systems—clusters and symmetric multiprocessors—without the rose-colored classes usually coloring most views of those subjects.

History

This book began several years ago, while I was a participant in an internal IBM work group. Formed from members of several development laboratories and Divisions of IBM, the group's charter was to figure out what to do with, or about, the groups of computers being called *clusters*.

Clusters had, of course, existed for many years as commercially available products from several computer vendors, although just how common they were none of us really understood at that time. They appeared to have been, if not niche products, at least outside the mainstream of the greater computer milieu. But now they seemed to be popping up all over the place. These new clusters were not formal products from vendors but rather informal bunches of computers assembled by customers. Those worthies were using bunches of computers in a number of ways that were both technically interesting and, we hoped, commercially useful and exploitable. In addition, there were some group members making deep, or at least loud, arguments in favor of clusters as a particularly efficient and attractive product offering.

Interesting stuff. My own interest was less than overwhelming, however. This was not because of the topic, but because of the situation. I was jaded. This was far from the first working group on various parallel architectures that I'd been involved in. I could tell it wouldn't be the last, either, since like most of the others, it was going nowhere fast. A basic problem was that this collection of generally rather high-level, intelligent, and experienced computer architects, software system architects, technical strategists, product designers, researchers, and market analysts didn't know what in Sam Hill they were talking about.

No, that's actually wrong. We did have a problem, but it was the nearly the exact opposite of that one. Each individual knew precisely what he or she was talking about. They were (mostly) rather smart folks and were earnestly expressing worthwhile, useful points. But each person's point of view, and often what they meant by seemingly common words, was completely or (even worse) subtly different from most of the others. So the discussion was going in circles and everyone was trying, with decidedly varying intensity and success, to believe that everyone else was not a complete dolt.

Communication was just not happening because we differed at every possible level: feasible market and application areas, appropriate performance measures, the amount and type of software support necessary, whether that support could be "open," what "open" meant in this context, what if anything all that implied for hardware, what the "natural" hardware (whatever *that* was) implied for software, where applications and subsystems were going to come from, and so on *ad nauseam*. Nobody could even use what seemed simple terms (for example, "single system image") without significant misunderstanding by others.

It was probably fortunate that I was bored. If my mind hadn't been wandering, I probably would have "contributed" more, listened less, and never realized that this meta-problem of communication was lurking below the surface of the more obvious morass. Since anything was obviously better than actively participating in yet another accursed work group, I began to work out how some of the various positions were different and what their relationships were.

That lead to my collecting in an organized form various aspects of "clusters," whatever that meant, simply to give us the common vocabulary without which progress was impossible. The outcome was a presentation that was at first short, but incrementally expanded to include possible hardware organization, aspects of software support, a number of examples, and finally a definition of the term "cluster." As I picked up more information or realized something else, I just kept fitting it into the presentation's organization, massaging that organization as necessary to make things flow logically.

The original work group was soon enough disbanded; this had become a personal project with a life of its own, and it was becoming larger than I realized at the time. I gave parts of the presentation several times, in various circumstances, and the whole thing exactly once. Yes, to Another Work Group. To my amazement, one of the audience observed when I concluded that the complete presentation took approximately 16 hours, spread over two days. That time did include a large amount of lively discussion; otherwise I'd probably still be hoarse.

I concluded that the circumstances leading to my having a captive audience for that long were at least unusual, and certainly unlikely to be repeated. If this material was to be of use to anybody, it had to be in a different form. So I stayed home for two weeks of intense effort and wrote out in prose a lengthy white paper based on that presentation.

That white paper, an internal document completed in the early fall of 1992, was version 1 of *In Search of Clusters*. I made about 100 copies, informally distributed it to people who I suspected might be interested, and, well, just stopped. There were other things to do.

I later found out that the copying machines had been busy. *In Search of Clusters* had become, informally, what amounted to required reading in the newly formed Power Parallel Systems group in the IBM Kingston laboratory, as well as in the Future Systems group in Austin and several groups in IBM Research. Not that they agreed with all of it or even modelled their projects after its precepts, but it apparently had succeeded in providing a useful set of common terms and concepts in their contexts. Comments and suggestions, both pro and con, of course began arriving.

About a year later, members of the IBM AIX Executive Briefing Center in Austin contacted me. They had been requested to provide the IBM field and marketing forces a paper that would clear up what the differences were between various forms of parallel, distributed, and clustered computing—one of those so-called market "positioning" statements. After spending several months attempting this themselves, they had come across *In Search of Clusters*. It had the information they needed, and they wanted to distribute it. This implied some work to eliminate the company-confidential elements, but at one year old those were history anyway. So, I did that, added a good amount of information I'd collected over the intervening year, did some substantial re-editing, and published it electronically by placing softcopy on the internal IBM distribution facility called MKTTOOLS.

That was version 2 of *In Search of Clusters*, an "IBM Internal Use Only" 80-page document completed in September of 1993. About 1500 people obtained copies from MKTTOOLS. The copying machines have also been busy again, since it's not the simplest thing to print a 70 page document in the field in IBM, especially one translated into the common IBM printing format from PostScript® (this process usually creates huge files that print at an incredibly slow rate). I also made it available within IBM development by an easier-to-access electronic means that does not keep track of requests; from inquiries back to me, I know that has seen substantial use. I estimate that at least 2000 copies got into circulation within IBM.

Along with that circulation came a stream of electronic mail and telephone calls from the field with many comments, a fair number of kudos, and could I please make a version that wasn't "internal use only" so they could give it to customers? In addition, word inevitably began to leak out of IBM. I saw several postings to USENET discussion groups on the Internet of the form "I hear there's this paper on clusters or something that somebody in IBM wrote. Anybody know where I can get a copy?" It sounded like time for a completely unclassified version 3.

Well, somehow despite my day job I managed to put that version together. In the six months that had passed since version 2, the entire chapter on "Examples" had been made obsolete by new product announcements; but the basic structure and content had stood up well. Comments from readers indicated that several other chapters needed expansion, so that was done along with some further general tweaking. By this time it had grown to over 140 pages. Problem. This was too long to be a white paper. I was wondering what to do with it when I accidentally heard of a seminar being run by the Austin IBM "Technical Author Recognition Program," a seminar for anyone who interested in publishing books—at which representatives of publishing companies would be present. Bingo.

What you are holding is essentially version 4 of that original 16-hour presentation. It's been greatly expanded, brought up-to-date, and reshaped by feedback from a large number of internal IBM readers. The book format—translation: more words than I ever thought I'd write—has allowed me to make the treatment of most topics much more self-contained than the original, which more or less assumed that the reader was a competent, practicing computer hardware or software architect. It also allowed me to include several new nonbackground elements, such as the chapter explaining why we need the concept of a cluster.

It's been a long, interesting trip for me. I hope you enjoy the ride, too.

Acknowledgments

I am very grateful for the rather enlightened policy IBM maintains towards book authors, which provided both support for writing this book and motivation to complete it. None of the views expressed herein are necessarily those of the IBM Corporation, of course.

I am also grateful for the support of my family, who gracefully put up with the seemingly interminable periods of seclusion I needed to get this done: my children Danielle and Jonathan, and, of course, my wife, Cyndee Stines Pfister—who said this was probably her only chance to get her name in a book. There it was.

My thoughts about clusters and symmetric multiprocessors, and this book in particular, have benefitted tremendously from discussions over many years with a large number of people, both within and outside IBM. There are too many to mention all of them individually, but a few deserve special mention. The elaboration of workload characteristics occurred in discussion with Tilak Agerwala, who set me on the topic of clusters to begin with. (I originally didn't want to do it, since it involved all that ugly "distributed stuff.") Recognition that there were levels of single system image first occurred in discussions with Patrick Goal; a number of "at large" discussions with Patrick also contributed greatly. Jim Cox helped further my understanding of single system image concepts, along with other members of the Yet Another Work Group that met in the fall of '92. Jim also contributed to my understanding of system management issues. None of these fine people are to be blamed, of course, if I mutilate their knowledge in this book.

But the people who are most to be thanked are the IBM customers I met with during the summer of 1991, as part of a kind of technical market-survey exercise primarily targeting another set of issues. I began that exercise with a specific notion of what a "cluster" was. The customers I met had myriad other, very different notions. The disparities between the many expressed views are what first sent me in search of clusters.

Greg Pfister
May, 1995
Austin, Texas
pfister@austin.ibm.com

Part 1:

What Is a Cluster, and Why Use Them?

Introduction

There are three ways to do anything faster:

1. Work harder.

2. Work smarter.

3. Get help.

Work harder is familiar to all of us. Ancient Sumerians probably worked extra hours for the last few days before a Priest-King's inspection of a Ziggurat. "Crunch time" has been with us forever and applies to artistic-intellectual tasks as well as physical ones: Michaelangelo carried his lunch with him up the scaffolding so he wouldn't have to stop while painting the Sistine Chapel ceiling. We may not like it, but we've all done it and we know it works.

But working harder often isn't enough. It's nearly always better, and often necessary, to find a way to reduce the amount work needed to accomplish something. That's what *working smarter* is all about. Management consultants found it particularly profitable to hawk this one in the United States during the last decade's preoccupation with oriental competition. Despite such hype, doing anything more efficiently has a positive flavor; everyone likes to get more with less effort. Large examples, such as Henry Ford's automobile assembly line, have become cultural icons.

Finally, if you can't do it fast enough alone, no matter how much you sweat or how much intelligence you apply to the problem, you can always *get help*. This works, too, whether it's a road gang or an army. But this method has a curious ambivalence associated with it. Several people can almost always dig a ditch, build a house, or write a big computer program faster than one. Committees, however, are notorious for wasting time and producing inferior results; "the right way, the wrong way, and the army way" is proverbial; and bureaucrats, who are necessary to coordinate large group efforts, are universally satirized as slow, bumbling, incompetent, and wrong-headed—except, of course, by other bureaucrats. Getting help certainly works, but everyone is well aware that it can go awry.

And so it is with computers:

	In a computer:
1. Work harder.	processor speed
2. Work smarter.	algorithms
3. Get help.	parallel processing

1.1 Working Harder_____

Simply making the basic guts of a computer run faster, as often measured rather imperfectly by its clock speed, works very well indeed to increase performance. The beast simply *works harder* on everything, all the time. It has the electronic equivalent of a faster metabolism.

The advances that have been made in this area, and can reliably be predicted to continue, are nothing short of astonishing. Intel, for example, has increased the speed of its X86 architecture microprocessors 450 times between the introduction of that architecture in 1978 and mid-1994 [Hal94]. This is an astonishing 47% annual cumulative growth rate (CGR) over 16 years. Vendors of RISC architecture workstations have done even better over a shorter haul. Virtually every member of that club—Hewlett-Packard, MIPS, IBM, and Sun in particular—have declared that they will double their system performance every 18 months. That corresponds to a 60% CGR. Never in recorded history has any human-created process increased its speed at a sustained rate like this.

The end is not yet in sight for the advances in circuit technology, semiconductor processes, lithography, and the other assorted techniques that enhance basic circuit speed, resulting in ever faster computers. Economic empires are rising and falling as a direct result—and don't think for a minute that the last shoe has dropped or the fat lady has sung. There's more in store than anybody realizes, because no one is mentally equipped to truly comprehend the exponential growth that's involved here. If we were, we wouldn't be annoyed that a personal computer or workstation purchased five years ago is now virtually worthless.

Not all of this speed increase arises just from clock speed, the purest manifestation of *working harder*; very significant aspects of the other two techniques are involved in a major way inside the microprocessors themselves. But it all does ultimately stem from improvements in basic circuit technology and, for our purposes here, is considered as a unit.

As will be discussed at length later, this book would never have been written if the speed increases described above were not occurring. The topic treated in this book is ultimately one of the consequences—possibly not even the most important, but quite certainly interesting and useful—of this continued rapid growth of microprocessor performance. But how that growth is coming about, and why, will not be discussed here. The saga of the circuits must be found elsewhere.

1.2 Working Smarter

"Using a better algorithm" is a direct translation into mathematico-computer jargon of the phrase *working smarter*. The increases in speed made possible by better algorithms dwarf even the feats of semiconductor integrated circuit technology.

No one would ever, for example, look a name up in a phone book by turning to the first page and checking the first name listed, then the second name, and so on up to the name that's wanted. Well, not unless the town were extraordinarily small. Nearly all phone books would be useless without a better search method (algorithm) than that. A one-at-a-time search takes time related to the number of names: 100 looks on average for 200 names, 100,000 looks for 200,000 names, and so on. The usual alphabetical search, in contrast, takes time related to the number of *digits* in the number of names: 3 looks for 100, and only 6 looks 100,000 names. (In the jargon: It's proportional to the logarithm of the amount of data.) The difference between 6 and 100,000, or 8 and 10 million, and so on, is gargantuan. Using the right algorithm can mean the difference between possible and practical, now; and impossible, ever, on any computer.

Choosing or discovering appropriate algorithms is therefore supremely important. We should be extremely careful that using any of the other techniques does not require us to use an inferior algorithm. But other than that caution, and the citing of a specific violation or two later, this book is not about that topic, either.

1.3 Getting Help

That leaves *getting help*, known for computers as parallel processing or, as it is sometimes called, concurrent computing (among the alliterati).

Some forms of parallel processing are covert: They reside hidden inside the processor, manifesting themselves only as increased processor performance on a single programmed stream of instructions. Covert parallelism is a very significant constituent of the increased processor performance mentioned above. It is advertised with terms like "superpipelined," "superscalar," "very long instruction word" (VLIW), and so on. This book is also not about covert parallelism; instead, it lumps this form of parallel processing in with processor performance.

If parallel processing is not covert, it is overt. Software—really, the programmers of the software—must at some level explicitly form multiple streams of instructions to "manually" (as it were) exploit overt parallelism. When the unqualified term "parallel processing" is used in this book, it means overtly parallel processing.

Like "getting help," its social counterpart, (overtly) parallel processing has, or, after discarding the hype should have, an aura of ambivalence about it. There's an old joke in the field that parallelism is the wave of the future— and always will be.[1] There is a tendency to feel that way because the history of the area has not been the smooth upward climb experienced by the two other techniques mentioned above.

Parallelism, of both overt and most covert forms, was explicitly considered and rejected by Von Neumann during the birth design of the modern computer in the 1940s [BGvN62]. There were of course excellent reasons for this rejection, but nevertheless it was not precisely the best possible start. The basic computer architecture he and his team devised, now known as the Von Neumann architecture, has dominated computing ever since. It contains an intrinsic, internal performance limitation called the "Von Neumann bottleneck" that all forms of overt parallelism, and some forms of covert parallelism, attempt to overcome. More will be said about this later.

---

1. The first time I ever heard it was in approximately 1982, from Creve Maples, who was then at the Lawrence Berkeley Laboratory of the University of California. I think he attributed it to someone else, but who that was I do not remember.

Nevertheless, a number of fairly early parallel designs were attempted, often using replication not for speed but to overcome the reliability problems of that era's hardware. Parallel processing to do a fair range of things faster—not just specific, one-off applications—probably emerged into its first great visibility in the late 1960s with the ILLIAC IV project at the University of Illinois [BBK+68]. This was not just parallel processing in the sense of getting a couple of friends to help paint the house. It was highly, or massively, parallel processing: recruiting an army of computational elements to do much more massive calculations than were feasible on conventional computers. Nowadays, if your army is merely tens strong, you're certainly not in the club; better make it hundreds or thousands.

ILLIAC IV suffered a number of problems, not all related to parallelism by any means; it also advanced basic circuit and other technologies significantly. It faded into obscurity, finally being extinguished in the early 70s. The field remained an active, collegial area of research at many major laboratories and universities, with results reflected in a number of interesting projects and products that will not be described in this brief overview. It was just less highly publicized and, at least in massive form, it was not terribly successful in the marketplace.

Thanks to that continuing effort, the field was well prepared when a very different sort of demand arose for parallel processing of the highly, massively, build-an-army persuasion. Such processing was one of the significant elements of the Japanese Fifth Generation Project, begun in the early mid-80s. Again the justification was, as it always is, to provide vastly more computation than was feasible with conventional computers. Countervailing projects in the U.S. and Europe were begun, including several efforts of the massively parallel persuasion.

Even though the Fifth Generation's goals didn't appear to require numerical processing (as far as anybody could tell), the more traditional scientific and engineering parallelizers seized the moment. Among other events, an official, government-approved list was made of problems of intense economic or scientific interest, significant problems that were so large they just had to have massive parallelism for their solution: the Grand Challenge problems [Exe87]. This was and continues to be used to justify government promotional programs.

The Fifth Generation also faded and was extinguished (again, by no means entirely, or even mainly, due to problems with parallelism). Most of the countervailing projects followed suit, although some have survived and most left a legacy of interesting computer designs and pathways to government support.

Through all of this, the hype and the front-page newspaper articles ebbed and flowed, as is inevitable surrounding projects to build the biggest, fastest, most colossal of anything, including computers.

Starting in the late 70s and early 80s, the parallelizers had noticed, along with everybody else, that microprocessors had superb performance for their price compared with larger computers. They just weren't very fast individually. Well. Talk about a tailor-made situation. All You Have To Do Is Just gang up a huge whacking lot of them, and you get massive amounts of computer power for relatively little money. Almost all the Fifth-Generation-Era projects were microprocessor-based.

The problem was, always was, and still is, that All You Also Have To Do is program the dang things to work together. Why that's a daunting task is a question to which we will return in far more detail. In the meantime, just consider the effort needed to coordinate large numbers of people to do anything and the mistakes and frustrations typical of dealing with the bureaucracy necessary for control of large organizations. Programming costs money, much more than hardware, and is furthermore in a chronic state of crisis; so if all parallelism gets you is cheaper hardware, it's no bargain. These didn't make it commercially, either.

Then, in the early 90s the continuing rise of microprocessor performance made itself felt. The business end of an exponential growth curve is really just rising as usual, but it feels like it's "kicking in," and kick in this one did. Rather suddenly, large but practical-sized agglomerations of microprocessors didn't just equal big machine performance or provide it more cheaply. They clearly became the way to exceed even the biggest and super-est computers' speeds by large and ever-increasing amounts.

This is a horse of a shockingly different color. Byzantine programming or no, there are an adequate number of people willing to do quite a lot for significantly faster computers than anybody else has. They range across a very broad area.

> Scientists want to verify or disprove things they couldn't before, and just incidentally get the work done faster so they can publish first, establish precedence, get tenure, and receive the other rewards of scientific excellence.

> Engineers want to simulate more of a car, airplane, drug, or whatnot in ever greater detail so they can remove their mistakes before embedding them in expensive prototypes, trials, or even more expensive production; this avoids really ugly economic decisions.

➤ Retailers want to examine every one of roughly a gazillion sales records so they can tailor, for you alone, every individual one of you, a whole series of offers so good you just can't refuse them.

➤ Airlines want to make sure a "full" short-hop flight really has room for that one more person who's using it to get to a high-profit trans-continental connection.

➤ Financiers want to make an obscene amount of money because their probabilistic analysis of future projections of multilevel tranches of mortgaged-backed securities is 0.1% faster than their competitors'.

➤ And, as far as I can tell, nearly everybody on earth wants to ware-house a huge number of movies for immediate, interactive down-load to your home, making a high profit at this because absolutely everybody else hates having to return rented video tapes.

That's where things stand as this book is being written. Highly parallel com-puting is finally becoming a commercial success. Established companies like AT&T GIS (NCR), IBM, and Fujitsu have joined in. Early-riser startups like NCube are at least in less danger of folding. Intel's Scientific Supercomputer Division (sell lots of chips at once!) is rumored to be making money. Tradi-tional vendors of supercomputers and superminis like Cray and Convex, following the trend or in self-defense, have begun marketing massively par-allel machines based on the newly potent microprocessors. It is not all roses. Post–Cold War military downsizing is hurting the market for the largest numerically-oriented machines, so company failures still are occurring, but a far more lucrative commercial market for massive parallelism is arising, abetted by parallel database offerings from several of the powerhouses of database software: Oracle, Sybase, Informix, IBM, and others.

Massively parallel processing is the wave of the future again, and this time it actually seems to be making money. There is an aura of satisfaction in the air, at least among those not wedded to shrinking defense spending, and not a little relief.

Of course, the publicity machine remains in full gear—although at a tad lower volume now that fewer folks have to be convinced that real profits are possible. It's easy to hype the biggest, fastest, most powerful. Everywhere you look you can see yet more grandiloquent claims in a continuing battle for the front pages of newspapers. Unusual programming is still required, but hey, get used to it: It's the wave of the future.

There is a wholly justifiable fascination with huge computer systems. Cathe-drals, pyramids, and other Grand Challenges are legitimate objects of awe and rightfully the province of efforts correctly described as "massive." To quest for the biggest and the fastest, to push back the boundaries of the possible—this is to be involved in a grand cause. It feels wonderful, especially when after all those years one finally (knock on wood) is winning. Trust me, I've been there [Pfi86, PN85, PBG$^+$85]. The lure of large numbers is powerful.

But this book is not about *that*, either.

For in the hullabaloo of the highly massive and the excitement of finally making it, something seems to have been forgotten. When I've previously tried to point it out I feel, well, not like Banquo's ghost, since what's under way is considerably more energetic than even a medieval banquet. I really feel like a single person, pushing open a huge door and wandering into big hangar-like factory bustling with frenetic activity. Reverie on:

> "Oh, guys..."
>
> "Gangway! Omega Network comin' through on this fork lift!"
>
> The operator of the large, bright yellow fork lift loaded with a tall, skinny unpainted wooden crate slams on the brakes beside me, screeching to a stop.
>
> "Yeah, watcha want?" he shouts down to me over the din.
>
> "Um, the microprocessors..."
>
> "What about 'em?"
>
> He turns away from me and shouts across the room to someone I can't see. "Hey, Harry, UltraMassive just announced a 40,000-way!" Turning back, he leans on the fork lift's steering wheel and tips back his company logo work cap. It's grey, with a square, black, iron-on cloth badge on the front bearing a gold V. *Vishnu.* The Ultimate Destroyer. The Thousand-Armed One. He wipes his forehead.
>
> "Jeez, now we gotta figure out how to get 80,000 into our box without frying 'em all. At least 80,000. Maybe two-stage turbine fans. So, what's this about the micros?" His eyes wander about the vast, dim, open space of the plant. Big things are moving around very quickly. It's hard to tell what they are.
>
> "Well, er, they're still getting faster."
>
> "Eh? Yeah, 'course they are. Great! So what? Just makes us faster! Quick, duck!"
>
> An overhead gantry swings a huge dirty white cylinder through the space my head and shoulders occupied a moment earlier. While picking myself up, I smell concrete dust.
>
> "Was that a concrete pylon?" I ask, standing up again and brushing dirt off my clothes.

"Yeah, gotta stock 'em for big systems. The copper in the network wiring alone weighs 3 tons. But we'll go optical real soon now. We've gotta. The pylon inventory's a pain." He continues to stare out into the plant, watchful for more large events.

"Oh. Well, anyway, the way the microprocessors are getting so much faster, almost nobody needs more than a dozen or so any more. I guess there are some people who still need lots at once, but..."

I stop, because without moving his body he's swivelled his head towards me, glaring over his shoulder.

"What? Son, we do massively, got that?" he says, swiveling his body towards me and thumping the steering wheel "*Massively* parallel processing here." He starts turning away, his eyes scanning the open space again. "Maybe you can sell a whole buncha those nice *little* systems, but—"

Oh, not again. He's not going to say it. Not the standard formula defined to end discussion. Oh, hell. He is.

"—that's not our mission."

Sitting up straight again, he snugs his cap back down onto his forehead and reaches for the fork lift's controls. "Niceta meetcha, but I've gotta run. There's a level 1 synchronization problem out at the NRITB lab! That's a big account!"

He guns the fork lift. After punctuating its start with a short, sharp tire chirp, it silently accelerates, races forward, smoothly up a ramp, with no hesitation off a sudden edge and into empty space. Before it can fall he touches the logo badge on the front of his cap. The rig, its load, and he dissolve into a radial starspray. Looks like 32, no, 64 simultaneous paths.

A slight sour ozone tang in the air is all that remains. It smells like bumper cars at an amusement park. No one else even notices. 64? Highly fault-tolerant, I guess. Or maybe for the bandwidth...

Back from reverie. The march of processor power has already made smaller parallel systems, mere *clusters* of computers, very potent. Many installations already exist, and in fact the notion is not new at all. What is new is their power and viability. These will inexorably increase, so that while there will always be a market for highly parallel systems, the other end of the scale—for want of a better term, *lowly parallel systems*—will be adequate for an ever-increasing majority of the market.

That, finally, is what this book is all about.

Not the armies, the conquering hordes, the multitudes recruited for the grand exploits of whole civilizations, national economies, or massive individualized mail-order campaigns. This is about construction crews, tightly knit teams, small departments. Groups big enough to handle the majority of jobs today, and even more tomorrow when they're composed of ever-growing giants.

There would, however, be no point to this book if this were all happening smoothly, if there were not difficulties or issues to be resolved. There are. While many will be discussed, two of them stand out in particular.

First, there already is a highly visible, entrenched lowly parallel architecture. The symmetric multiprocessor (SMP) has been around since at least the early 70s. It is the workhorse lowly parallel architecture of both commercial processing and much engineering and scientific processing, the *de facto* industry-standard lowly parallel system. SMPs have at present some very significant advantages over clusters, but they have disadvantages, too. Are they competitors, or possibly synergistic?

There are characteristics of clusters that SMPs cannot have that will cause clusters to survive; SMPs alone just aren't good enough. The same is true of SMPs relative to clusters. But SMPs are getting all the attention in the industry press. What exactly is the relationship between SMPs and clusters? The comparison is crucial. It appears later in this book, arguably its climax, after an awful lot of preparation.

There's an element of the SMP issue that's particularly nasty. How you program these two lowly parallel architectures is different. It is so different that it builds a significant barrier to anyone who would like to move between them. In the jargon: their programming models are different. If one explicitly exploits SMP architecture in an application, it's essentially impossible to use that same program to efficiently exploit clusters. The situation is not quite symmetric, however: If an application explicitly exploits cluster architecture, SMP use is merely degraded, at present rather significantly, and the main features of SMPs are not exploited.

Open systems standards do not bridge the gap. There are, or will be, standards—one set for SMPs, and another for clusters. So the bad old days before open systems, when programming locked you into an architecture, are still around.

Beyond the question of SMPs, there's a completely separate, second problem. It is a distinctly odd one. Despite the fact that clusters, like SMPs, have been around for decades, they're invisible. In a very real sense, they don't exist.

1.4   A Neglected Paradigm _____

Is there really such a thing as a *cluster* of computers?

To the users and administrators of the hundreds of thousands of clusters in production use, that must seem a remarkably stupid question. Of course there are clusters. You can purchase them ready-made from many sources— Tandem, Digital, Hewlett-Packard, IBM, Sun, Pyramid, Sequent, and others; or you can roll your own using nearly anybody's computers and widely deployed distributed and parallel computing facilities—distributed file systems, network operating systems, parallel programming packages, and the like. What's the problem?

Consider:

On the one hand, material on clusters enjoys a respectable if not particularly large presence in the technical literature, in the form of papers, books, and chapters in books. These describe individual cluster implementations: how they are built, how they are programmed, what they are used for. The books usually amount to reference manuals for specific cluster products. Individual cluster incarnations are described in conferences on parallel and distributed systems and are occasional case studies in textbooks.

On the other hand, there is silence about characteristics shared by clusters in general. There are no textbooks or textbook chapters that are not case studies; there are no conferences other than product user groups (although small workshops have begun to spring up). There are no standards, benchmarks, programming tool kits, and other desiderata specifically for clusters. Instead, the paraphernalia of distributed and massively parallel computing is applied helter-skelter, occasionally modified (kludged) to fit the context of some particular cluster system.

Recently, there have been some market studies of clusters by independent consultants as the economic importance of clusters has become more evident, but these are few, limited, and concentrate on individual products and partial features such as high availability. In fact, I can offer no documented evidence for the claim above that there are "hundreds of thousands" of installed, production clusters. I can't count them because the requisite market studies simply haven't been done. That number used above is based on my personal knowledge of the install base of a few cluster products, extrapolated to the many products that exist and the amount of time they've been in the market (see Chapter 2 for the basis of this). It is certainly an underestimate.

In short, the topic of clusters is not recognized as a coherent discipline. Its current state mirrors that of the state of geography in the Middle Ages as described by Daniel J. Boorstein, a time when there wasn't even any common synonym for the word "geography":

> Lacking the dignity of a proper discipline, [it] was an orphan in the world of learning. The subject became a ragbag filled with odds and ends of knowledge and pseudo-knowledge, of Biblical dogmas, travelers' tales, philosophers' speculations, and mythical imaginings. [Boo83, p. 100]

It surely is overstatement to apply this to clusters, of course. There are no religiously held dogmas, are there?[2] We don't draw our product-positioning maps of clusters with Eden, the unreachably magnificent, at the top, labelled "East" (...with the massively parallel systems)—do we? The sales force is certainly imaginative, but can we credit them with truly mythic capabilities? Depends on their budget, I guess.

But clusters aren't being used because of metaphysical speculation. There is a relatively recent, rising trend to clustering, but it's actually following a path long trod by makers of mainframe and midrange computers, who have been grouping machines for decades. The general motives are the usual reasons advanced for all types of parallel and distributed computing: Clusters provide users with enhanced performance, capacity, availability and price/performance; in addition, these qualities are extensible—they increase, within sensible limits, as the size of the cluster grows.

There is nothing new about such motivations. They comprise a standard litany that is always trotted out and recited as the list of reasons for parallel and distributed systems of all stripes. But although clusters' general motivations match traditional paradigms' motivations, other reasons for clusters, as well as clusters' characteristics, do not. It is a thesis of this book that clustered systems are not very well described by current computer system paradigms. As a result, they are not well served by existing tools, their ability to fulfill their promises is curtailed, and they will continue to be underutilized until their differences are recognized, supported, and exploited.

This is slippery ground. Paradigmatic distinctions in the realms of distributed and parallel systems are notoriously difficult to make and are usefully ignored in not a few contexts. For example, some recent textbooks (e.g., *Modern Operating Systems* by Tannenbaum [Tan92]) explicitly label all multiple processor systems of any type "distributed," on the grounds that coupling techniques form a continuum, as indeed they do. On the other hand, practitioners of the parallel art have been heard to refer to all multiple-com-

---

2. For those who are not involved in this field at all: This is rather heavy-handed sarcasm. There are more religiously held-to dogmata in parallel and distributed processing than there are fleas on the Pope's dog.

puting-element systems as parallel, which of course in a sense they are. It is all one, big field that invisibly grades from one style of computing to another, so this reductionist logic is impossible to refute on its own terms.

However, there is also, to pursue an analogy, a continuum between the Great Salt Flats of Utah and the Swiss Alps. One could refer to all topography as hills of different magnitudes. No one does, because distinctions such as flatlands, mountains, and rolling plains are useful and necessary. If they weren't, we would cross Kansas using the cog railways of the Alps—or use secure remote procedure calls to communicate inside a symmetric multiprocessor. We obviously don't do either.

One class of foothills has been commonly accepted as a useful subparadigm of distributed processing: the client-server paradigm. The unique needs of client-server systems are addressed by a number of tools and techniques, notably the remote procedure call, threads, distributed naming techniques, security services, global time services, and so forth.

Clusters are similarly a sub-paradigm of the parallel/distributed realm. But their unique needs are not being addressed. This is a neglected paradigm. More: The very concept of a cluster, as a unique type of thing of itself, is missing.

Product developers and researchers work on massive parallelism, (massively) distributed processing, or SMPs. Relatively few work on clusters, and when they do, they hide it or continually have to defend their efforts because they're not part of the recognized mainstream of the computer industry.

This lack of an intellectual framework for clusters is not without costs that range well beyond the frustrations of some eccentric and atypically stubborn workers. Broadly used performance benchmarks, lacking the concept of a cluster, give information most people misunderstand and misuse when the benchmarks are used to compare clusters to other types of systems—even though the situation is quite explicitly defined. Research and development efforts are misdirected, wasting effort and losing the recognition and market presence that should rightfully be their reward. There are issues in computer science which remain confused when they might be clarified by considering clusters. Products are maladapted to the greater market they could serve because developers, lacking an appropriate framework, concentrate their efforts on the wrong things.

A later chapter will explicitly address each of these items to show just how much we need the concept of a cluster.

1.5 What Is To Come _____

So just what is a cluster, anyway? Well, I'm not going to tell you. Not now anyway. There is a reason for this reticence.

Since it's not commonplace to consider clusters a separate sub-paradigm, the first task must be to give examples, focusing on aspects common to the cluster genre. Then the technology trends that lead to clusters and lend them ever-increasing importance will be discussed. The intent is to build up the characteristics that a definition should try to capture, hopefully creating a focus on the thing rather than on its definition. After that background, a surprisingly simple-looking definition will be offered, and the nontrivial distinctions that follow from it will be highlighted.

The bulk of the discussion then begins. Starting with hardware, both of clusters and of SMPs, we will continue into software and finally converge to systems—for all overtly parallel issues, be they cluster, massively parallel, or distributed, are system issues, not hardware or software alone, but their alliance.

The hardware discussion will cover the myriad possible forms of clusters and what's needed to build a good one of any of several varieties; how they differ from the competitive symmetric multiprocessor (SMP) architecture; what an SMP is, really; and in some detail, the amazing things one has to do to build a shared-memory machine that can run programs which exploit industry-standard SMPs—and not just wind up with a "shared-memory" computer, which in general is *not* the same thing as an SMP.

Then it's off to software: what these systems can be used for and how easily, the ways they are programmed, a demonstration of difficulties parallelism adds to programming, the great continuing debates in the area, how differing "computational models" can trap you into an architecture, and how commercial, not just technical, parallelism works; and finally, the subject of "single system image" (whatever that means).

The convergence to systems then interrelates what has come before in an SMP-cluster comparison. Finally, examples of where we are going wrong without this concept—clusters—will be addressed in detail, and some conclusions drawn about what we should be doing to better exploit the paradigm.

On the tail end, I've also included some annotations that briefly describe each bibliography entry. This description is necessary if anybody is to use this information, because it covers a wide spectrum—from brain-twisting logical details of proving the equivalence of computer interprocessor synchronization classes to the cartoon-illustrated exploits of Zog the Martian as he explores the dense jungle of distributed computing.

This is a far longer trip than I anticipated when I began this project. I hope you can stick around for the ride.

In Search of Clusters ✳

Examples

2.1   The Farm _____

Deep within the densely wooded, hilly terrain of northern Westchester County, just a bit to the north of New York City, lies a very long, skinny, black building. It doesn't look terribly long and skinny from the outside, because it's gracefully draped into an imposing black curve around a manicured, grassy hilltop that's surrounded, at a discreet distance, by dense woods. But those who work inside it, and have to walk a good part of its length to reach the cafeteria for lunch, are very aware of its true shape: long. And skinny. They're members of IBM's Research Division, and this is its home location, the T. J. Watson Research Center.

Except for a holdout in the flatter eastern reaches of Westchester, nobody has farmed this region since pre-Revolutionary times. Back then there was no choice. Settlers arriving at New York piled up in Westchester along the eastern bank of the Hudson River, since crossing the river meant dealing with decidedly uncooperative natives. Once those had been "pacified," the settlers took off to the west and never returned. The trees they cleared have been growing back ever since. I don't blame them for not sticking around, since how they actually managed to farm that area I don't understand.

When I lived a bit to the north of there, I once tried to clear the rocks out of a plot for a vegetable garden. After several hours of work I had a large pile of rocks, the level of the ground had dropped about an inch, and I was staring down at just as many rocks as when I started. I gave up. The early settlers obviously didn't have that option or found better locations; when the leaves are off the trees, the stone fences that separated their plots are still obvious, crawling up and over the hills like great, grey, demented snakes.

Inside that long, curved black wall of a building there's some farming going on that doesn't require rock removal. It's in response to the full-time, production, computationally intensive needs of the Research Division's work in physics, semiconductor device technology, and other fields. They no longer use large mainframes with heavy-duty vector units; those are too expensive. Instead they use what's officially the "Watson Research Central Compute Cluster," but is known to everyone as "The Farm": a cluster of 22 high-performance workstations.

Insofar as possible, the Farm is run as if it were a single machine. For example, a user doesn't log onto any specific machine, but rather onto the Farm as a whole. This is done, as illustrated in Figure 2-1, through a terminal server on a master workstation. The server automatically selects the least loaded of the workstations that function as compute servers. Any user's job must be able to run on any compute server, so the same programs and data are available on all. Common data access is achieved by using an everyday distrib-

Figure 2-1   Use of The Watson Farm

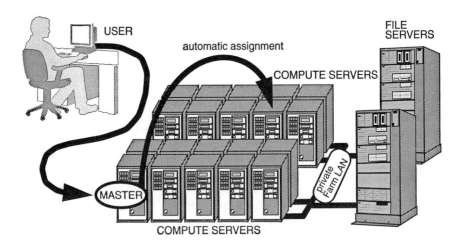

In Search of Clusters ✳

uted file system: All user files are mounted from file servers in a standard-by-convention position in every compute node's file hierarchy, while each compute server's own disks hold only system software, swap space, and a small amount of temporary (**/tmp**) space.

As implied above, the Farm's workstations are partially specialized in function: One is a gateway, the master machine mentioned above, connecting the campus LAN system to the local farm LAN(d); two are file servers with about 15 Gbytes of disk space each; and the remaining 19 are compute servers with large amounts of memory (512 Mbytes or more). While the file servers are rack-mounted machines, to conveniently provide large disk storage capacity, the master and the compute servers are deskside, floor-standing machines. Seeing those 20 in compact rows leaves little doubt about why this type of arrangement is universally known as a workstation farm.[1] The term was probably suggested by a precedent: Back when disk drives were the size of washing machines, large floor-covering arrays of them became known as "disk farms."

What new software was written for the Farm, and that was deliberately minimal, was written to facilitate its use as a single computing resource. This software was the terminal server mentioned above, a central accounting system that provides daily usage summaries across all machines, and a high-level scheduling mechanism called *Share*, which helps distribute compute time based on prior allocations. *Share* does its job by using standard UNIX facilities such as **renice**, which alters running jobs' priorities. Everything else is assembled out of distributed and open systems technology that is standard, commonly available, and quite broadly deployed. Graphical output is delivered straight to users' workstation displays, using again standard X Windows facilities. Thanks to the Farm, those users can get by with far smaller personal systems than would otherwise be feasible.

Very little software development has yielded a bountiful crop of eminently usable MFLOPS.

2.2 Fermilab

Illinois has really good dirt. You learn to appreciate stuff like that when you live in places like Eastern New York and Central Texas. (A major difference between those two is that the Central Texas rock hasn't been broken up.)

Illinois is also really flat. This makes the building in Batavia, southwest of Chicago, dominate the horizon for miles around with its curved thrust tens

---

1. In Texas: a workstation ranch.

of stories tall: Fermi National Accelerator Laboratory. This is the home of the Tevatron particle accelerator, and also of a standard Fermilab joke: The bison living in the restored prairie area within the accelerator ring are *not* cattle mutated by synchotron radiation.

Good dirt and a big, flat area means megafarms. While amusingly coincidental, this obviously has absolutely nothing to do with the fact that Fermilab runs one of the largest workstation clusters currently known: about 400 Silicon Graphics and IBM workstations. Unlike the Watson Farm, the workstations here are all small desktop units, mounted in racks that stretch wall-like across rooms. All were chosen by virtue of their having the best cost/ performance on the primary Fermilab application, the analysis of subnuclear particle events recorded by huge, multistory, underground detectors of exceedingly tiny things. Analyzing any one of those events, and a whole lot of them have been recorded, has nothing to do with analyzing any of the others; so there's no reason why many analyses can't be done at the same time. That's parallel processing, and that's what the Fermi cluster is used for. Analyzing each individual event doesn't require a lot of memory or storage, so no individual machine in the cluster has to be big—but it does have to be computationally fast. Therefore, they use many small but powerful workstations; each has large raw floating-point performance without paying for large addenda to bigger machines: space for more memory, robust input/ output subsystems, and so on.

Fermilab researchers are interested in physics, not the computer science of making large numbers of machines cooperate. If writing parallel software is as difficult as has been implied, something had to have been done to make such a collective simpler to use. It was. The Fermilab solution is to do something very similar in spirit to the techniques long used to domesticate parallelism in commercial systems: Users simply don't write parallel programs at all. Instead, the system provides the parallelism. How this works is illustrated in Figure 2-2.

The physicist-user writes an ordinary serial program that analyzes a single accelerator event. That program gets the data for one event, munches on it in complex ways having to do with the physics involved, and delivers output describing what happened in the event. This analysis procedure is then given into the care of a Fermilab-developed subsystem called Cooperative Processes Software (CPS), which causes the procedure to run many times, simultaneously, on multiple machines. CPS reads accelerator events data from input tapes and feeds that data to those multiple instances of the user's analysis procedure, one event's data for each instance. As each individual event analysis finishes, CPS collects the results and writes them to storage, to be perused by the user.

Figure 2-2   Fermilab CPS Operation

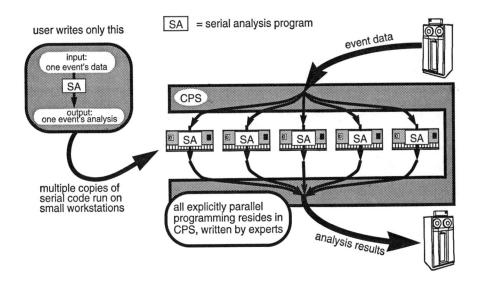

CPS is a parallel program. It was written and is maintained by a coterie skilled in parallel programming, not necessarily physics. That one supervisory parallel program, however, allows many physicists to get the benefits of parallelism without the pain: Many serial programmers are reaping the benefits of a select few parallel programmers.

This is a common pattern. Subsystems like transaction monitors and database systems fill the same role in business and commercial use of clusters and other forms of parallelism: An application programmer writes a (comparatively) simple serial program, a program containing no parallelism; the subsystem runs it many times simultaneously, in parallel, and has the job of keeping the many instances from interfering with each other. Perhaps less obviously, operating systems and batch monitors also provide this service for stand-alone programs that don't visibly run under the care of a parallelizing subsystem; the system provides the parallelism.

This **serial program, parallel (sub-) system (SPPS)** technique is by far the most common way for business and commercial computing to use *any* of the forms of overt parallelism: cluster, symmetric multiprocessor, highly parallel, you name it. By "hiding" the parallelism from the run-of-the-mill user, SPPS effectively turns overt parallelism into a higher-level form of covert parallelism. This is a very common way for many forms of computing to implicitly use parallelism. Rather than splitting a single program into simultaneously active, parallel parts, instead separate, different programs are run at the same time. In this form, when done particularly on a single processor (overlapping I/O) the technique has long been known as multiprogramming. The individual programs don't go faster. But they wait less for the resources they need, since those resources have been multiplied (parallelism) or their use has been overlapped (single processor). The Watson Farm described above effectively uses parallelism that way. Up to now, a term for what is here called SPPS parallelism has been missing.

Fermilab to the contrary, SPPS parallelism is a rather uncommon way to get individual technical programs to run faster. Most technical problems aren't as obviously composed of many independent tasks, and single common structures usable by many are not common. As a result, aside from multiprogramming whole programs, it is more common to find users applying parallelism within their programs. A number of tools and techniques have been developed to make that easier; these will be discussed later.

Fermilab has developed some software which, while very representative of a general technique of exploiting parallelism, is in the technical computing realm uniquely suited to the atomistic nature of their problem. Of course, it's not just Fermilab's problem; it is *the* data processing problem of high-energy physics, common to all particle accelerator laboratories—CERN in Europe, SLAC (Stanford Linear Accelerator) in California, and so on. There is definitely motivation for some unique development that harnesses as much computing power per dollar as possible, because the colliders have created their own kind of information overload, There are quite literally warehouses full of tapes holding collider-generated event data that have never been processed, simply because the required computing capacity isn't available. There's just got to be a Nobel Prize hidden in there *somewhere...*

2.3 Many Others

The two projects described above typify a class: user-assembled technical computing clusters. They also represent two ends of a spectrum of ways to use such clusters. The Fermi cluster is primarily used to execute parallel applications, that is, individual jobs that simultaneously use at least several of the clustered machines. The Watson Farm, on the other hand, is primarily for multiprogramming: Multiple different jobs are run on the clustered machines. Neither is a pure type—each does some work of the other sort— but together they represent endpoints of the spectrum.

In one respect, however, those two clusters are quite atypical of clusters being assembled today. They were some of the earliest practitioners of the art of assembling clusters from high-performance workstations and therefore had to roll their own software support almost completely. Today, cluster assemblers have a much easier time of it; they can pick and choose among a good range of commercial offerings that provide the necessary functions of cluster-wide batch queueing, interactive login, and parallelization. Examples of these products are listed in tables that accompany the discussion of each class of facility in the sections that follow.

One area that these products do not yet address well, however, is system administration. Keeping a flock of dedicated workstations in line is nowhere near as bad as doing the same to a huge crowd of individuals' personal machines. The latter is like trying to sweep up ants, while cluster management is more like herding sheep. An administrator can enforce far greater uniformity within a cluster, because the machines don't have individual owners who are free to mess around with their machines or demand to be different. This uniformity means that there's a much higher likelihood that the same command, performed on each machine, will yield the same result; this simplifies the problem immensely. Nevertheless, you still need a sheep dog or two. Trading the administration of a single, large machine for the administration of eight, ten, or more requires forethought and work. In assembled clusters, this task is usually accomplished by a combination of standard distributed-system facilities (such as Sun's NIS and NIS+ [Ram93]), judiciously chosen "mount points" for shared file data, and a local collection of Shell Scripts from Hell that actually use those tools to do what's required.

The product offerings that do exist, and there are a fair and growing number, would not have been developed in the absence of customer demand, and demand there certainly is. While the exact number, or even a good estimate, isn't known, it can safely be stated that there are at least thousands of assembled clusters out there, primarily in technical settings: universities, industrial research laboratories, government laboratories, and so forth. For example, Florida State University's Supercomputing Research Institute (SCRI) has a large heterogeneous cluster containing workstations, massively parallel machines, and a conventional supercomputer. Philips Research Laboratories in The Netherlands has a cluster based on Hewlett-Packard hardware for computer-aided design support; in this case, most users have only X-stations (UNIX graphics terminals); all the "real" work is done on a cluster of machines that provide login, computing, and file services [vDR94]. Among many others, Cornell has a cluster, as does Lawrence Livermore National Laboratory. Eugene Brooks of that laboratory has been quoted as saying "One computer center after the other is lining up to put a cluster of microprocessors on the floor. Their budgets are shrinking and these systems are much more cost-effective [than traditional supercomputers]." [Mar94]

For a while, a list was kept within IBM of clusters that IBM had helped assemble from its workstations; as of October 1993 it had nearly 100 entries for clusters in the United States, Europe, and Japan. That's a list only of some of the "mostly IBM" clusters, and IBM is scarcely alone in this. For example, CERN's cluster is mostly Silicon Graphics machines; Hewlett-Packard is also quite active; and Sun Microsystems' workstations are also commonly clustered

While system vendors can be facilitators in this category, they are for the most part not the ones doing the work. Users and administrators are creating clusters, using software and hardware that is generally available. However, there's obviously a product opportunity here, too, so several vendors have begun marketing clusters-in-a-box that make what are really assembled clusters more compact and tolerable—"preassembled" clusters, in other words. Those are by no means the only cluster system products. With others, they'll be discussed in the next section.

2.4 Cluster System Products _____

Many manufacturers offer products that group their machines in clusters; a number are listed in Table 2-1 on page 28. Software-only products and products devoted primarily to high availability are discussed later.

In a number of cases, the products provided are rather straightforward. Those cases are the vendor-packaged preassembled clusters mentioned above. For those offerings, versions of the companies' main-line products are simply sold in groups, usually with little if any modification. For example, the HP Apollo 9000 and the current DEC Advantage Cluster consist of those companies' high-end workstations with the displays removed, repackaged to allow them to be conveniently placed in a rack or similar enclosure, connected by standard communication offerings such as Ethernet, FDDI, or Fibre Channel Standard, and packaged with third-party software offerings pre-ported to the platform; the spectrum of those software offerings will be described later. HP's preassembled cluster is typical; it's shown in Figure 2-3. For IBM, small versions of its Scalable Parallel series of systems fill this role and offer IBM-supplied software that makes system administration somewhat simpler.

Preassembled clusters have an advantage for both the vendor and the customer that can make it advantageous to buy (and sell) even a one-machine cluster rather than the corresponding workstation. This is true even though the singleton workstation is likely to be a bit less expensive; after all, the workstation price does not include the cost of the larger rack or the less-common (and therefore more expensive), single-machine packaging used in the cluster.

Figure 2-3   HP Apollo 9000 Computational Cluster

The advantage arises because the whole cluster is typically labelled with a single serial number. This sounds trivial. But it makes the purchase of additional machines an upgrade, not a new purchase. Upgrades of existing systems typically do not require the bureaucratic approvals needed for new machine purchases, approvals that would be required if another stand-alone workstation were purchased. In addition, software license arrangements are typically resolved at the outset for the entire cluster, making that aspect of adding a new machine easier, too. This is a wholly artificial distinction, but it makes a practical difference.

Preassembled clusters will not be discussed further; they're noted in the table by having a "no" in the "Special Hardware/Software?" column.

But minimalist preassembled cluster products are by no means the only ones offered for sale. Very elaborate, well-supported cluster systems have been on the market for some time. Sometimes they're explicitly called clusters, and other times they're not. Those are noted with a "yes" in the "Special Hardware/Software" column of Table 2-1. The next section discusses some of the more prominent offerings.

Table 2-1   Some Cluster System Products

Who	What	Type[a]	Special Hardware / Software?
DEC	OpenVMS Cluster	general-purpose cluster system	yes
	Advantage Cluster 5000	compute and availability cluster	no
Encore	Infinity 90	OLTP and DB	yes
NCR	NCR 3400 and NCR 3600	OLTP and DB query system	yes
HP	HP Apollo 9000 Computational Cluster	compute cluster	no
IBM	JES2, JES3 clusters	commercial batch and OLTP	no
	Sysplex	commercial batch and OLTP	yes
	service offerings	compute cluster	no
Sequent	Symmetry 5000 SE90	OLTP and DB	no
Sun	SPARCcluster 1	NFS File Server	no
	SPARCcluster 1000 PDB, SPARCcluster 2000 PDB	OLTP, DB, high availability	yes (lock manager)
Tandem	Cyclone, CLX, Integrity, Himalaya	OLTP and DB system	yes

a. Legend: OLTP is On-Line Transaction Processing; DB is database processing; NFS is Network File System

2.4.1 Digital OpenVMS Cluster

Digital Equipment Corporation offers what is arguably the most complete general-purpose cluster system currently available: the OpenVMS Cluster [Dig93]. Introduced in 1982 as the VAXCluster [KLS86, KLSM87, Sha91], a name change was appropriately made when this clustering technology was extended to heterogeneous mixtures of VAX and AXP systems; today virtually any AXP or VAX system can be part of an OpenVMS Cluster—large, small, uniprocessor, symmetric multiprocessor, workstation, whatever.

OpenVMS Clusters, in contrast to assembled clusters, are often connected by sharing input/output devices: Multiple computers are attached to the same disk or tape devices and the computers can read or write all the devices. Obviously something has to keep them from stepping all over each other's handiwork, and that's the OpenVMS Cluster software—which does much more, as will be discussed below. The hardware aspect of this sharing is supported by Digital's Star Coupler and CI Interconnect, a shared device interconnect reaching 45 meters at 70 Mbits/second; and Digital Storage Shared Interconnect (DSSI), a less expensive shared-disk reaching 6 meters at 32 Mbits/second. In addition, OpenVMS Clusters can also be connected by Ethernet or FDDI. Multiple types of interconnect can be mixed in the same cluster. This is illustrated in Figure 2-4: Several workstations, AXP systems, and VAX systems combine with terminals over an Ethernet; the APX and VAX systems share access to a collection of common disks attached via CI and Star Coupler.

Figure 2-4   Digital OpenVMS Cluster

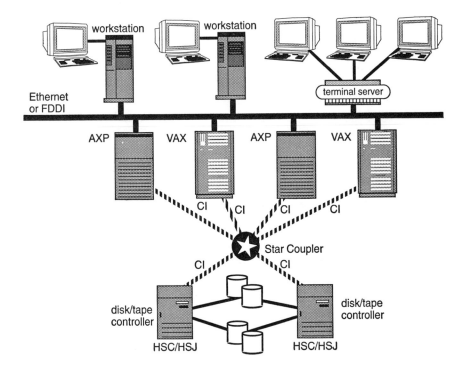

And the whole conglomeration is made to look very much like one computer.

What this means is: When you log on, you get put somewhere in the cluster. Unless you explicitly ask, you may never find out where, nor, in most cases, will you care. Those three terminals on the top right side of the figure, seemingly hanging in midair, aren't attached to any specific machine—they're attached to the cluster-as-a-whole; the "terminal server" shown is typically a small computer that serves only as an attachment point and communication concentrator. When you submit a batch job, it gets done somewhere—again, don't know where and don't care because the same environment is available for all jobs: I/O devices have cluster-wide single names, and their use is the same from everywhere; the file system is likewise universally available, through shared disk if that's used; and to the outside, the cluster as a whole has a single "alias" to DECnet. Administration is similarly made uniform: all operations on user information, security, software installation, and so forth, are performed as if the cluster were a single, albeit extended, machine. Monitoring facilities allow all jobs running across the cluster to be seen, as well as the load on individual machines. In effect, the image of a single system is created across the cluster.

Digital's OpenVMS Cluster is based on an "open"-interface-supporting but basically proprietary operating system, OpenVMS. Like other proprietary systems, VMS and with it the VMScluster are now fighting a defensive and probably losing battle against the market preference for open rather than proprietary systems. Announcements that are recent as this is written indicate that Digital is now starting to pursue extensions of its preassembled clusters, connecting clustered machine with a new "Memory Channel" communication scheme developed in conjunction with Encore [Dig94], and providing database support through an initiative with Oracle Corporation, a major open-systems database vendor with a cluster-supporting product set.

Nevertheless, the OpenVMS Cluster must be regarded as a highly successful product on several grounds.

First and most basic, they've sold a lot of them. According to Digital, there are over 25,000 installations world-wide [Dig93 page 1-3]. This number must be interpreted in light of the fact that many cluster installations arise because a customer has outgrown the biggest machine a vendor makes. So, in all likelihood, many of those 25,000 represent multiple copies of Digital's largest machines. The hardware "drag" generated by this software is therefore quite considerable.

Second, this market success spawned important technical advances in the form of several cluster-supporting database systems—systems that provide the image of a single database across multiple machines and pass that image down to ordinary serial programs via the SPPS (Serial Program, Parallel Subsystem) technique mentioned in the discussion of Fermilab's cluster. In addition to Digital's own Rdb, Oracle originally developed the Oracle Parallel Server for what were then VAXClusters, and Ingres similarly developed parallel support there. This heritage is reflected in the structure of those systems: They require disk systems shared by computers, as is provided by CI/Star Coupler in OpenVMS Clusters (and in other ways on other vendors' clusters). More recently designed database systems—Sybase's Navigation Server, IBM's DB2/6000 Parallel Edition, Informix' DSA—eschew shared disk, targeting conventional intermachine communication such as LAN instead. Which is better—"shared disk" or "shared nothing"—is a hotly debated topic that will be discussed in more detail in Chapter 9.

Third and finally, coupling this database technology with the robust performance of Digital's Alpha AXP processor-based symmetric multiprocessors has allowed OpenVMS Clusters to demonstrate rather considerable aggregate commercial performance. In May of 1994, Digital announced that a four-node OpenVMS Cluster composed of DEC 7000-650 AXP machines, each of those a five-way symmetric multiprocessor, all running DEC's Rdb cluster-parallel relational database, achieved a new world record in the standardized TPC-A performance benchmark: 3,692 tpsA, at a system cost of $4,873 per tpsA. This was stated to have exceeded all other relational database systems' performance by a factor of at least three.

Digital has recently announced that it is, in effect, "migrating" OpenVMS Cluster's functionality to another operating system base: Microsoft Windows NT. This extremely interesting cluster product will be discussed under "Operating Systems" on page 40.

2.4.2 Tandem Himalaya

Tandem is well known for selling fault-tolerant, on-line transaction processing (OLTP) systems. What is perhaps less well known is that all their systems have always been clusters. That it's less known is partially explained by their preference for referring to smaller configurations as "loosely coupled multiprocessors." Nevertheless, all their machines down to the smallest are composed of multiple uniprocessors that happen to be packaged in a single box, just like a preassembled cluster. Tandem calls the individual separate machines "cells," or "processing cells." The structure of a current high-end Tandem system, the Himalaya [Tana] is shown in Figure 2-5. Tandem uses clustering for both increased performance and for fault tolerance, an aspect not emphasized in this book until now.

As it must, fault tolerance begins with detecting the faults; if you don't know something's wrong, you can neither fix nor tolerate it. Fault detection in a cell is provided by, among other things, duplexing processors in each cell: two processors are run in lock-step, and if their outputs disagree, a fault has been found. That alone is neither clustering nor any other form of parallelism; no benefit other than fault detection accrues from the second processor. (Fault detection is, of course, not a trivial function to provide.) Once a fault is detected, fault tolerance is achieved by switching the affected operations to another cell—"failing over" to another machine in the cluster that is running a synchronized backup copy of the failed function.

Figure 2-5   Tandem System Architecture

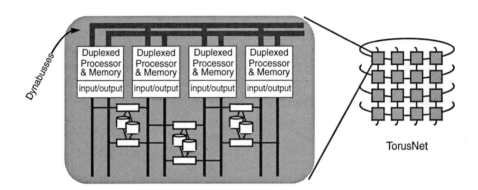

Failover and fault tolerance are assisted by providing internode disk multitailing; as shown in Figure 2-5, two machines can access each disk. However, this connectivity is not used the way it is in the DEC OpenVMS Clusters. In VMSclusters (and in systems running the databases that were originally developed for VMSclusters), multiple machines simultaneously read and write disks to obtain and update shared data. This is not done in Tandem systems, which instead use the "shared-nothing" approach: Only one machine "owns" and is allowed to use each disk at any time; if a non-owner needs to do something to data on a disk it doesn't own, a request is sent to the owner, who then performs the requested operation. The multiple access that's provided is for fault-tolerance only: If the owner dies, and so is definitely not using the disk any more, another machine can take over as the owner. Multiple access is also used for the same fault-tolerating purposes in OpenVMS Clusters and the commonly provided availability clusters discussed in a later section.

Increased performance on OLTP and database applications is achieved by parallel operation of the clustered cells [EGKS90]. This proceeds in multiple levels [Tanb]: Four "cells" are connected by a Dynabus [HC85]; four of them are connected by TorusNet 40Mbyte/second horizontal connections to form a 16-cell (machine) "node." Vertical connections are then made with 4 Mbyte/second connections, forming up to a 14-node (225 cell) "domain." Domains can themselves be connected to achieve systems with more than 4000 cells.

Tandem's NonStop Kernel, as well as their database system, makes such collections of units again appear to be a single unit for administrative and programming purposes. Once again we see cluster support provided in the context of an "open"-interface-supporting, but basically proprietary, operating system; like all other proprietary systems Tandem must adopt a defensive market posture at present.

Tandem's systems must also be considered a success. Initially regarded as a "niche player" in a small fault-tolerant market, they have garnered a multi-billion dollar share of the commercial transaction-processing market. Beginning in the mid-80s, as the performance disadvantage of smaller machines relative to mainframes began to be felt, Tandem was able to leverage its multiple-small-machine, cluster-based technology for very significant performance. One of the larger and more publicized cases of this was when they overwhelmingly defeated IBM mainframes in the performance requirements of the California Department of Motor Vehicle. The mainframes couldn't handle the processing requirements, while the cluster could. (That the implementation of this system is now running into problems typical of intractable huge-scale software system development does not detract from the basic achievement.)

Tandem is in the benchmark race like everyone else. On July 5, 1994, they announced that they had achieved world-record performance on the TPC C standard benchmark—by what they state is a factor of almost ten over the closest competition: 20,928 tpmC at $1,532 per tpmC. Another new world record for a cluster, this time by a factor of ten.

Three comments about this are in order:

First, this is not the same benchmark mentioned before with respect to Digital; this is TPC-C, that was TPC-A. Digital won the javelin throw and Tandem the shotput; they both get gold medals. (The Transaction Processing Performance Council's TPC benchmarks are discussed on page 341, in the chapter titled "Why We Need the Concept of 'Cluster.'")

Second, the system used to reach that mark was a 7-"node" system, where each "node" contained its full complement of 16 "cells" (machines). This is a total of 112 processors; but it was benchmarked as a 7-element cluster, treating the groups of 16 as if they were single machines—"loosely coupled multiprocessors," in Tandem's terminology. This, as will be explained in that same later chapter, is quite significant.

Finally, Tandem has put some publicity-garnering spice into the game. So sure are they that others will not be able to surpass them soon that they've publicly made a wager: Should any company beat their record within a year, they'll donate $20,928 to the charity of the winner's choice.

2.4.3 IBM Sysplex

The concept may boggle the mind of those attuned to microcomputers, personal computers, and workstations, but huge, room-spanning clusters of physically large mainframes have been used for a very long time. IBM's Job Entry System (JES) has eased the task of distributing work to a user-constructed cluster of mainframes since the mid-1970s; enhancements over time produced JES2 and JES3 [IBMb]. In 1990, the IBM Sysplex (for **sys**tem com**plex**) was introduced to ease administration and simplify cooperative processing. The year 1994 saw the introduction of additional hardware and software providing data sharing and parallelism; this is officially an "enhanced Sysplex," but that's techno-bureaucrapoop. Even the IBM documentation simply calls it a Sysplex [IBMd].

A Sysplex is a cluster of up to 32 MVS/ESA systems running on System/390 (S/390) mainframes; a "small" one is illustrated in Figure 2-6. The multiple machines get access to shared data through ESCON Directors: I/O switches that simultaneously provide access to disks (DASD) and other input/output devices from multiple sources. (ESCON, "Enterprise System CONnection," is the normal 12-Mbyte/second I/O connection to S/390s.) ESCON Directors serve much the same function as Digital's Star Coupler, but at significantly higher performance because they allow multiple simultaneous data transfers. The Sysplex Timer provides a common real-time reference for all systems, making it simpler and more efficient to provide consistent date/ time stamping of transactions, file modifications, and so on to occur across the complex. The Sysplex Coupling Facility is a hardware assist for performance enhancement. It provides cluster-wide locks, and also stable electronic storage for caching Sysplex-wide common read/write data; that stable storage also holds Sysplex-wide lists such as global work queues. The Timer and the Coupling Facility are the hardware that defines an "enhanced" Sysplex.

Cluster-wide parallelism making use of the Coupling Facility and Timer is now, or will be, embedded into numerous subsystems, allowing widespread use of SPPS techniques. The list is Acronym City, but it can't be helped: IMS DB (Information Management System Database Manager), a hierarchical database product, now provides SPPS use; DB2 (Database 2), IBM's flagship

In Search of Clusters ✳

relational database product, will do so in a future release, as will VSAM (Virtual Storage Access Method), a data access method; the latter will enable CICS (Customer Information Control System), a transaction monitor said to be the native language of over two million programmers worldwide. The security facility RACF (Resource Access Control Facility) now uses the coupling facility for greater performance, as does the JES2 job entry system and the VTAM (Virtual Telecommunications Access Method) network access facility.

System administration in a Sysplex is achieved through a number of specialized tools, all of which allow creation of a single point of control—one console from which their target area can be managed and administered for the entire cluster. For example, the ESCON Manager monitors and manages I/O configuration and status; RMF provides Sysplex-wide performance monitoring and capacity planning; CICSplex System Manager monitors and controls CICS (transaction monitor) resources across the Sysplex. There are many others [IBMd].

Figure 2-6   IBM Sysplex

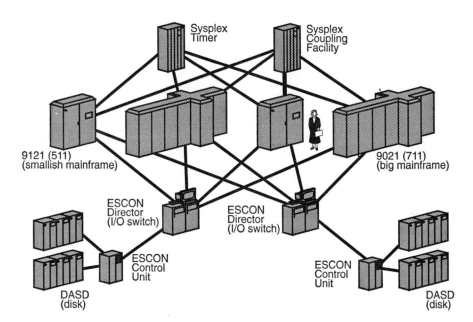

The success of enhanced Sysplex as a product is impossible to gauge at present, since it is new to the market. Similarly, dramatic statements of performance on benchmarks have not yet been made and will probably wait until more subsystems are available in Sysplex- (or cluster-) enabled form.

2.4.4 Sun SPARCclusters

Sun Microsystems announced in late 1994 three cluster products about which little detailed technical information is currently available.

The SPARCcluster 1 [Sun94b] is targeted at high NFS file server performance. It consists of two to four nodes, each a SPARCserver 10 Model 40, coupled through a high-speed Ethernet switch making use of specialized ONT (Optimized Network Throughput) software to make the cluster configuration work better than independent servers. It is stated that the SPARC-cluster 1 delivers more NFS operations per second than any other machine on the market, and better NFS throughput than servers costing twice as much.

The SPARCcluster 1000 DB and SPARCcluster 2000 PDB are, on the other hand, targeted at high-performance, high-availability database operation [Sun94a]. The difference between the 1000 and the 2000 is that the 1000 series is composed of multiple SPARCcenter 1000 nodes, while the 2000 series, logically enough, is composed of multiple SPARCcenter 2000 nodes. Both will be initially offered in 1995 as two-node systems, eventually to be expanded to eight-node systems. Members of this series provide shared access to disks by means of redundant Fibre Channel Standard switches. (See Chapter 3, particularly the section titled "Fibre Channel Standard" on page 63 and the "Discussion" on page 66.) There is no single point of failure, performance of a single database across the cluster is provided by Oracle Parallel Server and later by Informix and Sybase (see later in this chapter), and a special multithreaded lock manager is used to enhance performance.

A comprehensive suite of cluster management tools is stated to be part of the SPARCcenter PDB products, but no details about these tools were available at the time this is written.

2.5 Cluster Software Products_____

Except for Sun's offerings, all the cluster system products looked mired in proprietary implementations. Are most cluster system products vestiges of closed system badolddays? Where are all the open system cluster products?

They're primarily software, and that's how it should be.

The unique proprietary cluster systems are characterized by unique, usually quite powerful, methods of connecting and synchronizing multiple machines: Digital's CI/Star Coupler, Tandem's Dynabus and TorusNet, IBM's ESCON Directors and Coupling Facility. In open systems, on the other hand, the most essential element to be standardized is communication. As a result, connecting open-system machines is simply no big deal; one just uses off-the-shelf adapters for any of a number of communication media: ethernet, token ring, FDDI, ATM, HiPPI, Fibre Channel, or whatever. That leaves the field wide open for anybody to develop software clustering tools. As mentioned earlier, many have done so.

A number of the software products for clustering are briefly described, by category, below. Many are treated in considerably more detail in later chapters. The tables provided should be considered only a sampler, since new products and entrants are arriving regularly.

2.5.1   Batch and Login

Several products for batch submission to clusters exist, from the venerable JES system mentioned above, which works on IBM and compatible mainframes, through more recent systems based on modern distributed processing software. Many also support interactive login in the manner described for the Watson Farm.

Examples of the more recent systems include DQS, the Distributed Queueing System developed at Florida State University SCRI (not a commercial product, but widely available "freeware"); NQS/Exec from The Cummings Group; and the IBM LoadLeveller. The latter was announced with IBM's Scalable Parallel systems, but runs on any collection of IBM, HP, and Sun workstations that communicate using the *de facto* industry standard IP (Internet Protocol); the same is true of the other packages. A number of other systems provide similar functions; several are listed in Table 2-2.

These systems provide job submission to a cluster, perform at least rudimentary load balancing, and allow users to query the status of jobs. The degree to which they hide the multiple-machine nature of the cluster varies widely. Some (for example, IBM LoadLeveller) also provide checkpoint/restart facilities for more reliable operation; others (for example, The Cummings Group's NCADMIN) provide cluster-wide administration and accounting services. At this time, only one provides multistep job submission or conditional job step execution: Utopia Load Sharing Facility from Platform Computing. At this time, none can be really considered a complete, full-function commercial batch system with conditional job steps, step monitoring, priority queues, resource enqueueing, and so on. This may change, and in any case the systems now available are certainly adequate for some commercial and most technical use.

Batch systems of course have the major advantage of being SPPS: They allow clusters to be effectively used without altering applications in any way. Normal (serial, not parallel) jobs can be submitted to a cluster and run without further ado. Some batch systems (e.g., IBM LoadLeveller) have facilities for running parallel jobs too, but it's not required in order to make effective use of the cluster. These issues are discussed in more detail in Chapter 7.

Table 2-2   Some Cluster Batch and Login Systems

Who	What	Description
Freedman Sharp & Associates Inc.	Load Balancer	batch queueing, interactive login
IBM	Loadleveller	batch job submission; runs on heterogeneous collections of machines
	Job Scheduler for AIX	batch job submission with multiple queues and other features; runs on IBM's AIX only.
Platform Computing Corp.	Utopia Load Sharing Facility	batch queueing with multiple job steps, interactive login, development
The Cummings Group	NCADMIN, NCLOGIN, NQS/Exec	accounting, managing, reporting, and such; load-balanced interactive login; batch job submission

2.5.2 Database Systems

As Table 2-3 indicates, every major vendor of open systems database software (and proprietary vendors, too) either now has, or has in development or plan, a version of their database that operates across multiple computers—in other words, across the machines of a cluster. In doing this, these systems effectively merge the machines into a single database entity for application and database administration purposes. Oracle's Parallel Server has been delivered for several years now [Llo92, LC94]; IBM's DB2/6000 Parallel Edition [Fec94] is in beta test, as is Sybase's Navigation Server [Ber94]; and Informix-Online's DSA (Dynamic Scalable Architecture) [Chr94] has been described. The different techniques used by all of these, and they all do differ significantly, are discussed in Chapter 9.

In Search of Clusters ✳

Table 2-3   Some Cluster/Distributed/Parallel Database Products

Who	What	Description
IBM	DB2 Parallel Edition	Relational Database; OLTP, Query for open system clusters and parallel machines
	IMS for Sysplex	Hierarchical database manager for IBM Sysplex
	DB2 and VSAM	Relational DB and storage management, statement of direction for Sysplex support
INFORMIX-Online	Dynamic Scalable Architecture (DSA)	Relational Database; OLTP, Query for open system clusters
Oracle Corp.	Oracle Parallel Server, Oracle Parallel Everything; Oracle V7 on NCube	Relational Database; OLTP, Query; many installations on clusters and highly parallel systems
Sybase/NCR	Navigation Server	Relational Database; OLTP, Query

Like the batch systems mentioned above, such database systems are also SPPS, and hence are application transparent: No change to the application is required. This enormous advantage, and other aspects of the whole issue of exploiting parallelism, will also be dissected in detail in Chapter 7.

2.5.3   Parallel Programming Facilities

There are also packages available that enable applications to be programmed to run in parallel, that is, to run faster because they've been reorganized to execute simultaneously on multiple nodes in a cluster. Examples, listed in Table 2-4, include Parasoft's Express [Kol91], Scientific Computing Corp.'s Linda [CG89], Applied Parallel Research's FORGE 90, and two popular "freeware" packages: P4 from Argonne National Laboratory [BL92, LO87] and the very popular, highly portable package from Oak Ridge National Laboratory and the University of Tennessee, PVM (Parallel Virtual Machines) [GS93, BDG$^+$91]. A standard program interface for message-passing parallelism is also being developed, called the MPI (Message Passing Interface) standard [Wal93, Mes94]. MPI is being defined by an international *ad hoc* group called the Message Passing Interface Forum that is very well supported by many industrial members, universities, and research laboratories. Many other systems for parallelism, particularly message-passing parallelism, have been developed; for example, there's also PARMACS [Hem91], CHIMP [Edi91], EUI [FBH+92], and so on.

Table 2-4   Some Cluster Parallel Programming Facilities

Who	What	Description
Argonne National Laboratory	P4	portable parallel C and FORTRAN programming; free package
Oak Ridge National Laboratory.	Parallel Virtual Machines (PVM)	portable, heterogeneous parallel C and FORTRAN programming; very popular free package
Parasoft Corp.	Express	parallel C and FORTRAN enablement; message-passing, collective operations
Scientific Computing Associates, Inc.	Network Linda	parallel C & FORTRAN enablement; a relational-database-like shared memory is emulated
The MPI Forum	MPI	Widely-supported, highly detailed proposal for a standard C and Fortran interface for message-passing parallel programming.

Many of these facilities began life as university or research laboratory projects in providing programming support for massively parallel systems; Express, Linda, and P4 are examples of this. They were then were ported to collections of workstations connected by LAN, simply as an expedient way to allow multiuser program debugging that didn't use up expensive and/or limited time on a massively parallel machine. The workstation/LAN version proved to be a valuable tool in its own right, to say nothing of a profitable product. PVM was different: Its avowed original purpose was to support parallelism across heterogeneous clusters of machines.

The installation rate of these systems is at least as large as the rate of installing assembled or preassembled clusters. Virtually everybody with one of those clusters at least thinks they want to explicitly exploit its parallel capabilities, too. As has already been emphasized, explicit parallel programming is not for the faint of heart (or the credulous). Circumstances in which it is feasible and warranted are discussed in Chapter 7.

2.5.4 Operating Systems

The products previously described are tools or subsystems that run under the native operating systems of the clustered machines, one copy of the operating system per machine, hooking them together as a unit for some specific purpose. There are also, in contrast, at least the beginnings of extensions to operating systems themselves that start to make multiple machines look unified in general, not just for one specific purpose. Those are listed in Table 2-5.

Table 2-5   Some Cluster-Supporting Operating Systems or Extensions

Who	What	Description
Chorus Systemes	Chorus/MiX Operating System	Microkernel-based system, Unix SVR5 personality; transparency among machines
Digital Equipment Corp.	Digital Clusters for Windows NT	Extensions to Microsoft Windows NT that provide the function of VMSclusters
Locus	Transparent Network Computing (TNC)	Microkernel-based UNIX process, device, etc., transparency between machines
Open Software Foundation	OSF/1 AD TNC	Microkernel-based Unix OS for massively parallel technical computing; uses Locus TNC. Different, modified versions of this are used to support the Intel Paragon and Convex Exemplar massively parallel multicomputers.
QNX Software Corporation	QNX	Microkernel-based system for real time and control operations spanning multiple machines
Santa Cruz Operations	SCO CHORUS/ Fusion	Extension of SCO kernel for real time and clusters

While there is an exception, these for the most part provide the internal bare-bones requirements for cross-machine operation. In the jargon, they implement unified name spaces: The name for something is guaranteed to be the same, and unique, across all the machines connected. For example, files are globally named, processes (running programs) likewise, normal forms of communication inside an operating system work between machines with no application code change, new processes are created on different machines in accordance with load balancing, and so on. These are necessary technical underpinnings for SPPS execution of general programs on a cluster, not just programs submitted to a special cluster-wide batch system.

Locus Computing's Transparent Network Computing (TNC) does this for the UNIX personality of a microkernel [Thi91, PW85], and has been included in the Open Software Foundation's OSF/1 AD TNC product used by Intel Scientific Supercomputers' massively parallel offering [WLH93]. A prior non-microkernel version of Locus' technology was used in an IBM product, Transparent Computing Facility (TCF), which made a single system out of S/370 mainframes and PS/2s all running UNIX [WP89]. Convex uses similar Locus-derived OSF/1-based support to emulate Hewlett-Packard's HP/UX across their highly parallel machine. Chorus Systemes' Chorus/Mix is another microkernel-based approach to distributing UNIX [A+92], and Santa Cruz Operations has announced that they will be providing similar capabilities based on their UNIX kernel. In addition, QNX markets a microkernel-based system of the same name, particularly targeted at embedded and control applications, that provides a large degree of single system image across multiple machines [Hil93].

While these systems provide a way to run applications across multiple machines, they seldom if ever adequately tackle the larger, more amorphous, and highly practical problem of similarly modifying the parts of operating systems not talked about in operating system textbooks: system management and administration facilities. This and related areas are further discussed in Chapter 10.

There is an exception to the general comments above. Digital announced very recently (while this book was in review) that it is creating a a software package, "Digital Clusters for Windows NT," that extends Microsoft Windows NT operating system as a LAN server system the way Digital's VMSCluster product extends the VMS operating system. That is to say, multiple machines running Windows NT can be managed as if they were one machine and will appear to client machines as if they are a single system: Files and other services, resources, and objects residing anywhere within the cluster can be accessed by clients that treat the group as if it were a single entity. Clients connect to the cluster, not to any single machine; the computational load is automatically balanced across the machines; and should one (or more) of the machines in the cluster fail, client systems need never even know that fact—the others will automatically pick up the load, without clients requiring to reconnect or perform any other non-ordinary action. Unlike Digital's VMSCluster, this will operate on any machines that host Windows NT, using standard communications media among the clustered machines. The host machines specifically include mass-market PC server systems; such systems are obviously the primary target of this product.

They estimate that a complete, highly available cluster system may be marketable for less than $25,000.

Digital's NTcluster (which it will obviously end up being called) falls in a half-way zone between the current category of operating systems and the next. It isn't a full operating system; rather, it wedges into the articulation points of the Windows NT operating system, extending it into the cluster dimension.[2] Although the current NTcluster descriptions stress availability, NTclusters promise to have much more function than the pure "availability clusters" that are the subject of the next section. Those tend to focus strictly on actualizing the availability latent in any collection of machines, and unlike Digital's cluster products, they do not address system management and uniform addressability of resources.

Last, literally on the day the final, copy-edited text for this book was sent to the publisher, Tandem announced that it had arranged a source license agreement with Microsoft for Windows NT Server and would be using that as a base for new, highly-available, scalable products.

2.6   Availability Clusters_____

As indicated by Table 2-6, virtually every manufacturer of commercial UNIX systems has some facility for coupling at least two machines to attain higher availability by what is called *failover*: The machines listen to "heartbeat" signals from each other, and when one stops the other takes over its work. Hewlett-Packard, Sun Microsystems, Sequent, Pyramid, IBM [IBMa], and so on all provide such systems. At least one manufacturer (Sequent) considers this facility important enough to designate it as a specific machine model (Symmetry 2000/990), rather than as a feature or software offering.

This is similar to the failover used in Tandem systems, but nowhere near as fast. Tandem provides the ability in its own database system to keep a process on another machine (another Tandem "cell") synchronized and up-to-date; that process is effectively on a trip-wire ready to take over very quickly. In contrast, these systems usually have to restart the application (and possibly the database system) on the backup machine before it can take over. Some of them even start the failover process by booting the backup machine from scratch; this can take half an hour or more when booting involves the traditional UNIX file system check (**fsck**) and the file system is large. Others, using more modern file system technology, can complete the

---

2. The fact that Windows NT has articulation points at the proper places for cluster additions, as did Digital's VMS, probably has more than a little to do with the fact that both systems had the same software architect: David Cutler.

failover process and be completely operational in as little as 20 to 30 seconds; the Pyramid and IBM products are examples of the latter, faster category. DEC has indicated that their DECsafe Available Server environment can fail over in 18 seconds, which they state is a leadership position [Dig94]

Table 2-6   Some Cluster High-Availability Products

Vendor	Product
Data General	Data General High Availability
DEC	DECsafe Available Server Environment
HP	Switchover UX
IBM	HACMP/6000 (High Availability Cluster Multiprocessor)
NCR	NCR Lifekeeper
Pyramid	Pyramid Reliant
Sequent	HiAv Symmetry
Sun	Open*Vision High Availability
	SPARCcluster 1000 and 2000 PDB availability support
	Fusion High Availability (third-party software product)

Obviously, these systems don't provide the continuous availability characteristic of traditional fault-tolerant machines. They are therefore not appropriate for highly critical applications like real-time transportation control systems, where even a very short outage can lead to disaster. But in many situations they are appropriate. For example, a 20- second outage of a warehouse inventory system is not likely to be a severe problem. There, and in other circumstances, the relevant requirement is to get things going again before anybody is tempted to wander off to the coffee machine or hang up while making an order; for that, outages of less than 20 or 30 seconds are adequate.

So, in appropriate circumstances, these clusters provide a quite usable higher level of availability than single systems. They're popular because they have the cachet of "open systems," unlike most hardware fault-tolerant solutions. They're also cheaper. There are two reasons for the latter: First, the open systems competition and volume have driven prices down to where two open systems can be cheaper than one proprietary hardware-fault-tolerant one. Second, the amount of availability purchased can be tuned to the situation, in the following sense. Most manufacturers allow failover to be between machines of different sizes. So, for example, a large system can be the primary, and the secondary can be a smaller, less expensive machine. Response time and other performance characteristics certainly won't be as good when running on the backup, but that's supposed to be the exceptional, temporary case. How much one wants to support that case can be considered an aspect of risk management, like buying insurance; not everybody needs, wants, or can afford total blanket coverage.

There's another advantage of these systems over hardware fault-tolerance approaches that is a positive gain, and very important: They can provide at least some detection, and thence tolerance, of software failures in addition to hardware failures. Since software failures are now very much more common than hardware failures, coverage of the more likely failures is significantly improved. Software failure coverage arises in an obvious way: The failure-detecting heartbeat signals are generated by software. If the most usual failure mode of software occurs—it goes catatonic—the heartbeat isn't generated and a failure is detected. One might imagine manic failure modes that spew forth spurious heartbeats while ignoring real processing requests and shredding vital data, but the accidents of coordination needed to make that happen are exceedingly unlikely.

The degree of software failure coverage varies among the available products. All implicitly provide detection of operating system failure, since if that's brain-dead, there's no communication at all, including the heartbeat. Some also provide for installation-specific heartbeat generators that can be installed in subsystems (databases) or in applications; these additional heartbeats are then monitored in addition to the basic hardware/operating system heartbeat, allowing action to be taken when these other software components fail. Pyramid's system is one example of this.

The overall system configurations supported by these systems also vary. Some provide only a simple hot standby; others provide rotating standby, mutual takeover, and so on. The more complex configurations, which typically involve more than just two machines, lead one to expect higher performance, in addition to availability; that does appear.

The most common performance extension, since this is primarily a commercial market area, is for higher performance on batch or OLTP/database processing. Assuming the underlying support is there, one simply runs one of the parallel/cluster databases or a distributed batch/login system on the collection. The result is a larger system that simultaneously provides higher availability. Since larger systems tend to be depended upon by larger numbers of people, this combination is particularly felicitous.

Where these systems have a weakness is (as usual) in system administration and management. Not a whole lot of additional administration is required for a simple duplicate system used as a backup. However, as these systems are used for higher performance in addition to availability, the number of machines in the cluster rises and the multimachine administration required becomes a deterrent to sales. It is hardly surprising that commercial customers, buying multiple machines for enhanced availability, are unwilling to entrust their corporate jewels to Shell Scripts from Hell.

Availability clusters are in widespread use. At this writing there are, for example, over 700 HACMP/6000 installations worldwide, and the rate of installation is growing rapidly. Furthermore, the rate of announcement is fierce; five of the ten systems listed were either newly announced or upgraded during a two-month period in the fall of 1993 (Digital, IBM, Pyramid, Sequent, Sun). If anything similar happens a year later, this section of this book will be seriously out of date even more quickly than anticipated.

2.7   Not the End

An amazing thing about clustering is how widespread it is. There's just so much of it going on, and it's been going on for so very long. There are so many products, so much new product development right now, and such significant market presence. The author was, frankly, flabbergasted at how much there turned out to be in this chapter. In fact, this has been an exhausting if not impossible chapter to write, because clusters seem to be announced faster than they can be catalogued and documented by any one person. For example, there is a new Hewlett-Packard FCS-connected cluster recently announced (last week as I write this) about which I've been unable to find enough detail to describe with any reliability; and on the day the final text of this book went to the publisher, Tandem announced its use of Microsoft Windows NT Server.

An obvious question to ask at this point is: Why?

What makes clustering something that people just *do*, continually, with a steady, high-speed flow of new product enhancements and announcements, conspicuously *without* all the bandwagons, eye-catching front-page announcements, high-profile government research grants, and other assorted hoopla that surround the other forms of overt parallelism?

That's the topic of the next chapter.

3

Why Clusters?

It should be apparent from the prior chapter that there are many clusters out there, and that vendor-supplied and user-developed tools for using clusters of machines are being developed apace. There are a number of reasons why vendors, research labs, and computer service departments should go through the bother and expense of creating clusters—and certainly it is a bother and an expense; many "simple matters of programming" are involved, and the technical issues involved are certainly not simple. There are both general reasons and specific reasons for going to that trouble. The general reasons arise because clusters are a form of parallel or distributed system. As such, they inherit many of the reasons for which their more recognized brethren are pursued. These general reasons are by now neither particularly new nor even exciting, but they are not to be brushed aside; they also apply to clusters and form a broad general motivation for their development.

But why, specifically, clusters? The general reasons can't explain that. Are there specific factors that exist now favoring clusters as opposed, for example, to ever larger symmetric multiprocessors or massively parallel machines? There are. Those are the specific reasons, the reasons why clusters are actively being assembled now and expanding their sweep, rather than dying out in the face of significant competition.

Most of both the general and the specific reasons have actually already been mentioned in the "Examples" discussion. This is where we pull them all together and examine them as a whole.

3.1 The Standard Litany _____

Every time anybody tries to sell a parallel or distributed system, or obtain funding for the development of a new one (which amounts to the same thing: selling), a fundamental collection of standard reasons is always recited. This litany hasn't changed one whit for 30 years. Slotnick probably used it when he went for the money to build ILLIAC IV. Dewy-eyed neophytes declare themselves by chanting it with ingenuous enthusiasm. Here it is.

> ➤ **Performance:** No matter what form or measure of performance one is seeking—throughput, response time, turnaround time or whatever—it is straightforward to claim that one can get even more of it by using a bunch of machines at the same time. In some cases there is a proviso that a wee bit of new programming is involved for anything to work. Those cases are best avoided.

> ➤ **Availability:** Having a computer shrivel up into an expensive doorstop can be a whole lot less traumatic if it's not unique, but rather one of a herd. The herd should be able to accommodate spares, which can potentially be used to keep the work going; or if one chooses to configure sparelessly, the work that was done by the dear departed sibling can, potentially, be redistributed among the others.

> ➤ **Price/Performance:** Clusters and other forms of computer aggregation are typically collections of machines which individually have very good, if not industry pace-setting, performance for their price. The promise is that the aggregate retains the price/performance of its individual members. While this, like the other reasons, can be true, it always makes me think of committees…

> ➤ **Incremental Growth:** To the degree that one really does attain greater performance and availability with a group of computers, one should be able enhance both by merely adding more machines. Rolling an old, smaller computer out and rolling a new, bigger one in should not be necessary. This collaterally avoids the attendant trauma of justifying a whole new computer, to say nothing of getting everything to work again on the new one. Good show.

> ➤ **Scaling:** The marketing community, ever alert for new synonyms for "good," has seized on "scalable" as the buzzword of the mo-

ment for open commercial systems. As a result, its definition has devolved to the point where it means little. It actually has (or did have) something to do with how big a computer system can usably get. Since there's no limit outside a buyer's pocketbook to how many machines can be stacked side by side, parallel and distributed systems in general and clusters in particular are good… er, I mean offer great scalability. This will be discussed at far greater length later, since despite the marketing hype it's a crucial element in the differentiation between clusters and symmetric multiprocessors.

The above is the Classic Standard Litany. There is an addition to it that was spawned with the wide deployment of personal workstations and computers. Adding it to the above results in the Enhanced Standard Litany.

> **Scavenging:** Every Information Services (I/S) manager on earth possessing two neurons to knock together lusts after all those "unused cycles" spread across most organizations' personal computers and workstations. As the saying goes: Computers may grow ever cheaper, but unused cycles are *free*. Putting those spare cycles to productive use appears to be just another application of clusters, since the collection of all those personal machines is "just" a large, rather diffuse cluster. For reasons to be discussed later, however, rounding up spare personal cycles into a usable herd complicates cluster support very significantly.

The rather jaded rendition above to the contrary (well, partially), the standard litany is real. The benefits promised are without question highly desirable and are actually being accomplished—gradually—by aggregate computing in general and clusters in particular. This was demonstrated by the examples in the last chapter.

The important points are that the litany is certainly neither (a) new, nor (b) accomplished by merely waving a parallel-hardware magic wand. Hardware provides potential, and potential alone; fulfillment lies in the software. Painstakingly incremental development of the requisite software has proven to be required, has been going on for years, and will continue. Software is not riding the same kind of exponential growth curve that hardware has, so there is no business end of an advancing curve to "kick in" and make recent advances ever more spectacular.

In addition, the litany explains why parallelism or distributed computing in general has always been desirable. It does not explain why assembled clusters have become very popular recently. One must still answer the question "Why *now?*

3.2 Why *Now?*

There are three reasons why clusters' popularity is now increasing and will continue to increase.

1. **Very high-performance microprocessors.** Current workstations have performance that is a large fraction of the power of a mainframe or supercomputer and, in some cases, exceeds that power. The result is that only rather few of them, say tens, need be coupled to produce aggregate performance that is very impressive. This is in contrast to the situation only a few years ago, when hundreds or thousands of microprocessor-based systems had to be ganged up to achieve interesting aggregate performance levels. On top of that, the other shoe is about to drop: Mass-market, inexpensive microprocessors, originally segregated from technical workstations, are about to crawl up the tail pipe of the workstation market just like workstations crawled up the tail pipe of larger machines. This will make the few machines needed even less expensive.

2. **Standard high-speed communication.** Communication technologies are rapidly advancing, allowing off-the-shelf, industry-standard parts to achieve levels of performance that previously were possible only with expensive, proprietary techniques. This technology saw a jump in capability starting a few years ago with the start of the introduction of fiber optics. The introduction of such standardized communication facilities as Fibre Channel Standard (FCS), Asynchronous Transmission Mode (ATM), and the Scalable Coherent Interconnect (SCI) is raising intercomputer bandwidth from 10 Mbits/second through 100 Mbytes (not bits) /second, and even gigabytes per second. It is significant that these advances are approaching, and in some cases may exceed, the internal speeds feasible between processors of an SMP. This will dramatically increase the range of applicability of interconnected systems.

3. **Standard tools for distributed computing.** The requirements of distributed computing have produced a collection of software tools that can be adapted to managing clusters of machines. Some, such as the Internet communication protocol suite (called TCP/IP and UDP/IP) are so common as to be ubiquitous *de facto* standards; others, such as the OSI standards, are struggling to happen. But higher level facilities built on that base, like Sun Microsystems' ONC+, are extremely widespread; and others, like as OSF's Distributed Computing Environment, will soon make available a comprehensive tool set and may have comprehensive manage-

ment tool sets (such as the Distributed Management Environment, DME) built on top of them.

Later sections of this chapter discuss each of these three cluster enablers in greater detail. An important aspect common to the three is that all, for reasons having nothing whatsoever to do with clustering, will be enhanced over time: There will be faster microprocessors, faster standard communication, and more functional tools for distributed computing. This means that if these factors do indeed favor clusters of machines, and there appears to be little question that they do, clustering bids fair to become even more common.

However, clustering is in fact not the most prevalent kind of computing today. The thousands of installations mentioned in prior chapters are but a drop in the Brobdingnagian bucket of the computer industry. The reasons for that need to be examined also.

3.3   Why *Not* Now?

So if they're so good, why haven't clusters already become the most common mode of computation? Two reasons:

> ➤ **Lack of "single system image" software.** Replacing a single large computer with a cluster of, say, 20 smaller ones means that 20 systems have to be managed instead of one. The only reasonable response to that is a feeling of intense nausea. The distributed computing facilities currently available are piece parts; they are toolkits, not solutions providing "turnkey" single system management and administration. A study by International Data Corporation [Int94] which surveyed hundreds of actual midrange UNIX installations in the United States and Europe showed that the largest component of cost, around 50% of the total, is not hardware, software, or maintenance—it is staffing. As staffing is intimately related to system management and administration, an increase in system management workload is a huge cost disadvantage for assembled and preassembled clusters.
>
> Digital's OpenVMS Cluster, Tandem's systems, and possibly IBM's Sysplex are exceptions that probe this rule. But each of them is a unique solution, both tailored to and a product of its unique hardware/software surround; as a result they have not spread beyond their proprietary bounds and are not likely to. The VMSCluster code, for example, cannot simply be dropped into the middle of a UNIX system; it depends heavily on the internal structure of VMS, which is quite different from that of UNIX.

This general lack of "single system image" effectively limits the use of open-system-based clusters either to very small installations—minimalist two-way availability clusters—or to technically sophisticated sites with the expertise to construct and maintain the required solutions using the available tools. This restricts nonproprietary clusters to technically sophisticated sites—usually universities and large laboratories that both have the required expertise and place a low enough value on system robustness to entrust it to Shell Scripts from Hell.

Difficulty of programming. Full exploitation of clusters requires that major applications and subsystems run across all the nodes in a parallel fashion, fully enabling the SPPS mode of operation that moves user parallelism to the covert domain. Batch with login systems exist, as was documented; but of databases only the Oracle Parallel Server, born a decade ago and nurtured in the VMScluster creche, is now in regularly deployed, production operation on a wide range of platforms. The others are in various stages of development from direction statements through announcement to initial market penetration and will require substantial tuning time before they fully take their place in the fold.

This is a direct result of the substantial difficulties that arise in parallel programming, difficulties that are further reflected in the lack of single-system-image software mentioned above. Everyday sequential software is already notorious for being the bottleneck in computing of all kinds; parallel is substantially more complex. A later chapter illustrates this in great detail.

The reasons "why," listed in the prior section, were all hardware. The reasons "why not," listed above, are all software. In other words: **The problem is not hardware. It's software.**

This fact bears more than a little emphasis.

Any number of hardware products and proposals for clustered or parallel systems continually appear, willy-nilly, especially for intermachine communication. Strange communication architectures and switches appear to be particularly fun for engineers to design and build—there are so many of them proposed. Their proponents all universally chant the Standard Litany of advantages listed above; some—especially those using optical fibre—have even progressed to the Enhanced Standard Litany. *All such claims are intrinsically without merit unless the proposed hardware facilitates solving the real problems, which are all in software.*

To date, no cluster hardware organization has demonstrated any such ability to simplify software, other than the distinctly neutral advantage of doing standard things faster or more cheaply, without appearing different; the lack of being different supports existing software with minimal fuss.

This situation—easily proposed and constructed hardware, recalcitrant software—has been true of parallel and distributed systems since their inception. In the colorful phrase of a colleague,[1] two blind men and a lame boy can assemble the hardware for a cluster. But programming it takes sophistication, experience, and gumption—and the time of people with all three is very expensive.

The rest of this book delves into these issues in greater detail. A word, first, about the exception.

The statements above could be taken to apply to any and every parallel or distributed system. That would be incorrect. For one parallel system, software issues have been addressed to a great degree, and in the process it has become an industry-standard organization: the symmetric multiprocessor (SMP). It alone has the single-system-image management required (and by the way, its hardware organization requires this), and for it alone has the necessary parallelization been performed on virtually every major subsystem required for effective general use: databases, file systems, communication subsystems, and so on.

The SMP, therefore, obviously becomes the benchmark for clustered systems, as well as for any parallel or distributed system, and must be discussed in some detail. A later lengthy chapter is devoted to explaining the hardware of SMPs; this is in support of another chapter specifically comparing clusters and SMP systems.

But first, let's talk about those cluster enablers in greater detail.

3.4 Cluster Enablers

As mentioned above, three things have changed that make clusters a more attractive proposition than has previously been the case: microprocessor performance, standard interconnect performance, and the availability of tools for distributed computing. Each of these will now be discussed in more detail.

---

1. Justin Hall, then of the IBM RISC System/6000 Division in Austin, TX.

3.4.1 Microprocessor Performance

Microprocessor performance is, more than any other aspect, the primary reason for the popularity of assembled and other "open" clusters. This issue has two elements. One has already come to pass, while the other shoe has not quite fully dropped.

Workstations: The First Shoe Has Dropped

Microprocessor-based open systems have fully crawled up the tail pipe of traditional large machines—minicomputers, mainframes, and supercomputers—and begun lunching on their innards. Anyone doubting this must be living in an alternate universe where IBM stock is not sold. These are not, however, the garden-variety, sold-in-millions microprocessors that power personal computers. They are the rather robust, relatively limited volume, "boutique" microprocessors originally developed to power high-performance technical workstations and make them "supercomputers on a desktop." Since their introduction in that market, they have spread from their origins into the far more lucrative open-systems commercial computing market, largely but not entirely in the form of SMP systems.

While these systems succeeded in their power challenge and *coup d'etat* because they were dramatically more cost-effective than the larger systems, they had to cross a threshold before they did so, and that threshold was not one of cost-effectiveness, alias price/performance. Even the earliest microprocessors, back in the 70s, had fantastic price/performance, and it took nearly 20 years before they really were challengers. The threshold was, rather, plain vanilla performance, period—the absolute performance of each microprocessor singly, measured against a single larger machines. That didn't have to equal the performance of large systems, it just had to come adequately close. This is most easily documented for the case of technical computing, so that will be discussed first.

Technical Computing

The absolute performance of microprocessor-based workstations like the IBM RISC Systems, HP 700 series, Silicon Graphics MIPS-based machines, DEC Alpha AXP machines, and so on, has reached a point where each workstation realistically exhibits a very large fraction of the performance of a supercomputer.

For example, users of just the first midrange IBM RISC Systems, introduced back in 1990, routinely reported performance on the order of 20% of that obtained on the then-contemporary Cray Y-MP systems. For some applications, workstations actually exceed supercomputer performance; but it's not necessary to assume that level of performance to make the point being made here, which is the following: At a routine 20% of supercomputer performance, a group of only five workstations has a potential aggregate performance equal to that of a machine whose annual maintenance cost usually exceeds the total purchase price of all five of the workstations.

This is a very major change. In the mid-80s, literally hundreds of workstation-class processors had to be used in aggregate before minimally "interesting" performance levels such as this could be obtained.

The effect of such a reduction in numbers dramatically affects the practicality of multimachine systems in a vast number of ways: Communication, synchronization, load balancing, administration, generality, and virtually all other aspects of multiple-machine computing become intensely easier when one is dealing with only a few machines rather than hundreds or thousands. That alone makes clusters a more accessible way to be granted the litany of parallelism benefits.

In addition, this level of individual machine performance has another, perhaps less immediately obvious effect: Rather modestly scaled clusters can be used in a very different manner than highly parallel systems.

Highly parallel machines are inevitably designed, and their software support arranged, to reduce the turnaround time of individual applications. Their purpose is to support applications that have been modified to run in parallel, most often with high degrees of parallelism, so their parameters and organization are chosen with that in mind. It is indeed desirable to run some applications in parallel on clusters, and clusters of workstations are very competitive with supercomputers on parallel benchmarks [BBDS94].

The point here, however, is that it is not a requirement to parallelize programs in order to obtain benefits from clusters. An extremely viable use of clusters is to instead run plain, serial programs, a different one on each cluster node, to obtain greater throughput. (This is elaborated on in Chapter 7, "Workloads.")

That this kind of SPPS use is made of clusters is hardly a new revelation; it was illustrated back in the first case described in Chapter 2, "Examples." The issue here is why that is the case.

What makes that kind of SPPS use feasible is the *absolute* performance of the *individual* microprocessor-based machines, not any form of combined, parallel-execution performance or cost/performance. By enabling effective SPPS operation without *any change* to the application software, that single-machine performance makes clusters a much more accessible form in which to be granted the standard litany of parallelism benefits.

This would not be true if most individual uses of large machines actually used to the limit the full capability of those machine. But they do not.

The hardest evidence I am aware of for this statement is contained in data obtained at NCSA (the National Center for Supercomputer Applications in Champaign, Ill.) that was part of their 1991 report to the National Science Foundation. They did something that everybody says is a good thing, but seldom does: actually measured what was going on inside their systems, for a period long enough for the measurement to be meaningful. (This was done as part of the justification for acquiring a workstation-farm-style cluster, by the way.)

What they found was that the vast majority of jobs run were not well "vectorized," that is, reorganized (or perhaps reorganizable) into a form in which they attained anywhere near normally benchmarked (LINPACK) speed of their supercomputer, a Cray Y-MP.[2] It was NCSA's estimation that many of the jobs run will do equally well on a midrange scientific workstation. Thus, no matter how long most of the jobs in the workload run, their turnaround time will not be substantially worse on a workstation than on a supercomputer. This is numerically by far the largest number of jobs and, therefore, the dominant source of user satisfaction.

CPU performance is not everything, of course; the jobs must also fit into memory and adequate I/O must be available. The memory installable for such workstations now routinely exceeds 512 Mbytes, which NCSA found quite adequate for their workloads, and the compute-bound nature of that workload put little strain on input and output.

But what about big, well-tuned jobs? What will happen to the time it takes them to complete—their turnaround time? Measurements again made at NCSA showed that it took roughly 2.5 times as long for jobs to return to the users—turnaround time—as the jobs required in actual run time.

This result would not be very interesting in this context if the difference were due to I/O or some other intrinsic characteristic of the jobs being run, but that was not the cause. Nearly the entire expansion factor was due to simple waiting in job queues. This correlates well with anecdotal evidence I have heard; users often gripe about week-long waits in supercomputer job queues for large, long-running jobs.

Obviously, queue waiting time in a cluster can be reduced to a negligible amount by the simple expedient of installing more machines. They're cheap.

---

2. These results are a little dated at this point. In particular, Cray definitely makes faster, more cost-effective machines by now. Then again, so does the workstation competition.

(Relatively, anyway.) For simplicity, consider the case were it actually is reduced to zero. The clustered machines could then be 2.5 times slower than the large machine and still give the same turnaround time. Put another way: The clustered machines, simply because they are more available for use, act as if they were 2.5 times *faster* than they actually are.

Now, if workstations are really 40% the speed of large machines—and that is a rather low estimate today—an "availability multiple" of 2.5 makes them effectively 100% of that speed.

So, parallelization of individual applications is not a necessary precondition for effectively using moderate-sized clusters of workstations; both un-tuned and highly optimized jobs can see a benefit without moving into the dimension of parallelization. This doesn't mean that running jobs in parallel on clusters isn't meaningful. The ability to take particular problems of interest and parallelize them is legitimately a factor in the purchase of clusters; supercomputer-level computing resources, while more typically used for batch throughput, are very often justified and purchased on the basis of one or a few large applications that will be tailored to the purchased system by experts. The absolute power of the individual nodes has a large effect there, too, due to an factor usually referred to as Amdahl's law [Amd67]; this law will be discussed in a later chapter.

To sum up:

The increase in microprocessor performance to a large fraction of big machine performance makes smaller groups of machines—clusters—a particularly easy way to be granted the entire litany of benefits of parallelism for the broad range of technical applications, whether they by short-running, long-running, or important enough to explicitly tune to parallel execution.

Commercial Computing

There is a similar tale to be told with respect to commercial performance. While it's impossible to find non-company-confidential data as explicit as that obtained at NCSA, it is at least logical if not obvious that big commercial systems also routinely run multiple applications at the same time, none of which individually saturate the system.

There are obvious exceptions, situations where single large applications do soak up whole huge systems. But those exceptions are primarily applications running under subsystems—database management and transaction processing systems in particular. Those subsystems are appropriate to parallelize for clusters, and that is being done or, in some cases, has already been accomplished. Since parallelizing them helps many users via the SPPS paradigm, they are particularly important. The arguments from Amdahl's law figure here, making the absolute speed of individual processors an important issue also.

Thus, only a few dramatically less expensive machines, each running just one or a couple of applications, can be an effective substitute, if each provides a sufficient fraction of a large commercial systems's power. They do.

Table 3-1 validates this assertion. It lists the published performance on the industry-standard TPC-A benchmark of two mainframe systems: An IBM ES/9000 742 running MVS/ESA and IMS Fast Path, a hierarchical database; and an IBM ES/9000 511 running TPF, a special-purpose operating system developed specifically to run on-line transaction processing blazingly fast. Then it lists several microprocessor-based systems, giving their performance ratio to the two mainframe cases.

Table 3-1   Some Comparative TPC-A Results

System	Throughput (tpsA)	$ per tpsA	Ratio to IBM 511 (TPF)	Ratio to IBM 742 (IMS/DB)
IBM ES9000 Model 511, with TPF (special OLTP operating system)	3504	$ 7,964	100%	246%
IBM ES9000 Model 742 with IMS Fast Path	1427	$13,438	41%	100%
DEC 7000 Model 660 AXP with Oracle V7	1079	$ 5,850	31%	76%
HP9000 Series 890 with Oracle V7.0	710	$ 6,767	20%	50%
DEC 7000 Model 620 AXP with DEC RdB V6.0	529	$ 5,498	15%	37%
IBM RISC System/6000 POWERserver R2 with Oracle V7	354	$ 7,334	10%	25%

Whichever mainframe case you choose to compare with, the microprocessor-based systems clearly are now running at a large fraction of mainframe performance. As was noted earlier, clustered microprocessor-based systems have already exceeded these marks. However, the systems listed are not clusters. They are, except for IBM's entry in the microprocessor-based set,

SMPs. These results are quite volatile, and will undoubtedly be exceeded by the time this book sees print.

Workstations do not have to beat mainframe performance, just come close enough, and be less expensive. The table does not appear to support lowered expense, however; the "$ per tpsA" column does not indicate the kind of very large difference one would expect, given the technical price/performance measures achieved. This is, however, affected in ways one might not expect from the benchmark definition. The TPC-A benchmark's price/performance strongly favors those who can find cheap terminals and disks; as a result, central system price/performance is often not visible. (One can argue till the cows come home about whether it is good or bad to include terminal and/or disk cost in these comparisons; the only conclusion I've ever seen to such an argument was an agreement that no benchmark can be perfect.)

Same discussion, same argument as was made for technical computing. Case closed.

The Other Shoe

Andy Groves, the CEO of Intel, stated at the 1994 Spring Compcon conference that Intel would be marketing a board containing a complete six-processor SMP, using its next-generation processor (widely known to be code-named "P6"), that would achieve an aggregate of 1000 MIPS.

Why should this be greeted with other than a yawn? The implied rate of 1000 / 6 = 167 MIPS has already been grossly exceeded by many microprocessor systems. For example, the SPECint92 record holder as this is written, Digital Equipment Corp.'s Alpha AXP 21164, is claimed to achieve 1.2 BIPS, otherwise written as 1200 MIPS. That's a tidy bit more than 167 MIPS. It's even more than the 1000 MIPS SMP aggregate rate Groves mentioned, and SMPs will probably be built from the 21164.

But it does indicate that microprocessors produced in huge quantity are attaining speeds that are a large fraction of the speeds of the "boutique" microprocessors used in technical workstations and midrange commercial UNIX systems. It may not seem that 167 is a large fraction of 1200, but these numbers are MIPS, about which the old joke goes that it does not stand for "Millions of Instructions Per Second" but "Meaningless Indicator of Processor Speed." In all seriousness, MIPS is not a useful measure.

Using the newer industry standard SPECint92 measure, which is rather more meaningful, the AXP 21164 weighs in at 330, and a 90 MHz. Intel Pentium—on the street now, in real systems—attains 90. That's 27%, by any standard a large fraction. More dramatically, consider the PowerPC 604, claimed on Oct. 10, 1994, to be 160 SPECint92: that's 160=48% of the leader, and in sample quantities costs $549. The PowerPC chips are the product of a consortium of IBM, Apple, and Motorola, used in Apple's PowerMACs and to be used in a variety of machines, from commercial UNIX servers to PC price-class machines from 13 manufacturers, including IBM, Apple, Motorola, Canon, Hitachi, Groupe Bull, members of the Taiwanese New PC consortium, to name a few. Intel or clones of Intel's processors are of course used by virtually innumerable companies.

The differences in quantity is quite substantial. Intel says it will sell six million Pentiums in 1994, against the total sales of all technical workstations, adding them together, of 749 thousand [QD94]. Sales of Apple PowerMACs alone—and PowerPCs are used in other systems, too—are estimated to be one million in 1994; more than all the technical workstations put together, including some from IBM that actually use PowerPC chips. Hewlett-Packard's recently announced alliance with Intel to produce what is touted as "post-RISC" VLIW systems underscores the recognition that sheer quantity makes a huge difference.

Quantity has an obvious effect on price. The Alpha AXP 21164 is at this writing (Oct. 1994) priced at $2669 in sample quantities. What the "P6" will cost is not known, and will vary over time like any other microprocessor's price, but a similar initial price is likely to be well under $1000; several hundred is more likely. The PowerPC 604 is currently (Oct. 1994) $549 in sample quantities; its predecessor, the 601, is priced at $165 in large quantities [IBM94].

But processor price alone, it can be argued, is not a whole computer, and cannot make the largest difference in the total cost of a server system; it is overshadowed by the cost of memory, disks, and the supporting hardware: I/O controllers, cache controllers, caches, and so on. This argument is both wrong and irrelevant, as illustrated in Figure 3-1.

The argument is wrong because some of those additional elements—I/O controllers and cache controllers—are designs that are unique to the processor. If the processor successfully participates in mass-market economies and competition, the support chips do, too, driving their cost down—and their cost can be a very appreciable part of the machine cost, equalling if not exceeding the processor cost. The argument is also wrong because while the total purchaser's cost may be dominated by memory and disk, one must ask where those items were purchased. By no means do all of them come from the original system manufacturer. Memory and disk sales can be a profitable side business, but base system configurations—not including huge memories and disk arrays—must pay for themselves and provide the revenue that enables the next leap in a business where everyone is leap-frogging everybody else in performance. Sooner or later, lacking the revenue, somebody's not going to be able to leap.

Figure 3-1   How Processor Volume Drives the Rest of the Computer

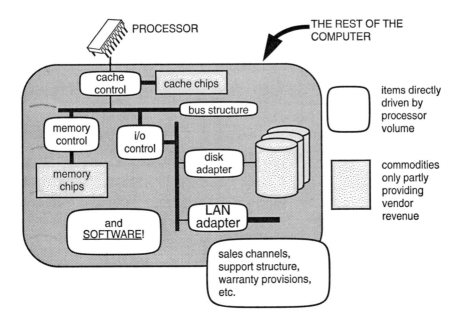

The irrelevancy of the argument arises because it looks only at the hardware, not the entire picture. The entire economic model for mass-market systems is different from that of boutique systems. They are not sold the same way, purchased the same way, or supported the same way; as a result, the overhead involved is drastically cut down from the traditional "boutique" economic model.

Consider the sales channels used. A clerk in a retail PC store does not, for example, command a large enough salary to keep a high-level traditional manufacturers' sales rep supplied with the golf clubs necessary to make sales where they're usually made. This reduction in overhead translates into a massive reduction in markup and, therefore, a price lower than even the quantity-derived economies of scale would imply.

Furthermore, the concomitant proverbial "razor-thin" profit margins mean that the entire design philosophy of these systems is different. The entire development focus is not performance, it's cost: Given a cost as the primary target, the secondary questions become how much performance, and how many features, can be wedged into a box. This is a design philosophy that has yet to infiltrate the standard textbooks on computer design, which are traditionally focused on how to make things go faster. Its implications are more than initially meets the eye.

The result of all this is a dramatic decrease in system price. And these are the systems whose actual performance is now creeping up to a sufficiently high *absolute* level that they can challenge the more-expensive, limited-edition systems. For example, Compaq, the current market leader for PC clients and servers, recently announced that it was entering the database arena with a "transaction blaster" version of its SMP server system.

The benchmark results from that entry are at least interesting. On the industry-standard TPC-B benchmark, a two-processor Compaq ProLiant 4000, using 100 MHz. Pentium processors, achieved 306.1 tpsA. In comparison, on the same benchmark with the same operating system (Windows NT) and database, a two-processor Digital Alphaserver 2100, using 200 MHz Alpha processors, achieved 308.8 tpsA. Both of these results were announced in May 1995. This is clearly more than just a challenge. Why didn't the much faster processor show a much better result? Because the other system elements—memory subsystem, I/O subsystem—are more dominant factors in total system performance than the processor alone. (A big car engine doesn't help if your tires are slipping.)

And then there's software. Software for large-quantity systems can have its development cost amortized over many, many more sales than that designed, or even ported, to the smaller-market boutique systems. Even if the software vendors charge more for licenses to run on big machines—and there's no reason they shouldn't, since on larger machines the software runs faster and supports more simultaneous users—that price is in effect subsidized by the mass-market low end, if it requires no effort to put it on the larger system. This again lowers the total system price to the user.

A very important additional point must be made about these mass-market systems: The most dramatically low-priced versions will be client, not server, systems because the clients have the volumes. As a result, whatever inexpensive support chips come along for the ride will not be ones targeted to adequately support SMP systems with many processors. There will be some SMP support, whether it's used in the majority of clients or not, but it will be the easily-provided bus structure, cache control, and memory organizations that adequately accommodate two- to four-way systems, not the heroic measures—massive caches, complex cache control schemes, muscle-bound bus-driver electronics, and other elements—needed to get performance, not just heat, out of eight or more SMP processors. Those items will not participate in these economies of scale. Why such measures are required, and describable as "heroic," will be discussed at length in Chapter 6.

3.4.2   High-Speed Interconnect

In some cases, the reduction in numbers wrought by workstation performance makes the issue of interconnect for clusters almost a moot point. It is simply not very difficult to connect a few workstations. Very inexpensive off-the-shelf LAN technology, for example Ethernet or token ring, can be and has been used quite successfully. Nevertheless, interconnects are an important factor for clusters for two reasons.

The first reason is the use of clusters to run actual parallel programs, as mentioned above. Aside from winning supercomputer-oriented sales by having a macho interconnect, programming a system with a faster interconnect presents fewer difficulties and can have significantly higher efficiency; this is further discussed in Chapter 8.

The second reason why interconnect is important is I/O. In a cluster, a program will often, if not always, be running on a computer other than the one with its data files attached. If an application does significant I/O, the interconnect can easily become a bottleneck.

Standard interconnects with much higher speed than traditional LAN are rapidly becoming, or have already become, available to meet this need. Three of particular note are Fibre Channel Standard, Asynchronous Transmission Mode, and the Scalable Coherent Interconnect, each of which has the obvious TLA (Three Letter Acronym). They're described below. As will be noted, not all the aspects of these communications schemes are positive for clusters.

Fibre Channel Standard

Fibre Channel Standard (FCS), now in the final phases of ANSI standardization, is also proposed for ISO adoption. It is a one Gbit/second maximum speed facility, capable of delivering 100 Mbytes/second of data both into and out of a node simultaneously, and doing so over a 10 km. distance with a bit error rate of 10^{-12}. Quarter-speed and half-speed versions have also been defined, and implementation of all the speeds is under way. Both connection-oriented (circuit-switched) and connectionless (packet) classes of service are part of the standard, as are broadcast and multicast. While most current available implementations are quarter- or half-speed, full-speed versions are expected on the market this year.

The IPI-3 disk protocol is embedded as a higher level in the standard, fostering the use of FCS as a means of attaching high-speed disk storage. Rooms full of RAID-based disk subsystems immediately come to mind, as does the possibility of mammoth shared-disk systems (which may or may not be used as such; see Chapter 9).

FCS is a switched system, unlike LANs and busses that are broadcast media. This means that multiple data transfers, in both directions, each at 1 Gbit/second, can occur simultaneously if the switch used can support it. At least one implementation (the Ancor CXT 1000) allows this simultaneous transmission in as large as 64-way switch. This means that, counting each of the two directions as a connection, 64 simultaneous connections are possible, and any connection can be made if the input and outputs used are free (in the jargon: It is a 64-way nonblocking crossbar switch).

Hewlett-Packard, IBM, Sun, and other companies have announced support for FCS and have formed the Fibre Channel Initiative, a forum which now numbers about 50 members. Its purpose is to enhance FCS' acceptance by defining a "standard footprint" within the standard that is implemented, tested for cross-company compatibility of implementations, and so on.

Asynchronous Transfer Mode

The very existence of "Asynchronous Transmission Mode" (ATM) [Bou92, HM89] proves one thing beyond the shadow of a doubt: Somebody is even worse at naming products than IBM.[3] Even a four-digit number would be preferable to "Asynchronous Transmission Mode." ATM displays other camel-like characteristics betraying its heritage as a grand international compromise. For example, its basic transmission unit is 53 bytes long. That is not an even power in *any* number system; it is a prime. (I foresee a run of basically silly patent applications for clever ways to count to 53.) I have been told that this occurred because the Americans and the Europeans couldn't agree over whether the basic data item length should be 32 or 64 bytes. The compromise was to split the difference—48 bytes—and having split it, added 5 bytes of header. This is a good story and rings true for me, but I can't personally vouch for its veracity.

None of this matters when behind ATM is a consortium of over 200 companies, stretching over both oceans: the ATM Forum. ATM is happening. Virtually every system vendor already offers ATM adapters, and the price for third-party adapters is already being driven down into the few-hundred-dollar range for lower speed (155 Mbits/second) versions. Not all of the offerings interoperate yet, but that's because vendor enthusiasm and desire to gain market presence and experience have run ahead of the standardization process.

ATM originated as a way to support Broadband Integrated Service Data Network (BISDN) (another great name) offerings, which are to provide com-

---

3. Well, worse than IBM used to be, anyway. "Thinkpad" is a really good name. So is "PowerPC."

munication of multimedia, video telephony, bulk data transfer, video, HDTV, and so on. It is basically high-bandwidth telephony gone digital— not just digital trunk lines, which are common now, but digital all the way to the handset or its computer adapter-card equivalent. No more modems: Those take digital data and encode it in an analog signal; that is then re-encoded digitally far from the handset for transmission; at the receiving end the process is reversed. When ATM is used, the analog stage goes away completely, resulting in great efficiency benefits. There are other techniques new to telephony that are used in ATM, like the switching of fixed-length data packets (fixed at 53 bytes). But for our purposes, most of the details don't matter.

What does matter is speed, distance, and how many things you can connect. ATM data rates start at 155 Mbits/second and potentially rise to 4.8 Gbits/ second, depending on the class of service. The distances and quantities covered are potentially globe-girdling, since ATM is a telephone system and promises to connect directly to everything—from company-local PBXs (Private Branch eXchanges) to Metropolitan- and Wide-Area Networks (MANs and WANs). A continent-spanning 4.8 Gbit/second leased line is not going to be cheap, however; lower-speed T3 leased lines currently run up to four-digit (US$) prices per month. So don't plan on building a massively parallel multicomputer out of a multinational company's branch office computers quite yet.

There are many efforts attempting to use ATM as a LAN. This is not immediately trivial because standard LAN protocols—particularly IP, the Internet Protocol—rely on broadcasting. This is an obviously good match to Ethernet, which broadcasts everything; and to token ring, which slides everything past everybody. But ATM is a switched, point-to-point, communication system like a telephone without a party line; you don't talk to anybody without dialing a number (although multicast is defined, and in some implementations). The ATM Forum as well as independent research work is addressing this problem [CGST94]. In addition, work has already begun on ATM-based software implementations of the similarly broadcast-preferring, collective communication of parallel processing [HKM94, HM] (collective communication is discussed in Chapter 8). Naturally, the inevitable plugging of ATM-connected workstations as grand-challenge-style parallel supercomputers has begun [KSS+91].

Scalable Coherent Interconnect

The Scalable Coherent Interconnect (SCI, ANSI/IEEE standard 1596-1992) [Gus92, Ins93] provides a very different kind of communication than do either FCS or ATM.

Where FCS and ATM grew from the I/O-attached conventional communication domain, SCI arose from the IEEE Futurebus standards effort, an attempt to standardize internal processor-memory connections within computers. As a result, SCI-connected computers do not have to use I/O operations to communicate; they can use ordinary **load** and **store** instructions to directly access each others' memory.

SCI defines electrical interconnect standards allowing 1 Gbyte/second transfers over distances of 10 meters, and a fiber-optic serial interface that equals FCS full speed over kilometers. As part of its role as a memory interface, SCI also includes a distributed shared-memory cache coherence protocol; what this means, and how SCI works, is discussed in Chapter 6.

SCI is also real. A 1 Gbit/second implementation of SCI is available as an SBus adapter card from Dolphin [Dol95] (this is not a direct memory connection, but still has the data rate); it uses support chips available from LSI Logic [Cos94]. Convex uses SCI to connect its massively parallel system, the Exemplar.

Discussion

After one finishes translating between Mbits/second and Mbytes/second, it becomes apparent that the intercomputer data rates that exist now or will soon be available are reaching an appreciable fraction of the bandwidth available *inside* computers, on the buses that connect processors in SMPs. For aggressive SMP systems, those bandwidths are currently edging up to the 1 Gbyte/second range (further discussed in Chapter 6). FCS is 100 Mbytes/second in each of two directions, ATM is 19 MBytes/second to 600 MBytes/second, and SCI is currently implemented at 125 MBytes/second, going to 1 GByte/second: the ratios are 0.1:1, up to 0.6:1, and 1:1.

The ATM and FCS rates don't sound as impressive as SCI or the SMPs, but don't forget that ATM and FCS are not buses; they use switches. As a result, each link to a machine can, with a good switch design, independently carry that rate, so there can be many full-speed simultaneous transfers going on. In fact, within the switch fabric's limits, the aggregate bandwidth goes up as the number of connected machines rises.

The SMP bus systems and SCI numbers, on the other hand, are aggregate rates shared by all processors;[4] they can't be exceeded even if everybody talks at once (especially then, in fact).

---

4. For SCI, this statement assumes the common simple loop topology; it's possible to use switches instead and thereby increase aggregate bandwidth.

A collection of 16 machines connected, for example, by an FCS fully connected (crossbar) switch, could be holding 16 concurrent "conversations" when one counts bidirectional transfers. See Figure 3-2. (FCS is, of course, not the only medium with which this trick can be pulled.) Theoretically, that could exhibit an aggregate peak rate of 1.6 Gbytes/second. This is unlikely in practice, but so is using attaining the peak rate of the shared-media systems. What it means is that 16 connected uniprocessors would, in some sense—aggregate raw bandwidth—be *more tightly coupled* than those same 16 processors *inside* an SMP.

Figure 3-2   Internal vs. External Bandwidth Available

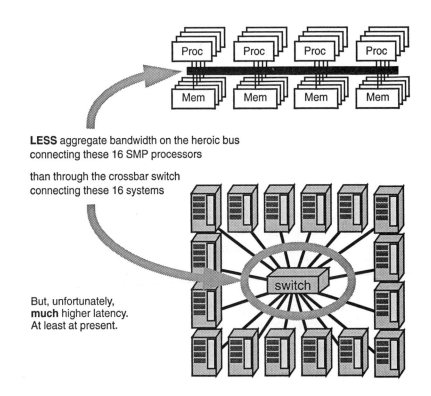

That is an utterly amazing statement to be able to make.

It has long been the case that many, many machines connected by switches could exceed the bandwidth within an SMP. For example, if you add up the bandwidth available through all the modems connected to all the PCs in the world, the figure is undoubtedly astronomical. But now the same number of machines is involved: 16 in each case.

This is another one of those differences whose effect is hard to overstate. The most commonly deployed intermachine communication is in the range of 1 Mbyte/second on Ethernet LAN, and goes up to tens of MBytes/second even on some massively parallel systems. An increase of one to two orders of magnitude *potentially* makes parallel software significantly easier to construct than it is now and expands the domain of applicability tremendously. Greater communication between machines than within a machine turns any number of basic architectural and design positions inside out and upside down.

But only potentially. There is a very ugly fly in this ointment, and this time it's not wholly software. Data rates like those becoming available present a significant challenge to both the hardware and the software of workstations.

Most hardware I/O systems simply are not designed to handle, for example, the two simultaneous 100 Mbyte/second streams a single FCS connection can produce. The aggregate data rates can often be met, but I/O systems are not equipped for the data hemorrhages implied by such massive streams— they're more attuned to the intermittent, temporarily distributed "death of a thousand cuts" wrought by a very large number of much slower devices, taking small quantities over time. Such massive data motion will bring their operation to a shuddering halt.

On the software side, neither operating systems nor communications protocols were designed with these very high speeds and very low error rates in mind. In fact, they were specifically, and for the time and for many current cases correctly, designed to be robust in the face of high error rates and low transmission speeds. They capitalized on those transmission speeds by burning CPU cycles for integrity, a correct trade-off under the circumstances.

As a result the computational overhead, time spent by the processor weaving a protocol through an operating system, time which can be used for no end-result computation, is in the millisecond range even for "null" messages containing no data [SGDM94, DOKT91, HM]. Compare this with the nanosecond ranges for interprocessor data transfer inside an SMP. This intermachine communication overhead can be improved; it is clearly not entirely the "fault" of the protocol or of the operating system, but rather of the way the two interface with each other.

Nevertheless, it goes without saying that the wrong set of trade-offs have been made for using communications systems that operate at or faster than the internal speeds of the machine and have very low error rates. For general use—as opposed, for example, to special-purpose, multimedia extravaganzas—it will be very hard to tell that one has even purchased fast communication hardware unless something about this situation changes quite dramatically.

SCI's memory-based architecture would appear to fix this problem. It is difficult to have a lower software latency for passing a message than a single **store** instruction. This is not, however, a completely positive story. In the first place, that **store** instruction may entail more overhead than is apparent, as is discussed in Chapter 6, particularly Section 6.5 on page 158. In addition, software that makes direct use of SCI's features is not yet in general availability; there is, of course, the major exception of Convex's highly-parallel support on the Exemplar. As will be discussed after more background is covered, however, the cache coherence that is a major feature of SCI has properties that are a significant challenge to commercial SMP-derived software (Chapter 6); and from a cluster point of view, cache coherence is a decided detriment to availability (Chapter 11).

3.4.3   *Distributed Processing Facilities*

The final element making moderate-sized clusters a growing phenomenon is the availability of standard facilities for distributed processing. For example, it is highly unlikely that assembled clusters would ever have been constructed without distributed file systems like NFS being virtually ubiquitous. Such file systems are typically the way that all the elements of a computational cluster get access to their data and the programs they are running. This is, while immediately usable and convenient, not without its limitations, a point that will reappear regularly. It can be anticipated that the deployment of more comprehensive systems will make the organization and construction of clustered systems easier than it is now.

Since the capabilities of distributed systems are generally well known and well-described elsewhere [for example: CP93, Edd94, Ope93, Pek92, Ram93], little more will be said about them here.

But one perhaps nonobvious point, to be belabored later, must be made: Distributed system technology is not primarily targeted at clusters of workstations. Rather, it is focused on problems of larger numbers, such as the management of interconnected networks of thousands of essentially autonomous workstations. These are real problems, and customers are demanding (and willing to pay for) good solutions to them. However, they are not the same as the management problems of workstation clusters, partly because they must cater to the essential autonomy and individuality of the many workstations they manage. Clusters, in contrast, are usually kept as internally uniform as feasible. More about this later, particularly in Chapter 10.

In the meantime, now that we know why clusters are coming, it's more than time to say something about what they are.

4

Definition, Distinctions, and Initial Comparisons

Having given more examples than was perhaps needful, and pointed to the reasons for clusters and some of their problems, a definition of a cluster is in order if not rather grossly overdue.

The definition in itself is not complex and may initially appear rather vague. This is at least in part because it is attempting to avoid being prescriptive. I am not attempting to define what a cluster "ought to be" or how it "ought to be constructed" independent of what others may be (misguidedly) doing.[1] Rather, the definition tries to be descriptive of what many are constructing, informally or formally, as clusters. I have seen too many, too dogmatic definitions of the term "cluster," all contradicting one another, to be a prescriptivist in this area. Furthermore, without some grasp of the breadth of possibilities, it is impossible to make an intelligent choice of what might be pursued.

---

1. I once gave a presentation whose theme was that there are many ways to build a cluster. I was immediately followed by someone who began by saying (approximately) "Greg may be right that there are many ways to build a cluster, but there's only one *right* way. That way is..." Sigh.

While being descriptively inclusive, the definition must distinguish "cluster" from the traditional realms of parallel processing and distributed computing. The definition in fact does that, but why it does so requires more explanation. That is why the rest of this chapter is devoted to distinctions between clusters and other forms of parallel and distributed computing.

4.1 Definition

A cluster is a type of parallel or distributed system that:

> ➤ consists of a collection of interconnected whole computers,
> ➤ and is utilized as a single, unified computing resource.

The term "whole computer" in the above definition is meant to indicate the normal combination of elements making up a stand-alone, usable computer: one or more processors (symmetric multiprocessors, SMPs, are acceptable cluster nodes), an adequate amount of memory, input/output facilities, and an operating system.

Well, that seems simple enough. (Earlier versions I used were much more complex.)

But it may not be immediately apparent that this definition does effectively separate clusters from other forms of aggregate computing. Distinctions in this area are notoriously difficult and under some circumstances they are usefully ignored. However, the intention is not to define clusters as something different from parallel or distributed systems, but rather to distinguish them as a *subspecies* or *subparadigm* of distributed (or parallel) computing. The next sections discuss the distinctions more fully.

4.2 Distinction From Parallel Systems

There is an analogy I find interesting and surprisingly useful in this context.

Here is a dog:

Figure 4-1   A Dog

She seems a friendly type, though a bit close-mouthed. Figures 4-2 and 4-3

below, on the other hand, show a pack of dogs and their competition, a Savage Multiheaded Pooch[2].

Figure 4-2   A Pack of Dogs

Figure 4-3   A Savage Multiheaded Pooch

Dog packs and (pardon the abbreviation) SMPs are both more potent than just plain dogs. They can both bring down larger prey than a plain single dog, are more ferocious at guarding things, eat more and faster than a single dog, and so on.

These two dog organizations differ in important ways, though. It's rather difficult to get a whole dog pack to follow "at heel," for example; and if you command the entire pack to fetch a stick, the most likely result is wood shavings. Both of those are fairly easily done by an SMP, once the heads decide to cooperate—and they had better learn that at a very early age (pity the bitch that whelps one). In general, obedience training is likely to be eas-

2. This savage pooch is, by the way, no relation to the well-known Kerberos who guards both the gates of Hades and distributed systems (an interesting equation, that). The Grecian pooch has only three heads.

ier with the SMP; and, of course, you only have to walk an SMP once. Another difference is that the SMP must have a bigger body than each of the pack dogs' bodies, since that one body must support several heads; if it has smaller heads, that of course isn't the case. (And larger dogs are more likely to suffer from infirmities like hip dysplasia.) Yet another distinction: If one dog of the pack is put out of action, the rest of the pack can certainly continue to function at a good fraction of its peak effectiveness. An SMP can do the same if what's hurt is a head—assuming the other heads don't get too distracted by the pain. But if the SMP is wounded in a leg, or the heart, it's had it. Also, it's very likely possible to form a usable dog pack that has a far larger headcount than any one Savage Multiheaded Pooch.

The analogy should be rather obvious: Like dog packs, clusters are composed of whole entities—whole computers—while the lowly parallel symmetric multiprocessor SMP is formed by replicating only *part* of a computer, namely the processor.

This has a number of implications: The rest of an SMP must be made larger (a bigger body), to keep the system in balance and allow the extra processors to do some good. Problems must be solved in that bodily scale-up (hip dysplasia) that modest-sized dogs aren't prone to. The SMP is somewhat more tolerant of faults than a single machine, but nowhere near as broadly as is a cluster. It's a lot easier to do system administration (obedience training, walking) with an SMP than with a cluster; and so on. Since the SMP-cluster comparison is of singular importance, it will be pursued in greater detail later, after the characteristics of SMPs have been discussed in some detail. But the dog pack vs. savage multiheaded pooch analogy is rather better than it appears at first glance.

This distinction—whole computers vs. replicated computer parts—also serves to separate clusters from other parallel systems. For example:

➤ SIMD, or instruction broadcast machines such as Masspar systems or early Thinking Machines systems (but not later versions) replicate only an arithmetic and logic unit (ALU), along with registers and some memory. (This type of system is described further in Chapter 8.)

➤ Massively parallel multicomputers such as the Intel Paragon, Convex Exemplar, Cray T3D and the IBM Scalable Parallel series replicate whole processors and memories, and each has an I/O system. This makes them quite akin to clusters, and in some circumstances they shade over into clusters with attendant confusion of marketing focus. But usually not all nodes have complete I/O resources; there is usually less than adequate memory for a stand-alone machine at each node; and until the Intel Paragon, and later the IBM

SP series and the Convex Exemplar, there was no attempt to provide access to complete conventional operating system facilities at each node.

So, like distributed systems, but unlike most parallel systems, clusters are composed of whole computers. That's not to say that parallel systems cannot be made out of whole computers; they can. When that's done, what you get is a cluster used for parallel programming.

4.3 Distinctions from Distributed Systems ___

The distinctions between clusters and many distributed systems are somewhat more devious. They come in several areas, discussed below.

4.3.1 Internal Anonymity

Nodes of a distributed system necessarily retain their own individual identities. For example, it is quite important to the functioning of a node in a bank's distributed system that a particular node is the one physically located in the office in East Overshoe, Maine. That physical location is an intrinsic part of its function; it's there to serve customers living and working in East Overshoe. Equally, it is important that the workstation in my office is physically in my office; that is key to the response time it provides to me. There are other important aspects of individuality; for example, particular distributed nodes may have software licensed to them that are unique to that node.

The elements of a cluster, on the other hand, are usually viewed *from outside the cluster* as anonymous; as much as possible, they are "cogs in the system," facelessly and interchangeably performing a function, much as the processors of an SMP are not individually addressed from outside the machine. Hence the phrase "single, unified computing resource" in the definition. There may be functional differences between a cluster's nodes—one may have a vector unit or communications facilities that others lack; and it is common to designate one or more nodes as "keepers of the data," specialized with large disks to hold the cluster file system, while the others provide computation (but see below). From the outside, however, one would like to log onto the cluster, not cluster node 4; submit a job to the cluster, not to node 17; and so on.

Current distributed system facilities do not support this notion of internal anonymity very well. This will be discussed more completely below.

4.3.2   Peer Relationship

Another distinction between clusters and traditional distributed systems concerns the relationship between the parts. Modern distributed systems use an underlying communication layer that is peer-to-peer: There is no intrinsic hierarchy or other structure, just a "flat" list of communicating entities. At higher levels of abstraction, however, they are popularly organized into a client-server paradigm—a two-level hierarchy, with clients as the leaves and servers as the root(s). This results in a valuable reduction in system complexity. It also serves as a distinction from clusters, but one that is deliberately not part of the definition used because it is not universal: a peer-to-peer relationship between the cluster elements themselves.

The reason this distinction is not universal stems from the common use of specialization among the cluster nodes, particularly the use of file-serving cluster nodes within assembled and preassembled clusters. Being built out of the distributed-systems kit of parts, these often use distributed file systems following the client-server paradigm: A cluster node is designated the file server and equipped with large disks; the other nodes are the clients and have little if any disk storage.

This arrangement is adequate for processor-intensive technical computing, which uses relatively little input/output, and this is the use to which many assembled and preassembled clusters are put at present. But the disk bandwidth available within the entire cluster is thereby limited to that of a single node—actually, it's limited to the bandwidth of the communication between the file server and the other nodes; this bandwidth is typically LAN speed, in the low Mbits/second. So, this arrangement is inadequate for I/O-intensive commercial computing.

This inadequacy is recognized by the creators of many commercially oriented clusters and cluster subsystems (the Open VMS Cluster and various distributed database systems in particular), which instead access data in a peer-to-peer fashion, as illustrated in Figure 4-4. In a typical distributed, client-server file system the clients access files on the server; they do not access each other's files directly. In commercially oriented clustered systems, on the other hand, the files are typically a mutually shared resource: By hook or by crook, every machine must access most (if not all) the data in the cluster; if it cannot, the ability to balance the workload within the cluster and hence achieve scalable performance is curtailed.

In practice the need for mutual data access has lead to two organizations, illustrated in the figure. On the one hand, there are shared (multi-tailed) disks that all machines can physically access—used for example in the VAX-Cluster, Oracle's Parallel Server database system, and many availability-oriented clusters. On the other hand are "shared-nothing" systems in which requests for disk access and other I/O requests are "shipped" to the appropriate machine—used for example in Tandem systems and several database subsystems such as Sybase Navigation Server and DB2/6000 Parallel Edition. Either way, the cluster elements are peers; there is no hierarchy among.

This is one area where clusters are singularly ill served by distributed system technology. Disk sharing is simply anathema in that regime, for good and sufficient reasons; it's hard to scale disk sharing up to hundreds or thousands of nodes, and similarly hard to share disks over physically large distances.[3] The effect of I/O shipping could be obtained by having each machine be a file system client of all the other machines and a file system server to all the other machines. But managing such partitioning under a dynamically changing load is an administrative nightmare unless appropriate administrative tools are available. They generally are not.

Figure 4-4   Client-Server Hierarchy vs. Cluster Peer File Systems

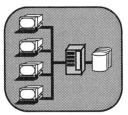

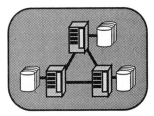

Client-Server
One-level Hierarchy

Cluster
Peer Access
Physically Shared Disk

Cluster
Peer Access
Shared Access by I/O Shipping

4.3.3   Clusters Within a Client-Server Organization

The above should not be taken to imply that internally peer-to-peer clusters adequate for commercial workloads cannot be a part of client-server distributed systems. A cluster running a peer-to-peer file system can serve quite well as a scaled-up file server, for example, as illustrated in Figure 4-5. Here the cluster is (most desirably) viewed as a single "node" of the distributed system; any of the clients can use it as a whole, without necessarily indicat-

3. However, disks attached through Fibre Channel Standard can be kilometers away, and there can be lots of them. There are other reasons, though, why such sharing may be nonoptimal; see Chapter 9.

Figure 4-5   A Cluster as a Server: Logically One Distributed Node

ing which node they access it through, to get at any of the data on any of the attached disks.

Viewing a cluster of machines as a single node is another area not well served by traditional distributed system technology, although some support exists. There are commonly available naming schemes—both Sun's ONC+ and OSF's DCE, for example, provide this—that decouple the physical location of a resource from its designation, allowing a logical name to designate any of several sources of the desired resource. A prospective client queries the name server, which could (for example) respond with the physical location information of any of a cluster's nodes. This approach has two difficulties when clusters are considered, both problems of modularity:

➤ First, it places the primary load-balancing decision outside the cluster, in the naming facility. The cluster itself is the natural location of such decisions for many reasons. For example, the cluster might be able to dynamically move work from one internal node to another to better balance the node. But the client, having obtained a name translation, is using a physical node designation and cannot easily change it.

➤ Second, it similarly places decisions about reaction to failure outside the cluster, in the naming facility. This is an appropriate thing to do for the catastrophic case of whole-cluster failure, but part of the Classic Standard Litany of reasons for clustering is to allow failure of a part without failure of the whole. How this is done and how it affects clients is more naturally encapsulated within the cluster itself. In some ways this is the ultimate dynamic load-balancing act: all the work must be moved from one node onto others. The difficulties involved are similar to those mentioned for load balancing, but if anything more severe. (How node-locked program licenses, or license servers, "fail over" in the event of an internal cluster failure is another interesting issue not well addressed by any system the author is aware of.)

This is not to say that these functions completely cannot be done within existing distributed computing facilities. Turing still reigns. For example, the cluster could keep the name server continuously updated regarding its internal load status, in the form of changes to the most desirable target(s) of resource names; or a second level of name indirection could be performed by a client, with the cluster's help, to determine who to talk to; or the cluster can "masquerade" one node as another by taking over its low-level (IP) address—which will fool most of the clients most of the time, but not all of them all the time (this is actually done in practice in some availability clusters, such as IBM's HACMP). These are practical responses and reflect what any implementation must do at some level. It's just not "architected in" to distributed system support technology, and that technology does not have the architecture to support it in a modular fashion. You can't do everything for everybody. And cluster considerations—or even consideration of a single machine with more than one communication adapter, which would have helped—were an item left out.

So, there is no conflict between clustering and distributed client-server; they are mutually useful. But they are also clearly different; and to the extent that distributed computing remains focused on client-server, it is a clear indication that clusters are different from, and not particularly well served by, distributed computing tools.

4.3.4 Clusters and Three-Tiered Database Applications

Clusters also appear to be arising in a natural way in the evolution of distributed systems. Look again at the part of Figure 4-4 illustrating a typical distributed client-server file system. That same system organization has been used for client-server database systems: The clients run the application code, which requests and updates data in the database system much as a file system would be accessed (but, of course, with very different access techniques, durability guarantees, etc.).

However, a funny thing is happening as the database applications implemented in this manner become larger and more sophisticated, extending their reach throughout large enterprises. The applications are actually starting to do some substantial work. In the process, they're getting too big for the clients—or, equivalently, increasing the cost of the very voluminous clients with their large multiplicative cost factor. The alternative of performing the entire application on the "back-end" database engine is also problematical, since as the enterprise grows it runs out of capacity.

Figure 4-6   Three-Tiered Distributed Hierarchy, a Cluster

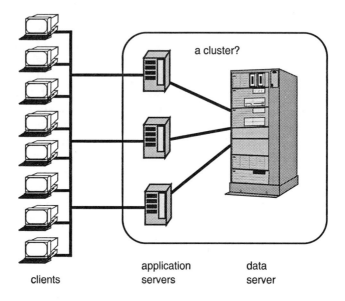

| | application | data |
| clients | servers | server |

A response to this conundrum is an organization with three levels, as shown in Figure 4-6. This organization is, for example, used by the whole-business application suites sold by SAP and Baan. On one end, client workstations concentrate on the human interaction, parsing users' inputs and displaying results by using graphics in an appropriate manner. On the other end, the database engine grinds away, making sure everything is consistent and stably stored. In the middle, application servers, a new class, perform the application work itself. The middle tier is a server to the workstations and a client to the back end.

This whole arrangement sure looks like a cluster to me.

4.4   Concerning "Single System Image" _____

A term that may appear conspicuously absent from the cluster definition provided is "single system image." There are two reasons for that.

First, "single system image" turns out to be an interestingly complex subject that is, at least in part due to prior overly simplistic renditions, subject to some controversy. There is a whole chapter devoted to the notion: Chapter 10.

Second, and highly related to the complexity of the issue, clusters can be very useful entities even though they lack much of what might be called a "single system image." Database systems that operate against "raw" disk devices, for example, may neither require nor usefully utilize a single cluster-wide file system. At some level a single system image should still be present, of course—a statement that anticipates the discussion to come.

The phrase "utilized as a single, unified computing resource," on the other hand, appears to capture the intent of clusters without raising the complications that the term "single system image" entails.

4.5   Other Comparisons

Further distinctions between clusters, distributed computing, and parallel systems are summarized in Table 4-1.

Table 4-1   Comparison of Cluster, Highly Parallel, and Distributed

Characteristic	Highly Parallel	Cluster	Distributed
number of nodes	thousands	tens or less	thousands
performance metric	turnaround time	throughput and turnaround time	response time
node individualization	none	none	required
internode communication standards	proprietary, nonstandard is OK	varies depending on type; proprietary often used	strict standards adherence required
node size	smaller (< 1 problem)	larger (≥ 1 problem)	larger (≥ 1 problem)
inter-node security	nonexistent	unnecessary if enclosed; required if exposed[a]	required
node OS	homogeneous	varies depending on type; often homogeneous	must be heterogeneous

a. "Enclosed" and "exposed" are defined in the next chapter.

The distinction drawn here is between "highly parallel" and cluster, rather than the general parallel area and cluster, because the only interesting "lowly parallel" system is the symmetric multiprocessor (SMP). A summary comparison of SMPs and clusters was given earlier (woof!), and a detailed comparison of clusters and SMPs appears later.

Some of the rows in that table require explanation.

In the "number of nodes" row, the point being made is that neither highly parallel nor distributed systems are particularly interesting if they are not designed to scale to thousands of elements; the same is not true of clusters. This factor eliminates from the hardware of clusters many constraints that exist in highly parallel or distributed systems. For example, communication by multi-tailed access to disks is a clustering technique that has been used more than once, is in common use now, but, because it does not scale to thousands, is disparaged in the parallel and distributed arenas.

"Node individualization" is meant to indicate whether individual nodes are typically personalized and/or different from others. For highly parallel and cluster systems, this is not usually the case, whereas for distributed systems it is a necessary characteristic—even if the node hardware and software is homogeneous in the sense of being the same hardware and software models.

In another metric, clusters are closer to distributed than to highly parallel systems: Since highly parallel systems typically spread a single problem across many nodes, each node need not be capable of running an entire job. Nodes of clusters and distributed systems, on the other hand, must be able to run at least one entire job at a time. Clusters must do this because they are often used for execution of serial jobs, often in a batch execution mode. Distributed nodes must do so because, while parts of a job (like file access) may be performed elsewhere, the bulk of the work of a job is typically performed in a single place. That is the point of the "node size" row.

"Internode security" refers to whether communication between nodes must be made secure for either the proper functioning of the system or for protection against illicit access. Within highly parallel systems, no security firewalls are present any more than they are between a processor and its memory—which is to say, they are probably there but the situation is tightly controlled, with hardware support that allows them to exhibit very low overhead while maintaining high integrity. Distributed computing, on the other hand, deals in communication that is in general exposed to external view, so its communication generally requires protection from malicious or unintentional tampering. Clusters may or may not need internal security measures, depending on the type of cluster ("enclosed" and "exposed," terms that are defined in Chapter 5).

In Search of Clusters ✳

4.6 Reactions _____

At this point I have hopefully convinced the majority of readers that a cluster is a subtype of aggregate computer system distinct from the traditional parallel and distributed varieties. The intent here was not to be legalistic. As has been noted before, there are clearly senses in which all aggregate computing scenarios are parallel, and equally valid senses in which all aggregate computing scenarios are distributed. But to the extent that there are useful distinctions to be drawn at all in this area, "cluster" is as distinct as any.

If there is still confusion or disagreement, it is my experience that it resides in the minds of active practitioners of the arts of parallel and distributed computing.

Parallel computing specialists have typically responded to the distinctions being drawn by remarking that they can clearly see a difference from distributed computing, but there's no distinction from parallel computing. Conversely, distributed computing mavens readily acknowledge a distinction from parallel processing, but state that there's no distinction from distributed computing.

Part of this is undoubtedly simple territoriality; I've yet to see a definition of distributed computing, for example, that did not implicitly claim all of parallel processing in its bounds—despite the fact that the actual day-to-day concerns and operation of parallel systems use techniques that are foreign to the distributed world, and vice-versa. Another part of this disagreement is submergence in the Turing tar pit that afflicts all of computer science: Any computer or type of computation can, with (ahem) *sufficient* ingenuity, motivation, effort, and resources, be made to look like any other.

There is a final interesting comment I've received from some of the members of both camps: There may be a distinction from where their field used to be, but there is no distinction from where it is heading. This sounds quite deep and is possibly very revealing, but I fear I'm really not quite sure what it means and certainly am not ready to herald the coming of a Grand Unification.

Part 2:

Hardware

A Cluster Bestiary

A more detailed discussion of the hardware of clusters and of their competitor, the SMP, is the topic of this and the next chapter. The chapters following those two deal with software; then the threads of discussion rejoin for system discussions. The divergence begins with this chapter, which purports to describe all the ways that clusters can be built.

It may seem odd to treat cluster hardware first; after all, it's been emphasized that the primary issues facing clusters are software. There are several reasons for doing so.

First of all, it's the simpler topic, and so the easier one to get out of the way. Also, the treatment here and in the other allegedly "hardware" chapter consists only in part of hardware issues. Several of the distinctions made are far more relevant to how clusters must be programmed than to the hardware implementation, which can vary quite a bit within the classes to be mentioned. The limitation of clusters to combinations of whole computers also forces a nontraditional view of the topic. The traditional views of types of parallel machines will be covered, both for completeness and to show that many of them have little relevance to this discussion, in one of the software chapters: Chapter 8, on programming models. Another, rather plebeian reason for "hardware first" is that it's hard to talk about software without knowing what kinds of contraptions the software is supposed to make into something useful.

A somewhat more interesting reason for treating hardware first is that you have to start somewhere. Clusters, like all of the forms of overt parallelism, is neither a hardware nor a software issue; rather, it is a *system* issue: an issue that involves the interaction of the software and the hardware with each other, each affecting the other in nontrivial ways. Many of the items presented in this book, and the way they are presented, are in fact the result of having gone 'round and 'round in circles from software to hardware to software to hardware... more times than anyone should admit to. This is a primary reason why these issues have historically been so difficult to explain; it's not simple to untangle this knotted mass of threads into a nice, linear presentation. Hardware just happens to be the thread that my mental fingers happen to seize first. I've tried to keep things as linearly readable as possible, but be prepared for a large number of references to the software chapters from the hardware ones, and vice versa; or busting out into code in the midst of greasy hardware details; or discussions of hardware effects while wallowing in software.

That's why hardware is the first topic. Before we begin, however, another digression is in order. This one is to explain why this allegedly survey-like, all-encompassing chapter is so short.

There are two types of people. Aside, that is, from those who think there are two types of people and those who do not. Old joke. Anyway, the two types I'm thinking of differ in their mental apparatus.

There are, on the one hand, people who glory in diversity. They love the richness and multiplicity of the many heterogeneous variations of things that are presented to us by the world, be those things people, other living entities, natural objects, or artifacts. Simplicity, including the simplicity created by organization, bores them; there's not enough of it. They tend to be chemists (particularly organic chemists) not physicists, cataloguers rather than taxonomists. They like the unstructured, repetitive documentation that typically accompanies GUIed programs, but they never read it, rather dipping in here and there. In the words of a colleague of mine, they luxuriate in the Dionysian richness of androgynous, chthonic nature. And they have mental machinery that easily, pleasurably, remembers and recalls a multitude of examples of that variation, which fact probably has more than a little to do with why they like all those examples. They are far better equipped to know than to deduce.

On the other hand are people who glory in structure. They like having one rule that rings them all, that unifies all the heterogeneity they can see, and like to think that such rules "explain" that variation. Unconstrained diversity bores them; it's just mush. They tend to be physicists (particularly particle physicists) not chemists, taxonomists who relate things to one another rather than cataloguers who insist on listing them all. They don't understand how anybody can sit down and read the documentation that typically accompanies GUIed programs (probably nobody does, but these folks try). Again in the words of that colleague, they typify Apollonian, Western males. And their mental machinery has an absolute *blast* "understanding" specific cases by spontaneously flashing down a deduction chain, dynamically generating any of a combinatorial explosion of individual cases by intensely massaging a few logical rules; which fact probably has more than a little to do with why they like those rules. They are far better equipped to deduce than to know.

I am a structure guy. A physicist-type. A taxonomist. I actually try to read the documentation of GUIed programs from front to back, linearly (with exceptions, it's usually incredibly boring, unstructured, and repetitious). In mental structure[1] I am a typical, Apollonian, Western male, and unrepentant about it. I deduce like a madman, and I remember nothing.

And I hate surveys.

Particularly surveys of parallel computers.

I am bored to tears by compilations of seventy-three "interesting" variations of partially fault-tolerant, multipath parallel interconnection networks, all treated in that academically diplomatic style that implies they're all equally good, to say nothing of worth mentioning. I have an identical reaction to the eighty-fourth of the limitless possible recombinations of arithmetic and parallel communication gear, none but an infinitesimal number of which could possibly be programmed by anyone but a graduate student starving for a thesis topic. (A significant but thankfully declining number of graduate Computer Science thesis titles can be best translated as "How I Actually Managed to do X on the Y Machine My Advisor Thought Up.")

In short, I could never write a typical parallel processing textbook.

So this discussion of possible cluster hardware will not be typical. It instead consists of a small number of dichotomies, two-way distinctions, that indicate axes along which cluster hardware can vary, with a few examples illustrating the differences highlighted. In one case, two pairs of dichotomies are coupled, creating what I suppose might be called a quadrichotomy, but it's still dichotomous at heart. Combine these at will to create variations on the theme of "cluster." Anything that doesn't fit I've felt free to ignore.

---

1. But not necessarily politics or sociological attitude, please.

By the way, structuralists like to say that there are two types of people. Diversity lovers always disagree.

5.1   Exposed vs. Enclosed _____

The first distinction to be made is decidedly nontraditional. It refers to the security characteristics of intracluster communication: As illustrated in Figure 5-1, intracluster communication can either be **exposed** to outside view, or **enclosed** within the cluster itself.

Figure 5-1   Exposed and Enclosed Clusters

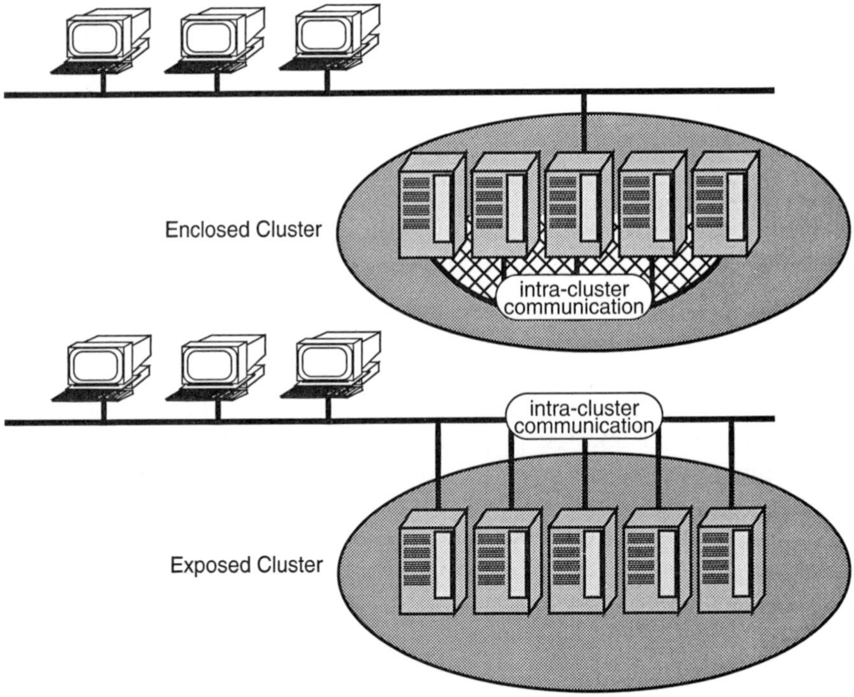

An exposed cluster shares public communication facilities with other computers not part of the cluster. This sharing has several consequences.

> ➤ The cluster nodes necessarily communicate by messages, since public, standardized communication is always message-based.

> ➤ Communication has fairly high overhead, since it must use standard protocols designed for robustness in the face of adversity.

> The communication channel itself is not secure, so additional work must be done to ensure the privacy of intracluster communication that carries security-critical data.

> Since public, potentially widespread communication channels are used, this type of cluster more naturally enables "scavenging" of otherwise unused workstation cycles across a campus or enterprise.

> It's really easy to build. In fact, you often don't have to build it at all. All you have to do is pick some workstations on a LAN, say "I dub thee a cluster," and start writing and/or buying software.

An enclosed cluster, on the other hand, has its own private communication facilities. Those facilities could be standard ones; for example, a second Ethernet or token ring residing solely within the cluster could be used. The important thing is that it is private. However, the possibilities are broader than standard communication techniques.

> Communication can be by a number of means: shared disk, shared memory, messages, or anything else.

> Communication has the possibility of having very low overhead because designers' imaginations need not be limited to standard mechanisms. Those mechanisms also don't have to be agreed upon by an international committee, so they can be defined and implemented faster.

> The security of the communications medium is implicit, so data can be transferred between nodes with only the same security provisions used, for example, between sections of an operating system kernel. Which is to say: very low cost security provisions; in many cases, none at all are necessary. (Advocates of capability-based operating systems will disagree with that last statement, and I might join them.)

Figure 5-1 on page 90, used to illustrate this concept, also implies that the cluster has only one communications path to the outside world. That need not be the case. Other paths were left out only to make the enclosed/exposed distinction graphically self-evident in the figure. (Multiple paths into a cluster are also not well supported by the current wave of distributed programming, though, as was mentioned in Chapter 4).

While the above distinctions are interesting and useful, they are not the major reason for making this distinction. That is: It is markedly easier to implement cluster-enabling software on an enclosed cluster.

Communication can easily be faster and cheaper, which always helps a lot. Security is not an issue (or at least much less of an issue), which helps tremendously. It can be made at least highly unlikely, if not intrinsically impossible, that the cluster will be accidentally partitioned into two or more separate, individually survivable parts, which then later have to be merged; this is an unbelievably big help. In addition, it is possible to make use of shared storage to hold what would otherwise be replicated distributed data structures. The latter is not a theoretical issue; there are well-known techniques for maintaining such structures correctly that do not rely on the seeming crutch of actual shared storage media. But it is definitely an issue of implementation difficulty. It is far easier to whack a lock around a block of storage than to debug an asynchronous algorithm that reliably replicates data structure with multiple sources of updates.

Putting this another way: The programming of an enclosed cluster does not have to surmount all the challenges traditionally associated with distributed systems.

Unfortunately, to take advantage of this relative simplicity, the hardware designers often have to convince the software engineers to do nonstandard implementations. This is an enterprise fraught with difficulty and "full plate" syndromes, since software is usually fully occupied adding function to the "standard" facilities in a race with their competition. This is a reason why extraordinarily fast, *and standardized*, communication is such an important piece of the cluster puzzle.

Speaking of fast standards: Facilities like Fibre Channel Standard and ATM require care when applying the enclosed/exposed distinction. It is possible to implement communication switches that themselves provide security, allowing only certain endpoints to connect to other endpoints. (At least one such FCS implementation is currently under way, and it is being actively discussed in the ATM context.) This ability to embed partitioning implies that a single communication switch could, despite looking to all the world like a widely used common communication facility, host one or more enclosed clusters, each with their own private communication. At the same time, it could be hosting a multitude of randomly communicating nodes that can, along selected paths, communicate with the cluster(s).

The multi-kilometer reach of such technology also dissuades one from assuming that any cluster, exposed or enclosed, is necessarily geographically compact. At least it will until the software overhead gets down to a point where one can detect the fact that the speed of light isn't infinite.

Of course, assembled and preassembled clusters are very often exposed, primarily because the hardware for doing so is usually already sitting right in front of the assemblers, ready to be dubbed. That and the "standards" argument account for the reason why much home-grown open system cluster software is designed to run on exposed clusters, even though that makes it much more of a challenge to write.

5.2 "Glass-House" vs. "Campus-Wide" Cluster

While I was discussing clusters with one of the pioneers in the assembled-cluster area,[2] he mentioned that all his users' individual workstations were part of his cluster.

"Then why," I asked, "do you have a room with a rack full of machines?"

"Because we ran out of desks. If we could use [the machines] as plant stands in the lobby, we'd do that, too."[3]

This points to another distinction between cluster types: Whether, on the one hand, the nodes are fully dedicated to their use as a shared computational resource; or, on the other hand (the case above), the nodes are also used as personal systems that must provide the response time that's characteristic of local, personal, dedicated workstations. In the first case, the cluster nodes will typically be located together in a geographically compact arrangement for ease of management: a "glass-house" arrangement. In the second, they will generally be scattered across a campus. Hence the dichotomy: "glass-house" clusters vs. "campus-wide" clusters.

The attractiveness of campus-wide clusters lies in their potential for scavenging unused computing resources from personal workstations, which, like private automobiles, have notoriously low average utilization. This is the additional verse that turns the Classic Standard Litany into the Enhanced Standard Litany of reasons why parallel/distributed computing is good. To repeat the old saw mentioned in Chapter 3: While the workstation cycles that form the basis of cluster cost/performance are cheap, unused workstation cycles are *free*.

Two factors distinguish campus-wide clusters from glass-house clusters: Nodes of campus-wide clusters operate in a a less-controlled environment; and they must quickly and totally relinquish use of a node to a user.

The campus-wide environment is less controlled in several ways. It is less reliable in the sense that power cords are accidentally unplugged, machines

---

2. Dennis Duke of Florida State University's Supercomputing Computation Research Institute.

3. Product planners take note. How do your systems rate on the plant-stand requirement?

have coffee spilled on them, are bumped into, have inexpert users messing around with system configuration files, and so on. It is also obviously a less physically secure environment. In addition, there are likely to be uncontrolled variations in the configuration of the nodes: storage, availability of software, and so on, will vary widely. For example, how does a campus-wide cluster batch system ever find out that a user has installed more memory or disk storage, or upgraded to a new, buggy beta release of a compiler? It cannot—unless control is exerted over users' systems, more control than is often the norm.

Enforcing such control requires a loss of autonomy, perhaps rather substantial, by the individual workstation owner/user. In many cases, the owners will gladly give up that control in exchange for lessening their burden of system management—or for the benefit of using others' machines for their long-running jobs. Other owners regard their workstations as being as personal as their toothbrushes and will be harder to convince. In the end, this is a sociological issue: Commercial enterprises are in general more likely to enforce the requisite control than are universities or independent laboratories whose populace has a culture of intellectual independence. Industrial research labs are an interesting middle ground.

The second of the two factors differentiating campus-wide from glass-house clusters is the need to totally relinquish use of a node when a local user wants it. This might appear to be a simple matter of scheduling priorities on each node: Give the scavenging job such a low priority that it doesn't get in the way.

However, even an idle scavenging job is using up local resources—operating system data structures, buffer space in memory, paging space on disk, and so on. Also, private workstations are often sized to just barely handle an owner's personal needs—and if they're larger than that initially, such an oversight is always temporary; Gresham's Law applies, and the needs grow to the maximum that can be accomplished with the available tools, even if the "need" is a new collection of humorous screen savers. Amusing cases aside, the full capabilities of one's workstation really must be available. No user who understands the situation is going to allow some *thing* to come in from who knows where, essentially at random and, for example, use up the paging space needed by the desktop publishing system that must be used to turn out a report in ten minutes.

The issue is not how to turn down the scavenger's use of resources, rather it is to how make it completely *gone* at the tap of a space bar, the twitch of a mouse, or in more sophisticated cases, the reaching of some resource threshold.

That this is not so simple is indicated by the several solutions that have been applied where it has been attempted. Here are some examples:

> ➤ The Condor system of the University of Wisconsin takes periodic checkpoints of scavenger jobs; these are sent to a separate controlling site. Then, when a user implicitly requests his machine back, the scavenging job instantly commits suicide and is reborn somewhere else from a prior backup. This is used in IBM's LoadLeveller batch system [IBMc].

> ➤ The Piranha system of Yale, based on the Linda programming paradigm [CG89], sends a scavenging job an "exit" signal on return from which the job is instantly purged. The programmer of the scavenging job must write appropriate code that executes in response to that signal if the scavenging job's work is to be partially or wholly saved.

> ➤ Sprite [O$^+$88, DOKT91] and Locus [PW85] (the latter used for the IBM TCF facility [WP89]), do cross-machine job migration when a user wants his/her resources back. This is the best solution from the point of view of the scavenger, since no forward progress is lost and no special code must be written. But it is far more complex. In addition to memory contents, open files, threading, and so on, must be moved. Also, it relies an significant surrounding infrastructure (a "distributed" operating system) and is possibly slower to relinquish the local machine than either of the other two.

Just like the prior distinction made between exposed and enclosed clusters, the primary reason for distinguishing glass-house from campus-wide clusters is not whether one or the other versions is feasible in the sense of a Turing machine; in principle, anything can be programmed. Rather, the issue is the sizeable number of nontrivial, additional problems that arise when one wants to scavenge computer time in a campus-wide cluster. Such clusters are by no means impractical—they see very significant use—but they are more difficult to program into fully robust, usable life.

A factor not yet mentioned is that campus-wide clusters will assuredly be heterogeneous, composed of nodes using hardware and software from differing vendors. The issues involved in heterogeneous systems have been beaten to death in the distributed computing context; there is no point to rehashing them here. Suffice it to say that this also can certainly be solved, but it nonetheless increases the general overhead and makes life more difficult for the programmer.

Of course, once again the nonstandard/full-plate software syndrome enters the picture. Unlike the enclosed/exposed case, this one will probably only be resolved when clusters are considered a legitimate paradigm that must somehow be shoved onto the plate, too.

Finally, a question: Are campus-wide systems actually clusters? Earlier it was stated that the definition of a cluster implied that internal nodes were anonymous as viewed from the outside. There's a bit of a problem here. Where's the "outside" of a campus-wide cluster? To me, my workstation obviously isn't anonymous, but yours is just another resource.

Individual office workstations in a campus certainly are not anonymous from the point of view of the owner. But from the point of view of a batch submission system wanting to use a workstation for a job, each workstation is indeed anonymous. It might be said that what is involved here is a "virtual cluster" that can occupy part, but not all, of the machines on which it is hosted. So the workstations involved have a split personality; it's even been called schizophrenic computing [SSCK93]. The difficulties discussed above are caused by the need to switch between those two personalities and the tension between them. If it hasn't happened already, somebody should call such a system "Eve."

5.3 Cluster Hardware Structures _____

Describing all the possible hardware structures usable for clusters is difficult and quite possibly silly, because every conceivable technique for gluing computers together has been called a "cluster." When a hardware designer is not even limited by worries about scaling to large numbers—a cluster of four, or even two machines is quite usable—all kinds of strange and wonderful things are both feasible and practical. About the only thing they all have in common is that they are most definitely *not* symmetric multiprocessors, that is, they are not composed of processors with equal, uniform access to main memory and I/O (this is further discussed in Chapter 6.). Beyond that, well, there must be 60 ways to build a cluster.[4]

There are many ways to attempt to organize this unbridled chaos, and most are probably equally good. Here I will use an organization based on two nearly orthogonal characteristics: the method of attachment to the whole computers involved; and whether the communication medium is or is not some form of shared storage. How these "paired dichotomies" related to each other is shown in Figure 5-2, which also gives some examples of each type. By no means is that example list anywhere near complete; your per-

---

4. Slip the data out the back, Jack / send it on a LAN, Stan / a store to employ, Roy / but not an SMP. / Drop it on a bus, Gus / no need for coherence / share it on DASD / set those hardware jocks **free**. *Pace* Paul Simon. Sorry. I couldn't resist.

sonal pet version probably does not appear. Also, hybrid systems that simultaneously use multiple quadrants are definitely feasible, so this categorization is not mutually exclusive (and neither is any other categorization I am aware of). The most common hybrids will be discussed below.

Figure 5-2   Categories of Cluster Hardware

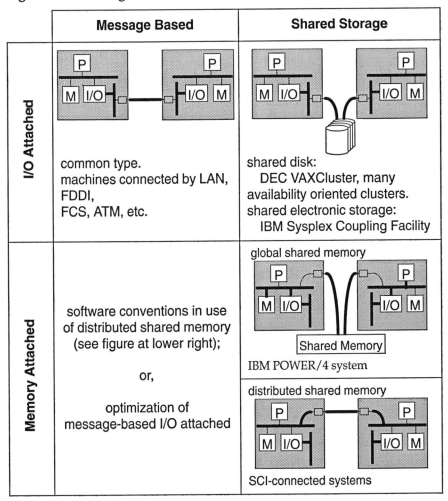

P = Processor
M = Memory
I/O = Input/Output

5.3.1 The Four Categories

Clusters are composed of whole, conventional, traditionally organized computers. Such machines have a limited number of places at which connection to other such computers can be carried out. In fact, there are exactly two such places: at the I/O subsystem and at the memory subsystem.

In the case of I/O attachment, communication is performed by using I/O operations that are usually mediated by an operating system. In the case of memory attachment, processor-native, memory-based **load** and **store** operations result, possibly indirectly, in data motion between nodes. Memory-mapped I/O may appear to smear this distinction, but really does not. Memory-mapped I/O **load**s and **store**s don't affect the real memory hardware subsystem; they get trundled off to diddle hardware that is nowhere near the usual memory attachment point but rather is on a (usually slow) path to a standard I/O bus. Therefore the hardware attachment points remain distinct.

The properties of the communication medium itself are largely independent of where it is attached. That forms the basis of the second distinction: whether the communications medium does or does not contain explicitly used shared storage of some sort.

If there is no explicitly used shared storage, the system is referred to (here, at least) as message-based or message-passing. In such a system, communication is completed when data have been received by the target node. A message-based system may contain incidental storage—pipeline registers and the like—used to hold data during its transfer to another node; such storage is not explicitly used in programming the beast. In shared storage systems, by contrast, communication from a node is complete when the data is placed in the shared storage; the location in the storage is explicitly used by the processor as the target of communication.

Unfortunately, from the point of view of simple dichotomizing, the shared storage category admits of a few subcategories. The shared storage can, for example, be electronic (fast memory); or it can be electro-mechanical (slower, disk); that difference, while very practically significant, does not affect the system structure, only the data rates—possibly by orders of magnitude, so this is not a trivial distinction. However, there is another distinction, this one structural: where the shared storage is located. In particular, is it distinct from each node's own main storage, or is it part of them? This is a structural distinction that is quite significant, which is why the lower-right entry of Figure 5-2 has been split to accommodate that distinction.

Each of the possible combinations of those two characteristics, attachment point and type of medium, are discussed in the sections that follow.

5.3.2   I/O-Attached Message-Based

I/O-attached message-based systems are the most common and the most fundamental. Clusters connected by common LAN, FDDI, ATM, and FCS fall into this category, as well as clusters connected by proprietary switching systems. They are fundamental in that all the other combinations also include some form of this attachment, at least at the level of a simple inter-node interrupt that can inform another node when data is waiting for it somewhere. They are also the easiest to construct because off-the-shelf hardware can be used.

5.3.3   I/O-Attached Shared Storage

The most common manifestation of I/O-attached shared storage systems is the shared disk system. In this case, a disk controller is able to take commands from two (or more) computers, each of which can read data the other has written onto the disk. The DEC Open VMS Cluster is a well-known example of such a system, as is the IBM Sysplex, and the SPARCcluster x000 PDB series, and anybody else who wants to run Oracle's Parallel Server systems (which is a nontrivial collection of commercial UNIX system vendors).

Many of the "availability clusters" mentioned in Chapter 3 are also of this type, but not all, even though all of them contain cables to disks from multiple machines—multi-tailed disks. The reason some are not of this type is that in several cases, only one machine at a time ever uses a given disk; the multiple tails are there only to allow one machine to take over the disk if the other one buys the farm. Since only one machine ever accesses a disk at once, it obviously is not being shared.

In addition to disk sharing, various forms of semiconductor store can also be shared in this mode. The IBM Sysplex Coupling Facility is an example. The ill-fated IBM POWER/4 RPQ, a very short-lived, limited availability product, was also of this category; it had in addition a special cluster-wide "lock box" providing fast cluster-wide synchronization facilities, like some of the features of the Coupling Facility. (Some SMPs implement locking hardware in this fashion also.)

Systems sharing I/O attached storage, like systems sharing any form of storage, require some way to adjudicate ownership of segments of the storage, so they do not step all over each other's data. (How this can happen, and ways to get around it, is discussed in more detail in Chapter 8, "Basic Programming Models and Issues" on page 187.) This arbitration is usually done by some form of software-based coherence control, since one machine may have in its memory a block of data that has been updated but not yet written back to disk; particularly when semiconductor storage is used, however, hardware assists may exist [IBMe].

5.3.4   Memory-Attached Shared Storage

Memory-attached shared storage systems come in two varieties: those with at least one physically common block of shared storage separate from the storage of the individual nodes; and those in which the storage contained in the individual nodes is shared. Systems connected via the Scalable Coherent Interconnect (mentioned in Chapter 3 and described in more detail in Chapter 6) will usually be of the latter type, although it is logically possible to use SCI to access a common storage module. The IBM POWER/4 RPQ (RIP) was an example providing only a common shared storage block, with no accessibility between individual node's local memory.

Shared storage of this type can also be "logically shared," as is the case with Encore's (Gould's) Reflective Memory facility, which is the basis of DEC's newly announced "Memory Channel" facility mentioned in Chapter 2. In that case, writing into the shared Reflective storage region results, at some point, in each processor seeing that data—but the actual data storage is replicated at each node. In effect, a **store** into Reflective Memory is "reflected" from a node's the local copy into the copies at all other nodes.

5.3.5   Memory-Attached Message-based

The fourth category of cluster hardware, memory-attached message-based systems, contains no current examples that I am aware of. It's possible that this is the case because any hardware vendor making an intermachine memory connection is likely to want to trumpet it as having "shared memory," even if the system actually uses this connection only to pass messages. Software can obviously use memory under conventions that limit it to message-passing; this is common in SMPs and perfectly possible with SCI (along with other memory-based systems) but the hardware base in those cases is nevertheless shared storage.

Designers of I/O-attached, message-based systems are continually frustrated by the system and software overhead required to use their facilities, however, and have regularly proposed attaching their fast communication facilities directly to primary system memory buses or to intermediate "mezzanine" busses. In this they are no different from designers of graphics hardware, who share the same frustrations. The graphics designers, thanks to a mass market of millions of systems and continual comparisons in popular magazines, have succeeded; witness the "local bus" graphics now common on IBM-compatible PCs. The now-emerging PCI bus may end up being the solution to both problems in that market arena.

5.3.6   Discussion

All of the above communication strategies can and have been used for clusters of machines. Which is best depends on the application area and the available software support.

I/O vs. Memory-Attached

I/O-attached message-passing is currently the only way to construct clusters from heterogeneous machines. For only that case have standards been created and deployed that allow meaningful data transmission between machines from different manufacturers running different software systems. In theory, SCI should allow such heterogeneity for memory attachment (why else make it a *de jure* standard?), but the many levels of software protocols required to make such attachment safely usable have not yet been addressed. One can only imagine the chaos that would result if, for example, a Hewlett-Packard HP/UX operating system and a Sun Solaris operating system could write willy-nilly into each other's memory. In all likelihood, neither would survive the boot process.

Memory attachment in general is harder to accomplish than I/O attachment, for two reasons:

1. The hardware of most machines is designed to accept foreign attachments, such as communication devices, in its I/O subsystem. This attachment point is generally a well thought-out, architected interface that does not vary too much, at least within a single manufacturer's line. Memory subsystems, on the other hand, generally have more stringent hardware attachment requirements and are usually not "architected," in the sense that they change dramatically from one machine model to another within a single manufacturer's line. Thus, different memory-attachment hardware may be needed for different models of the same machine. This is not a good situation.

2. The software required for the basic functioning of memory-to-memory connection is more difficult to construct. Again, I/O is where attachment is expected, in hardware as well as software, and device drivers for new attachments are routinely written to an explicitly designed interface. The corresponding support required for the bare functioning of memory attachment usually reaches deep into the operating system kernel, affecting at the very least its memory management subsystem; these are not externalized inter-

faces, and changing them may require pervasive changes in the operating system.

Once memory attachment is operational, on the other hand, it can potentially provide communication performance that is dramatically better than that of I/O attachment, because unlike I/O, memory subsystems are designed for efficient access directly from user-mode applications. Intrauser protection at the memory access level has extensive, optimized, hardware support built into virtual memory-mapping mechanisms. Interuser protection at the I/O level, on the other hand, is largely semi-interpretive, most usually enforced by disallowing direct user-mode access. I/O-attached communication (and graphics) is therefore usually in a pitched battle with system software over latency reduction. This potential advantage of memory attachment can of course be dissipated if the necessary communication protocols—always necessary at some level—are not extremely lightweight, if not completely "compiled away."

Shared Storage vs. Message-Based

Which of shared storage or message-based systems is preferable is the subject of a long-running heated battle with techno-religious overtones that is not likely to be settled any time soon. The dispute is most often over shared electronic memory—we'll cover it in Chapter 8—although shared disks also participate, as will be discussed in Chapter 9. To quickly summarize that argument: Shared storage advocates claim that because their computational model is closer to the traditional uniprocessor model, it is easier to program and furthermore is more efficient, particularly in aspects such as load balancing. Message-passing advocates claim their solutions to be far more portable and adaptable to larger-scale systems with more nodes, as well as being simpler to debug, and if our minds weren't polluted by conventional programming we'd all understand that fact intuitively. Each disputes the other's claims, and neither position is provable at this time.

Finally, note that the above has been primarily a hardware discussion. All these things being Turing machines, the appearance that software puts on any hardware can be arbitrary, specifically including the exact opposite of the hardware's innate characteristics. Such cross-dressing is rather more common than one might expect. Here are some examples.

> Reference has already been made to shared storage systems being made to appear as message-based systems; a particularly important example of that is communication techniques of the Mach microkernel operating system [BRS+85, Ras86]. Every entity in that system communicates by messages, no matter what the hardware. To speed the passing of large messages between processes residing on

the same machine, a message may be "passed" by remapping the memory of one process into another.

➤ In the other direction, the technique of distributed virtual memory has been developed to give the appearance of shared memory between machines connected only by message-based hardware. These, and related issues, are discussed later (Chapter 8).

➤ Disks are not immune to software cross-dressing, either. The appearance of shared disk storage can be obtained when there is none, as was mentioned in Chapter 4, in the discussion of cluster file systems. This technique was originally developed for databases, where it is known as "I/O shipping." More about this in Chapter 9.

5.4   Communication Requirements_____

Something none of the above has yet addressed is how much power any of these interconnection schemes must have to create a usable system. The answer is naturally quite dependent on the use to which the system is put— the workload—and also bears on the perennial shared storage vs. message-passing issue.

5.4.1   Computationally Intensive Workloads

For long-running, computationally intensive, serial jobs executed in a batch environment, the machines may as well be connected by wet string. They don't exchange enough information often enough for the robustness of the interconnect to make a significant difference in the overall performance on their workload. That is why the many systems like the IBM Research Farm or the Philips Research cluster mentioned in Chapter 2, along with a host of other assembled and preassembled computational clusters, make sense in their context: One or a few file servers within the cluster provide adequate access to data, even though the aggregate disk capability of the whole cluster is limited to a conventional LAN's throughput and latency; the demand for data access is simply quite small.

5.4.2   I/O-Intensive Workloads

Commercial and technical workloads that intensively use input/output facilities are another issue altogether.

It is straightforward to show that adequate internode communication bandwidth of a cluster for such workloads *should equal the aggregate bandwidth from all other I/O sources that each node has.*

To be crystal clear about this: Suppose a computer can, for the workload of interest, achieve a total, aggregate bandwidth of N Mbytes/second when you add up the contribution of every disk, tape, graphics device, or other I/O thingamabob attached to it. If that computer is to be used in a cluster that performs the same kind of workload—just more of it—the internode cluster communication should provide an *additional* N Mbytes/second between nodes.

Of course, the system will still work if that bandwidth isn't there. It'll just run the workload substantially more slower than you would expect, unless you have the Great Galactic Genius as your job scheduler, and maybe not even then.

This surprising and seemingly overwhelming requirement can be derived by considering two different I/O-intensive workloads: batch processing, and distributed ("parallel") query processing. Latency requirements are a bit harder to get a grip on at the present time.

I/O-Intensive Batch

First, consider commercial batch jobs, or, more generally, I/O-intensive batch jobs. Such jobs' execution time is dominated by how fast they can move data in and out of the computer, not by how fast the processor is; that might as well be a lump of putty, except for its role in scheduling I/O (and more than occasionally, its role in sorting the data). As we'll see (Chapter 7), serial batch jobs of any kind are potentially a very usable workload for clusters, one to which cluster designs should cater.

Drop such a job down in a cluster. How likely is it to land on the node where all its data resides? Not very, for two reasons.

The first reason is that a convenient cluster organization is to specialize some nodes for storage and others for computation. No user job goes on the storage nodes; therefore the user jobs have to get their data from the storage nodes and will slow down if they don't get it as fast as they did when it was local. That doesn't sound good. While a functional split like that may be very useful for administrative or other reasons, it is clearly not optimal for an I/O-intensive batch situation. So let's assume that every node is a combined compute-I/O server, running something like the true cluster file systems mentioned in Chapter 4.

Then a second reason comes into play: Optimizing the placement of a job on a node so that both its computational needs and its storage access needs are satisfied is an exceedingly difficult task and in general will be impossible to perform. What can even a perfect scheduler do, for example, if a job needs data that's attached to two different nodes? In general the job will not be on the node where its data resides. Since its execution time depends on how fast it gets its data, it will slow down if it can't get its data equally fast no matter where it is. That means each node must be able to supply that data at the original, stand-alone speed, as well as receive it at that same speed.

Conclusion: For I/O-intensive batch systems, the inter-node bandwidth should at least equal the aggregate I/O bandwidth of each node, or throughput and turnaround time will suffer. The processor overhead required to use this bandwidth cannot get out of hand, either, since no system is used purely for one type of workload or another and the processor requirements of the other jobs will be compromised. The "at least" qualifier is there because in addition to end-use job communication, there undoubtedly must be some communication related to running the cluster itself; how else can the cross-node scheduler work? Telepathy?

Query Processing

The second case concerns database query operation.

Anticipating some of the discussion in Chapter 9, a large relational **join** (for example) may be split up so that is performed partly on each node of a cluster (without any user reprogramming, by the way); each node performs a subset of the operation by working on the subset of the whole table that's directly attached to that node (or, with shared disk, primarily used by that node). The data for that local subset is streamed off disk into memory as fast as its I/O system can pump; the database was specifically written to do this.

While that's happening, the data being read is **join**ed with data from another table—**T**—and the result sent to another node. **Join**ing finds rows that match and creates new rows that concatenate the matching rows: In other words, whenever a **join** finds a match, it outputs a row bigger than the rows either table had. Suppose table **T** happens to be sufficiently small that it all fits in memory. Then the outgoing data, if there are a lot of "hits" in the **join**, will be *larger* than the original data being read: There can be more data that needs to be sent between nodes than can be read off disk at its maximum rate.

There is actually no theoretical limit to the multiplier that can be applied here. But something on the other end must absorb that stuff, and dump it onto the receiver's disk. (There's always more data than fits in main memory in a database system.) Since the receiver can't get rid of the data any faster than it can write it, the maximum it can receive—so the maximum that it makes sense to send—again turns out to be equal to the maximum aggregate I/O bandwidth of a node.

Transaction Processing: Latency and Overhead

Transaction processing, at least as typified by popular benchmarks, does not intensively use I/O bandwidth. It does, however, stress the ability of a system to initiate a large number of I/O operations, each not transferring much data. This assuredly implies requirements on internode latency and overhead.

However, those requirements are hard to pin down, at least in part because of the large differences in software architecture used by different database systems; that variety is discussed in Chapter 9. The currently normal millisecond-level latencies for standard communication, however, will surely be a drag on this use of clusters. Proprietary systems, such as those of Tandem (Chapter 2), have apparently solved them.

5.4.3   What Can Be Done?

The requirements described above are fierce. They may also be somewhat overstated for the I/O-intensive batch case, since systems often provide more I/O bandwidth than any real program can use because the need to connect many devices may boost aggregate bandwidth beyond usability. Inter-node bandwidth need only add an amount equal to real aggregate programs' use, of course. Even if the full, possibly overstated goals are accepted, however, clusters do not have to be consigned to a compute-intensive ghetto or restricted to proprietary, special-purpose communication hardware and software.

Shared-disk clusters, accessing all disks equally, today at least come close to meeting the bandwidth requirements, if not completely meeting them in some configurations. They are currently the undisputed leaders of commercial cluster architecture, and meeting this bandwidth requirement is part of the reason. They do have their own difficulties, as will be discussed in Chapter 9, but they are certainly in the right ballpark, if not always in a scoring position, as far as bandwidth is concerned.

As for techno-politically-correct "shared nothing" systems, well, this explains at least part of the enthusiasm evident in Chapter 3 over the new, fast, standard communication techniques. Those at least potentially offer the bandwidth demanded by the most lucrative markets for clusters—which is also, of course, the most lucrative market for any other computer systems. (Their role in technical computing is also very nontrivial.) There are still hardware and software challenges, as were mentioned back in that Chapter 3. A new challenge came out here: A good handle on communication latency and overhead requirements of commercial computing, particularly transaction processing, would be a rather interesting piece of data. The rewards for meeting all those challenges may well be great.

A final comment: This chapter contrasts very strongly with the one following, which deals with symmetric multiprocessors. In that one, not only are the requirements clear (although not well understood outside a limited technical coterie), but also a huge number of incredibly sophisticated techniques for meeting those requirements have been developed, published, and will be described.

Such are the wages of not being a recognized, coherent discipline.

CHAPTER 6

Symmetric Multiprocessors

Symmetric multiprocessors (SMPs) and clusters are the two primary forms of lowly parallel computing. Since they address approximately the same range of parallelism, they can strongly overlap each other in aggregate performance and other characteristics. Yet they differ, grossly in some ways—overall system organization and programming model, for example—and more subtly in others, such as their utilization of memory. Since their overlap often makes them competitors, a comprehensive discussion of the differences is very important. That comparison appears several chapters later, because it must be a system discussion incorporating both hardware and software issues.

It's obviously impossible to understand such a comparison without understanding the relevant characteristics of SMPs. Hence this chapter, which is not about clusters at all. It is a discussion of the characteristics of the other lowly parallel system, the SMP.

Unlike the salient characteristics of clusters, which are at present primarily external to a whole computer (or are software), the crucial characteristics of SMPs are deep in the heart of the hardware. What an SMP looks like to software—its *architecture*—is very important, as will be discussed. But the things that have to be done create that appearance, to implement that architecture—the *machine design*—are where the meaty comparison issues lie. So this chapter gets rather deeper into computer hardware innards than most other parts of this book.

It's not going to be that hairy, however, and there's a reason beyond cluster comparison for paying close attention to this chapter: Inoculation against processor architecture hype. You'll notice that, like much of this book, this chapter is about performance. But it doesn't say much about processors, only about memory systems. In fact, the performance of a computer is now almost entirely dependent on memory system performance rather than on processor performance. If the processor is fast enough to push the memory to its limit—and most of them are, as will be explained below—its architecture may not matter very much. What will always matter, however, is how fast and clever the memory subsystem is—a part of the computer that is woefully unsung in the current atmosphere of RISC/CISC/VLIW wars.

6.1 What Is an SMP?

A symmetric multiprocessor, an SMP, is a computer variation that, well, has multiple processors that are symmetric.

Figure 6-1 Simplified Diagram of a Symmetric Multiprocessor (SMP)

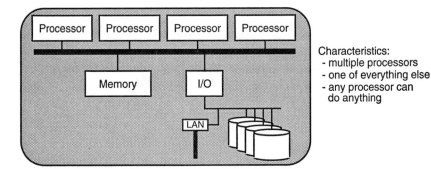

Being a bit more informative (also, see Figure 6-1):

> ➤ **It has multiple processors.** And *only* multiple processors. It does not have multiple I/O systems, it does not have multiple memories, it does not have multiple anything else, either, like cabinetry. Actually, any of the above can be physically packaged as multiple units, but that is not visible to any program that runs on the machine: application, subsystem, operating system, or whatever. Figure 6-2

shows an example of a multiprocessor that is not an SMP because it has multiple separate memory systems.

The fact that there are multiple processors, however, definitely *is* visible to programs running on the machine, although that fact can be hidden from some software by other software. A prime example of a program that hides multiple processors is the operating system. The OS must be exquisitely, intensively aware down to its bones that there are multiple processors, but by default hides that fact from applications. If an application wants to be multiprocessor aware, it can perform operations that find out there are multiple processors and exploit that fact; but by default they think they're running on a uniprocessor. This is true of every commercially available SMP operating system. It doesn't mean you can't use the multiple processors, just that by default no single program does. Multiple programs, running simultaneously, may. Many database systems are MP-hiders, too. They find out from the OS that there are multiple processors but hide that from their applications. This hiding of the parallel nature of the hardware is key to the SPPS paradigm, which allows plain jane serial programs to make effective use of SMPs.

Figure 6-2   Two Multiprocessors That Are Not SMPs

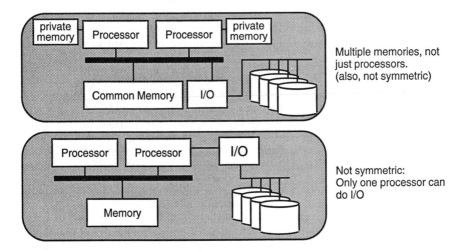

Multiple memories, not just processors.
(also, not symmetric)

Not symmetric:
Only one processor can do I/O

> **Those processors are symmetric.** What this means is that each of the processors has exactly the same abilities. Therefore, any processor can do anything: They all have equal access to every location in memory, they can all equally well control every I/O device, leap to any interrupt at a single bound, and so on. In effect, the rest of the

machine looks the same from the point of view of each processor; hence the term "symmetric." There are multiple-processor systems where this is not true. In a common variant, also shown in Figure 6-2, all the processors can access all of memory; but only one has the ability to do I/O. Not too surprisingly, these are called *asymmetric* multiprocessors, or, historically, attached processors (referring to the processor that can't do I/O). Such systems can have slightly simpler hardware than SMPs but are less efficient at doing I/O (big surprise) and slightly more difficult to support with system software.

Deviations from these two characteristics are often related, because the most popular way to incorporate multiple memories or I/O systems into a computer is to associate them (tightly) with each of the multiple processors. The top example in Figure 6-2 illustrates this. There are three memories, which violates the first requirement. However, what primarily makes two of the memories separate is that only one processor can access each—in other words, a violation of symmetry.

SMPs are occasionally referred to as "tightly coupled multiprocessors," as distinct from "loosely coupled systems," the latter being more or less the systems referred to in the book as clusters. These names open the door to variations on the adjectives—firmly coupled, very loosely coupled, and so on. I have avoided this terminology because it implies that the types of system described are architecturally similar, differing in only one dimension: the mysterious "coupling." In fact SMPs and clusters differ tremendously along many dimensions, including most of the important issues that concern how they're programmed. Therefore, terms not implying similarity are better. (The "firmly," etc., variations also differ tremendously, a fact hidden by the terms.) Also, the term "tightly coupled" completely misses the necessary emphasis on symmetry that is a crucial element of SMPs; the asymmetric processors mentioned above were, in fact, tightly coupled.

The definition of an SMP is more than just a sterile academic description of one of the legion of possible parallel machines. This definition has teeth because it is what software expects an SMP to be. In the jargon: It is the *programming model* to which software has been written.[1]

If a machine does not adhere to this programming model, the difference can in some cases be wallpapered over by system software. For example, suppose only one processor can do I/O. The operating system can run jobs any-

---

1. There will be later chapters devoted to programming models. Also, there are elements of the SMP programming model not mentioned here, such as sequential consistency, that are covered later in this chapter.

where until they request input or output, at which point they're effectively stopped and rescheduled onto the I/O-enabled processor. This is not as trivial as that sentence makes it sound, but is certainly feasible and has been done. It allows applications and possibly subsystems, like databases, to run on a machine supporting only a non-SMP programming model, with at least some performance degradation.

But in this age of portable system software—UNIX, OS/2 for PowerPC, Windows NT, Machine-Independent NetWare, Linux, and others—you must count the cost of altering that standard system, since it has been written assuming the SMP programming model. That will more than likely be far more expensive than just giving in and doing a true SMP, especially when you consider keeping that modified OS up-to-date with every new software release.

That's it. Except for one little thing. Just how many is this "multiple"? How big can an SMP get? *Do SMPs scale?*

There are very possibly few, if any, limits on how many processors sharing memory in some manner can be coupled together. Having to preserve the complete SMP programming model, including total symmetry of memory access, presents graver problems. It is certainly possible that very big SMPs can nevertheless be built, but the cost of maintaining that programming model will increase ever more rapidly as the maximum system size increases.

The question of SMP scaling will be taken up again when SMPs and clusters are compared in Chapter 11, after a great deal more preparation. For one thing, it's necessary to say exactly what "scale" really means. This chapter provides the background needed to understand how SMPs work and therefore to appreciate why there might be difficulties building really big SMPs out of ever more powerful processors. That background begins, of necessity, with a discussion of computer memories and caches.

6.2   What Is a Cache, and Why Is It Necessary?

Memory access and cache memories (or just *caches*) are at the core of many of the issues with SMPs. This section describes caches and relevant aspects of how they work, starting with the question of why they're used in the first place.

Despite the fact that this whole discussion will appear to go into incredibly gruesome detail, it comes nowhere near doing full justice to the richness and complexity of this topic. Caches have been around for a very long time; their first use was on the IBM Stretch 7090 project in the early 1960s. Since then, many extremely intelligent people and a veritable army of lesser lights have spent their entire careers inventing and simulating variations on the theme of caches—simulating, because no completely satisfactory, closed-form mathematical analysis has been devised, although everything from simple linear equations to fractals has been tried. The result of all this frenetic, high-quality effort is an immense store of hard won information about myriad cache mutations and rococo embellishments. This chapter does not even try to cover them all. Rather, it focuses only on the key structural elements of caches relevant to SMP design. That alone is a lot; this became—not by design, by any means—the second longest chapter in this book. I've added a section that at least hints at some of the complexity not covered, both to salve my technical conscience and to avoid being pilloried by the experts, but that section need not be read to understand the overall picture. Far greater detail is available in existing textbooks on computer architecture [HP90, Man93].

6.2.1   The Processor-Memory Speed Problem

Figure 6-3 shows the basic problem that caches were invented to solve: There is a huge mismatch in speed between memories and processors. I really do mean huge. Current, typical memories are at least 20 times too slow for current typical processors. Why this happens is described below.

Main memory is commonly built out of inexpensive, large, dense memory chips called Dynamic Random Access Memory or DRAM chips. When such chips are asked for the data stored within them, they take (at present) 50–100 nanoseconds before disgorging the information requested. In the jargon: their access time is 50–100 nanoseconds To keep the discussion simple, let's

Figure 6-3   Processor and Memory Speeds: What's Wrong With This Picture?

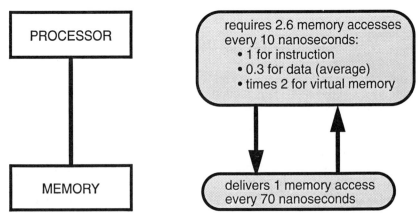

say such chips take 70 nanoseconds. While that's how fast the memory chips themselves operate, it actually takes much longer to access a large bank of memory chips, correct (or at least detect) errors that might be there, and pass the result to a processor. Thus, 70 nanoseconds is really a gross underestimate, but the problem is quite bad enough for the current discussion if we pretend that the whole memory system runs at chip speeds. So let's do so.

Processors, on the other hand, currently run with a clock speed anywhere from 50 MHz to several hundred MHz. This means that their internal cycle time (1/clock speed) is somewhere between 50 nanoseconds and around 2 nanoseconds Again to keep things simple, let's take 10 nanoseconds as a typical cycle time, corresponding to a 100 MHz clock.

A modern, superscalar RISC processor works quite hard, and often succeeds, at executing *several* instructions in *one* of those cycles [Joh91]. Some CISC machines whose developers have deep pockets work hard at this, too, and the latest highly-hyped phenomenon in town is "very large instruction word" (VLIW) machines that may attempt to do tens of instructions, or more, every cycle. But you certainly don't always get several instructions executed simultaneously. How many do get done depends heavily on the processor, compiler, other hardware factors, and very heavily on the particular program being executed. As a result, on a good RISC you can get anywhere from three or more cycles/instruction to 0.2 cycles/instruction (five instructions/cycle). Again, rather than deal with ranges, let's pick a simple number: one instruction per cycle.

So, what we've got here is a processor able to execute one instruction every 10 nanoseconds and a memory that can respond to a request every 70 nanoseconds This is starting to sound bad. Now: Every instruction (10 nanoseconds) requires at least one, and usually more than one, memory reference (70 nanoseconds). This is rather obviously a major problem. Why are all those references to memory required?

Well, you first have to fetch the instruction itself. That's one reference to memory right there. In addition, the instruction might tell the processor to reference memory—for example, a **load** instruction saying to copy a memory location into a processor register or a **store** doing the opposite (for a RISC machine, those are practically the only such instructions). Not all instructions will require a memory reference, but enough do require one that the effect is definitely noticeable. Typically, somewhere around 25%-30% of all instructions are **load**s or **store**s referencing memory [HP90, Joh91]. That means up to 30% of all instructions require an additional memory reference. Adding the reference to the instruction itself, gives us 1.3 memory references (on average) per instruction. Wish we were done, but we're not.

In addition to the above, we have to account for the fact that with modern "general-purpose" computers and operating systems, all but a tiny fraction of memory references are *virtual*—meaning that the memory address given by the instruction (or the program counter, for instructions) isn't really the address in the memory. I'm not going to explain all about virtual memory here. It's a standard technique allowing programs to be written as if there were much more memory than really present; it also keeps programs from stepping on other programs' data, to say nothing of stepping on the other programs themselves. See a textbook on operating systems, such as [Tan92], for more details.

For our discussion, what's relevant is that the virtual address (the one in the instruction or the program counter) has to be checked against a table of bounds for validity and then "relocated"—have a number added to it—to get the real address in memory. Those bounds and the numbers added are kept (where else?) in memory. So every time the processor references memory, it really does so twice: once to get the virtual-memory checking and relocation information, and then again to do the reference that the programmer asked for in the first place. Actually, more than one reference is necessary to get that bound and offset information, but for illustration here we'll just use one; that's bad enough.

Having to get the virtual-memory information means that our original 1.3 (on average) memory references per instruction is doubled. The processor somehow has to do $1.3 \times 2 = 2.6$ memory accesses for each instruction. Each one of those memory accesses takes at least 7 times as long as we'd like the whole instruction to take. Since $7 \times 2.6 = 18.2$, we are trying to fit nearly 20 lbs. into a 1 lb. bag.

There is absolutely no point to having such fast processors if they are hobbled by this slow memory. It's like supergluing an eyebolt to a tortoise's shell and chaining a hare to it. What can be done to fix this problem?

6.2.2   Why Faster Main Memory Alone Doesn't Work

Something that obviously suggests itself is using faster memory chips. There are such chips. They're called Static Random Access Memory chips, alias Static RAMs or SRAMs. They operate at the same speed as processors because they're made out of the same kind of circuitry as the processors, rather than the different, smaller ("denser") and slower circuitry used in DRAMs (Dynamic RAMs). This solution has been used in the past on expensive supercomputers. Seymour Cray, the famous supercomputer architect and designer, is alleged to have said "You can't fake what you haven't got" (actually referring to caches), when equipping his original machines that way.

But SRAM chips are far more expensive individually than DRAMs, and you need more of them because each chip holds fewer bits (they're "less dense"). For example, I recently purchased 4 Mbytes of DRAM memory for a PC, packaged on a card, ready to plug in.[2] Those 4 Mbytes cost me $132. At the same time, 256 Kbytes of SRAM cache cost $76. This was from the same source, for the same machine, under the same price structure, and like the DRAMs, the SRAMs were packaged ready to plug in. So SRAM in that form costs $76 × 4 = $304/Mbyte, while DRAM costs $132/4 = $33/Mbyte. This is nearly a factor of 10 difference. At those prices, if I had bought 4 Mbytes of SRAM rather than DRAM it would have cost me $1216—which is more than the entire computer cost me including 8 Mbytes of DRAM memory. SRAM main memory is not a solution for people lacking very deep pockets.

All microelectronics is, however, continually getting faster and cheaper. Will DRAMs catch up with processors? Will SRAMs get so inexpensive they can be used? DRAMs are getting faster, and variations on the DRAM theme are appearing which are even faster For example, there's Rambus [Ram] and synchronous DRAM (SDRAM) that's available at slightly higher cost than normal DRAM from many manufacturers, and EDO (Extended Data Out) is starting to catch on in PC circles. This will help and may in fact help quite a bit. But speed relative to the processor is what counts, and the trend is for processors to speed up even faster than DRAM memory does. SRAMs are also getting less expensive, but not fast enough. The problem isn't going away and is more likely to get worse than to get better.

Even if the problem were going away, who wants to wait? The problem exists now. Also, don't forget that processors need more than one memory access per cycle; so fully solving the problem means the memory must somehow be faster than the processor. Forget that. If the memory were made out of some kind of new, faster stuff, everybody would instantly turn around and make the processors out of the same stuff, bringing us back to square one.

In part this is a vicious (or possibly virtuous) circle: Because caches work so well, as described below, designers are more motivated to improve density (bits per chip) and therefore cost ($ per bit) than to improve speed. This makes caches even more crucial, therefore more universally used, further decreasing the motivation for really fast memory, and so on.

2. By publication date, the prices quoted for memory will hopefully seem large; but the ratios should stay about the same.

6.2.3   Locality of Reference and Caches

There is a rather inexpensive way to fix the memory-processor speed problem that works quite well and, as a result, is used by just about everybody, from PCs to mainframes: cache memory. To understand why it works, we must begin by looking not at hardware but at the behavior of most programs.

Programs don't access memory here and there, willy-nilly, in a random fashion that scatters across the entire memory. Instead, they repeatedly read and write a relatively small collection of memory locations over and over again; then they move to a new collection of memory locations and access them over and over; then they move again, and so on. That this is a reasonable assertion can be seen by considering a simple program loop. The instructions in the loop are used over and over until the loop finishes. The same is true for at least part of the data used in the loop: temporary memory locations that hold partial results are reused each time the loop is executed. This behavior of programs is called *locality of reference*. Not all programs have good locality of reference—some really do access memory in a nonrepetitive fashion—but the vast majority have quite a bit of this quality.[3]

It is this program behavior that suggests a solution to the memory speed problem.

Suppose you kept just a small amount of the data from memory, specifically the most recently used part, in a small amount of that fast, expensive memory (SRAM). Snuggle that fast memory up close to the processor, inserting it between the processor and its memory, as shown in Figure 6-4. Now, whenever the processor requests a memory reference you don't go directly to memory; instead you first quickly check the small, fast memory. If it's there, you return the answer right away—at speed comparable to the processor's speed. If it's not, you trundle off to memory as usual to get the data. But when the main memory (finally) gives you that data, you do two things: Give it to the processor as ordered, and tuck it into that small, fast memory. That way, subsequent references will find it in the fast memory. Locality of reference means you'll find it in the fast memory quite often and will seldom have to go to the slow main memory. As a result, on average you get much faster memory access. And note: The program doesn't have to change one bit to make use of this; it's fully automatic.

---

3. What's described here is more specifically known as "temporal locality," since it operates over time. There is also "spatial locality," which asserts that when a program references one memory location it's pretty likely to reference nearby memory locations too. Spatial locality comes into play later.

Figure 6-4   A Cache Memory Between Processor and Main Memory

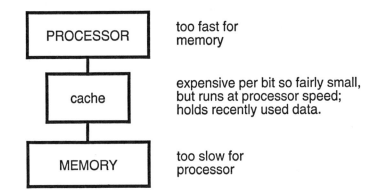

That small, fast memory, holding recently used information, is what is called a **cache memory**. Caches work better than we have any right to expect. How well they work is expressed by what's called the **cache hit ratio**. This is the fraction of the time the desired data are found in the cache, normally expressed as a percentage: 100% is perfect: everything's found in cache; 50% means half the time you find what you want in cache; etc. The opposite ratio (0% is perfect) is symmetrically called the **cache miss ratio**. The exact numbers achieved for hit ratios vary and depend very strongly on the size and other qualities of the cache memory, as well as on the specific program being run. But computer hardware engineers and others concerned with performance get decidedly bent out of shape if cache hit ratios fall much below 90%. So at least 90% of the time, your machine acts like it has that expensive fast memory, while you've only paid a very small fraction of the cost. This is one heck of a deal, otherwise known as a wonderfully good engineering trade-off.

But we noticed that each instruction requires more than one memory reference. As discussed above, you can't go faster than the SRAMs; if you could, you'd build the processor using whatever it was that was faster, and so the memory wouldn't be faster any more. The solution is to use more than one cache and get data out of all of them simultaneously. Result: modern processor-memory subsystems are positively dripping with caches of various types.

For example, Figure 6-5 shows a system with three caches: One holds instructions, one holds data, and one holds the virtual memory translation information. (The latter is usually called a "translation lookaside buffer" for obscure and primarily historical reasons; it's still essentially a cache). Using all three caches simultaneously, the processor can get an instruction, and data, and the virtual memory translation information it needs, all at the same time and all in a single one of its own cycles. (Yes, something special must be done with the translation lookaside buffer if two translations—instruction address and data address—are to be done in a single cycle.) (And doing more than one instruction at a time can get even trickier.)

Figure 6-5   A Processor Festooned with Many Caches

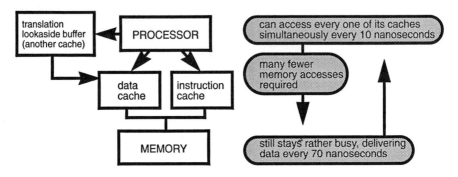

Here's a specific example of the difference a cache can make: The IBM RISC System/6000 model 530 is an aggressively superscalar (five instructions/cycle peak) cached machine. In doing dense linear algebra, it's been demonstrated that the machine can do about 44 MFLOPS when its peak performance[4] is 50 MFLOPS—if it is explicitly programmed to take advantage of the cache [AGZ94]. By such explicit programming, I mean doing two things: First, organize the program so that you reused data in the cache as much as possible (this will be discussed in "Chunking and Blocking" on page 221 in Chapter 8). Second, include carefully positioned, seemingly useless **load** instructions whose results you do not immediately use. Their only purpose is to cause data to be moved into the cache ahead of time, so the data are there when they actually are needed. These **load**s don't slow things down because the RISC System/6000 (in common with other manufacturers' designs) simply keeps doing other instructions until it comes to one requiring the data **load**ed. Eliminating just the seemingly useless instructions that prefetch data, but keeping the reorganization, causes performance to drop from about 44 MFLOPS to around 36 MFLOPS—a 22% loss of performance. Eliminating both optimizations can cause performance to become very bad, since completely loading a full cache line (defined later—a hunk of data)

---

4. Jack Dongarra of the University of Tennessee, Oak Ridge National Laboratories, and LINPACK benchmark fame, has defined "peak" as the performance the manufacturer guarantees you cannot exceed.

from memory to cache can take 18 cycles on that machine, and its memory system is rather aggressive compared to others.

6.2.4 Level 2 Caches

As I hinted a while back, and showed in the example above, I've dramatically understated the slowness of main memory. By the time you send a request to memory, do the access, and send the (multiword) cache line back, it really isn't 7 times slower than typical processors. More typically, memory is 10, 20, or even more times slower. This means a processor is really out to lunch when it has to get data from memory rather than cache—implying a very large cache is appropriate, since the larger the cache, the less often you "miss."

But very large, very fast caches have very large price tags. Another alternative is often used to keep the cost down, called the **level 2 cache** [BW89]. This is, as its name suggests, a second cache inserted between the other caches (now called **level 1 caches**) and memory, as illustrated in Figure 6-6. The level 2 cache is intermediate in speed between level 1 and memory. For example, it might respond in 5 to 7 instruction cycle times, rather than 10, 20, or more. In addition, there aren't several of them to provide multiple

Figure 6-6   A Processor with a Level-2 Cache

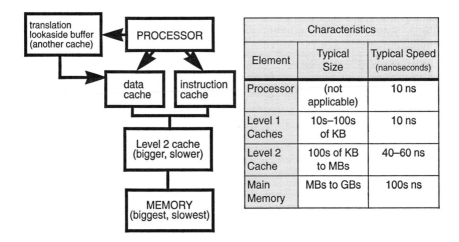

Characteristics		
Element	Typical Size	Typical Speed (nanoseconds)
Processor	(not applicable)	10 ns
Level 1 Caches	10s–100s of KB	10 ns
Level 2 Cache	100s of KB to MBs	40–60 ns
Main Memory	MBs to GBs	100s ns

simultaneous accesses. The trade-off is that it can be larger, which helps immensely in running anything other than tiny programs on tiny data. Commercial processing (database systems, for example) and operating systems aren't small programs and don't operate on small amounts of data, so they can benefit significantly from a large level 2 cache. "Large" in this case is typically somewhere from half a Mbyte to 8 Mbytes, depending on the system's target price and application domain. In contrast, when level 2 caches are used, the level 1 caches are typically in the 8 to 32 Kbyte range. Some manufacturers have opted for extensive large level 1 caches instead (Hewlett-Packard in particular), but that is the exception rather than the rule.

Level 2 caches are particularly common in systems made from PC-class CPU chips, such as the Intel X86 series or the PowerPC, because those chips incorporate small (level 1) caches on the chips themselves. The level-1 caches included are fine for "client" programs and data, but application servers and database systems (to pick two examples) will find their performance improved with additional, hence level 2, off-chip caches.

6.2.5   Cache Lines

Another aspect of caches that will become important in our discussion of SMPs is how much data they get from memory at a time. They certainly don't get only what the CPU asked for, which could be as little as one byte; among other problems, that would require them to manage variable-sized pieces of data, which is hard.

Instead, they grab a fixed- and convenient-sized hunk of data surrounding the address requested. "Convenient" means a power of two and can range from 4 bytes to 64, 128, or even 256 bytes for an aggressive level 2 cache (which typically takes bigger bites than a level 1 cache). **Cache line** is the term for that hunk of data moved between the cache and memory. The term has no mnemonic value I can detect, except for the fact that it is deliberately not the same as "word" or "byte," the units the processor operates on. A cache line is usually at least several consecutive words, all moved in and out of memory and at the same time.

Good-sized cache lines are a good thing for two reasons.

> ➤ First, they exploit *spatial locality* of programs. When the processor asks for an instruction, guess which instruction it's most likely to ask for next? The one right after it in memory. If the cache gets a hunk of memory surrounding the instruction, it's quite likely (but not guaranteed) that when the processor asks next, what it wants will already be there in the cache. Data also exhibits spatial locality, although not to the extent that programs do.

> ➤ Second, they allow a designer to get more data faster out of the DRAMs. Many chips can be cycled at once, getting more data in the same time. In addition, most DRAMs have a mode of operation

("page" or "nibble" mode) that takes less time to get data if what's asked for is right next to what you asked for before. So, you can whip out more data faster if you ask for it in larger chunks, like cache lines.

It's possible to carry this good thing too far, though, which is why I said "good-sized" cache lines above, rather than "big" cache lines. If all the program really wants is one byte and it never refers to any of the other bytes near that one byte, then you've wasted time, and space in the cache, by getting a big hunk of memory rather than a smaller amount. Overall, cache lines at least several words long are a good bet and therefore commonly used.

6.2.6 Now, Let's Simplify Things

All of this complexity of multiple caches with multiple levels and cache lines can be intimidating. Thankfully, it's not necessary to keep it all in mind. In fact, for the remainder of this discussion, we'll ignore the presence of anything but a single data cache, simply labelled "cache," as shown in Figure 6-7. All the issues we're discussing come up there; nothing is lost.

Figure 6-7   What to Keep in Mind

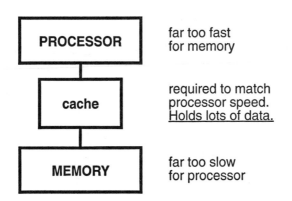

Also, remember that there can be a lot of data in a processor's cache—in many cases, megabytes of it, in fact. And it's kept in hunks, cache lines, bigger than a typical word.

The rest of the discussion above was to prove it and tell you why. Those few things are all you really need to keep in mind.

6.2.7   The Cache As a Messy Desk

Well, almost

There's an aspect of how caches operate that is crucial to SMPs and has been glossed over so far. It concerns how they function, rather than their size and speed.

Cache memories effectively "know" when the processor starts using some data, since new data isn't in the cache. But caches have no way of knowing when the processor is finished using a given piece of data.[5]

As a result, caches operate using what might be called the "messy desk" principle. Here's the analogy suggesting that name: Suppose you walk into an office and start to work on some project. You dig the files out of a desk drawer or cabinet, put them on your desk, and work. Then you start something else. No, don't put the old stuff away; restrain your tidiness even if you completely finished the previous job. Just get out the new things you need, find an empty spot on your desk, and work there. Do the next task in another empty spot, and so on. Eventually, of course, your desk will be a mess with no more room left on it. That's when you clear some space off by putting some of the items on your desk back in the files—but only clear enough space to do the next thing you need. Gradually, the next task's stuff replaces older stuff on the desk.

Notice that the desk never ever gets clean. In fact, except for the initial period when you first start using it, the desk is always completely filled with "old stuff" of various ages. Sometimes this saves you time, since a new task may refer to things you already have out on the desk. In fact, you're maximizing the chance of that by never cleaning things up. (I personally find this a delightful rationalization for the usual state of my own desk.)

Cache memories work exactly like that messy desk: Nothing is emptied out of them until the space it occupies is required for something else.

How this works for caches is illustrated in Figure 6-8 and Figure 6-9, which show the life cycle of a cache line.

As illustrated, the life of a cache line has four phases.

1. **Get the cache line.** Initially, let's assume there's nothing in the cache. The processor kicks things off ① by asking for location 23.

---

5. An oversimplification. Several systems have specific instructions allowing the processor to tell the cache to just wipe some stuff out ("**purge**" it) or write it back to memory and then clear the space. But for the most part they're only used in special circumstances; programs aren't usually written to use those instructions.

Figure 6-8   The Life Cycle of a Cache Line, Phases 1 and 2

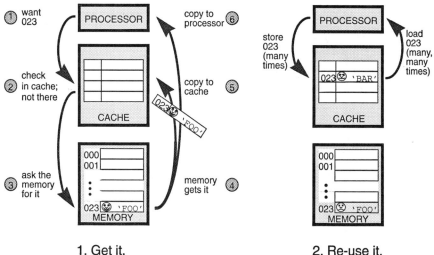

1. Get it.   2. Re-use it.

The cache is checked ② —nope, not there—so we go off to memory, ③ which after a while responds with the contents of location 23. ④ In the illustration, that happens to be the character string 'FOO'. The fact that memory location 23 contains 'FOO' is **stored** ⑤ in a slot in the cache; simultaneously 'FOO' is given to the processor ⑥, which has been waiting patiently.[6]

2.   **Reuse the cache line.** This is the phase that's the whole point of a cache. Assuming the program has reasonable locality of reference, the processor hammers away at location 23 for a while: It writes a new value into it ('BAR'), reads that again, forgets it and reads it a few more times, writes another value ('MUMB'), and so on for quite possibly many, many times. We want it to be many, many times, because each time we find the data in the nice, fast cache rather than that slow, old main memory. No waiting, runs fast, everybody happy.

3.   **Ignore the cache line.** (See Figure 6-8.) The program has moved on to other things, so the processor doesn't call on location 23 any more. The cache line for location 23 just sits there in the cache, bored, since nothing tells it to get out. This is the messy desk factor.

---

6. ...to wake up the cat ⑦ who jumps on the modem ⑧ pushing the dip switches ⑨ that put a squawk through the multimedia speakers ⑩ which wakes up the opera singer ⑪ whose scream breaks the monitor... oh, sorry, wrong strip.

Figure 6-9   Life Cycle of a Cache Line, Phases 3 and 4

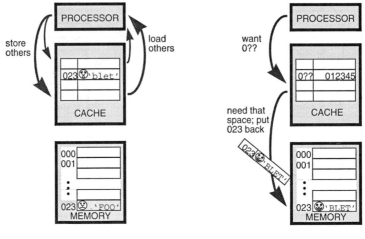

3. Ignore it.   4. Put it back.

4. **Put the cache line back in memory**. At some point, the space that location 23 is using in cache is needed for some new stuff. To clear out that space, location 23 is bumped out of the cache and written back into memory.

That's the life of a cache line.

But, wait a minute. Something odd is going on.

We've been watching the cache. Instead, take a look at the memory in the illustrations. Until the cache line was copied back, location 23 in main memory had the original value in it: `'FOO'`. The value in the cache changed to `'BAR'`, then `'MUMB'`, and so on, but the memory stayed `'FOO'`. So the value in memory is *wrong*. Only when the cache line gets written back does the memory change to the value the processor "thinks" it has—actually, and more importantly, the value the *programmer* thinks it has.

This doesn't matter, of course, because the processor always looks in the cache first, so it always gets the correct memory contents. Right? Right.

Watch this space.

6.2.8   Caches Do It at Random

Up to now, I've not said how caches decide which "old stuff" gets put back when you have to make more room on the messy desk. That omission was deliberate, to save a punch line: *Caches do it at random.*

You might think that it would be better to specifically pick the oldest item (really, the least recently used one) and put that away. It would be better, but nowhere near as much better as untrained intuition would indicate. The reason follows from relative sizes.

Even a small cache holds several thousand items (cache lines) from main memory. If you were to close your eyes and randomly pick an item to put away out of several thousand, chances are that you would not pick the exact one you need next, or even one you need pretty soon. Sometimes you'll be unlucky; that's why this method isn't perfect. But most of the time it works rather well—and boy, is it cheap. So it's not optimal, but it is an excellent engineering trade-off.

An effect of this randomness is that some of the things left on the messy desk can get very old indeed. In fact, you can't predict how long anything will stick around in a cache. It's random! Some things are booted out early and have to be obtained again from memory almost immediately (bad luck; done in excess, it's called "trashing the cache"). Other things could be **load**ed into the cache when a machine is first turned on, used exactly once, and then stay there until it's turned off—days, weeks, or months later—just because, at random, they weren't picked to go back into memory.

Those wrong values in memory are corrected only when things are moved out of the cache. That means that values in memory might be quite recent (with a trashed cache) but they can be wrong for a very long time, too. At random. Since caches can be big (especially level 2 caches), many locations in memory—megabytes—can be randomly wrong. But it doesn't matter, since the processor checks the cache before looking in memory. (Keep watching this space.)

An update to the "What to Keep in Mind" diagram is now appropriate. See Figure 6-10, which points out that main memory is not only slow, it's measled with incorrect values at random locations.

So much, finally, for caches.

6.2.9   An Aside for the Incurably Precise

The topic of caches is one of the more embellished in computer architecture. To simplify the explanations above, I've made some approximations that stretch the truth a tad, and I've ignored much of the diversity of cache design that exists in contemporary computers.

If you don't care a fig about that, skip to the next section; this one is not necessary to preserve the flow of the discussion. This section may, however, explain a few terms you've heard elsewhere, and fixes some of the inaccura-

Figure 6-10 What Else to Keep in Mind

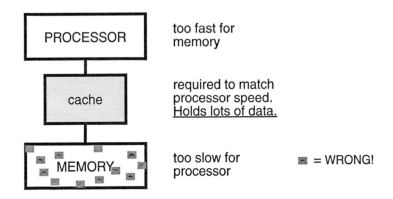

PROCESSOR — too fast for memory

cache — required to match processor speed. <u>Holds lots of data.</u>

MEMORY — too slow for processor   ▓ = WRONG!

cies for those who already know something of this area. For a far more thorough description, please see a textbook on computer architecture such as [HP90]. Unfortunately, such textbooks all seem to stop short of a good discussion of SMP-related cache issues, which will be our next topic. I suppose there are only so many hours in an undergraduate degree.

First topic: All right, I lied. It's not really random. An algorithm is used, so cache replacement is at best pseudo-random. What happens is that the address of the referenced data is pummeled and mashed to pick a location in the cache memory. If the desired data is there, then you've got it. (You find out it's the desired data by storing the full address in an associated memory called "tag memory" along with the data, reading that address out and comparing it with the desired address.) Otherwise, whatever's in there is put back in memory, and the desired data is fetched from memory and put there.

The picking of the location in the cache's memory is the element that's effectively "random." That location is chosen by shredding the address given by the processor: A scattering of bits from that address is taken; their order is switched around; and they're mixed up with each other by exclusive-ORing (XORing) some of them together. The process is repeatable: Give it an address, and it will pick the same cache location. Nevertheless, no programer can make effective use of that algorithm to predict what's left in the cache, so it might as well be considered truly random. The exact algorithm used—which bits, switched how, XORed with what—is seldom if ever published and in any event changes from machine to machine, both between manufacturers and within a manufacturer's product line. Don't get the impression that you can pick any old address bits, do any old thing with them, and get a cache that works well. This is very deliberate, careful shred-

In Search of Clusters ✳

ding whose exact characteristics are established only after a nontrivial amount of work.

Another topic: What's been described above is what's called a direct-mapped cache. This is the simplest variety. There are also set-associative caches, which pick a group (set) of 2 (or 4, or...) items at (pseudo-) random as described above. Then within the chosen group, the least recently used one of just the 2 (or 4, ...) is picked and put back in memory. This is a bit more expensive than a direct-mapped cache; figuring out which is least recently used costs circuitry, although not much since it's done over just a few entries. However, it does work better in most circumstances than a direct-mapped cache. For example, going two-way set-associative more or less helps keep data from kicking instructions out of the cache. The general designers' rule of thumb is that a two-way set-associative cache needs half the size of a direct-mapped cache to achieve the same cache miss ratio [HP90]; since SRAM is expensive, this is an extremely good thing. Note that the choice for replacement is still mostly (pseudo-) random: There are thousands of sets, versus a small number (2, 4, ...) of things from which the hoariest is picked.

In addition to direct-mapped and set-associative caches, there are also, or at any rate used to be, fully associative caches. These really do figure out the least-recently used of all the data and chuck it out. The expense of figuring that out limits them to very small caches, appropriate in some circumstances but seldom used more generally. Translation lookaside buffers are usually small enough that fully associative techniques are useful and often, but not always, used there.

Yet another topic: The whole running theme that the memory contents can randomly be wrong is a description of a particular cache policy called "write back": The cache remembers that the data has changed and writes it back into memory when that part of the cache is needed for something else. (It never writes back stuff that hasn't changed; why bother?) There's another policy, "write through," that writes data into memory every time the processor writes into the cache. In effect, every **store** (write) goes "through" the cache to memory. A write-through policy is simpler and therefore cheaper, because you don't have to remember which cache lines are changed—you never have to "write back" anything when making room. This is good. It also keeps main memory correct. This is also good. But it requires more main memory cycles, often many more, which is unbelievably bad in the SMP context we are about to enter. SMPs using it—there are a few in PC-land—are so focused on cost that they don't care at all about performance. (An arguably valid design position, by the way.)

Finally, I've undoubtedly given the impression above that use of a cache always results in faster system performance. That is almost always true and will probably become even more generally true in the future, because processor speeds are increasing faster than DRAM memory speeds. But there are exceptions. If you're running a program with very little locality of reference (it may be incredibly pathological to everybody else, but hey, it's your program), the presence of a cache can slow you down. There's no need to take the time to check whether data's in the cache, for example, because it never is. And the cache will pull a whole cache line out of memory, taking additional time, when your program might use only the first byte out of (for example) 64 bytes; that can *really* hurt. If execution speed is an issue, however, the near-universal deployment of caches makes it wise to look at ways of rewriting that program to increase its locality of reference. You'll probably end up with a more complicated program, but it could end up running 10 or 20 times faster on nearly every computer made.

6.3   Memory Contention _____

We've almost reached the first main point of this chapter. Plug a second processor with all its caches into a memory, and *voilá!* we've got a multiple processor system, as shown in Figure 6-11. And boy, are we in trouble.

In the first place, even if you could just "plug in" another processor (the memory has to be built to allow that), the whole reason for caches is that a single processor is quite capable of completely overwhelming a memory all by itself, thank you. Remember that a processor's memory appetite is like 20 lbs. trying to fit into a 1 lb. bag, and that was an underestimate. One twentieth is 5%. If only 5% of the processor's memory accesses "miss" its cache, that memory is *used up*. It is running at full speed and can't produce any more data. Now you know why system designers get bent out of shape when cache hit ratios fall below 90%.

Actually, the situation isn't quite as bad as the above description makes it seem, in good part because processors and the programs running on them aren't so boring as to miss cache accesses on a uniform, regular schedule. They smack on the memory a lot, running slowly; then they run full tilt, hitting solidly in the cache with very few misses; then smack the memory some more, and so on. All in all, cache misses have a generally rather jagged behavior profile. (This is why fractals once suggested themselves as a modelling tool.) As a result, one can be smacking away at the memory while the others are buzzing along using cache or at least buzzing a bit between smacks.

Figure 6-11 A Naive Multiprocessor System with Caches

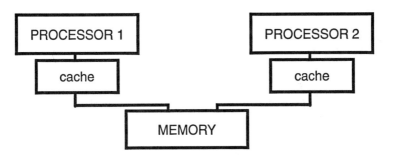

Nevertheless, the processors can't run as fast as they could when they were alone. On an irregular but statistically predictable basis, each processor will have to wait because another happens to be using the memory. In other words, the processors now must contend with each other to gain access to a single resource, the memory. That's why this is called "memory contention." It is always mentioned as the conventional canonical reason why SMPs don't scale. (That thinking ignores a great number of interesting things that can be done, as we'll see.)

This particular form of contention is often referred to as the **Von Neumann bottleneck.** It was Von Neumann's original design—and a good one, too— that separated the processor from the memory and put everything, data and instructions, in the "memory organ" of the computer. But if you naively add more processors, you quickly find that the system speed is limited not by the processors but by how fast the memory can produce data: the connection to memory is a bottleneck. As was hinted earlier, with modern (particularly superscalar) processors, it can be a bottleneck for a single processor, too.

6.3.1 Great Big Caches

Without caches, the SMP situation would be hopeless. Well, it would be hopeless with even one processor, so big deal. But with caches, there is the option of making them bigger and bigger until they contain essentially all the data and instructions most programs' locality requires. If the processors very seldom use memory, they aren't likely to run into much contention.

The term "most programs" is particularly application dependent in this case. There are nontrivial programs that just sit and grind on a fairly small amount of data for a rather long time: Start one of those programs on each processor, and all the processors can buzz along at full speed for quite a while, even with tiny caches.[7] Obviously this doesn't make any of those programs run faster—you get greater throughput rather than faster turnaround time—but at least they don't go slower than they would on a uniprocessor. The system *scales* in performance when running those programs.

Scientific and engineering programs are generally the most likely to have this property of running mostly out of cache. There's no standard term for it, so I'll call it "processor bound" here. (It's not the same as "compute bound," which can have cache misses galore, just no significant I/O.) Not all technical programs are processor bound. Seismic data processing for oil exploration, which literally uses truckloads of tapes[8] as input, is the standard counterexample. Some commercial applications fill this bill, too. For example, I was recently surprised to find that with sufficiently large caches (for example, 4 or more Mbytes per processor—obviously they're L2 caches) many systems that are used to keep track of hotel, car, and other reservations are processor bound, even running under commercial databases. That, however, is the exception rather than the rule for database applications.

Other programs are not processor bound either because they do more input and output operations (we'll get to I/O eventually), or they're parallel and talk among themselves a lot. Or, they may just refer to more data than fits into the processor's cache. That last type may still have decent locality of reference; they've just got a rather large locale. Examples of the latter include operating systems, database subsystems, and communication subsystems. Since such programs are rather widely used, rather large caches appear to be a good idea for SMPs.

This, by the way, is the first indication of why there's a larger cost *per processor* in larger SMPs. If a system is to support more processors, it needs bigger caches to help reduce memory contention. There's a limit, of course; it seldom helps to have much more than 8 Mbytes of cache per processor. But 8 Mbytes is much larger than systems need if they're not designed to scale up. As we've seen, the SRAM memory required makes large caches expensive.

---

7. I know of one program that ran for an entire year at multi-Gigaflop rates and produced as its entire output exactly one single-precision, floating-point number. It was a *very* interesting number. (To be fair, they did do checkpoints, too.)

8. A major oil company actually did the calculation and concluded that, for the distances they were interested in, the highest possible data bandwidth was achieved by 18-wheel semitrailers loaded with tapes. That's as opposed to jumbo jets full of tapes, or all possible electronic transport available to them at the time.

6.3.2   Line Size, Memory Banks, and Pipelining

There are ways to alleviate memory contention that are independent of caches. They rely on understanding a distinction that could be sloughed over up to now (including in our discussions of intermachine communication). The distinction is that between **latency** and **bandwidth**.

Latency is how long something takes. Bandwidth is how much of it you can do in a given time. They're related, but different. Imagine passing buckets of water from person to person in a bucket brigade from a well to a fire. How long it takes any specific bucket to pass down the line from the well to the fire is the latency. How many buckets of water per minute get dumped on the fire is the bandwidth.

The original single processor-memory speed problem is primarily, though certainly not entirely, a latency problem: The memory can't produce a result fast enough. If we've got a cache-memory combination that adequately fixes latency for a single processor, adding more processors is primarily a bandwidth problem. The data can make the trip fast enough; more of it just has to get there simultaneously. How can this be done?

One way to move more data is to increase the cache line size, the amount of data passed to the cache on a miss, and widen the data path over which the data travels—use more wires, so the pipe is wider. This works, but has other ramifications to be mentioned later. It also costs more, since it uses additional pins on the chips; and pins are often more precious than silicon area.

Another technique is to use or increase pipelining in the memory subsystem. Pipelining is exactly like the bucket brigade in the latency/bandwidth example. In this case, you divide each memory operation into successive stages and do each stage simultaneously. For example, one stage might receive requests from the cache, while the next actually runs the DRAMs to retrieve the data for the previous request, another checks for errors on the request before that, and yet another sends the checked data for an even earlier request back to the requesting processor. The only problem here is that the speed is limited by how fast the slow guy in the middle—the DRAMs—can do things. But it definitely helps and only costs a little more in control logic.

Yet another technique is in the category of "blindingly obvious." If you need more water than a well can deliver to a fire, set up another bucket brigade to another well. If you need more data, use more pipelining to more memories. All the processors have to be able to access all those "memories" equally, though, or you've broken the SMP programming model. So, arrange it that there's only one memory as far as the processors are concerned—one collection of addresses—but it's divided into independent units. These are called **banks**, each able to independently and simultaneously read and write data.

This doesn't make any individual memory any faster; the latency stays (about) the same. However, processor 1 can be reading or writing data from bank 1 while processor 2 is doing the same to bank 2. They're not contending with each other as much. That's true at least part of the time, anyway; the rest of the time they want to get at the same bank and so do contend.

Figure 6-12   A Multiprocessor with Interleaved Memory Banks

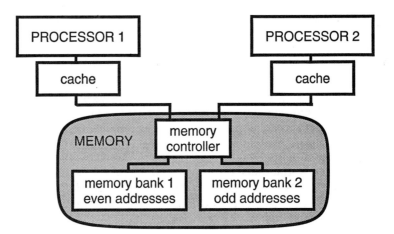

Figure 6-12 illustrates this. Requests come into a central memory controller from each processor and are directed to one or the other bank depending on the address. Figure 6-12 also shows the typical solution to a problem banks of memory bring about, namely: Which memory locations do you put in which bank of memory?

You could, for example, put the first N locations in bank one; the second N in bank 2; the third N in bank 3; and so on. That would work, but it starts to bend, if not break the programming model because getting the bandwidth required to scale now means explicitly programming the location of information in memory relative to the banks.

Instead, banks are typically interleaved: odd-numbered locations (really, cache lines) are put in one bank and even-numbered locations in the other. This can clearly be extended to four, eight, or even more banks. With interleaving, there is decent average behavior without explicit programming. It won't be perfect, but you can increase the effective bandwidth of memory quite a bit.

The memory controller shown in the figure is more important than it might appear at first glance. It has to be able to satisfy one processor's memory request while at the same time satisfying the other's, at least whenever they don't go to the same memory bank. See Figure 6-13. Proc1-Bank1 while Proc2-Bank2 should be possible, but so should the cross-connection: Proc1-Bank2 while Proc2-Bank1. The idea is to allow everything that's possible, but that doesn't mean everything is possible. The controller must delay cases where multiple processors want to get to the same memory, as also shown in Figure 6-13, while maintaining fairness—never "starving" any processor.

Figure 6-13   Data Flowing in a Crossbar Memory Controller

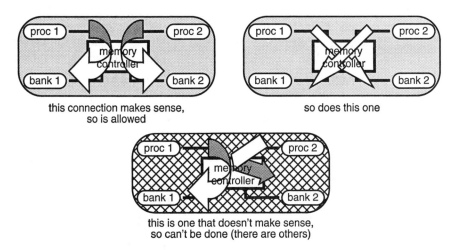

this connection makes sense,
so is allowed

so does this one

this is one that doesn't make sense,
so can't be done (there are others)

Keeping all the possible paths available at the same time and not allowing the forbidden ones means that this controller must walk, chew gum, pat its head, and rub its stomach all at the same time, or the system will not get the benefits possible from interleaving. This gets more complex the more processors and memory banks there are.

All possible nonconflicting permutations can be simultaneously allowed; it just takes more hardware. The primary data path hardware required, known as a **crossbar switch**, goes up in size as the square of the number of processors: Double the number of processors and memory banks; the switch doesn't just get two times as big, it gets four times as big. This rather quickly gets very expensive. As a matter of fact, going up in cost with the square of the size is the primary reason why crossbar switches are conventionally considered not scalable.

For reasons to be discussed in the next section, the kind of memory controller described above is seldom used in that form in SMP systems. It was presented here to allow considering it separately and more simply. We'll use the concepts later. Rather than having multiple points where processors attach, there is more usually a single input point, shared by the processors (and that sharing involves other complexities). The back end of the controller still talks to multiple banks with a (smaller) crossbar. Now, to get the higher bandwidth, you absolutely must use pipelining; that's the only way to get all the banks going at the same time.

6.4   Cache Coherence

Even without considering memory bandwidth, there's another problem. It's far more serious than the memory bandwidth problem, since that is "merely" a performance problem that "merely" inhibits scaling the system up in size. This problem is one of correctness. You can build computers or write programs that go really, really fast if they don't have to get the right answer.

Remember that space I told you to watch? We're there now.

Figure 6-14   The Cache Coherence Problem

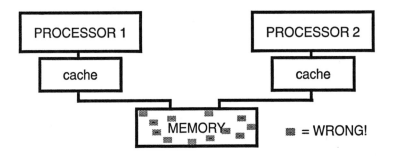

See Figure 6-14. Thanks to the messy desk effect, the memory has random wrong data in it. What happens when a program running in processor 1 **load**s data from a memory location that was last written by processor 2? The value in memory might be the correct value, meaning the one most recently **store**d, because, at random, it just recently was written back out of the cache. Then again, it might not. The system might run for hours or days, getting the right value each time. Then, at random, it gets the wrong value. Whatever the final outcome is, it won't be pleasant. Unrepeatable, randomly occurring errors. Everybody just hates when that happens.

This difficulty is referred to as the memory coherence or **cache coherence** problem: The system must somehow provide a coherent, uniform view of the memory to all processors, despite the presence of local, private cache storage. If it doesn't, it's not an SMP because it's not symmetric: It doesn't look like it has one memory. That means standard system software will not run on it, so you might as well not build it. (And you certainly shouldn't buy it if you are using it for conventional purposes.)

Cache coherence problems are not an odd occurrence that happens only infrequently. Even if they were, the threat of their occurrence would warrant taking care of them. But **load**ing something that another processor **store**d happens all the time, although hopefully it is not extremely frequent for reasons that will become clear later. It arises in several common circumstances.

1. **Process migration.** A running program (otherwise known as a *process*) is executing on processor Archie. For any of a number of possible reasons, it stops running there and is moved ("migrates") to processor Buela. All the data it happened to leave in Archie's cache has to be read Buela. With a big level 2 cache, this could be multiple megabytes.

   - Process migration could occur, for example, because the running program initiated an input or output operation. When that happens, the operating system stops running the program because it will be waiting for the device for some time. Later, when the I/O operation is over and the program is to resume execution, the place where it used to run (Archie) might be busy doing something else while Buela is twiddling her thumbs. Rather than wait for Archie, you'd like to use Buela to continue execution.

2. **Parallel communication.** If a program is actually written to run simultaneously on multiple processors at the same time, it is a parallel program. The parts of parallel programs running simultaneously must invariably communicate with one another. On an SMP, this is done when one processor reads data that another processor has written.

   - At least one such parallel program always exists on every SMP: the operating system. For example, when it begins running a user process on one processor, the operating system had better let every other processor know that process is being executed; it wouldn't do to run it twice. (It would probably end up charging you double.) Heavily used subsystems, such as databases, are also often written to run in parallel on symmetric multiprocessors.

3. **False sharing.** This one is reminiscent of a slapstick routine. Suppose two processors never have anything to do with one another. They never read or write the same memory locations. They can still get in trouble if they simultaneously work on *different* data that happen to be in the *same* cache line.

   See Figure 6-15. Two processors **load** the same cache line. One **store**s into one part, the other **store**s into another. One is **flush**ed to memory. When the other **flush**es, it wipes out the first one's **store**. This stepping on each others' toes is called **false sharing**. Obviously, the longer the cache line size, the more false sharing you'll have. This is why an earlier comment was made: long cache lines can be too much of a good thing.

So a multiprocessor system does not have to do things that are in any sense exotic to run into the cache coherence problem. It's there all the time. How do we get around it?

Figure 6-15   Coherence Error Due to False Sharing

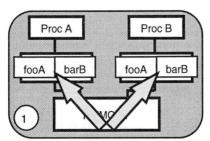

Both get the same cache line.
A needs only fooA, B needs only barB.

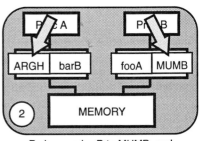

B changes barB to MUMB, and
A changes fooA to ARGH.
Neither touches the other's stuff.

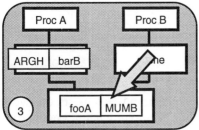

B's copy is written back to memory
(or A could go first; doesn't matter).

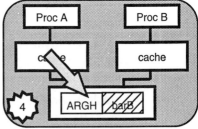

Then A's copy is written back,
clobbering B's data.

6.4.1 "Fixing" It in Software

It is possible to build a usable, cached, multiprocessor system with just a little bit of hardware and a sufficient quantity of software. Just add two instructions to the processor: The first immediately forces a cache line out of the cache and back into memory; this is known in the jargon as a **cache line flush**. The second just empties a cache line in the cache, without writing it to memory; this is a **cache line purge**.

Now the software can take care of itself. It just **flush**es things out when it's finished with them, in particular when a process migrates or information has to be passed to another processor. The **purge** is used in the opposite direction: If a processor is about to start using something that it might have touched before and not **flush**ed, there might be old data left around in its cache; **purge**s get rid of that data. Software also must be careful to avoid false sharing. This isn't hard for nonparallel application programs manipulated by the system; it's rather a bit more tricky for parallel programs like the system itself.

A good thing about this approach is that it allows you to use one of those crossbar memory controllers that was discussed earlier under "memory banks." This lets you have lots and lots of memory bandwidth, so considering only hardware and assuming a captive collection of tame programmers, it could scale well in a raw "break the Von Neumann bottleneck" sense. This is all some application areas need.

But there are a few problems.

> ➤ **The software must be inhumanly careful not to mess up.** Because of the random nature of cache contents, errors in cache management are of the nasty sort: unrepeatable and transient. They'll never be visible in the lab; instead they'll always happen in the field, during your best customer's peak busy period. In general, mere mortals should not be allowed to explicitly program cache management.

> ➤ **The approach is inefficient.** A process that is to be migrated, for example, may have accessed many megabytes of data. Some of that data might, at random, still be in even a small cache. Which is left around? The only thing to do is execute cache line **flush**es on all the megabytes to make sure none of the data is still there.[9] Alternatively, there could be an instruction that allows scanning the cache itself, rather than searching it for memory addresses. But caches can

9. Games can be played with the virtual memory system to reduce this inefficiency somewhat. See my forthcoming book, *Stupid Virtual Memory Tricks*.

themselves contain megabytes, so it's still a long scan. Another alternative: Don't migrate the processes, or at least do so only under extreme circumstances. This avoids the inefficiency mentioned above but runs into another. Because process migration is more painful, you now can't balance the computing load as evenly among the processors. As a result, the system won't scale as well. It would obviously be better to move only the data required, and then only when necessary, but the random nature of caches makes this impossible for software.

➤ **The approach breaks the SMP programming model** to smithereens. SMP programs expect to see one consistent memory, and requiring use of **flush** instructions makes the caches into visible private memories, one per processor. This is another one of those things that could be wallpapered over by a deeper level of system software,[10] but the system software will have the two problems mentioned immediately above, along with the cost of being different that has been discussed earlier. In this case the difference is rather major.

The next several sections will describe ways to maintain cache coherence automatically, in hardware alone, which is what the industry standard is.

6.4.2 Central Directory

With only one processor, memory could be incorrect without catastrophe because the processor always checked the cache first. That remains the basic answer to the cache coherence problem: Check the caches first. *All* the caches, on all the processors. If somebody else's cache has what you want, somehow get it from that cache, not from the memory. And better be quick about that checking, because you're adding an additional delay to the amount of time it takes to get data from memory.

There's an implication to the phrase "get it directly from that cache" that could be missed. In a uniprocessor, a cache is its own master. It services the processor, moves things to and from memory, and just keeps busy on its own. It never gets rid of something until it decides that it needs the space for something else. In an SMP, however, somebody else must be able to come in from outside and say "gimme!" On demand, lines from their mother cache must be untimely ripp'd. Each cache must serve at least two masters: its own processor, and the collective will of all the others. This is certainly not impossible to do, but: First, it's yet another element of expense; the hardware itself may not be that large, but whenever you serve multiple things

---

10. *Ibid.*

the interactions become complex, making design, simulation, and test harder. Second, you lose efficiency. Obviously, when the cache is serving the "others," it's not serving its own processor, which as a result has to wait and can't do useful work. This was the reason for the earlier comment that **load-ing** data another processor has **store**d hopefully would not be too frequent an occurrence. We'll touch on this issue again before the chapter's out.

So, we've got caches that can give back the data they hold, whenever some-body demands it. Next question: How do we know which cache to ask for data, or whether any cache has it at all?

There is a technique for doing this that's extremely fast. It's also quite expen-sive and gruesomely complex. That technique is to have a single central unit that maintains a centralized collection of tables—a **directory**—of whose cache has what data. Everybody's cache. Everybody's data. Lots of tables. Rather than ever directly going to memory when data is needed, you instead request the data from that central unit. It "knows" where everything is and so can get it from the appropriate place, be that the memory or any of the other caches.

A diagram of a system with such an all-seeing, -knowing, and probably -singing and -dancing central unit appears below as Figure 6-16, with a cou-ple of memory banks for a typical situation. At the level of detail of the dia-gram, it looks deceptively like the relatively simple, multiple-banked memory of Figure 6-12 on page 134, but there are two major differences from that situation.

Figure 6-16   A Central Directory Scheme

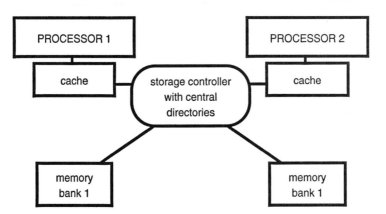

> First, additional data transfer paths are required, because data must be transferred between all the caches directly, as well as between caches and memory. This has more crossbar-ishness than the original (see Figure 6-13 on page 135). It will be even more expensive.

> Second, unlike the other crossbar, this one is smart. It doesn't just stuff data directly where directed, it looks up referenced addresses in internal tables and figures out where they are. It can know where everything is because everything flows through it: For example, whenever it delivers a line to processor A's cache, it notes in an internal directory that processor A in fact has that line. When it sucks that line out of A and gives it to B, it deletes the entry from its A table and puts it in its B table.

One thing making this method particularly interesting is that it has to do everything at once. All the processors could miss in their caches simultaneously. To avoid increasing memory delay, it has to be able to do all those lookups and transfers at the same time. Doing this requires another increase in cache complexity, too, since the cache has to be able to disgorge a line at the central unit's request while it is waiting, itself, for a line it has requested. This, by the way, just happened to come up at this point; all the other hardware coherence schemes also require it from their caches.

Another important optimization: Much of the information that processors get from memory never gets modified by the processors. Programs, for example, are never changed by the processor (not any more anyway, and except for special circumstances like compilers and loaders). So, it is quite correct and reasonable for more than one cache to have a copy of some information. If everybody has recently run the same program (like the operating system scheduler), then bits of that program and its data are probably in everybody's cache. But you never really know that it's just a program, and there is, in addition, nonprogram data that everybody looks at without changing. So, a processor can turn around and decide to write into a line that everybody has a copy of.

Interesting things must then happen. All the copies in all the other caches have to either get marked "invalid, wrong, not correct, don't use me any more" or they all have to be updated. Which of these two is best is the subject of endless simulation, and in some cases schemes have been proposed that adaptively change from one technique to the other [CF93]. But whichever is used, in the technique being discussed here the central unit coordinates it all, including yet another amusing case: Two processors might just happen to want to **store** into the same location at the same time. (**Load**ing and **store**ing simultaneously is just about as bad.) Somebody's got to go first—having a memory location with two different values is the no-no all this stuff attempts to solve—and it is the central unit that picks the winner and sequences everything.

The rather complicated central directory unit that's been described is known as the **storage control unit** of the big, bad mainframes of yesteryear. It, and not the processors, was undoubtedly the most complex element of those systems. Its size and complexity grows tremendously as the number of processors and memory banks increases. For a small number of processors, it can be so efficient it is frightening. It certainly does not scale. It is no longer used.

6.4.3 Snoopy Bus

Rather than have a central authority that knows everything, another alternative is to have every cache continuously tell every other cache what's going on. This solution, called **cache snooping**, is currently the overwhelming winner of the technical popularity contest for best solution to the cache coherence problem. It trades a central active unit for a central broadcast communication channel called a snoopy bus.

The snoopy bus is like a telephone conference call to which every cache and every memory unit is attached. Systems working this way necessarily have all the processors and all the memories on one bus, as shown in Figure 6-17.

Figure 6-17   SMP With a Snoopy Bus

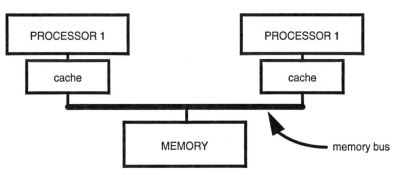

The way snooping works is illustrated in Figure 6-18. When a cache wants to read something from memory, it talks: grabs the bus and broadcasts a read request for that particular location. The memory, listening to the bus, hears this request and begins to respond. But all the other caches are listening, too; they're snoopy. They proceed to check their own caches to see if they've got the data being requested. If one of them does, it essentially pretends it's the

Figure 6-18   Snooping

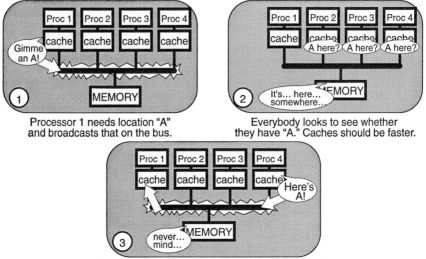

Processor 1 needs location "A"
and broadcasts that on the bus.

Everybody looks to see whether
they have "A." Caches should be faster.

Processor 4's cache had "A," so broadcasts it back
to 1. If no cache had it, the memory would have it.

memory: It grabs the bus itself, puts the requested data there, and in the process implicitly tells the memory to forget that request. The requestor sees that the data is there and gobbles it up. There's never a real race between the caches and the memory because the caches are so much faster. It doesn't matter if the contents of memory are wrong because you always get the most recent value direct from a cache. If this is all done correctly and things line up right, you can even get data faster than you would otherwise: you're getting it from (someone else's) fast cache rather than from the slow memory. It's not as fast as your own cache, because the snoopy bus is slower than the processor-cache connection, but it's faster than memory.

That's the basic idea. There are, however, a cornucopia of variations on this theme. They come in two classes: Fixing things up when the cache is not faster than memory; and reducing the number of times a cache has to broadcast something on the snoopy bus.

The first class seems odd given the discussion so far. How can the cache be slower than memory? It's not—when accessed from its associated processor. But when accessed via a secondary path from outside the processor, the cache can be slower, particularly compared to an aggressively pipelined memory system.

One way to fix this, which happens to be used in the Hewlett-Packard T500 [AR94], is illustrated in Figure 6-19. A request is made as usual. The mem-

Figure 6-19   Snooping with Slower Caches

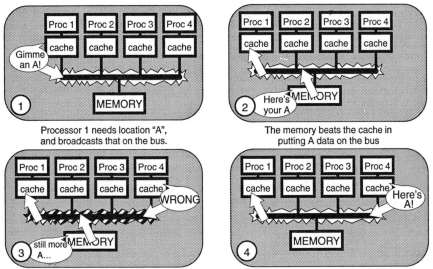

Processor 1 needs location "A", and broadcasts that on the bus.

The memory beats the cache in putting A data on the bus

Processor 4's cache had a new "A" value, so indicates that the data being sent is wrong.

After memory's done, Processor 1 discards the old data and Processor 4 sends the right stuff.

ory, however, always wins and puts its data on the snoopy bus. While that data's being transferred, one of the caches might come along and indicate, through some additional control lines on the bus, that the data being transferred is wrong. This doesn't stop the transmission from memory; that's a fixed operation. After that transmission is over the receiving processor discards the (wrong) data from memory and instead receives data from the other processor's cache, using another bus cycle. Other techniques for solving this problem exist, including updating the data in memory and then retrieving it from there, perhaps a second time. All have the common property that they result in lower performance when data must be obtained from another processor's cache. The reason is that more than the minimum number of bus cycles must be used. As will be discussed in a later section, this is not a desirable property when the target workload is a commercial database or transaction processing system (see "Commercial Processing: Cross-Interrogation and Shared Caches" on page 156).

The second class of refinements, those aimed at reducing the bus traffic, cover a wide range. For example, suppose a cache already has a line and the processor wishes to modify the data in it—do a **store**. In the general case, the processor would have to broadcast that write request on the bus. Other caches might have their own copies, which must be **purged** or rewritten with the new value. But if the writer knows it has the only copy of that line in any cache anywhere, it can just go ahead and write, quietly, without broadcasting anything. This is a valuable optimization because different processors often end up running programs that have nothing to do with each other—they're just separate programs and share no data. Under those circumstances the caches might never, or hardly ever, have to broadcast a request to write.

A cache can know it has the only copy by maintaining a small amount of information about each cache line, referred to as the line's **state**. Suppose, when a line is first **load**ed, it came from memory; that can be determined in a number of ways, including having the memory transfer the data on the bus with a marker indicating "from memory." Since it's from memory, it's the only copy in any cache—otherwise you'd have gotten it from some cache. The cache receiving that line from memory thus has exclusive use of the line and records that fact. But the owner keeps snooping the bus; if anybody else issues a read requesting that same line, it dutifully provides it (to speed things up) and changes the line's state to "shared." If the owner of a line wants to write data into the line, it first checks the state: Exclusive? Just do it, quickly and quietly. Shared? Grab the bus, broadcast that you're writing, and don't write until everybody says they've **purge**d it (or done something else to update everywhere).

The particular collection of snoopy bus messages and responses a machine uses to maintain coherence is called its cache protocol. There are lots of cache protocols, using varying amounts of state information per line. A popular one is called the MESI protocol (pronounced "messy"), after the four states of its cache lines: Modified, Exclusive (this is the only copy anywhere), Shared, and Invalid [PP84]. Others are named after machines or institutions: the Berkeley protocol [KEW+85] and the Firefly protocol [TS87] are two examples. Comparative surveys of cache protocols have concluded that the more complicated protocols, with the most states, produce the best performance [AB86]. This isn't terribly surprising. Chalk up another increase in complexity and cost the bigger you make an SMP.

Trading out a central controller for a snoopy bus to solve cache coherence is a good complexity trade-off, because the central unit, the bus, is passive, and the complexity that remains is focused in relatively simple units replicated in each cache controller.

The obvious weak point is the snoopy bus itself. Every processor's memory requests must traverse the bus, making it a classic Von Neumann bottleneck that inhibits scaling: Rather than being directly inhibited by memory speed, since memory can be readily built in multiple banks and pipelined—just attach multiple memory banks to the bus—the system is limited by the latency and bandwidth of the bus. If you keep the bus the same, you can increase the speed of the processors and caches forever and never go any faster.

The common response to this problem has been to haul out the electrical engineering textbooks, grease up the circuit simulators, and design some really heroic busses. Bandwidth is increased by making the busses wide: hundreds of wires are used (296 in one case [Gal93]). Width is limited only by "data skew": You have to wait until all the wires transfer their data, and the more wires there are, the more speed variation there is. Latency is decreased by making the bus physically short, so the signals take less time to traverse its length; even the speed of light matters, a lot. The Silicon Graphics Challenge [Gal93] and the HP T500 [ZR93], for example, halve the physical length of their buses by using a "midplane" rather than a conventional backplane: The bus lies on a central circuit board, and processor cards plug into both sides of it.

Such buses can achieve peak bandwidths at or well above a gigabyte a second, and should soon be delivered in production machines. They are currently used by Silicon Graphics, Hewlett-Packard, and Sun[CY93]. Even such very large speeds are only just good enough for the current crop of RISC processors, albeit with up to 36 processors [Gal93], or 20 processors [CY93]. How well these scale up in performance is at this writing still subject to some debate, since insufficient data has been published; you need more than one data point, all that's usually publicized, to draw a scaling curve. To see the difference processor performance makes, consider Sequent's 36-processor 50 MHz 486-based machine; it uses "only" a 280 Mbyte/second bus—less than a quarter the speed of the SGI Challenge's bus. What will happen when (not if) processors become considerably faster than they are now?

Another issue with any snoopy bus is that it is of necessity a shared bus. Recall that when a cache wants to read something it first grabs the bus. This "grabbing" alone takes some time. Somehow all the units on the bus must agree about who's going to talk now in the conference call. This bus arbitration, as it's called, can be made fairly fast. But its speed pales in comparison to not having to arbitrate at all—which is the case in uniprocessors and centralized systems. Up to 30% of the bandwidth of a bus can be lost by sharing, not just because of arbitration but also because of queueing delays that accrue because of sharing. (A switched system, since it has only point-to-point links, does not require this arbitration.)

Bus arbitration, bus and switch size, speed, and the packaging implied by those factors are thus a very significant way in which SMP systems increase in cost to support more or faster processors. A snoopy-bus-based SMP that is designed to support many fast processors must have a wide, aggressive, expensive memory connection—even if you only happen to plug one processor into it.

6.4.4   Snoopy Bus and Switch

One possible response to need to the make SMPs out of even faster processors appears in the IBM RISC System/6000 PowerPC-based SMPs, which are designed to work, not just with the current generation of processors, but also with the next two. This is forced upon IBM because of the very fast scheduled evolution of the processors: two generations, a factor of up to four performance, in a little over a year. Those systems use a combination of transfer methods: a snoopy bus, for cache coherence, and a crossbar switch to move the data. This organization is illustrated in Figure 6-20. Processors put memory requests on the bus where they are snooped as usual. In a pure snoopy bus system, the bus is also used to transfer the data from wherever it's found to the requestor. That transfer does not have to be broadcast and takes significantly longer than the request because there are more bits in a cache line than there are in an address. In this bus-and-switch arrangement, processors get off the bus after making the request and await the data through a separate path that does not have to be snooped—the switch.

Figure 6-20   A Bus-and-Crossbar Switch Combination

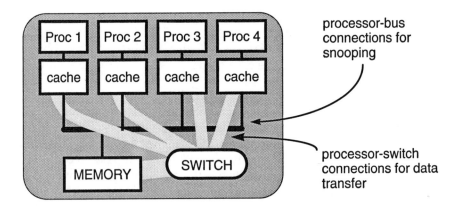

Since the bus is less occupied with each transfer and the switch can perform multiple transfers simultaneously, the result is larger aggregate bandwidth: up to 1.8 Gbytes/second, without using particularly heroic electrical engineering in either the bus or the switch. Furthermore, adding more processors increases the data transfer speed because more ports are used on the crossbar switch.

Figure 6-21 Operation of a Bus-and-Switch Combination

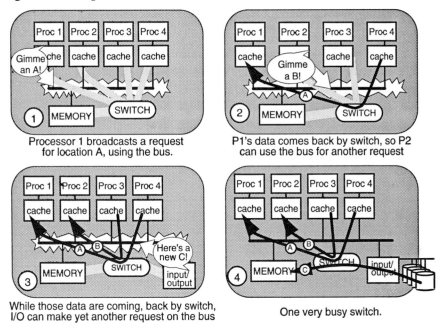

Processor 1 broadcasts a request for location A, using the bus.

P1's data comes back by switch, so P2 can use the bus for another request

While those data are coming, back by switch, I/O can make yet another request on the bus

One very busy switch.

The initiation of multiple transfers with such a system is an interesting operation. As shown in Figure 6-21 (part 1), a processor requests information as usual. While the data for that transfer is flowing back from another processor's cache on the switch, the bus is free, so another processor can make a request (shown in part 2 of Figure 6-21). Both of those transfers can be proceeding while yet another is requested, for example, from the I/O subsystem (part 3). So at its peak operation, (part 4), a six-port switch can be doing three transfers simultaneously.

There are several other things to notice here.

1. A switch like this is primarily good at transferring data between processors' caches. Notice that Figure 6-20 has only one path going to memory. If multiple processors go to the memory at the same time, processors still have to line up and wait. The switch port attached to the memory can be made more powerful than the others (it is, on the IBM systems: 800 Mbyte/second vs. 600 Mbytes/second.), but it's not going to be made so powerful it can handle all processors simultaneously. So, if there are many transfers to memory, everybody will serialize anyway. However, interprocessor data transfer is, for commercial workloads, extremely important

and often performance-determining; this will be discussed in more detail later.

2. Either the switch still doesn't keep up with processor speed, or the system is balanced in a radically different fashion from the ones already mentioned (not impossible; IBM should have learned something when building SMPs since 1974). Those 1.8 Gbytes/second are deemed only enough to satisfy 8, not 20 or 32, of the faster processors. (This is at least partly related to the point above; not all those 1.8 Gbytes/second can be used for memory traffic.)

3. It may be even more costly than a heroic bus. A less-potent snoopy bus may be cheaper, but the crossbar definitely adds significant cost.

4. Its bandwidth goes up when interprocessor traffic occurs; only then are the additional paths in the switch actually used. This is in contrast to the snoopy situation mentioned earlier, where effective bandwidth can actually decrease with interprocessor traffic, because more bus cycles are needed to transfer the incorrect, and then the correct data. (Again, this points to a different system balance point.)

Nevertheless, I would anticipate that other vendors will end up resorting to some form of switches, rather than pure buses, as processor speed increases. There's only so much pure buses can do, no matter how heroic the electrical engineering.

6.4.5   Distributed Directories

Snooping is the state of the art, meaning it is the everyday, standard solution to cache coherence that every competent SMP designer should have in his or her toolkit. At the leading edge are solutions that attempt to get beyond the shared bus bottleneck required by snooping. Two such techniques are currently being pursued. They are organizationally rather different, but both work by taking information about the location of cache lines—directory information—and distributing it more generally around the system.

The two systems are the Scalable Coherent Interconnect (SCI), which primarily targets massively parallel implementation, and DASH, which by the definition given at the start of the chapter is not an SMP. So why discuss them here? They indicate the kinds of complexity and the problems one runs into when attempting to circumvent the Von Neumann bottleneck inherent in SMPs.

Figure 6-22　Scalable Coherent Interconnect

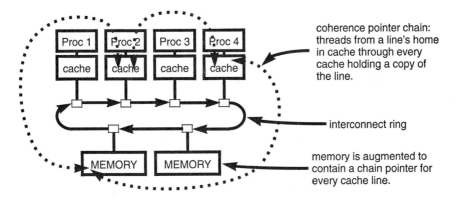

coherence pointer chain:
threads from a line's home
in cache through every
cache holding a copy of
the line.

interconnect ring

memory is augmented to
contain a chain pointer for
every cache line.

Scalable Coherent Interconnect (SCI)

The Scalable Coherent Interconnect [Gus92] is more closely associated with massive parallelism than with lowly parallelism. It replaces the snoopy bus with a ring (a circular bucket brigade), as shown in Figure 6-22. This has a number of good effects.

> Ring links are point-to-point, not arbitrated buses, so are easier to run faster. SCI links run a 1 Gbyte/second, and may go even faster in the future.

> Multiple ring links can be active simultaneously, so the total available bandwidth is higher than that of a single shared bus of the same speed. The ring is still a shared resource subject to contention, so processors do not each have 1 Gbyte/second available; but the bandwidth available per processor is nevertheless impressive.

> There is no limit to the number of processors and memories one can put on a ring, other than physical distance limits on each individual link. Since that limit is 10 meters, a very large system indeed can be constructed. Of course, if you put a large number of units on a single ring, the memory latency rises to impractical levels and processors become inefficient unless they run with quintessentially perfect cache locality.

> While the connection must look like a ring to SCI-conforming caches and memories, it doesn't actually have to be a simple ring. It could be a ring connecting to a switch of unrestricted topology, for example, or interwoven rings, or other topologies that have fewer stages between processor and memory than a single ring. This is the primary means of scaling to very large levels.

All of this is fine, but snoopy broadcasting is impossible and a central directory is impractical, so another solution to coherence had to be found.

The SCI solution is to use pointer chains (see the dotted arrows in Figure 6-22) to keep track of the whereabouts of cache lines. If a line is in a cache, the memory has a "pointer" to that cache that it keeps associated with the line. The pointer is a numeric identifier for the processor/cache unit. The chain continues if, as illustrated, the line's in more than one cache. The first cache associates with the line a pointer to the second, the second to the third, and so on, and the last back to the memory (which also has an identifier). The chain is actually bidirectional, meaning that each chain pointer is actually two, one to the next and one to the previous unit on the chain. This makes insertions and deletions easier: When a processor **flush**es a line from its cache, it (first!) uses the ring to notify both its neighbors to point to each other, thus snipping itself out of the chain. When a processor requests a line for reading, the memory links it into either the head or tail of the chain by (first!) notifying the head or tail unit to link the new one in, then sending the data back with information about who to point to. If the memory doesn't have an up-to-date copy, it tells the requester where to find one—the first cache on the chain. When a processor wants to write into a line others have in cache, messages must proceed around the chain that instruct each cache to **purge** its entry and snip itself out of the chain. All communication is, of course, done using the ring (don't confuse the ring with the chain!).

You know, this can get a little complicated. Imagine keeping things straight when two processors adjacent in the ring simultaneously decide to **purge** their copies of the line and snip themselves out. Similar issues are involved when two or more processors simultaneously request the same cache line. These cases certainly can be done correctly, but testing the implementations is guaranteed to be interesting. (Still, not quite as interesting as testing a central directory scheme.)

This can also take a long time. Boppin' 'round a ring alone takes longer than a simple bus broadcast, even though each individual bop may be faster than a bus transaction. In addition, many traversals are required: When a cache requests a line, it doesn't get it back straightaway. Instead, it gets an immediate acknowledgment that the request was received. This is done for reliability; it doesn't do to lose memory requests somewhere out there on multiple 10-meter links. Sometime later, after the memory DRAMs have done their thing and all the chaining is sorted out, the processor gets a message with the information requested; that message gets immediately acknowledged back to its origin, too.

The obviously worst comparison occurs when a cache must convert a widely-shared line from read-only to write. With a snoopy bus, the request is broadcast and every cache does its thing simultaneously. With SCI, it's a serial process: One cache after another must individually **purge** and detach from the ring. How bad this is depends heavily on the sharing characteristics of the programs running on the machine. If there's seldom any sharing, and then among few caches, the slow behavior of SCI in the worst case simply won't matter. There are too few implementations of SCI, and insufficient published data on the cache-line sharing characteristics of programs, to predict at this point how it will come out. However, at least one unrelated study indicates that on some applications, primarily scientific but including a sort, the degree of sharing is in practice so low that even software-implemented cache coherence is quite competitive with hardware [BMR91]. Some of the competing DASH system results are similarly positive, as mentioned in the next section. The authors of the study weren't looking at commercial workloads, as will be discussed later.

SCI is unique among cache coherence protocols in that it did not arise directly from published research or from product development. Instead, it was developed in committee as an IEEE standard. Standardization can potentially produce a valuable virtuous circle: multiple, compatible implementations compete, thus lowering the price, thus increasing use and raising the volume of sales, thus encouraging more companies to get into the market, increasing competition again, and so on. Formal IEEE *de jure* standardization between different companies at the memory bus level, however, seems a tad bizarre. For SCI to be a generally usable intercompany standard, many other much higher-level standards are required. Not only don't such standards exist, they're rather unlikely. Imagine competing operating systems—Sun's Solaris and Hewlett-Packard's HP/UX, for example; or, even more unlikely, IBM's OS/2 and Microsoft's Windows NT—married, coupled in the guts of their memories, **load**ing and **store**ing into each other's internal data structures, setting each other's locks, and generally mingling at the most intimate possible levels. The mind boggles. Software standards don't even exist that would support message passing by **load/store** through shared memory.

The explanation is that the SCI standard was driven by the high-energy physics community. This is not to say that large, serious computer vendors didn't consider this effort meaningful and participate quite actively. For example, Hewlett-Packard, Convex and lesser lights were active participants; many others including IBM lurked about the fringes with undisguised interest, and Convex has begun marketing a highly-parallel machine, the Exemplar, containing SCI technology (and not quite coincidentally using Hewlett-Packard PA-RISC processors).

But the reason for a formal standard rather than a public research project, the other obvious alternative, comes from high-energy physics. This community would dearly love to be able to buy processor and memory boards from the lowest bidders and sling them together into massively parallel machines that execute their application, under their chosen portable runtime system. They have both justification and inclination. High-energy physics, as a social entity, is very conversant with organizing people to move governmental institutions to their own ends; otherwise colliders would never get built. So, an institutional standards route naturally suggests itself. That's the inclination. The justification was described back in Chapter 2, in the Fermilab example: Warehouses full of data, unanalyzed; enough to make a grown man cry.

DASH

The second approach to getting past the snoopy bus bottleneck is being taken in a project at Stanford University called DASH: Directory Architecture for SHared memory [LLG+92].

Rather than taking individual processors as its building blocks, DASH uses whole, snooping, bus-based SMPs and connects them to form a larger system with an SMP requirement: a single uniform address space. The prototype couples Silicon Graphics POWER Station 4D/340 systems, with four processors each [BJS88]. Confusingly for this context, the DASH team calls these SMPs "clusters." In the discussion here I'll depart from DASH terminology and call them "nodes."

The nodes are connected as shown in Figure 6-23: Each snoopy bus has an attached directory unit that is connected to all the other directory units. The detail of the connection isn't relevant; anything able to carry messages could be used. The prototype happens to use a two-dimensional mesh. Each directory entry contains information about a cache line that is used outside a node. In particular, it contains a collection of "presence bits," one for each node in the complex; a bit is 1 if the line is present in the corresponding node. There is also a "modified" bit indicating that the value in memory is incorrect.

The directories are used to do a hierarchical search for cache lines. For example, suppose a processor issues a read request for data.

➤ If the cache line with the data is found in that processor's cache, you're done.

➤ If it's not, broadcast a normal request on the local snoopy bus. If that finds the line, you're done.

➤ If that doesn't work, go through the directory unit to the directory of the "home node" of the line, the place where it would be in memory; this location is determined by high-order address bits. If the

Figure 6-23 DASH

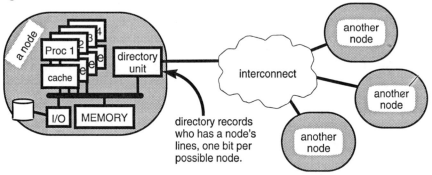

directory records
who has a node's
lines, one bit per
possible node.

home node directory says it's unmodified, a copy is shipped to the requestor and noted in the presence bits, and you're done.

➢ If the line was modified somewhere, the home node's directory requests it from the node that modified it through that remote node's directory unit. It's noted as being in two nodes, and the contents are returned to the requestor. Now you're guaranteed to be done.

If a processor attempts to modify a cache line, the process is similar. But if the quest reaches the home node, the directory unit uses its knowledge of where all the copies are—all the bits that are on in the line's entry—to reel them all in: It multicasts to the nodes holding copies a request to **purge** that line from their cache(s). Only when they've all finished that process does the home node directory grant the requestor write access and mark the line "modified."

In comparison to SCI, DASH deals with processors in nodal snoopy groups and can multicast, simultaneously sending requesting that everybody with a line copy get rid of it. That's obviously faster. But the process can still take a long time. In the prototype (which of course is just a prototype), a worst-case fill from a dirty (modified) remote node takes 132 processor clock cycles—compared with a best-case 8-cycle fill using the standard SMP snoopy bus within a node, or 1 cycle to access the first-level cache [LLJ+92, LLJ+93]. The time taken if many nodes must be **purge**d is not documented but must be substantially longer. And to think we were getting upset back at the start of this chapter because memory was only 20 times too slow; that factor of 20 corresponds to the 8 cycles mentioned above.

What that means is that DASH, while maintaining cache coherence, is not an SMP. This was mentioned previously, and it's actually pretty obvious; you may have noticed that it has multiple separate I/O units, one per node. But, in addition, the very large difference in memory performance between local and remote access means that programming must adapt to this regime or risk low efficiency. Experiments done on DASH support this conclusion. When there is little sharing of data or the sharing is local, individual parallel applications can achieve impressive results; applications with those characteristics achieve 30 to 47 times uniprocessor speed on a 48-processor system. Significant data sharing degrades performance to only a factor of 20, or even a factor of 7, on the same system.

6.4.6   Commercial Processing: Cross-Interrogation and Shared Caches

In the previous sections the discussions of latency and sharing may have left the impression that most uses of SMPs do not do very much actual sharing of data. Nothing could be further from the truth.

There is evidence, as was cited, that there is little interprocessor data sharing in at least some scientific and engineering problems that have been explicitly rewritten to run in parallel. But commercial processing—a much larger market—makes heavy use of database systems and transaction monitors. These, too, have been rewritten to run in parallel on SMPs. They share data. A lot. In fact, they slosh it back and forth between caches like madmen.

Why this occurs and what can be done about it (little, by system vendors) is treated in more detail later in "Commercial Programming Models" on page 259. For now, we'll just note that it happens a lot on commercial workloads. As caches get larger—1 or 2 Mbytes is usually adequate, and 8 is nearly always enough—entire programs and all local data structures are completely cached. This by no means caches all the data, which in databases can be gigabytes residing in main memory (there can be terabytes out on disk, of course). But while this irreducible memory traffic does not go away, it becomes a smaller overall factor. Intercache traffic can become the dominant use of a snoopy bus, exceeding cache-to-memory traffic and becoming the primary system performance limitation. This is a large enough problem in commercial systems to have its own name: the **cache cross-interrogation** problem.

As a result of heavy cross-interrogation traffic, the performance of SMPs on commercial workloads can actually be improved by doing something that, given the earlier discussions in this chapter, looks monumentally stupid: Have multiple processors *share* a single cache.

Using a shared cache, as illustrated in Figure 6-24, reduces the *apparent* bandwidth available to each processor, making the Von Neumann bottleneck worse: Access to everything—all programs and all data—is slower than if the cache were not shared, because the processors must now contend for access to a single cache. However, it may increase the *actual* bandwidth.

Data that's found in the shared cache is obtained more quickly than getting it from another processor; there's much more bandwidth between a cache and its processor—even when shared—than there is between units on the system bus. Data that's shared and found in a shared cache will therefore be obtained more quickly than if it had to be transferred on the bus. All you need is enough cross-interrogation to overcome the general loss of bandwidth that sharing produces for all other data accesses. There is very often enough shared data to overcome this loss—in commercial workloads.

Figure 6-24   Sharing Level 2 Caches

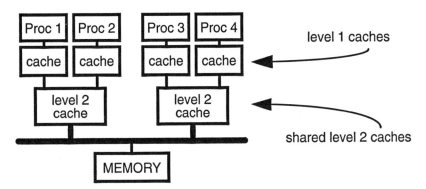

Whether shared caches make sense depends on the details of a system and the workload: the bus bandwidth, the time required for a cross-interrogation, the penalty incurred by the interrogatee, the amount of shared data, and so on. Whether it's the right solution for any given system is best established by detailed simulation of the system under the chosen workload. In general, it's easier to share caches at level 2 or higher; level 1 caches are simply too busy.

Sharing a level 2 cache, however, reintroduces coherence problems between the level 1 caches, since they no longer directly snoop the bus (or participate in other schemes). Since sharing is seldom among many processors and performance is an issue, a central directory scheme is often effectively embedded in the level 2 cache.

Shared caches might lead to less total expense because of smaller aggregate cache size: A shared cache holds the data of, for example, two processors, and therefore should be larger than a cache for a single processor to get the same hit ratio. But because programs and other data are shared, it need not be double the unshared size. The practical limitation of caches to power-of-two sizes can negate that advantage, however. The advantage can also be negated if the shared cache must be faster than an unshared one to avoid excessively degrading the base processor performance. In addition, the complexity of another coherence scheme within a level 2 shared cache will add to the development and design testing bill.

Systems incorporating shared caches can be SMPs. If the other requirements are satisfied (primarily universal access to I/O), the difference in memory access time between processors sharing a cache and processors in another sharing group is measurable, but small enough to be ignored. In point of fact, their whole purpose is to enhance the performance of programs that truly believe in the SMP model: All data is equally accessible, at any time, by any processor.

The technique of sharing a cache, brought about by the cross-interrogation problem on commercial database workloads, stands in sharp contrast to SCI and DASH. While those two techniques strongly differ in detail, they both make the same general trade-off: They have more memory bandwidth and so can support more processors, but the cost is increased latency—particularly latency in accessing global, actively shared data, that is, latency for cross-interrogation. This may be an entirely appropriate tradeoff for mathematical, scientific, and engineering workloads. The discussion in this section indicates that it is quite likely an inappropriate trade-off for database programs that are written to the SMP programming model.

A very different issue is whether DASH or SCI techniques can effectively support database programs written to other programming models. In other words, can they be the basis of good commercial clusters? Yes, they can, but then their entire *raison d'etre* vanishes: cache coherence is not desirable because it compromises another characteristic of clusters, availability. Both let you turn off cache coherence selectively, but why bother building something you want to leave turned off? This is discussed further in Chapter 11, which compares SMPs and clusters.

6.5   Sequential and Other Consistencies _____

Back in 1979, Leslie Lamport earned the envy of every scholarly person by publishing a two-page, straightforward paper with a catchy title that has been referenced countless times over the years since it was published. The title of the paper, actually published as a short note, is *How to Make a Multiprocessor Computer That Correctly Executes Multiprocess Programs* [Lam79]. It sounds eminently straightforward and is logically clear. But its implications are enough to make your hair curl, turn grey, and fall out. What that paper pointed out is that cache coherence is not the only correctness problem that SMPs face. There is also the issue that paper dubbed **sequential consistency.**

The consistency involved here has to do with the order in which **load**s and **store**s are performed. In a single processor, the issues appear simple enough. Consider the following, silly-looking code fragment:

```
y = 0;
x = 1;
y = 2;
if (y < x) then panic();
```

You would never expect **y** to be less than **x** in that **if** statement. That's because the **load**s of **x** and **y** in the **if** statement occur sequentially after the **store**s of **x** and **y** implied by the assignment statement. (A good compiler might not actually **store** either **x** or **y** in memory, keeping them in registers instead, but let's assume a stupid compiler for these examples.) This is uniprocessor ordering. Simply put, it means actions on memory take place in the order the program says they do.

But what about the order in which *another* processor sees them? Suppose, on one processor, the following even sillier fragment is executed:

```
x = 1;
x = 2;
x = 3;
/* etc., up to */
x = 99;
```

You would expect another processor to see these in the order they're programmed, too. So far, so good. Now consider that the other processor could be simultaneously executing a program that reads the values of **x**, so the following is going on:

Everybody starts with x = 1.

/* In Processor Able */	/* In Processor Baker */
x = 1;	y[0] = x;
x = 2;	y[1] = x;
x = 3;	y[2] = x;
/* etc., up to */	/* etc., up to */
x = 99;	y[99] = x;

The **store**s of **x** should occur in the order given. The **load**s of **y[]** should occur in the order given. But in what order should they occur *relative to each other*? They clearly can't be relied on to execute in lock step; a cache miss might occur in one and not the other, or a stray alpha particle could cause a short pause for memory error correction in one and not the other. Baker might, for example, execute **y[2] = x** before or after Able gets around to storing a 2 there. Will **y[2]** end up containing 0, 1, 2, or 99? Can't say. Could be any. Can anything useful be said about what's **store**d in array **y**?

Yes, but only if the multiprocessor involved obeys some rule about the order in which memory actions occur between processors. *This does not happen automatically.* Just because cache coherence has been maintained does not necessarily mean that processors will see the events in other processors in any useful order.

Lamport's sequential consistency is one useful rule, which actually turns out to be the strictest feasible one. To see what that rule is, imagine that the statements above have been written on ordinary playing cards, one to a card. Make two stacks of those cards: One with the **store**s of **x**, the other with the **load**s of **y[]**, each stack in the order shown in the code fragments above. Now shuffle the stacks together into one stack. Any shuffle at all creates a single stack that is a legal ordering of one processor's actions relative to the other's. You can interleave them, one from one stack and another from the other; you can put a bunch of one first, then interleave, then end with a bunch of the other; you can bunch, interleave, bunch, interleave, whatever. You can even put all of one on top of all the other. But—and this is the sticking point—you can *never, never, ever* alter the order of the cards relative to one another *within* either stack.

Processor and SMP designers just hate that rule. Why that's so we'll get to in a bit. First, what does it allow us to say about the contents of that array **y**? It lets us be sure that Baker never sees **x** values in decreasing order. Because the **x** stack can't be reordered, any change to **x** must be seen by Baker as an increase. The increase might stop for a while, or might never get started, or might be completely over before Baker even starts, but for sure **x** will never get smaller. So we can say something, anyway: $y[i] \leq y[i+1]$ within the array bounds.

Now, as it happens, a multiprocessor would have to be rather pathological for successive **store**s into exactly the same variable to get out of order. The problem is much more often encountered when multiple variables are involved. Consider the following, which is the standard example originally used by Lamport. It's far more typical of the convoluted logic typically found in this sort of thing:

Everybody starts with x = y = 0.

/* in Processor Able */	/* in Processor Baker */
x = 1;	y = 1;
if (y==0) print ("Able wins!");	if (x==0) print ("Baker wins!");

In Search of Clusters ✳

If sequential consistency is operational, only one processor will ever think it has won. It might happen that neither wins: they could both assign 1 before either test is done, causing both tests to fail. You surely can't tell which will win. But if there is a winner, it will be alone. Here's the logic behind that.

Assume that Able won. That means:

1. Able must have found **y** to be 0.

Since that's the case, two other things must be true.

2. Able must already have done **x = 1**, since that happens before testing **y**; and

3. Baker cannot already have done **y = 1**, since **y** is 0—it was just checked.

Since point 3 is true, we can conclude a third thing.

4. Baker cannot already have tested **x**, since that test comes after **y = 1**.

Now combine facts 2 and 4: **x** is already 1, and Baker hasn't yet looked at it. That means:

5. Baker must sooner or later find that **x** is not 0, and lose.

When we assumed that Able won, we were forced to conclude that Baker lost. Just turn it around to conclude that Baker winning means Able lost. So only one, at most, can possibly win. *Q.E.D.* and *voilà!*

Operations akin to the above, but even (gak!) more complex, keep multiprocess programs from making a mudpie out of shared data because they provide what's called **mutual exclusion**—they restrict access to one processor at a time. The "more complex" part comes from ensuring that somebody always wins, and nobody keeps losing forever, neither of which desirable characteristics is true above. The use of these operations for mutual exclusion makes them crucially important for the correct operation of SMP software. Numerous ways of doing mutual exclusion have been devised and published over the years, the first (or the first best known) by Dijkstra [Dij65]; an entire book of techniques has been published [Ray86].

But suppose that, somehow, sequential consistency is violated. In particular, suppose Able's **load** of **y** manages to complete before the Baker sees the **store** of **x**. The logic falls apart because fact 2 isn't necessarily true—from Baker's point of view. (It may still be true from Able's point of view.) Since it's not true, Baker could still look at **x** before seeing the **store**, find it 0, and declare victory too. One could readily conclude from this that letting **load**s get ahead of **store**s, or any other alteration of order, is definitely a Bad Thing.

But that's exactly what processor designers want to do, and for good reason: performance. Is there ever any other reason for anything in hardware? Oh, yes, cost.[11] Anyway, here's why processor designers hate these rules.

When a processor is told to do a **load** instruction, it will often have to completely come to a stop and wait for a while. This is true for even the most ambitious uses of covert parallelism to simultaneously do multiple instructions inside a single processor, because the **load** wouldn't have been requested were there no intention of using the data. Some later instruction is going to test that data, or add it to another, or something. That later instruction simply must wait until the data has arrived; you can't add what you haven't got. This is called in the jargon an **inter-instruction dependency**: the later use depends on the **load** having completed. Result: You would really like to get **load**s done as fast as possible. They hold you up.

A **store**, on the other hand, has no instructions depending on it at all (except later **load**s of the same data; we will get back to that). As a result, it doesn't matter when a **store** "really" happens. Could be immediately, could be sometime next year. We don't much care, because the processor will never have to wait for it to finish.

So to go as fast as possible, meaning to stop as seldom as possible, **load**s should get a higher priority than **store**s. High-performance processor designs do this. They let **store**s hang around in a **pending store buffer** while **load**s are done, even **load**s that appear after the **store** in the program. The notion is that at some future point, the program will probably be busy doing something that doesn't need memory access at all; the **store**s can be slipped in then, where they won't slow anything down. But do the **load**s right away.

This scheme works well, and it's not the end of this type of optimization. It's typically combined with other techniques that similarly allow entire instructions to execute out of order as long as a program can't tell the difference. Johnson [Joh91] estimates that such techniques can speed up program execution by as much 50%. That's definitely worth the bother; whole careers can be based on performance differences as low as 15%.

Of course, successfully pulling this off requires checking the pending **store** buffer whenever the processor does a **load**. You might be re-**load**ing something that's still hanging out, so you must get the correct data from the buffer and not from the cache or from memory.

Iiit's baaaaaaaack!

---

11. And a couple of other minor things like manufacturability, reliability, availability of applications, and so on. That was a joke, folks.

Remember that space I kept telling you to watch during the discussion of caches? We're there again.

A processor checks its own pending store buffer before going to cache, so it never sees the wrong thing. This time, however, the cache itself can be randomly wrong. All the cache coherence on earth can't help, because the cache never gets into the act.

This may seem a bit unfair and inaccurate, because store buffers and their ilk aren't the only places in a multiprocessor system where **loads** and **stores** can get out of order. A **store** could be aimed at one memory bank, and a **load**, another. If one bank happens to be busy, say, because it's responding to I/O, the actual access to the data can be out of instruction order. Systems with multiple stages of communication between the processor and memory, such as SCI allows, might wind up with a **load** and a **store**, or two **stores**, taking very different paths to different memories; so they may finally happen in who knows what order.

However, all such memory and communication-related reordering can be eliminated by a straightforward expedient: Just make sure the cache never shoves out a memory request before the previous one is finished. In systems with very long memory latencies, typified by SCI and DASH, this can result in a significant performance penalty. In a snoopy bus system it will have a much smaller effect, however, since the use of a single bus serializes lots of things anyway. (Unfortunately, I know of no published data that quantifies this issue. It must be out there somewhere. Sorry.)

In contrast, reordering inside the processor cannot be so easily fixed. All that's required is a processor aggressive enough to attempt some modest reordering and your goose has been cooked. That's any current high-performance processor design right down to the most recent PCs. So, in terms of most current SMP systems, sequential consistency truly is in the same space as cache coherence.

The consistency problem isn't quantitatively as bad as cache coherence, because the amount of data involved is much smaller. Pending store buffers are typically only a few entries long, as opposed to the kilo- or megabyte sizes of caches; the in-transit storage between cache and memory isn't large either, so relatively few memory operations are available for reordering. But qualitatively, it's just as bad. Get some of the crucial operations that enforce mutual exclusion out of order—the others don't matter—and interesting programs like operating systems and databases, which commonly run simultaneously on multiple processors, get into each other's shorts. *Whomp!* Down goes the system. Transient, random errors again. Everybody *still* hates when that happens.

What's to be done? The key lies in two points: First, sequential consistency isn't the only rule that lets you say something meaningful about cross-processor memory interactions. Second, the only place this really matters is when mutual exclusion is involved. Let's talk about the second one first.

Most programmers of parallel programs do not spend their lives spreading logic like that described above throughout their programs. They'd go insane, but, more to the point, the programs wouldn't stand an ice cube in hell's chance of working. Instead, they write—or, better, select someone who's both extraordinarily smart and extraordinarily careful (not the most common combination) to write—a small number of primitive operations that can be very strongly relied on to do the right thing.

For example, on an object-oriented basis the smart, careful one might create a "lock" object to be used by all. Send one of them a "lock me!" message, and you are guaranteed to wait until it is absolutely, positively certain that the running program is the *only* one coming out the other side, even and especially if two processors say "lock me!" at precisely the same time. What happens during the wait we will discuss later. Send a lock an "unlock!" message, and someone else is allowed through, but only one other; if multiple programs have said "lock me!" and are all waiting to get in, one and only one makes it. (Which one, we also get to later.)

Now suppose there's a shared object with a hunk of shared data to be updated. Embed a lock in it. Never touch it without a "lock me!" and always "unlock!" as soon as you're done. This alone is complicated enough to keep track of. Instead, it should, if feasible without unacceptable overhead, be embedded in the object protocols of accessing the shared object itself. That way, it's impossible to update the object without passing through the object's lock.

Much of the complexity involved here has little to do with sequential or any other consistency. How do you wait? Continuously re**load** and retest a word of memory in a tiny **spin loop** until somebody else sets it to 0? Sounds wasteful; the processor could be doing some useful work instead. How about going over to the operating system's scheduler and put the process on a queue, waiting, so the processor can do something else in the meantime? This has lots of overhead and takes a long time; the lock holder might unlock really soon now. Besides, suppose the lock-er is an application program; must every lock involve a system call to allow possible rescheduling? Let's try again, combining those two attempts: Gradually move from a tight spin to increasingly lengthy intervals between checks (for example, **exponential backoff**), eventually resorting to re-scheduling. Maybe. Sounds complicated, and this stuff has to be verifiably correct. Where's that careful genius? Also, you have to come out the other end of a wait with some amount of guaranteed fairness; it wouldn't do to have a process wait forever just because others kept butting in front of it. Simple spin locking doesn't deal with that issue adequately except in special circumstances.

The whole point is: This stuff isn't trivial.

With such complexity involved, encapsulation is a must. Any programmer who persists in spreading mutual exclusion logic throughout a program, rather than encapsulating it rigorously, is either certifiably insane, woefully ignorant, or never writes a program more than 20 lines long. In any event he should search for an occupation more suited to his capabilities (or she, hers).

Where I'm going with this is the following: In a sane world (heck of a qualification...) sequential consistency need not be enforced at all times. You just have to guarantee that it's true at certain crucial, encapsulated places in the code. So, at those places, and only at those, apply instructions whose purpose is curb all the covert parallelism going on—to fully serialize the machine. Those instructions wait until all outstanding memory operations are complete: Pending store buffers are empty, caches are updated, memory has acknowledged that all **store**s are complete. The program will be using special operations in those spots anyway, ones that are more convenient for constructing locks than basic **load**s and **store**s. Those instructions can have this "serializing" characteristic built in, or it can be a separate operation. This is the thesis of other ordering guarantees, such as weak ordering [AH90]; another, release consistency [GLL+90] is similar but allows greater overlap when accessing multiple locked blocks of data in sequence. Either is a relatively simple and efficient solution to the problem of sequential consistency.

You may have noticed that the solution proposed here is quite a bit different from that in the seemingly similar discussion concerning cache consistency. There, I railed against hardware-assisted software implementations. Here, I'm all for very similar solutions. But it's in the same space and can cause the same kinds of ugly problems. What's the difference?

The difference is in locality. After a lock is acquired, all access to the shared data is a cache coherence issue. It spreads throughout the code, not just in the locking itself. It can involve uncontrollably large quantities of data, whose movement through a machine is better handled by brute hardware, because the software can't know precisely where it all is (the messy-desk factor). In contrast, Locking and mutual exclusion involve a few key storage locations. Furthermore, simple access to shared data does not intrinsically involve complex, easily goofed-up logic chopping—once you've established an appropriate locking regime, anyway. Locking and mutual exclusion are logically complicated operations that had better be encapsulated or it won't matter if the machine is sequentially consistent; nothing will work anyway.

Unfortunately, in the not too distant past we were all woefully ignorant. "Heritage" operating and database systems are riddled with programs that assume a simple **store** can reset a lock. Even purveyors of reasonably modern systems, designed for the open systems market, can get a bit nervous over whether all of their hundreds of programmers were as religiously correct as they should have been about using standard locking primitives at every point where they might be needed. As a result, this issue remains at least somewhat open. Some newer SMPs are sequentially consistent or follow one of the similar sibling protocols. Others have taken the plunge to weak consistency.

One final note on this subject. If everything is under tight control, for example, with a big, bad central directory, corners can be cut and additional nontrivial performance enhancements are possible. The reason is that systems don't actually have to *be* sequentially consistent. They just have to *appear* sequentially consistent to *every possible* program. Like covert parallelism within a processor, this is committing the perfect crime: You can get away with murder if no program, or programmer, can detect that fact. And if you immediately see how to exploit this across a whole system, not just within a single processor, you were born in the wrong century. Grab a yarmulke and a time machine and make for the 12th century; you stand a good chance of becoming a definitive Talmudic scholar. This stuff gives me a splitting headache. Such distinctions were actually exploited in mainframe storage control units, where they distinguished between sequential consistency and **observable order**. Such techniques are the kind of thing required to make "heritage" programs run really fast. There is at least one whole textbook devoted to issues like this, and it is far from trivial [Col92]. There had to be some reason those mainframes used to cost a lot, didn't there? Just imagine trying to test such stuff ([Col92] tells you how). And pass the aspirin.

6.6   Input/Output

Input and output. The Rodney Dangerfield of computing. Everybody agrees that it's incredibly important, and it always gets stuck at the back of the chapter. Or the end of the design. There was one very large system project that had a virtually completed architecture and much of the "critical" hardware and software designed, before anybody bothered to tack any I/O at all onto it. This from within IBM, home of massive I/O. The project wound up a terrific success, by the way. I/O really does deserve more attention than it usually gets, but that age-old discrimination isn't really going to be rectified here.

The reason it's not is that there's actually not much to say about I/O that is unique to large-scale SMPs, other than: There has to be a lot of it, and it, too, must participate in cache coherence and consistency protocols.

There has to be a lot of it just because large SMPs are (intended to be) (or at least advertized as) powerful data processing facilities, and too little I/O means that the system can be limited by that rather than by computational capacity. "A lot" means many, because disks, tapes, communications adapters, and the like are fairly slow compared with the system speed. "Many" means enough space to plug it all in must be provided, and that requirement aggravates the need for even larger cabinetry. The many "slots" for I/O adapters that are needed necessitate large, long I/O connection buses which require that much more electronics to drive them. All of this really falls into the category of the (nearly) blindingly obvious. It's necessary, and therefore interesting, but not particularly intriguing except for the usual battles over how much of a machine's cost budget it gets to use.

I/O must also participate in cache coherence protocols, just like any processor attached to the memory. This might appear obvious on the surface. After all, reasonably intelligent I/O devices move data out of memory on their own; if they're not careful, they can pick up wrong values, too, just like a processor, only this time they'll make a nice permanent record of their error on permanent storage. They have to rip it out of processors' caches like any other processor. In the other direction, when the I/O system does its input, it had better act like any other processor doing writes; otherwise it is the processor cache contents that will be wrong.

There is a bit below the surface here, however. Doesn't this reasoning make a cached uniprocessor with its I/O subsystem effectively a two-way SMP? So, even uniprocessors have to do all that cache coherence and sequential consistency gorp? Not necessarily, but it doesn't hurt.

In a uniprocessor it's feasible, just not very pretty, to maintain the required I/O-memory coherence by explicit programming. This uses the cache **flush** and **purge** operations mentioned in "'Fixing' It in Software" on page 139. The reason it's feasible is the same reason it was feasible to "fix" sequential consistency with software: The complexity involved can be localized.

This time the locale is the operating system's device drivers or some generic "wrapper" programming surrounding all of them. Before initiating a transfer of data out of the memory, the device driver **flush**es it all from cache into memory; now memory is correct, so off we go. Transferring data into the system is the contrapositive: Potentially incorrect old data must be **purged** from the cache before any program is allowed to touch what was put into memory by an input device.

As with any form of software-mediated cache coherence, this operation had better be done very carefully (transient errors again), and it's less than optimally efficient. In addition, it makes device drivers more expensive to develop. But it can be argued that it's not grossly inefficient: You can do a whole lot of cache **purge**s while you're waiting for periods like 20–30 whole milliseconds for a disk's rotational latency. At least it's arguable until you find yourself doing a whole lot of I/O and discover this overhead is eating your processor alive.

Importantly, software-based coherence for I/O does not break the SMP programming model. Well, after all this is a uniprocessor, so that's a little hard to do. But portable system software is usually prepared to accept all kinds of weirdness, including things like this, from an I/O subsystem. Such oddities are expected to be encapsulated in the device drivers, which have to be rewritten for every new machine anyway; and so it is encapsulated. Therefore software-mediated I/O coherence is feasible and has been done.

Why not do the same on a large SMP? Well, such systems are often targeted at commercial workloads, so the threat of eating the processors alive with cache **flush**ing and **purge**ing is even stronger. But there's another reason.

Just which cache did you say the data is in?

If the system is a uniprocessor, you know the answer. It's in the cache. The only cache. But if cache coherence between processors is handled in hardware—and that's been argued for strongly enough already—the correct values to be transferred to a device could be scattered throughout all the caches. You just don't know where it is. It's not part of the SMP programming model to know this; data in memory are just in memory, the only memory, period, so the system probably being run has no idea. **Purge**s and **flush**es of all the processor caches in the whole system is just too much backbreaking overhead to consider.

So, in an SMP, I/O subsystems must participate in the cache coherence protocols used.

Oh, yes, and the entire discussion above was concerned with good old-fashioned slow I/O, like single disks, tapes, traditional communications adapters and the like. It did not discuss the new, really fast communication or really fast multidisk RAID subsystems. How that gets attached in is, as far as I'm concerned, a very interesting question. But it had better participate in cache coherence at least as well as a processor.

6.7 Summary

This chapter has been devoted to displaying both the problems that must be solved in building SMPs and the collection of tools available for solving them. The tool set presented here must be considered intrinsically incomplete; there are too many smart people feverishly working on this topic for any published record to be more than a belated snapshot.

The discussion did not encounter any adamantine "brick wall" prohibiting the enlargement of SMP systems beyond some set number of processors. It also showed how the tool set available to an SMP designer today is large, ingenious, and altogether admirable. But unless some genius works a miracle, it does not solve the problem that more and bigger versions of all the support gadgetry—caches, buses, switches, bus-driving transistors, protocols, and so on—are needed as the number of processors increases if the industry standard SMP programming model, the repository of multiple millions of lines of code, is to be maintained. "More and bigger" always means more expensive.

The implications of this will be discussed in Chapter 11, where SMPs and clusters are compared. But the background for a meaningful comparison is not yet completed. We must press on, entering a whole other dimension: Software.

Part 3:

Software

7

Workloads

All right, that's the hardware. So what? Hardware alone does nothing for anybody.

How can it be used? What do you have to do to use it? What good is it?

The next several chapters will address those and related issues, under the general and somewhat misleading rubric of "software"—misleading because the real topic is how that software can, must, or need not be aware of the hardware's characteristics. (*Systems* again.)

It seems appropriate to begin by discussing the goal of all this effort, namely, the kinds of work we can reasonably expect to perform on lowly parallel systems. That's the subject of this chapter. Subsequent chapters take up the issue of how that work is accomplished: parallel programming issues, programming models, and the avoidance of parallel programming. Finally, what is possibly the most significant issue for clusters will be discussed: single system image.

7.1   Why Discuss Workloads? _____

Installing a parallel system of any kind, or "scaling up" an existing parallel system with more processors or nodes, is not like installing the next-generation uniprocessor system. When you put in the new uniprocessor system, just about everything simply goes faster (an approximation, but good enough in most cases). Parallelism is nowhere near as uniform in its effects. Not all work will speed up, different types of work may speed up in different ways, and—depending on what exactly you did in adding parallelism—some things might actually slow down.

The reasons for this perverse behavior lie in how different types of work can exploit parallel hardware or, to put it the other way around, how well the hardware can work on different types of workloads.

So, it is worthwhile to understand the characteristics of those workloads and what kinds of workloads are reasonably targeted by clusters and SMPs. As indicated above, this is where that's done. The entire discussion is summarized in Table 7-1, which will be explained in subsequent sections. While the table and discussion appear fairly universal, they are both limited to the workloads typical of server systems. A similar categorization of client workloads, tasks for individuals' personal computers, would probably turn out to be different.

Of necessity, this discussion is in terms of "pure types" of workload. Of course, there is no such thing. Nearly all real systems must deal with a mixture of these types.

7.2   Serial: Throughput _____

There is no such thing as running only serial programs on a parallel computer system of any stripe. If you attempt to do so, the beast will at best just sit there and hopefully not destroy itself.

Some people are shocked to hear this. Those who are then react as if they've been tricked when it's explained that at a bare minimum, the operating system must be rewritten to run in parallel. "Oh. I thought you meant *application* programs." There is more than one kind of program in the world, and the degree to which the operating system is effectively parallelized will have a very strong effect on how well any type of program runs under its auspices.

Many if not most clusters, however, don't run an operating system that is parallelized across their nodes. Instead, they run multiple copies of operat-

Table 7-1 Workload Characteristics

Type	Purpose	Classes		Examples and Comments
SERIAL	throughput	no software application changes required	batch	Load Balancer, NQS/Exec, etc.
			interactive	NCLOGIN, etc.
			multijob parallel	boulder-size granularity; would be separate jobs on a uniprocessor
PARALLEL	turnaround time or response time	large software application effort is justified	Grand Challenge	no serial hardware will do it, so there is no choice
			research	parallelism is the wave of the future, and graduate students are inexpensive, intelligent, and motivated.
			heavy use: dedicated and/or widely reused	software cost justified by heavy use of a single important application or subsystem that will run often and/or long. some potentially significant commercial use of clusters examples: seismic migration, data mining
		little software application effort: mainstream parallelism	commercial	automatic exploitation of parallelism via SPPS techniques manually parallelized subsystems: OLTP, DB (SQL)
			technical	parallelized libraries special SPPS frameworks (HEP) automatic parallelization; requires language, programming change for good exploitation of parallelism (High Performance FORTRAN?)

ing systems, one on each node, and glue the assemblage together at a different, higher layer such as a cluster-parallelized batch system.

Given a parallelized operating system and/or batch submission system, serial application programs can of course be run on a parallel system. Many can be run simultaneously, each utilizing just one of the several processing units: one SMP processor or one cluster node. In this case they individually will not go faster than on a serial machine with the same processing facilities. So the appropriate measure of performance is throughput, the aggregate amount of work performed per time period.

This is an example of the SPPS (Serial Program, Parallel (Sub-) System) paradigm first introduced in Chapter 2. An important characteristic of this class is that there are no software changes whatsoever required for any application. Compared with the other general class, in which applications must be explicitly written in parallel, this is an enormous advantage.

Three types of serial workloads can be distinguished: batch, interactive, and what is here referred to as multijob parallel. They are discussed below.

This category is such a straightforward, immediate application of lowly parallelism that it might be asked why it's discussed at all. Its very straightforwardness is precisely the point: There is no magic; there is no heavy-duty high technology involved; it is perfectly plain and simple. And also extremely useful.

7.2.1   Batch

For batch processing, there are subsystems available today to handle batch submission of jobs to a cluster of machines. A sizeable list of them was given in Chapter 2.

It is clear that virtually any type of cluster or SMP is a natural for this workload. There are two issues to keep in mind, however: Does the system provide adequate I/O to match the job mix? Is the job mix perverse enough to run afoul of load balancing issues? Otherwise, this one is a natural.

As discussed in Chapter 5, the I/O issue is often a limiting factor for assembled and preassembled clusters, since distributed client/server, not cluster, file systems are all that are readily available. For technical workloads this is not a problem, but commercial batch workloads will often be hamstrung if they are limited to aggregate I/O equal only to the throughput of the LAN connecting to a file server. Cluster system products designed to run batch jobs against a file system, such as the Digital Open VMS Cluster and the IBM Sysplex, have software and hardware specifically designed to provide a file system across the complex; as a result, they do not have this problem.

7.2.2　Interactive

Two categories of possible interactive use are logging onto some subsystem or application, such as an OLTP or database system, and directly logging onto the native (for example, UNIX) operating system as a user. The reason for splitting this case in this way is that the application/subsystem case is covered under parallel applications and will not be discussed here further.

The second class, native login, can very nearly be considered a subset of batch processing, with the addition of standard distributed processing facilities such as X Windows and **rlogin**. You still run the same, unchanged serial applications; reprogramming is unnecessary. The "very nearly" aspect involves the fact that the load balancer involved needs some way to intercept a request to login and divert it to a chosen machine; this is effectively built into the scheduler in the batch case. There are, as were listed in Table 2-2 on page 38 in Chapter 2, a number of packages available to do this. This class makes little sense for low-computation, highly interactive applications such as editing, which are more reasonably hosted on a personal machine; however, for interactive use of a heavy number-crunching applications, for example, resource sharing using a cluster is quite a reasonable thing to do. The interaction comes in for "application steering": partial results are displayed as they're generated, and if things are found to be going awry early in the process, the application can be aborted, saving significant personal and computer time. This type of interaction is why an important measure of even these systems is throughput, although that may be perceived by a user as response time.

7.2.3　Multijob Parallel

Another category of basically serial workloads is what is called here Multi-job Parallel. This category is explicitly discussed here to separate it from the "true" parallel systems discussed below.

Members of this class consist of a number of very large, very loosely coupled steps. In terms of the parallel-processing metric of granularity (discussed in the next chapter), they may be said to have the grain size of Mt. Everest, or the rock (singular) that underlies central Texas. In general, they are so loosely coupled that even on a uniprocessor batch system they would have been submitted as separate jobs. Typically, they interact not at all during their execution; instead, each separate job step places its output in a file somewhere. A final cleanup job, often separately submitted, collects it all together.

Some forms of simulation fit this description, particularly those that check correctness or parameter sensitivity by reexecuting the same model many times. Each simulation run is done with different parameters, often pseudo-randomly chosen, and when they're all complete their output files are collected into a single unit for human perusal. Multiframe computer graphic animation also fits this description quite often: Each frame is a separate, large computation; there are a lot of them; and they don't interact with each other.

Multijob parallel is clearly another shoo-in for clusters (or SMPs), and most of the examples I'm aware of do not run afoul of cluster I/O bottlenecks—on the other hand, the ones I'm aware of are not commercially-oriented, either.

So much for serial or serial-like workloads. On to more conventionally conceived parallelism.

7.3 Parallel

In true parallel processing, a single application or subsystem is spread across multiple processing nodes, and there is communication between the parts during execution. The performance metric most usually applied is turnaround time. In the case of commercial parallel systems, response time (effectively a form of turnaround time), coupled in many cases with throughput, is used instead.

An unpleasant fact of life must be faced with regard to parallel processing: *It is hard to write parallel programs.* The design, debugging, and performance tuning of parallel programs are all significantly much more complex than the same operations performed on their serial counterparts. This will be demonstrated quite vividly in Chapter 8, "Basic Programming Models and Issues." This unpleasant fact is particularly vexing when one realizes that software is *always* the problem; software is in a state of chronic crisis; the software application backlog is notorious; and the software community's greatest challenge consists of dealing with the often overwhelming complexity of plain, ordinary, serial programming.

This is not to say that parallel processing does not work. On the contrary, it can be made to work very well indeed and is in regular use throughout the industry in a number of situations.

It does mean that quite significant justification is necessary before one embarks on complicating software even further by introducing parallelism. Therefore this workload characterization splits parallel cases into two subcategories: those where a large effort is justified, and those where it is not. Each is discussed separately below.

In Search of Clusters ✳

7.3.1   Large Effort Justified

There are three primary cases in which the effort required to use parallel processing is justified: Grand Challenges, research, and heavily used applications.

Grand Challenge Problems

The official, government-approved definition of the Grand Challenge problems, with examples, appears in Figure 7-1 [Exe87]. These are well-defined problems whose solutions have major scientific or commercial value, but which require so much brute computation that they cannot be done in a practical period of time on any existing serial hardware, and often not on any existing hardware at all. For purposes of having a number to hang on them, they have recently been referred to as requiring "TeraFLOP" levels of computation: 10^{12}, or a million million, floating-point operations per second (FLOPS). (Yes, it should be "TeraFLOPS," but everybody ignores that persnickety "S".)

Figure 7-1   The Grand Challenge Problems

> "A grand challenge is a fundamental problem in science or engineering, with broad application, whose solution would be enabled by the application of the high-performance computing that could become available in the near future. Examples of grand challenges are: (1) computational fluid dynamics for the design of hypersonic aircraft, efficient automobile bodies, and extremely quiet submarines, for weather forecasting for short and long term effects, efficient recovery of oil, and for many other applications; (2) electronic structure calculations for the design of new materials, such as chemical catalysts, immunological agents, and superconductors; (3) plasma dynamics for fusion energy technology and for safe and efficient military technology; (4) calculations to understand the fundamental condensed matter theory; (5) symbolic computations including speech recognition, computer vision, natural language understanding, automated reasoning, and tools for design, manufacturing, and simulation of complex systems."

Since no existing serial hardware will run these problems, if they are to be attacked at all, a parallel approach must be taken. There is simply no other choice.

These problems would be of very significant commercial utility were they solvable on a regular basis. Their other great utility—securing funding for highly massive computing—is declining in importance at present, in proportion to the post-Cold-War decline in the military and nonmilitary U.S. Federal research budgets.

This is not an arena in which clusters or SMPs play; they do not at present achieve the performance levels required. Wait a few years for processor performance to climb a bit higher.

Academic Research

The second case where large effort is justified is one in which the large, high-quality effort required is dirt cheap: academic research in parallel processing. Everybody knows parallel processing is the wave of the future, from the New York Times through federal grant-approving agencies. As a result, otherwise impractical parallel hardware can be quite effectively used as thesis-generating machines. Graduate students are generally substantially above average in both intelligence and motivation, and at the same time are notoriously inexpensive. So, normal economic rules are suspended.

Heavily Used Programs

The third case is the one of greatest economic importance. Certain applications or subsystems see extremely heavy use. Either systems will be dedicated to executing them, or they will be used on a very large number of systems, or both. Examples include database and OLTP systems in the commercial arena; or seismic migration, crash analysis, and general-use subroutine libraries (LAPACK, LINPACK, MASS, and others) in the technical area.

In this case, the additional software effort required for parallelism is economically justified because it produces an economic advantage. For a database vendor, his system produces greater performance on less-expensive hardware than competitors', in a field where price/performance is a very important sales advantage. For an in-house seismic application, an oil company can extract more from its existing fields, for less expense, when the fields are modelled more accurately and in a more timely manner.

The expense of tying up highly skilled application and (sub-) system programmers to parallelize such systems must always be justified. In this case, we are talking about cases where that justification, realistically performed, comes out in favor of parallelizing the application or subsystem—quite often heavily in favor of parallelization. Of the three cases where heavy parallelization effort is justified, this one alone represents a real, substantial, marketable economic opportunity for the use of parallelism in single applications for either SMPs or clusters.

In Search of Clusters ✳

7.3.2   Minimal Effort Justified

What about the multitude of Suzy Cobol and Freddy Fortran programmers out there? Is parallelism ready for the mainstream? In this case the use of parallelism must at the very least not increase the complexity of the programmer's task. There are definitely uses for true parallelism in some aspects of the commercial computing market, and at least a possibility in the technical market.

Commercial SPPS

Much commercial computing is done under the aegis of large subsystems, in particular OLTP (On-Line Transaction Processing) and database subsystems. As was noted above, those subsystems are good candidates for manual parallelization because of their heavy use. As a result of that work, applications running under those subsystems take advantage of parallelism with no effort. There are two categories: transactions and large database queries.

Transactions are computations with the property, guaranteed by the surrounding subsystem, that they are either completely done or completely fail; the idea is that your bank balance never gets debited without also crediting whomever the money goes to, which I, at least, consider a very good idea. Transactions are traditionally also considered fairly short but some can take minutes to perform; whatever the length, there are always a lot of them to do. A single cellular telephone call, for example, ends up causing tens to hundreds of transactions to be performed by the time you hang up and the billing information is generated. In this case, having lots of transactions is a virtue: the parallelized OLTP system "simply" runs many of them—in unchanged, serial form—simultaneously. No code changes needed. Pure SPPS parallelism. This is referred to as **inter-transaction parallelism**.

The second category, large database queries, requires **intra-application parallelism**, parallelism within a single database operation, to obtain the desired result: decreased turnaround time. The queries are "large" in the sense of requiring the processing of quite a lot of data; the application area typically addressed is decision support. For example, a product manager might want to know who his best distributors have been, for which product feature codes, over the last six months so that he can make sure they receive appropriate treatment. This is just one question, but the system might have to scan through lots of data to get the answer. Furthermore, there are lots of such questions that could be asked: Which distributors are fastest in paying? What about similar questions about suppliers? None of these individually is a heavy-use application, reused by many people in the firm. Even though the manager really wants the answer, he or she is alone in wanting that particular; so the justification for heavy parallelization effort doesn't exist.

In this case of parallelism, what saves the day is a standard high-level language for expressing queries: SQL (Structured Query Language). SQL provides a high enough level of expression that the database system can, without explicit action on the part of the application programmer, extract significant parallelism from queries large enough to worry about. The application programmer may eventually learn how to express queries for best parallel execution, which is a somewhat new discipline but not much different from learning the idiosyncracies of any compiler. However, explicit parallel programming is not required.

So, a significant fraction of commercial computing can make use of both SMP and cluster parallelism without running into the complexity of parallel programming. The reader should note that the complexity of the subsystems has not diminished; making them do inter- and **intra-transaction parallelism** well is by no means a simple task. Making them do both well simultaneously is at least a challenge.

Technical SPPS

How about technical computing? Remember that we are not here discussing large, important technical applications, nor similarly important widely used subroutine libraries, nor the amazing applications that graduate students tackle for peanuts. All those cases have been separated out into the "Large Effort Justified" category. We are instead talking about the numerical bulk of technical applications. As the NCSA case discussed in Chapter 3 indicates, that bulk is not even tuned to vector processing when run on conventional supercomputers, even though vectorization has been current in technical computing for decades. How can it possibly be parallelized?

Some is fruitfully tackled by making use of the large-effort subroutine packages mentioned above. This is partially an analog of the commercial case and works if the application spends the vast majority of its time in those subroutine packages. Otherwise it will run afoul of Amdahl's law, discussed later in this chapter.

There is one case of "minimal effort" technical computing that is interestingly unique: event reconstruction in high-energy physics, which, as discussed Chapter 2, can make good use of SPPS parallelism. This is the transaction processing of technical computing.

AMO Compilers

The only possible answer for the rest of the technical field is what one customer I spoke to referred to as "An AMO Compiler": You put a serial program in the front end, A Miracle Occurs, and a parallel program emerges from the nether end.

It might sound like this customer was an ill-educated fellow, since there are many automatically parallelizing compilers on the market. Cray, Convex, IBM, and literally every other vendor of SMP hardware, along with third-party vendors, sell them. But their output on the majority of unmodified applications (and *any* modification is prohibited in this category) is at best barely adequate to keep the few processors, say up to 4, of a modest SMP busy—and that is the simplest, easiest target of parallelism; any form of cluster, because of higher communication overhead, is more difficult.

The difficulty with automatic parallelization is not the fault of the compilers; even if the compiler were completely perfect, the same result would be obtained. The difficulty lies in the programs. They simply do not contain adequate parallelism in the expression of their algorithms.

A parallelizing compiler does not, and cannot, modify the algorithms of the program it is compiling. Users never want their algorithms modified at all. They worked hard to make them produce the desired result, and strange things can happen to boundary cases, numerical precision, and so on if compilers willy-nilly do algorithm modification. So, hands off. You can't replace serial algorithms with parallel ones (and by the way, it would be more than a little difficult to make such substitutions anyway).

And the algorithms expressed by programmers are likely to contain significant serial elements that block parallelism. The reason this happens is that current languages used for programming, the techniques used to think about and express algorithms, are entirely serial. There is no benefit to a programmer to choose, even out of equally good possibilities, an algorithm that is parallelizeable over one that is not. The language used must change to something that gives Freddy Fortran a good reason, in his own terms, to program in a way that puts possible parallelism into his work.

This is a tall order. There is a possibility: Fortran 90's array constructs allow scientific programmers to express algorithms the way they originally developed the mathematics—in terms of matrices and vectors. Therefore, it passes the Freddy test: It makes his life easier. In the process, it also implicitly expresses some parallelism, although not always the most usable form. Compiling this at least has hope of increased parallelism.

There are other attempts at languages, in particular High-Performance Fortran (HPF) [Ste93], that add to FORTRAN[1] constructs describing how data is distributed for message-based machines such as clusters. This enables compilers to produce correct parallel code for such systems. (Why the primary

---

1. At least one person has commented that no matter what programming language technical computing uses in the future, it will be called FORTRAN, or possibly Fortran.

issue is data distribution will be covered in Chapter 8.) This is a very useful thing to do, and undoubtedly will save much grief in the programming of applications and subroutine packages that pass the "Large Effort Required" test; in the process they will lower the value of "Large" and make the test easier to pass.

But that's not what's being discussed in this section. Such constructs, unfortunately, fail the Freddy test: Unlike array notation, they make expressing *parallelism* easier, but they do not make expressing the *problem* easier; rather, they are an extraneous complication.

So for the bulk of numerical parallel programs, there is some hope. But it will be a long pull, and mainstream technical parallelism will not come easily.

7.4   Amdahl's Law

A factor that affects parallel workloads and the parallel operating systems and subsystems used for serial workloads is known as Amdahl's Law. Gene Amdahl, who did not believe parallelism was a correct direction to take at all, expressed it first in a paper published back in 1967 [Amd67].

Basically, what Amdahl noted was that there is always some irreducible part of a job that cannot be split up to run in parallel. For example, after doing a large mathematical calculation, one must print (or display) the results; even if the calculation itself can be done in parallel, there are few if any printers that do not take a purely serial string of bytes as input, so that part must be done serially. A simple mathematical formulation of this is that the execution time of any program can be split into two parts: part that can be done in parallel, and part that cannot.

$$\text{total execution time} = \text{parallel part} + \text{serial part}$$

Suppose there are N processors available to do the parallel part. The best that can possibly be done, ignoring all overhead involved in coordinating and synchronizing those processors, is then

$$\text{total execution time} = \frac{\text{parallel part}}{N} + \text{serial part}$$

which is known as Amdahl's law.

This calculation is straightforward but has interesting implications. Suppose only 5% of a task is irreducibly serial. That sounds fairly good; but Amdahl's law implies that the most you can speed it up, no matter how many processors you use, is a factor of 20. If the number of processors (N) gets indefinitely large, the parallel part (divided by N) can get indefinitely small. So, say you use a lot of processors. You use so many that this part goes so close to zero it can't be measured. Then the total execution time just equals the serial part—and since that was 5% of the total to begin with, you are stuck with at best a factor of 20. Even with hundreds or thousands of processors.

Amdahl's law has obvious implications for parallel workloads, as was noted above, and is particularly applicable to highly massive parallelism. If something useful is to be obtained from using 1000 processors in parallel, for example, the serial part of the job had better be substantially below 0.1%.

For serial workloads and SPPS parallelism, there is still an effect from Amdahl's law, although it is somewhat less obvious. The serial jobs themselves constitute the "parallel part," since they appear to have nothing to do with any other job on the machine. This appearance can deceive, because the jobs can interact in their use of the operating system or hardware. For example, suppose the hardware used is not an SMP but an "attached processor" system in which only one processor can do I/O. Then all I/O done by any job becomes a piece of the serial part. Insufficiently-parallelized operating systems can produce similar restrictions, allowing I/O to be performed by only one job at a time (obviously, such operating systems are not suitable for commercial workloads).

SPPS exploitation of parallelism using parallelized middleware, such as a database system, similarly depends on adequate parallelization of the middleware. In addition, applications can themselves create a "serial part." For example, if every transaction executed in a particular application adds a row to one specific database table, there is little the database system can do; all the transactions, no matter how many processors there are or how many transactions could be done at once, must line up to alter that table. In this case, neither the hardware—SMP or cluster—nor the middleware is to blame. It is the application structure itself. As this book is written, there are two very well known and popular commercial database application suites that have this problem in a particularly severe form. Both are being rearchitected to solve it, but a year's worth of effort is expected to be necessary.

Amdahl's law is actually an aspect of serialization in general, which will be covered from a different angle in the next chapter.

7.5   The Point of All This _____

That lowly parallel systems exhibit a broad range of useful, practical applicability is hardly surprising. SMPs have been plowing this turf for a couple of decades, so the utility of lowly parallelism is very well established. In fact, it's so commonplace that it's justifiably considered rather boring by those engaged in research in this area. Lowly parallel systems cover most of the usable possibilities with the exception of the Grand Challenges, academic research, and "no effort justifiable" AMO compilers. The first is not now a commercially viable area, the second doesn't have to be, and the third looks pretty difficult from my vantage point.

What the point is, is this: The number of times the phrase "SMPs and clusters" was used, taking them together, when describing whether an area was amenable to parallelism. The broad utility of SMPs is matched just as broadly for clusters. Neither apply to Grand Challenges and research. Both apply to everything else, with one exception: Clusters are worse for "no effort justifiable" AMO technical parallelism. Although there are people who have devoted much effort to that case, in the broader picture I fear it's not going to make that much difference of itself; the analysis techniques developed as part of that effort are another story entirely, finding immense, practical use in instruction scheduling for covert parallelism—to pick just one example.

This is not to say that there are not missing ingredients and holes in cluster support. There is the I/O problem, and at present the cluster-enabled SPPS subsystems for batch, OLTP, and the like must usually be separately purchased. SMP support, in contrast, is included in very many systems at no extra charge. And of course there's the cluster bugaboo, system administration. But there are no massive technical challenges in applying clusters to a rather broad, immensely practical set of workloads.

So, why have two architectures that do the same thing? Because, at least potentially and with ever-increasing advantage, clusters can do it better, bigger, and cheaper than heroically large SMPs. But SMPs are here now in a form many customers find more usable.

However, clusters and SMPs also do it differently, which is a major theme of the next chapter.

Basic Programming Models and Issues

Back in the introduction, I mentioned that there was a particularly nasty issue involved between SMPs and clusters. That issue is both basic and crucial:

> Programs written to exploit SMP parallelism *will not work* on clusters, and programs written to exploit open, message-based cluster parallelism *will not work* on SMPs.

This is not like the bad old days, when everybody wrote programs in assembler language and was locked into a particular manufacturer's instruction set and operating system. *It's very much worse.*

It's not a matter of translating a program, algorithms intact, from one language or system to another; instead, the entire approach to the problem must often be rethought from the requirements on up, including new algorithms. Traditional high-level languages and Open Systems standards do not help.

As a result, application developers, middleware and subsystem developers, system developers, and through them all, users can wind up locked in, not directly to one manufacturer's system, but to a system architecture. If another architecture turns out to be dramatically more efficient, you can't use it without incurring significant rewriting costs.

Like all generalizations, this one requires qualification. SMP-parallel programs, if otherwise compatible with respect to operating system, programming language, and so on, will run on clusters—in the trivial sense that they'll run on one cluster node. Since that doesn't use the cluster to exploit the program's parallelism, it's close enough to "not working" to satisfy me. Cluster-parallel programs are trickier, since—again, if otherwise compatible—you can make them run on SMPs and exploit SMP parallelism. The problem is that they will be significantly less efficient than equivalent programs written specifically to exploit SMP parallelism as well as possible. That matters, since SMPs have a good market position; there are a lot out there, so many native SMP-based programs have already been developed. Cluster-parallel programs on SMPs must compete with those. In most cases, the cluster-based versions' lower efficiency will put them at a disadvantage. As a result, they might as well not work; you can't use them on SMPs and make money from it.

Unfortunately, the statement about being "locked in" requires no qualification. I guess high-level languages and Open System standards make the rewrite easier than in the days of assembler, but that's it.

The computer-science jargon for this intractable difference between SMPs and clusters is that they have different **programming models**. That topic is what this chapter and the next are all about. In the process of showing what a programming model really is by example, this chapter will also substantiate the oft-repeated prior claims that parallelism adds significantly to the difficulties of programming.

8.1   What Is a Programming Model?_____

A programmer is usually about as aware of using a programming model as a fish is of water. It is the all-pervasive atmosphere, the internalized set of assumptions about how a computer works that imbue every program written for that computer. Almasi and Gottlieb [AG94] make the rather good analogy that a programming model (they call it a "computational model") is the set of rules for a game. Programs and algorithms are then game plans or strategies; they indicate how to achieve particular goals within the game, but clearly they are not themselves the rules.

A bit more technically: A programming model is the architecture of a computer system, both hardware and system software, *above* the level that's hidden by traditional high-level languages—C, FORTRAN, COBOL, and their ilk. It is an application's high-level view of the system on which it is running.

Because there is virtually universal agreement on the serial (nonparallel) programming model that everybody uses—the Von Neumann model—the issue of programming models seldom arises except in parallel systems. Hence, the term "parallel programming model" can be taken as synonymous with "programming model," and as noted above, "computational model" is also used.

A large number of programming models have been invented. They differ in ways that are truly basic; in fact, the differences are radical enough to frustrate attempts to construct a completely satisfactory taxonomy of them or otherwise relate them. Not that taxonomizing hasn't been tried; we'll see a few attempts later. Thankfully, all this wild difference doesn't really matter because only three of them, currently implemented on widely available, production computers, matter in our context:[1]

1. the **uniprocessor model**, otherwise known as the Von Neumann model;

2. the **symmetric multiprocessor model**, also referred to in this book as the shared-memory model (although there are other shared-memory models);

3. the **message-passing model** (used in open-system-based clusters).

The SMP and message-passing models will be described in this chapter; it's assumed that the uniprocessor model is well known, even though most people aren't aware that they're using it. This will be followed by a section giving a brief overview of some of the other programming models that are possible, but for various reasons are not widely used, are *passé*, or never have been the basis of a practical system.

It is important to note that a programming model is not exclusively, and in some cases not even primarily, a quality of hardware. The hardware may have been designed with a specific programming model in mind, but since when has any hardware system ever been used the way the designers envisioned? (Or any software system, for that matter.) Software-induced computer cross-dressing has been mentioned before; it applies here, too. Turing guaranteed that this is always possible, even with the most conventional hardware and the most *outré* programming model imaginable (or, com-

---

1. For technical computing, there is arguably one more well-used programming model embodied in vector-processing facilities. While vectors are related to the SIMD model, discussed later, in this book vector processing is not discussed. This is primarily a pragmatic decision; were vectors included, a host of other topics unrelated to the main theme would emerge.

monly, vice versa). This scarcely makes this chapter's discussion irrelevant, since whether constructed by hardware, software, or a mixture (the usual case), some programming model must be used. Without rules, there is no game.

The treatment of programming models in the rest of this chapter is both different from and similar to that which can be found in more technical detail in textbooks on advanced and/or parallel computer architecture (for example, [AG94, Hwa93]).

It differs because rather than talking *about* the models, with a few examples, its focus is on *using* them: A simple example program will be constructed and reconstructed in different models to demonstrate the differences. In the process, many of the traditional issues of parallel programming will emerge: speedup, races, deadlocks, repeatability, and so on. These problems will be discussed primarily in the context of shared memory, simply because that's treated first; message-passing is by no means immune to such problems.

By the time we've finished, you may well be of the opinion that parallel programming is like trying to turn the Keystone Kops into a precision drill team. That's not far wrong; processing elements will trip over each other's feet at every possible opportunity.

The similarity between this chapter and most discussions of parallel processing is that it is implicitly about processor-centric technical computing, in that it says nothing whatsoever about input/output. That is why this chapter is called "*Basic* Parallel Programming Models." The chapter following this one, which discusses where and how different programming models are actually used, brings in those additional issues; they are obviously quite important for commercial applications (not that they aren't also important in some technical contexts).

By the way, particularly for the shared-memory model, many of the issues discussed are identical to issues arising in multi*programming*, especially within operating systems. In that context the term "process," for an active program, is appropriately used for the active entities. Since we're concerned with parallelism here, the term "processor" will be consistently used.

When we're good and sick of programming model details, we'll return to the reasons why this stuff is so crucial. Grounding ourselves in the examples will make the general discussion much more meaningful.

8.2 The Sample Problem

The simple sample problem used in this chapter comes from the mathematico-technical domain, because only there can we find something both simple and comprehensible that actually does something useful. The techniques we'll end up using definitely apply to commercial processing.

The specific sample problem is based on a two-dimensional grid of data values, as shown in Figure 8-1. What we'll do is keep the values along the outer edges constant—those edge values will be the input to the calculation—and attempt to set all the interior values in such a way that each value is the average of all its neighbors. Those interior values are our output. The fixed, outer edge values at the boundary are known, logically enough, as the *boundary values*, or *boundary conditions*.

Figure 8-1 A 2-D Grid of Values and a 4-Point Stencil

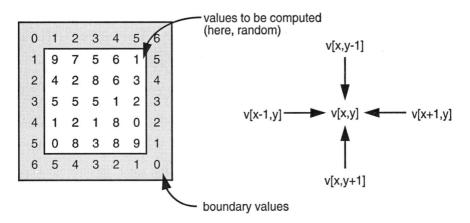

This task might seem like a waste of time, but it actually accomplishes something useful. When the interior values are successfully set to their neighbors' average, they satisfy a simple approximation to the two-dimensional LaPlace equation *(which you do not have to understand at all)*:

$$\frac{\partial^2 f}{\partial x^2} + \frac{\partial^2 f}{\partial y^2} = 0$$

where x and y represent coordinates in space, and f is the function, the values we're computing.

This equation predicts the shape of things that can bend and stretch when they're pushed or twisted. If you grab a piece of rubber balloon in both hands and twist it, the shape it takes between your hands is predicted by this equation; your hands supply the boundary conditions. Likewise, when an airplane wing, or a steel beam, or anything else is placed under load, its shape is predicted by this type of equation. So, think of LaPlace the next time you land in an airplane or see its wings flex.

Why setting the values to the average of their neighbors ends up satisfying that equation, God only knows. Literally. Nearly all differential equations are "solved" by guessing a solution and then showing ("proving") that the guess was correct. You usually leave some fudge factors in the guess; part of the proof is finding consistent values for the fudge factors (if there aren't any consistent values, you guessed wrong). Somebody—probably LaPlace—guessed averages, and that turned out to be right.

A couple of other things have to be specified before we start programming.

First: What does "neighbors" mean? We'll take the neighbors of a value to be the ones immediately above, below, left, and right of it. This defines what's called a 4-point stencil, also illustrated in Figure 8-1: the four points shown contribute to the average. There are other possibilities; for example, the entire box around a value, all eight values, could have been used. Four points is quite enough to illustrate the issues of interest here, which aren't really mathematical; the math is just a carrier for the discussion.

Second: When do we stop? We can't set each interior value to exactly the average of its neighbors, since that would require infinite precision. Instead, we'll be satisfied if it's "close enough." That will be another input, a value called **close_enough**. We stop when every calculated value—every value on the interior of the grid—is **close_enough** to the average of its neighbors. A value for **close_enough** that is, for example, less than 0.01% of the total range of boundary condition values is usually adequately close enough.

That's everything. Let's start. Put on some cast-iron mental hip boots, because we're going to beat this problem to death and in the process more or less deliberately step on every cow patty, mantrap, and land mine that parallel processing has to offer.

8.3   Uniprocessor

The way all those intertwined averages are actually computed is so simple it's practically embarrassing.

Want all those values to be nearest-neighbor averages? Go through them all and set them to exactly that: the average of their neighbor's values. Once that's done, ask a question: Did anything change when we did that? If the answer is no—nothing changed significantly, everything was already **close_enough**—then quit; obviously, all the values are now **close_enough** to the average of their neighbors, so we're done. If the answer instead is yes, something did change—some of the values were not already

close_enough—just go do it again, *starting with the last set of values computed.* Each iteration gets a bit closer to the mark, so sooner or later the program gets it right.

Figure 8-2 has the business end of some pseudo-code which does exactly that, ignoring the usual details of reading in the boundary values and writing out the output.

The nested loops that do the work go from 2 to N-1 over an array of values, **v[]**, that goes from 1 to N in both dimensions. The outer elements—row 1, column 1, row N, and column N—are skipped because they're the constant boundary conditions. They don't get changed.

In order to answer the "did anything change" question at the end of each complete pass through **v[]**—known as a full iteration—the program must keep track of the biggest change in value that it has seen. That's done using the variables **max_error** and **old_value**. **max_error** holds the largest change made to any element of the value array **v[]**. Before changing any element of **v[]**, we first tuck it away in **old_value**. Then we set **max_error** to the larger of two things: (a) whatever it currently is; and (b) the magnitude—absolute value, **abs()**—of the latest change done. That change is the difference between **old_value** and the newly computed value. After we've done all the points (completed both **for** loops), we look at **max_error**; if it's **close_enough**, we quit.

That's all there is to it.

Figure 8-2   Serial Program

```
do forever
    max_change = 0;        /* The largest error we've seen. Initially that's 0. */
    for y = 2 to N-1            /* do all rows, but not outer boundary rows */
        for x = 2 to N-1        /* do all elements in a row, but not boundary*/
            old_value = v[x,y] ;        /* record v[x,y] before changing it */
            /* replace each value with the average of its neighbors */
            v[x,y] = ( v[x-1,y] + v[x+1,y] + v[x,y-1] + v[x, y+1] ) / 4 ;
            /* keep max_change at the largest magnitude change we've seen */
            max_change = max(   max_change,
                                abs( old_value-v[x,y] )   ) ;
        end for x ;                      /* done with that row */
    end for y ;                          /* done with all the rows */
    if max_change < close_enough then leave do forever ; /* are we done? */
end do forever;
```

The technique described above is certainly not the only way to solve LaPlace's equation or ones like it, known as elliptical equations. This is what's known as an iterative technique, using finite differences: It repeatedly "iterates" some operation until the right answer appears or, rather, as close an approximation to the right answer as you like. There are also direct techniques; those don't iterate, they "directly" produce the correct answer. They involve creating banded matrices, inverting them, and other stuff that is, to me, anyway, not as much fun. Direct techniques sound much faster, but that isn't necessarily so in all cases; iterative ones are a perfectly valid, viable solution technique, and have the advantage that you can "dial in" the amount of accuracy you want, trading it for execution time as you like. There is a common variation on the iterative method used here, known as successive over-relaxation (SOR), that is far preferable if you're doing this stuff for a living; these and generally more mathematically rigorous parallel techniques for approaching the problem can be found elsewhere, for example, [FJL+88].

Another reason for using iterative techniques is that they're fun to watch. While it's traditional to begin the iteration with everything set to zero, that's boring. Figure 8-3 shows what happens when the program above is let loose on a collection of 24x24 essentially random points in the range 0 to 745,[2] with only four points tacked down as boundary conditions: the four corners. Initially, as expected, it's a mess. After just one iteration, a lot of the chaos has already dissipated; after 4 iterations it's already assuming a decent form, but is still pretty bumpy. It takes 61 iterations to get everything **close_enough**, in this case within 0.1 (out of a 0–740 range, that's around 0.01% accuracy), resulting in what's traditionally called a saddle-shaped curve.

You can also, by the way, have "boundary" conditions in the middle. Imagine taking a rubber sheet, stretching it between both hands, and bringing it down on top of a coffee cup. The top rim of the cup becomes a set of interior boundary conditions. It's straightforward (though a little tedious) to modify the program above to allow any point to be a fixed boundary position. That's what I did for Figure 8-4, which I intended to iterate to a Western saddle-shaped curve, complete with pommel. Owing partly to a lack of resolution on the 24x24 grid used and partly to having too high a pommel, I got a turkey curve instead.

---

2. Why that odd range of values? Since you can literally start these things out with any values whatsoever, I used my last 576 scores from the Microsoft Windows solitaire applet. Less boring than a random number generator.

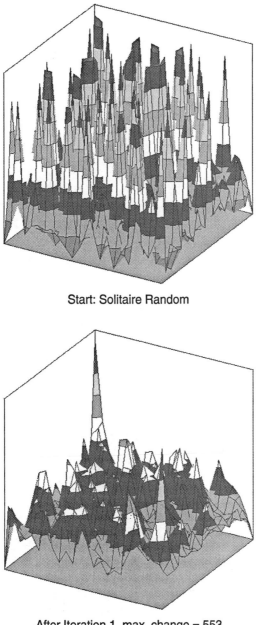

Start: Solitaire Random

After Iteration 1, max_change = 553
A swift reduction in "randomness."

Figure 8-3   Iterating to a Saddle-Shaped Curve

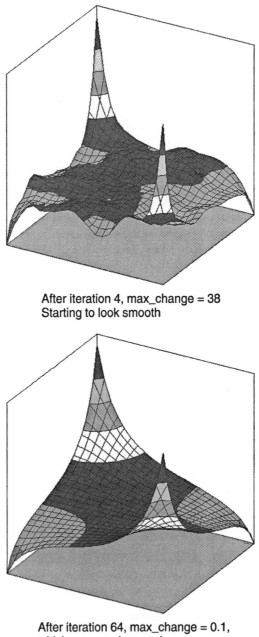

After iteration 4, max_change = 38
Starting to look smooth

After iteration 64, max_change = 0.1,
which was good_enough.

Figure 8-3   (cont.)   Iterating to a Saddle-Shaped Curve

In Search of Clusters ✳

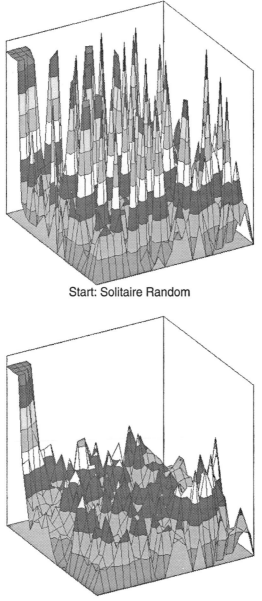

Start: Solitaire Random

After Iteration 1, max_change = 661
A swift reduction in "randomness."

Figure 8-4   Iterating to a Turkey Curve

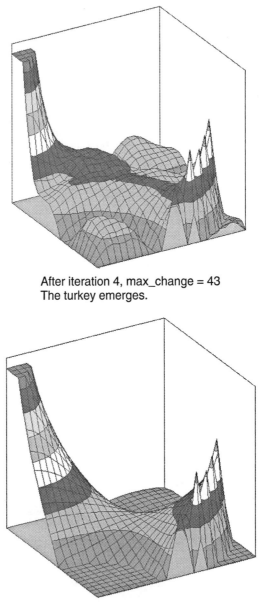

After iteration 4, max_change = 43
The turkey emerges.

After iteration 46, max_change = 0.1,
which was good_enough.

Figure 8-4   (cont.)   Iterating to a Turkey Curve

8.4   Shared Memory _____

All right, what parts of this can be done in parallel, meaning at the same time? The comparison of **max_change** with **good_enough** looks like something that cannot be done in parallel; it needs to intervene between iterations to determine whether to do another iteration. We've got a whole lot of averages to do during each iteration, so that sounds like a good place to start. The shared memory, SMP programming model is the first case we'll tackle.

Because all the data is available to all the processors in the shared memory, we can assume the program is still basically serial and just "turn on" parallelism at the points where it's useful. The parallelism, in other words, is primarily involved in the program's self-control—control parallelism, as distinct from what we'll see with message-passing.

To keep this discussion fairly simple, we'll assume some (seemingly) straightforward programming language constructs which do that. The first is the **forall** statement (elsewhere called **doall, foreach, pardo**, etc.). This is just like a usual iterative **for** statement, except that it doesn't actually iterate. Instead, it says "just get all these things done, in any order, using as many processors as are available." The number of processors available to the job may be specified or limited in some way, but that's usually outside the domain of **forall**; rather, it's in job initialization or some other parallelism support.

Simply using **forall** in a straightforward manner gives the program shown in Figure 8-5. It looks just like the original serial code, except for that **shared, private**, and **lock** stuff. Those additions are a direct consequence of the fact that several processors are going to be executing the code in the middle of the **forall** loops, all at the same time.

The **shared** statement indicates which data is actually accessed by all the processors using the same names. The **private default** statement reinforces the fact that sharing is not the default; only things explicitly **shared** are used in common, and every processor has its own private copy of everything else. This seems counterintuitive. After all, the hardware makes everything shared; something special has to happen behind the scenes to give each processor its own private copy of something, and even then it's private only by convention—the processors all have to agree to abide by the privatizing rules; nothing's forcing them to stay out of each other's turf. But sharing is tricky, as we shall see. Therefore, it's better programming practice to explicitly label the things that are shared, so there's at least that much of a reminder that they have to be treated specially.

Figure 8-5   Shared Memory Parallel Solution

```
lock max_change_lock;          /* declare a lock for max_change*/
shared v[], x, y, max_change;  /* indicate that v and max_change are shared, */
private default;               /*...and nothing else is. */
/***** The main loop *****/
do forever                     /* The outer main iteration loop is serial */
    max_change = 0;            /* Still serial. */
    forall y = 2 to N-1        /* do all rows at once, in parallel */
        forall x = 2 to N-1    /* do all elements in a row at once, in parallel */
            old_value = v[x,y] ;   /* record v[x,y] before changing it */
            /* replace each value with the average of its neighbors */
            v[x,y] = ( v[x-1,y] + v[x+1,y] + v[x,y-1] + v[x, y+1] ) / 4 ;
            /* keep max_change at the largest magnitude change we've seen */
            acquire ( max_change_lock ) ;  /* wait for access to max_change */
            max_change = max(   max_change,
                                abs( old_value-v[x,y] )   ) ;
            release ( max_change_lock ) ;  /* finished with max_change */
        end forall x ;         /* done with all columns*/
    end forall y ;             /* done with all rows */
    if max_change < close_enough then leave do forever ; /* are we done? */
end do forever;
```

8.4.1   Races and Locks

That special treatment of shared data is typified by the **lock**ing statements. For the program to work, **max_change** has to wind up each full iteration set to the maximum change made across every one of the elements of **v[]**. That means every processor has to test and potentially adjust its value, which is why the **max_change** adjustment is inside the nested loops.

But all will not be well if each processor simply whacks away at **max_change**. To see why, consider how a maximum is actually computed:

```
1       load reg_1 with newest change
2       load reg_2 with (old) max_change
3       reg_1 > reg_2?
4       Yes: store reg_1 in max_change
```

Two registers are **load**ed with the values to be compared, the comparison is done, and a **store** is performed if the new change is bigger than the old

max_change. This is straightforward. But it contains an assumption: It assumes that the copy of **max_change** in **reg_2** is the correct, current value during steps 3 and 4, where the comparison is made and the **store** is done.

That assumption is trivially true on a uniprocessor; you don't even have to think about it. But if multiple processors are whacking around on **max_change** at the same time, that assumption may be false. Somebody else could change it during that time it's held in the register.

The kind of thing that can happen is shown in Figure 8-6: Processor Able makes a copy of **max_change** at time 2. Processor Baker innocently makes its own copy at time 3, oblivious to Able's actions. Then, in the middle of Baker's comparison, Able goes and changes **max_change**. As a result, **max_change** does not end up containing the actual maximum change.

However, this is not always going to lead to an incorrect value. If both processors happened upon **max_change** when it contained 400, both comparisons would have failed and, since neither one did an update, no damage would have been done. On the other hand, if both processors happened upon **max_change** when it contained 75, Able would have stored its 100; but Baker's comparison would have failed, so it wouldn't have stored anything. Result: **max_change** ends up at the right value. So, sometimes the right answer will be produced.

That's much worse than failing consistently.

If the fool thing got the wrong answer *every* time, you would: (a) at least be certain something was wrong and not be tempted to attribute it to gremlins;

Figure 8-6   A Race Condition

Everybody starts with max_change = 0

time	processor Able newest change = 100	max_ change	processor Baker newest change = 10
1	load reg_1 with 100	0	
2	load reg_2 with 0	0	load reg_1 with 10
3	100 > 0?	0	load reg_2 with 0
4	Yes: store 100 in max_change	100	10 > 0?
5		10	Yes: store 10 in max_change

WRONG!

reg_2's copy of max_change is out of date

(b) be able to examine it, time and time again, meticulously checking all the possibilities, until the cause was determined. That's not possible if it happens only sporadically.

The kind of difficulty we're discussing is called a **race condition**, because whether the program works depends on the relative timing and speed of the processors involved—in effect, it is a race among them.To keep this horrible stuff from happening, we must only allow one processor at a time to get at **max_change**. This is mutual exclusion, as was discussed back in "Sequential and Other Consistencies" on page 158, and it's what the lock does.

A lock as we're using it has the effect of turning a block of code into a kind of voting booth: Only one processor can get in it at once; once one's in, another can't enter. Unlike a voting booth, a processor can stay inside it as long as it wants without getting other processors mad (but it may get you annoyed, stay tuned). Once out, somebody else is allowed in. The block of code is more formally known as a **critical section,** I suppose because it's "critical" that nobody else be in there.

The program we've written uses the procedure **acquire()** to "get" the lock ("acquire possession" of it) and be allowed into the critical section, and uses **release()** to "let go of" the lock, letting the system know that it's out of the critical section. There can be many different locks in a parallel program. Each has associated data needed to implement the locking function itself, which is why **acquire() and release()** take an argument; in the program, that's the data structure named **max_change_lock.**

Applying that lock to our race condition of Figure 8-6 results in the execution shown in Figure 8-7. The procedure **acquire()** is written extremely carefully; even if two (or more) processors call it at exactly the same time, only one returns. The other, or others, wait inside **acquire()** until the lucky one that got through calls **release()**; then, if anybody's waiting, exactly one more returns from its wait inside **acquire().** (If a "lucky one" forgets to call **release()**, or aborts for some reason, the program is in bad shape; other processors will wait in **acquire()** forever. Ominous parallelism bug #2769.)

The figure illustrates this process for the case in which Able and Baker both happen to call **acquire()** simultaneously, and Able won. Baker waits in **acquire()** until Able calls **release().** Now the assumption made by the "maximum" program fragment is correct: Nobody else can change **max_change** while a processor is in the critical section. It works.

It's also slower. Notice that in Figure 8-7, the program takes 11 time steps, not counting the time spent in the **acquire()** and **release()** procedures, which can be considerable. The original in Figure 8-6 took only 5 time steps, with

Figure 8-7   Race Condition Resolved With a Lock

Everybody starts with max_change = 0

time	processor Able newest change = 100	max_ change	processor Baker newest change = 10
1	call acquire(max_change_lock)	0	call acquire(max_change_lock)
2	load reg_1 with 100	0	... waiting inside acquire()...
3	load reg_2 with 0	0	... waiting inside acquire()...
4	100 > 0?	0	... waiting inside acquire()...
5	Yes: store 100 in max_change	100	... waiting inside acquire()...
6	call release(max_change_lock)	100	... waiting inside acquire()...
7		100	load reg_1 with 10
8		100	load reg_2 with 100
9		100	10 > 100?
10		100	No: do nothing
11		100	call release(max_change_lock)

no procedure calls. As usual, you can be really fast if you don't have to be correct; but there's something more going on here.

8.4.2   Serialization

As a result of the lock, which was necessary for correctness, all the processors have to line up to update **max_change**. That means that when they're updating **max_change**, they're not working in parallel any more: They've been serialized. This has been spoken of previously in the context of Amdahl's law; why it comes about has not been discussed, nor has there yet been any real indication of its effects.

Figure 8-8 illustrates the effect of a serial section like this on a program. Time flows downward in the figure; think of it as taking the program fragments of Figure 8-7 and eliminating all the detail, coloring the "useful work" white, the update to **max_change** grey, and the wait cross-hatched.

At first, all the processors are doing useful stuff in parallel. Then, they have to update something in common, such as our **max_change** variable. If the work is perfectly distributed to begin with, they'll reach the critical section at the same time, but only one will get through; as shown in the left side of the figure, that's processor 1. It does its thing, and then another gets in, followed by another, and so on. Now take a look at the right side of Figure 8-8. You might as well not have all those processors any more—one alone can do the job just as fast.[3] That's serialization.

Our program, however, doesn't execute like that diagram. We've got lots of averages to do, so when each processor finishes with the critical section update of **max_change**, it goes back and does another average—and then waits for the critical section again.

This is shown in Figure 8-9. Processor 2, for example, does some work; then waits; then goes through the critical section; then does some more work, waits, and so on. So does every other processor. In this simple case, they will eventually form a pattern. It generally won't be as clean and uniform as that illustrated, because none of the times involved are exactly repeatable; cache misses, memory errors, and so on will affect processing time pseudo- (or truly) randomly.

But notice something in Figure 8-9: Processor 1, the first one through, is finished a *second* time and waiting again before processor 5 has completed its *first* wait. Something is wrong here. If processor 1 gets back in the queue (and there is a queue involved, inside **acquire()**) while 5 and 6 are still in the queue, why bother having 5 and 6? All they're doing is spending time wait-

Figure 8-8   Serialization

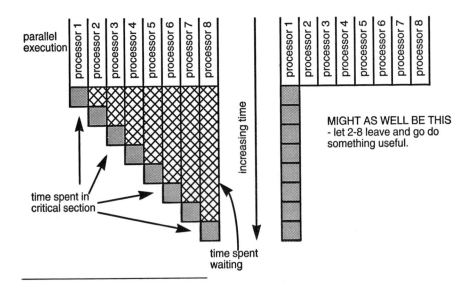

3. Actually, it can probably do it faster than many could, because it will have better cache locality. More about this later.

ing. Looking at the diagram more closely, you can notice (check the arrow) that only four processors are active at any given time. That says the same thing: Don't bother with processors 5 and 6. But there are potentially thousands of averages to do. Only four processors are useful no matter how much work is to be done? Is this an artifact of the diagram?

The specific number of processors, four, is indeed an artifact of the diagram. But limits like this are a general phenomenon. The issue is how much time is spent in serial code, compared with how much time is spent in parallel. Given N processors, once N × (serial time) > parallel time, you don't need any more of them—if they're running in the kind of pattern shown in Figure 8-9. That's one kind of pattern; there are many other possible patterns, and all have their restrictions. The point: Even if you have a ton of completely separate, different things to do, you can still be limited in the amount of parallelism available, limited by the need to keep the processors from tripping over each other's feet.

How long is our example's serial time compared with the parallel time? Actually, it's pretty bad. The only thing we're doing in parallel is a single averaging operation, and serially we're doing two things. One, updating

Figure 8-9   Re-execution During Serialization

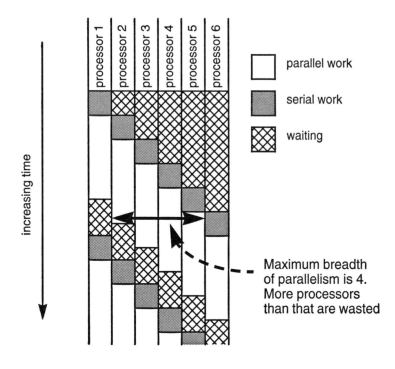

max_change, has been discussed. As to the other: Where did you think the values of the indices **x** and **y** were coming from? That's right. Hidden inside the **forall** implementation is a lock. The "**forall x=**..." statement must **acquire()** a lock for **x**, then increment **x**, then **release()** that lock on every iteration of the inner loop. The outer loop does the same for **y**.

This doesn't seem that bad. After all, the things we're doing in those critical sections are pretty trivial: taking a maximum, doing a single integer addition. The floating-point operations in the "real" work should, one might think, overwhelm that. Unfortunately, something else is going on in addition to that.

Recall the discussion about sequential consistency back on page 158. Suppose, in order to let the processor run fast most of the time, a technique like weak ordering or release consistency is used. This means that for the program to work at all—for example, for the correct value of **max_change** to be picked up when it's first loaded—the entire, mile-long, anthracite-loaded freight train of a processor's superscalar, pipelined operation has to come to a shuddering halt on each lock. That's what is needed to let the changed data values percolate through the system.[4] The **acquire()** and **release()** procedures must contain the appropriate, processor-specific instructions causing this to happen.

This means that a processor which could scream right along, completing a floating-point add every cycle, must wait, often as many as 10, 20, or more cycles when a lock must be grabbed. Synchronizing the data in the whole system, and that's what locking requires, is *expensive*.

Net: The program as so far written is in very bad shape serialization-wise. Fortunately, there's a relatively simple way to fix it: Don't try to use so much parallelism. We have lots of rows and lots of columns. Right now we're trying to use them simultaneously and tripping over our own feet in the process. Instead, let's use parallelism only on different rows and do each entire row serially.

That is what is shown in Figure 8-10, where the inner loop has been changed back into a serial **for** statement. This necessitated some additional changes: Now a running maximum change is kept in a private, per-processor variable, **row_max**. When an entire row is completed, **row_max** is used to update the global maximum, **max_changes**.

---

4. If it's not using those weaker orderings, it's running more slowly all the time, not just part of the time. Using a slower processor so you can be more parallel is almost never the correct tradeoff.

Figure 8-10   A Better Shared-Memory Parallel Implementation

```
lock max_change_lock;        /* declare a lock for max_change*/
shared v[], x, y, max_change;  /* indicate that v and max_change are shared, */
private default;             /*...and nothing else is. */
/***** The main loop *****/
do forever                   /* The outer main iteration loop is serial */
  max_change = 0;            /* Still serial. */
  forall y = 2 to N-1        /* do all rows at once, in parallel */
    row_max = 0;             /* reset running maximum for this row */
    for x = 2 to N-1         /* do the elements in a row serially */
      old_value = v[x,y] ;   /* record v[x,y] before changing it */
      /* replace each value with the average of its neighbors */
      v[x,y] = ( v[x-1,y] + v[x+1,y] + v[x,y-1] + v[x, y+1] ) / 4 ;
      /* keep row_max at the largest change made on this row */
      row_max = max( row_max,
                     abs( old_value-v[x,y] )   ) ;
    end for x;               /* done with one entire row */
    /* keep max_change at the largest magnitude change we've seen */
    acquire ( max_change_lock ) ;  /* wait for access to max_change */
    max_change = max ( max_change, row_max ) ;
    release ( max_change_lock ) ;  /* finished with max_change */
  end forall y ;                    /* done with all rows */
  if max_change < close_enough then leave do forever ; /* are we done? */
end do forever;
```

Instead of synchronizing on every point—N^2 times—the program will only update **max_changes** and get a new parallel index **y** on each row—N times. That's a factor of N reduction. As a result the program will run much faster and *by deliberately using less parallelism* be able to use *many more* processors. As a matter of fact, there is published evidence that this technique achieves the best speedup of any we will consider in this chapter: as much as 3.95 times faster on four processors [EY92]. Sounds pretty good.

Too bad it never gets the same answer twice in a row.

8.4.3   Consistency and Chaos

The program we've got so far will produce *a* correct answer; the values of **v[]** it produces will be **good_enough** averages of their neighbors. But for any one set of input values, there are any number of sets of **v[]** values satisfying that criterion. Running our current program twice, under exactly the same conditions, with exactly the same input values, will give two of those correct answers. Different ones. They will most likely differ down in the umpteenth decimal place; the harder you screw down **good_enough**, the larger "umpteen" will get; you might not even notice it unless your output format shows enough decimal places; but they will differ.

This kind of behavior can be disturbing. Lots of people expect computers to act like machines, after all, not like other people, and machines are alleged to do the same thing, time after time, except for certain specifically-designated, exceptional circumstances usually involving "random" number generators and Art.

Of course, if you don't know why the system is acting that way you've no guarantee it won't go completely nonmachine and give you a genuinely wrong answer, not just an alternative right one. That would be bad. So, why is this happening?

If something looks, smells, and acts intermittent, variable, and unrepeatable, it's probably a race condition. This is no exception. In fact, it's the mother of all race conditions. We don't have any controls in place that coordinate updating all the many values of the **v[]** array itself.

As a processor—call it Charlie—lays its stencil down on the array and computes an average for **v[x,y]** in the inner loop, it picks up values of **v[x,y-1]** and **v[x,y+1]**. It also uses **v[x-1,y]** and **v[x+1,y]**; those don't matter to us here, because they're in Charlie's own row and therefore under its own control. The **y-1** and **y+1** cases, on the other hand, are in the rows above and below the one Charlie's working on.

Those are possibly being whacked at by other processors, but, as usual, only possibly: There might be processors working the rows above and below Charlie's, or there might not; if there are, (see Figure 8-11) they could be consistently behind Charlie as it cranks across the row, or consistently ahead; or they could be neck-and-neck, duking it out for the same cache lines (about which more in a bit); or, since there are two other processors involved, one could be ahead and the other behind, or vice versa, or they could switch in the course of a row, or... you get the idea.

Things are pretty chaotic. The reason we get a correct answer at all has nothing to do with computer science, but rather with the mathematics of the iterative technique itself. It happens that Charlie never picks up a truly incongruous, random-like value because there are only two possibilities. For each value, either

> ➤ Charlie got there first, in which case Charlie gets the value that was in **v[]** before this full iteration started—an **old** value; or

> ➤ Charlie got there last, in which case Charlie gets the value that will be in **v[]** after this full iteration ends—a **new** value.

So all the possibilities for the input values to the averages aren't totally off the wall; they're at least on their way to a final solution.[5] Therefore, the averages computed from those values aren't bizarre either, which makes the next

Figure 8-11   Charlie's Fortunes in the New/Old Value Race

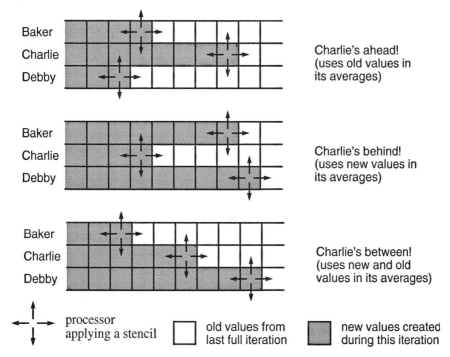

---

5. There is another hidden assumption here. The possibilities listed assume that when a processor writes into the array, it does so all at once; it doesn't write part of a value and then another part. This is called an atomic—indivisible—operation. There are systems in which updating a double-precision floating-point number is not atomic. In that case, Charlie could pick up garbage: a half-updated value, half old, and half new. This has happened, in actual practice.

✳ *Basic Programming Models and Issues*   **209** round of values reasonable, and so on. But the randomness of the situation produces different, but still correct, results each time.

It's a bit amazing to me that this method works at all, but work it certainly does. There's even a body of mathematical work behind it, complete with a formal name for it: chaotic relaxation. That mathematics, and not the "computer science," gives us assurance that it will work. There are many circumstances in which not only does it work, it converges to a solution faster than other methods. It even has been cited in cases of superlinear speedup: N processors produce a result in less than 1/Nth the time it takes one processor.

Before the marketeers start blowing this one to all four winds simultaneously: It doesn't always work. There are mathematical circumstances surrounding its use that have been quite carefully delineated, and I, for one, don't understand them at all.

In any event, most people don't like their computers acting this way. So how do we stop it?

8.4.4 Many Locks and Deadly Embraces (Deadlocks)

Locking got us out of a race condition before. But we certainly do not want to create an array of locks, one for each element of **v[]**, and lock the **y-1** and **y+1** elements before computing an average, for three reasons.

> We just finished removing one lock per element on the update; adding two doesn't sound terrifically smart. The serialization won't be as bad as the **max_change** case, because at most three processors are ever contending for a value and because many times they aren't even going to go after the lock at the same time. But there is still the intrinsic overhead of system synchronization on every lock operation.

> How many locks was that again? Just locking the values above and below isn't enough, because you somehow have to keep other processors out of the value being updated. It sounds like you have to lock the whole stencil. The overhead is now in the category of "tremendous."

> It just plain doesn't work. Say the program successfully locks everything in sight. Has it locked them before or after they've been updated? Will the average be based on old or on new values? This is the same problem we have without locks.

It sounds like we really don't want to lock each element. How about locking whole rows? There could be a lock for each row, and the code could grab all three row locks needed before doing anything, then do an entire row, then unlock them. This doesn't sound as ridiculous as locking every element; the overhead is back to reasonable amounts. Unfortunately, there are two reasons why this is a bad idea, too.

The first reason has to do with the danger, in general, of acquiring multiple locks. Suppose a processor—Charlie again—successfully gets the locks for its row, row c, and the one above. However, Charlie is blocked when it tries to get row d below; somebody else—Debby—already got that row. Oh, well, Charlie just has to wait until Debby's done.

Wait a minute. Debby also has to get three locks.

Suppose Debby successfully got row d, *and then tried to get row c after Charlie already locked it?* Charlie's stuck waiting on d; it can't ever let go of c. Debby's stuck waiting on c; it can't ever let go of d.

If that happens, Charlie and Debbie have locked onto each other, nevermore to separate. Their relationship is illustrated in Figure 8-12. They'll wait forever. The application locks up, because the iteration they're trying to do never finishes.

This kind of thing used to be called, rather evocatively, a **deadly embrace.** Nowadays it's more well known as a **deadlock.** The name change was probably done in pursuit of unnecessarily meticulous terminological exactitude,[6] since this situation can happen to more than two processors at once: Charlie's stuck on Debby's stuck on Pat's stuck on Charlie. "Deadly embrace" is "correctly" used when there are only two participants.

Can it happen here? As it turns out, it's possible. It depends on the details of the way program is modified to acquire those row locks. It might avoid the problem by accident, but a slight change in the problem statement could reintroduce them. Here's why.

To get a deadlock (deadly embrace), you need—as shown in Figure 8-12—a circular pattern, a cycle of references to resources of any kind, not just locks; all that matters is that only one entity can own each resource at a time. They could be tape drives or printers, for example. The circular pattern is the issue: No cycle, no deadlock.

To get the cycle in the example, Charlie had to ask for row c, then row d, and Debby had to ask for row d, *then* row c. They had to ask in the opposite order, creating a cycle in their lock requests, to get in trouble. If both had asked in the same order—say, d then c—there's no problem. Here's why.

---

6. To say nothing of a lack of imagination.

Figure 8-12 Charlie and Debby's Deadly Embrace

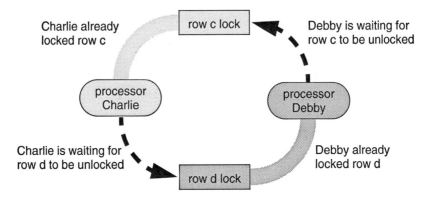

Since both ask for d before c, Debby (say) would get it and Charlie would wait there at d. So Charlie, waiting at d, can't interfere with Debby getting c. Debby would get c, work, and then release both c and d. As soon d was released, Charlie could get it and c, and do its work.

Now, one likely way to have programmed the locks is to have stuck these three lines in front of the loop that does a row:

```
acquire ( row_lock[y-1] ) ;
acquire ( row_lock[y] ) ;
acquire ( row_lock[y+1] ) ;
```

If this is done, all the row locks are always acquired in the "natural" order of their rows and in the same order by everybody. There are no cycles, so there will be no deadlocks. We win. Another likely possibility is to acquire the locks in the opposite order; that would have been just as good. We win again.

However, had it been programmed as

```
acquire( row_lock[y] ) ;
acquire( row_lock[y+1] ) ;
acquire( row_lock[y-1] ) ;
```

then there would be a potential deadlock, because no consistent order is followed in acquiring the locks. We lose. Several other inconsistent orders exist, too. Which order would you have written? (*Before* you read this.)

Even if a right order is (perhaps accidentally) chosen, the **acquire()** statements above will fail if the problem is changed slightly, to a common variation called "periodic boundary conditions." In that variation, there are no constant values on some pair, or both pairs, of sides. Instead, the requirement is that the top and bottom edges (for example) end up at the same values. The solution obtained with periodic boundary conditions is one that's valid for long strips or big areas: Copy after copy of the array can be pasted together at the edges, since opposite edges have the same values.

Computing the correct averages when using periodic boundary conditions is easily accomplished. Just run the averages around the edges of the array, "wrapping" the stencil from top to bottom (for example). This is done by computing the row indices **y+1** and **y-1** modulo the size of the array (if an index is greater than N, subtract N and continue; could do the column indices, too).

Unfortunately, this introduces a great big cycle into the "natural" way to acquire the locks, since the row indices now cycle around the whole array. Looking at it another way: The modulo'd value of **y+1** can be less than the modulo'd values of **y** and **y-1**, so we've lost a consistent order. It's admittedly extremely unlikely that the whole cycle, all the way around the array, will lock up at once; the longer a cycle is, in general the less likely it is to be encountered. But it still could happen and of course will happen at the worst possible time. It is still possible to acquire the locks in an overall total order, but special attention is needed—and, of course, the need must be anticipated.

As was hinted when the more general term "resources" was used in place of "locks," deadlock avoidance is clearly a far more general problem than this discussion has indicated so far. Operating systems, transaction managers, and database management systems must be alert to the possibility of deadlocks. Rather than deadlock avoidance or prevention, which has been discussed here, a strategy of deadlock detection is sometimes used: Occasionally the system fires up a subprogram that checks out all the locks (one lock for each resource), looks at who's waiting on them, and sees if there are any cycles. If there are cycles, one or more of the embracers in a cycle is told to give up: release all the locks it's holding, and start all over again. If this doesn't break all the cycles, another is told to give up, and so on. Once the cycles are broken, continued progress can be made. Obviously, this doesn't work unless the lock holders have specifically been written in a way that lets them give up and start over; in databases and transaction managers, for example, it's the required operation of "aborting a transaction," and the database or transaction manager provides that property for all applications running under it without their having to explicitly deal with it—as long as the applications only access information that's part of the data base; step outside, and anything could happen.

Now we know how to lock the rows in a way that avoids deadly embraces and deadlocks. This solves the first problem with using row locks. However, it was mentioned that there was a second. The second is much simpler and, unfortunately a little harder to deal with:

I've been leading you down a primrose path. Which processors get which rows is still the luck of the draw inside **acquire()** and can vary from run to run, so this method doesn't solve the problem we are worried about. The answers obtained will be somewhat more consistent from run to run, probably, but the program still isn't guaranteed to get the same right answer twice. Other methods have to be found.

8.4.5 Alternation Schemes

The difficulty we're having with consistency arises because some averages are based on old values present when the iteration started, others are based on new ones computed during the iteration, and there's no real control over which of the average calculations use which values. When the problem's stated that way, it's fairly obvious that some control must be exerted over exactly that aspect: who uses old values, and who uses new values. There are several ways to apply such control, all based on knowingly segregating old from new values and alternating between them.

A rather obvious way to segregate the new from the old values is to keep them in separate arrays, as illustrated in Figure 8-13. Every processor reads

Figure 8-13   A/B Alternation (Gauss-Jacobi iteration)

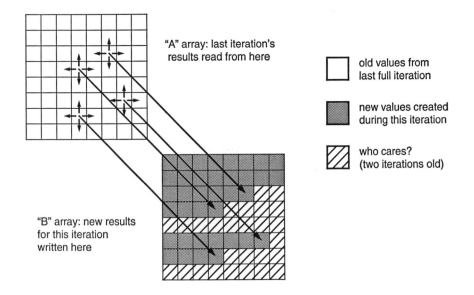

"A" array: last iteration's results read from here

☐ old values from last full iteration

▦ new values created during this iteration

▨ who cares? (two iterations old)

"B" array: new results for this iteration written here

In Search of Clusters ✳

values from one array, A, but never writes into it. Instead the new averages are put in array B. When B is completely filled, assuming another iteration is required you either copy B into A or, less expensively, exchange some pointers so now everybody reads from B and writes into A

The iterations now proceed through time by flipping from A to B, then B to A, then A to B, and so on. No matter what order the system does the averages, they're all consistently based on old values—because there's nothing but old values in the source array. The program will give same result with the same inputs, time after time. We have achieved complete, total consistency. Congratulations, us.

We have also used up twice as much memory. This is not good on general principles and is likely to get in the way when (not if) the calculation is done on a finer mesh (a bigger array) or extended beyond two dimensions to three.

Well, how about segregating old and new within the same array? That can be done, too.

The simplest way to do this with the program we started from is to divide the rows into two groups: odd-numbered rows and even-numbered rows. We'll call these "red" and "black" rows for a reason that will soon be clear. Now, we split each iteration into two phases. In phase 1, we read the red and write the black rows; in phase 2, we read the black and write the red—or, equivalently, flip what we call red and black.

Figure 8-14   Red/Black Iteration with Alternating Rows

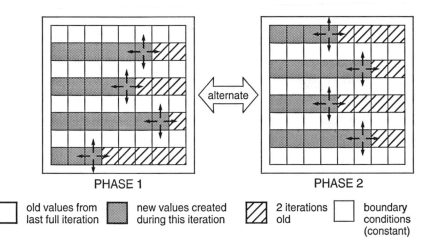

| PHASE 1 | | PHASE 2 |

| ☐ old values from last full iteration | ▓ new values created during this iteration | ▨ 2 iterations old | ☐ boundary conditions (constant) |

This red/black row alternation is illustrated in Figure 8-14. It also yields consistent results, because all the processors read only red (outside their own rows, anyway), and write only black. That means that during any phase their results never mingle, so the order in which they perform their computations doesn't matter at all.

That's not the only way to segregate within the array, however. We could also apply red/black labels like a checkerboard, alternating within each row, as illustrated in Figure 8-15. This is obviously where the red/black nomenclature comes from. It, too produces consistent results, for the same reason the row-by-row scheme does. Also, it will usually require fewer iterations than row-by-row because it percolates value changes more uniformly and quickly throughout the array.

Figure 8-15   Red/Black Checkerboard Alternation

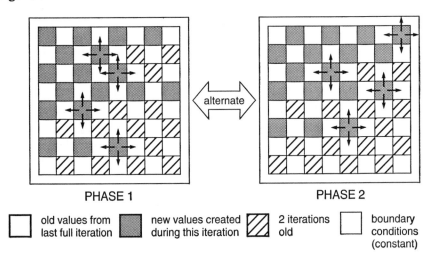

☐ old values from last full iteration	■ new values created during this iteration	▨ 2 iterations old	☐ boundary conditions (constant)

We now have a parallel program that uses no more storage than the original, except for locks and a few other minor things. It also runs fast and gives the same answer every time when given the same input. Pretty good.

The problem now is that the answer it gives is not the same one the original program gave. Groan.

8.4.6   What Went Wrong?

Once again, we're getting *a* correct answer; the values of **v[]** are all **good_enough**. We also get the same answer every time, which is soothing. But the answer produced is not *the* correct answer—the same one produced by the serial program.

In addition, the parallel program often takes more full iterations than did the original to get all the values into the **good_enough** range. Each of those iterations does go faster, but the fact that more of them are required cuts into the speedup we're getting. This is at least annoying and should be troubling.

Those two facts are linked. What's happened is that we changed the mathematical type of iteration being performed when we segregated the old and new values to achieve consistency.

The original program did *not* use all old values when it computed an average. Ignore the constant boundaries for a moment. As shown in Figure 8-16, whenever the program computed a new average for a value, the row above was already done; it contained all new values. That meant that the component at the top of the stencil wasn't old, it was new. Similarly, the program had already computed the previous point on the row, so the value on the left of the stencil was also new. The other two components of the average, the bottom and right parts of the stencil, hadn't yet been computed. So, they were still old. The original program used new on top and left, and old on right and bottom.

Figure 8-16   What the Original Program Really Did

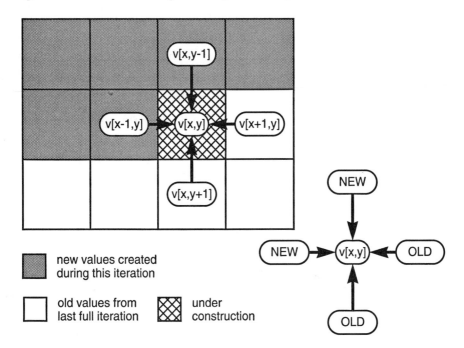

The red/black schemes, particularly A/B whole-array alternation, use all old values to compute each new average. This is not the same thing the original program did, so it's not surprising we get a different answer.

What may be surprising to those not heavily into the mathematics of iteration is that the different types of iteration used—the original program's and the alternating schemes—have been studied extensively. They even have names. A/B alternation is Gauss-Jacobi iteration, while the original serial program used Gauss-Seidel iteration. Unfortunately for us, while there are exceptions, the original Gauss-Seidel method is the superior one: It usually converges to a result faster (fewer iterations). There are even cases where Gauss-Seidel does converge to a **good_enough** result, and Gauss-Jacobi never does. Instead, Gauss-Jacobi ends up with two (or more) sets of values that it just keeps alternating between, never settling down to something **good_enough**. While unlikely, when it happens this is Very Bad. It is not nice to have programs that never stop. Our changes resulted in using an algorithm that is worse than the original.

This is not parallel processing bug #2769 or any other such high number. It is Classic Parallel Error #1: Parallelizing an inferior algorithm because it is the easier one to parallelize. While there may be a bizarre exception here and there arising from particularly crazed circumstances, it is virtually never the right thing to do. That was emphasized way back in the introduction, where I stated that "working smarter" meant using the best algorithms: "Choosing or discovering appropriate algorithms is therefore supremely important. We should be extremely careful that using any of the other techniques does not require us to use an inferior algorithm." This is where that statement comes home to roost.

While this error is committed regularly, one particularly egregious example stands out in my mind. It involved the publication, in a highly respected, widely read, quasi-popular computer journal, of a long article extolling the virtues of a particular massively parallel machine on the basis of how fast it was able to do a certain type of search. Literally tens of thousands of processors were used, and the authors were obviously quite proud of that fact. Very few months later, another article appeared in a more-or-less competing journal of the same type. It referenced the first article, and showed how exactly the same search could be performed, *much faster*, using a *single* processor instead of thousands—a processor that was exactly the same type and speed as just *one* of those thousands. Exactly the same total amount of memory and exactly the same input/output facilities were also used. A better algorithm was the difference. It was not as easily parallelizeable, but was more than 64,000 times faster.

Spectacular as it is, 64,000 isn't infinity. By switching to Gauss-Jacobi, our program doesn't just run slower. There are cases where it does not converge, meaning that **max_change** never gets less than **good_enough**. Therefore it will never exit the outer loop; it will just run forever. In effect, in those cases it runs *infinitely* slower. In all fairness, this doesn't always happen; the circumstances where it arises are not terribly common. Red/black schemes are practical and can be altered to use Gauss-Seidel iteration, too. Nevertheless, we need a way out of our current jam.

8.4.7   The Wavefront (Hyperplane) Method

If we want to get exactly the same result as the original program and keep its good mathematical properties, we obviously can't compute any old average at any time. What can we compute?

The analysis showing which stencil inputs are new and which are old provides a clue. Wherever the pattern shown in the lower right of Figure 8-16 is found—new on top and right, old on left and bottom—we can compute an average. That will preserve the new/old relationships of the inputs and produce the desired output.

When an iteration first starts, there's exactly one place where that pattern holds: The upper-left point, **v[2,2]**. (Figure 8-17, Step 1.) That's because the topmost and leftmost values, **v[1,2]** and **v[2,1]**, are the boundary conditions; because they're constant, they're always "new" (or old, take your pick). This is exactly what the serial algorithm does first. So wonderful, we can do one point. Big deal.

Figure 8-17   Which Points Can Be Done, When?

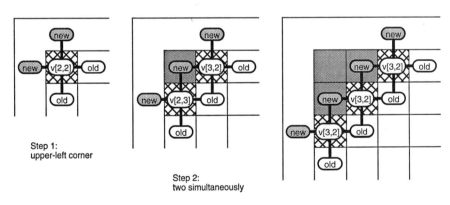

But after that one point is computed, there are *two* places where the new/old template holds (Figure 8-17, Step 2): **v[3,2]**, the next one the serial algorithm did; *and* **v[2,3]**, the one below the point just computed. That lower point wasn't used by the serial algorithm, but it can be computed immediately because the boundary, in this case **v[3,1]**, is available as a "new" value. So we can do both of those at the same time—in parallel—and still produce the same results that the serial algorithm produced.

Once those two are done, by the same logic we can do three at once; then four, then five, and so on. Now things are looking up. In effect, we can run a diagonal wave of computation through the array, doing everything on the "wavefront" in parallel as shown in Figure 8-18. This technique was originally described by Lamport [Lam], who described this wavefront as a hyperplane through the space of indices traversed by the loops.

Figure 8-18   Wavefront of Computation

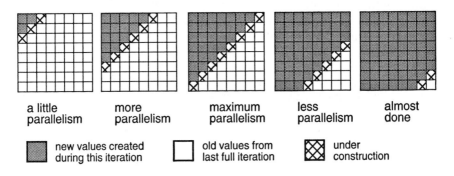

The parallelism available with this method isn't as uniform as in the previous techniques. It starts small, then increases to a maximum across the diagonal of the array, then decreases again. But the array size is likely to be hundreds or thousands square, so, after the first few wave steps and until the last few each wavefront will have more than enough points to keep all the processors busy on any SMP of rational size. (And, hey, it gets the right answer.)

How can we take advantage of this more irregular parallelism? As was the case with the rectilinear approach we pursued up to this point, there are several possible techniques. A few will be discussed below.

8.4.8   Let "forall" Do the Work

The first approach is simply to create a serial program that iterates along the diagonals and simply use **forall** to parallelize it, like this:

```
for max_x = 2 to N-1
    forall x = 2 to max_x
        y = 2 + max_x - x ;
        v[x,y] = ( v[x-1,y] + v[x+1,y] + v[x,y-1] + v[x, y+1] ) / 4 ;
    end /* of forall x */;
end /* of for max_x */;
```

That does the average computation, but what about keeping track of **max_change**? Locking it in the inner loop is bad because of serialization, and, unlike the previous example, there's no second-level inner parallel loop to turn serial to lower the overhead.

Notice: In any execution of the **forall** loop, each row is visited by a processor exactly once. (So is each column, but we'll use rows.) Suppose we do the following: Make an array of **row_max** values, one entry for each row, and maintain each entry as the largest change in the corresponding row. Because each row is visited exactly once, the **row_max** entries don't have to be locked when we update them inside the **forall**. An additional simple loop, or even a **forall**, can compute the maximum over that array; if a **forall** is used, we have exactly the same number of calls to **acquire()** and **release()** that the old **row_max** version did, and for the same reason: We're accumulating the result over rows again.

8.4.9   Chunking and Blocking

There's something wrong with the argument at the end of the last section. Just because there are the same number of calls to **acquire()** and **release()** doesn't mean the code is as efficient. Doing something as simple as a single maximum just has to cause serialization problems, and it does. It's obviously going to be much faster to compute a number of maxima serially, locking and combining them fewer times, like this:

```
forall i = 2 to N-1 by 200
    local_max = 0 ;
  /* Accumulate 200 of the maxima */
    for j = i to max( i+199, N-1)
        local_max = max( local_max, row_max[j] ;
    end /* of forall x */;
  /* Merge local_max with the global maximum */
    acquire ( max_change_lock ) ;  /* wait for access to max_change */
    max_change = max ( max_change, local_max ) ;
    release ( max_change_lock ) ;  /* finished with max_change */
  end /* of forall i*/;
```

Now we have 200 times less serialization than we had before and have lost no speed—in fact, the program is probably faster. This is a technique called "chunking": making each parallel iteration do a sizeable chunk of work to overcome the various overheads that must be built into locking and **forall**, which, if you recall, has to lock at least the index. Worse, it may, depending on the implementation, do system calls to recruit processors.

Speaking of speed, sorry to bring it up, but there's yet another problem this version has. (Won't it ever be right? We're getting close.) It has lots of parallelism, but as we add processors it does not speed up very much. It may even start slowing down. Where that behavior starts depends on the machine being used, but it can happen.

Part of the problem is again serialization. As in the computation of **max_change** above, there's serialization within the **forall** statement. A single average is just not doing enough to offset the locking serialization needed to update the index of that loop. All right, we know how to fix that: "chunk" the loop, so each time through the **forall** we do several elements on the diagonal.

That helps. We're now getting speedup. It's pretty fair when we compare this algorithm running on N processors against itself running on one processor. But try comparing it, not against its own one-processor speed, but against the original serial algorithm running on one processor. This is the only valid measure; beware people who compare against the one-processor version of a parallel algorithm. They are cheating (possibly without knowing it), and here's an example of why that's so: Our latest version, even chunked, is, frankly, in the toilet when you make that comparison. The versions that went across rows were much better (of course, if you don't have to get the right answer…). What's going on now?

Remember caches, cache coherence, and cross-interrogation? This wavefront version has a major problem with locality of reference.

Assume the rows are stored in a way that puts successive row entries next to one another in memory. Then, the versions that went across rows had at least reused cache lines when they loaded the left and right stencil elements and possibly also when they did a store of the new average value. Access to the up and down values, however, likely caused a cache miss because somebody else was storing in those rows. We had some cache reuse, but were doing a fair amount of cache line shuffling and cross-interrogation even there.

In comparison, the diagonal wavefront version is a cache-locality disaster. Will a processor *ever* use two things in a row that are close to each other in memory? Who knows? It's completely up to the luck of the draw of index values inside the **forall** statement. Chunking helps; successive diagonal elements do reuse some off-diagonal elements. But in general, the more processors we use, the less likely it is that a needed line will be found in the processor's cache. Result: cache lines are being ripped out of processors' caches at a fierce rate. This slows things down something terrible, as was emphasized in the earlier chapter about SMPs. It also has a nasty effect on speedup, of course: When the memory system is saturated, it doesn't matter how many processors you use; they don't determine the speed of the computation, the saturated memory system does.

In that earlier chapter, it was also mentioned that programs can be reorganized to get better cache locality. Here's where we do that.

Suppose, instead of each processor computing the average for just a single point, it did so for a rectangular block instead? That still follows the requirements of Gauss-Seidel iteration as expressed in the serial program. As illustrated in Figure 8-19, when a whole rectangular block is completed, work on the blocks to the right and below can begin. The upper-left corners of each of those blocks is enabled, which is all that's needed for the serial computation in the block; once the first row is completed, the second can begin because the left block acts like a boundary condition; then the third row can be done, and so on.

Doing work a block at a time will have a very salutary effect on cache locality. Consider:

When a processor traverses the first row of a block, the up and down elements of the stencil pull parts of two array rows into its cache, and the left and right elements pull in another (or possibly two others). The processor will miss a lot when doing this first row, but the fact that it's working on successive elements helps: several elements are undoubtedly in each cache line, so misses occur only every few repetitions of the inner loop. But when the next row's started, things get really good. Two of the three row sections needed are already in cache; only the bottom row need be brought in. You can even avoid waiting for the cache miss on that third line. If the processor is sufficiently clever (many are), there will be little or no overhead involved if the program references the data before it's needed. Doing so will load the line into the cache before it's needed, overlapping that load with the time the processor is busily computing on its current cache contents. This kind of thing is what was done in the cache prefetching mentioned in "Locality of Reference and Caches" on page 118.

Furthermore, this is the only processor reading or writing those sections of those rows, so it's got the only copy of those cache lines in the system. Remember the commonly implemented cache coherence optimizations that triggers? Before, when a processor wrote the average, it had to broadcast that it was writing, probably causing other processors to purge copies from their caches and wait for a system-wide "all clear" before continuing. But when it's got the only copy, a processor doesn't have to tell anybody anything—it just goes ahead and writes, silently, without bugging or waiting for anybody else.

The net of all this is that the processor can run almost entirely out of its own cache, interacting nearly not at all with other processors, pumping along at

Figure 8-19   Blocking and Block Edges

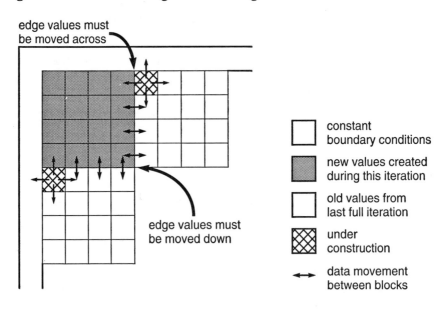

very much closer to full speed than was possible before. This is the nirvana of parallel processing—lots of work to do and little communication.

How big a cache is needed to pull this trick? Let's assume 8-byte (64 bit) data values. All we need in the cache are three rows at a time, so in a measly 8Kbytes we can fit a row segment that's 8K / 3 / 8 = approximately 300 elements long. That means with a square block, each processor is doing more than $300^2 = 90,000$ averages per block, with little overhead. You will be hard-pressed to find a system with so little cache memory that 8 Kbytes of data won't fit. If you do find one, don't buy it.

On the other end of the scale, how small you can go is limited by the cache line length. If you don't use at least one full line's worth of data from each row, you are wasting effort and inviting cross-interrogation. Very few systems use a line size larger than 256 bytes, and that size is usually in a level 2 cache. That's 32 of our 8-byte elements, yielding $32^2 = 1024$ averages per block. Is that enough to offset the cache re-loading needed when a new block is started? Quite possibly. It depends on how fast the system is at loading data from main memory into its cache; larger is better, as long as all three lines needed fit in the cache. A larger block also helps offset the synchronization overhead when a new block is started.

With the warning that larger is generally better, there is a very broad range—about 30 to 300 elements, a factor of 10—over which good efficiency can be obtained on most systems.

A square block was used in the above examples, but a square block has no particular advantage for maximizing cache reuse in a single processor. What should the aspect ratio be? Notice, as also shown in Figure 8-19, that the edge values of each block must be pulled into the processors doing the neighboring blocks. It is desirable to minimize the amount of data moving between caches; the less cross-interrogation the better. Since a square has minimum perimeter for a given area, a square block will minimize the number of array elements cross-referenced between blocks. However, this does not necessarily minimize the amount of data transferred in an SMP, because data are packed into cache lines.

Each individual value pulled into the computation of a block to the right requires a whole cache line. This happens because rows, we've assumed, have their values adjacent in memory. For that same reason, pulling a cache line into the computation of a block below one brings in several values; the exact number depends on how many data elements fit into a cache line.

Result: To minimize the amount of data transferred and the number of cross-cache interrogations, the aspect ratio of the block should be in proportion to the number of elements in a cache line. While this is obviously line-size dependent (as well as problem dependent), for our current problem making the block two or four times as wide as it is high will obtain most of the benefit. For example: four of our 8-byte data items fit into a 32-byte cache line. With a square 8x8 block, 10 cache lines must be transferred: 8 on the right, and 2 below. A 32x4 block, on the other hand, has four cache lines on each side; so a total of 8 lines must be moved instead of 10.

We're now down in the nits. Specifically dealing with a line-size dependent aspect ratio reaches the stage where cache-oriented tuning gives an increasingly smaller payoff. There is an exception: You need all the help you can get when using systems where cross-cache interrogation is particularly slow, such as in the envelope-pushing designs mentioned in "Distributed Directories" on page 150.

There is an important point to be noticed about this entire cache-related discussion: It is not optimization for a particular manufacturer's architecture. More could be done if it were; for example, the ideal block aspect ratio could be used, and the block width could be made an even multiple of the cache line size. But even without such detailed tuning, blocking within broad limits will yield very improved performance on any system with a cache. As emphasized earlier, for all practical purposes, that is all systems, period.

8.4.10   Load Balancing and a Global Queue

Our program is now rather good. It can get good real speedup compared to the original uniprocessor program, also (praise be!) gets the same answer produced by the original program, and even (Hosannas to the highest!) gets the same answer every time.

However, it still doesn't achieve "linear" speedup; it does not run N times faster when using N processors. This is partly inevitable; there is coordination activity in any parallel program that doesn't exist in the serial version, and that coordination overhead inhibits perfectly linear speedup. But even discounting that, we still aren't running quite as fast as seems reasonable.

The reason is illustrated in Figure 8-20. Suppose we have four processors. While the fourth diagonal is processed (iteration 4 of the **for x** loop), all four are in use; each is doing a different block down the diagonal. This cannot produce a speedup of exactly four, owing to inevitable variations in processing speed and the time to initiate each processor's work; but it can get very close indeed. No problem there.

Iteration 5 of that loop, when the next diagonal is processed, is a different story. All four processors chew up the first four blocks, again speeding things up nearly four times. But whoops, there's another block to be done. Whoever finished first—processor 3 in the figure—does that block. The

Figure 8-20   Another Source of Parallel Inefficiency

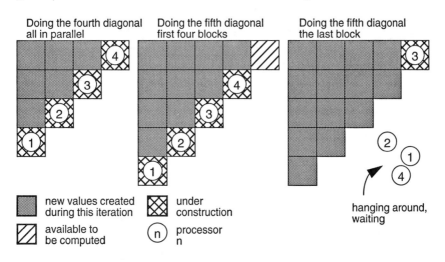

other three can do nothing but mill around the water cooler until processor 3 has finished. The result is a speedup for that diagonal of at most 2.5: The first four blocks are done in the time it takes to do one block (elapsed time = 1), the last block takes the time it takes to do one block (elapsed time = 1), for a total time of 2. In that time we did the work the serial algorithm would have done in 5 time units, one per block. So the speedup is 5/2, or 2.5.

This is a form of the **load-balancing** problem. If the amount of work each processor does is not the same as the amount every other processor does, you can't reach full speedup because part of the time some of the processors are idle; the "load" on each processor is not "balanced." Load-balancing problems are much more common where problems are decomposed into different functions, rather than splitting one function across processors as we are doing here. It is usually nearly impossible to evenly balance the processing requirements of different functions.

Load balancing gets better as the diagonals get longer—in other words, when there are more blocks available to do in parallel. For example, using four processors, a 31-block diagonal would do $4 \times 7 = 28$ of the blocks fully in parallel, in seven stages; and then it will do the last three at once. This is a (maximum) speedup of about 3.9, which is not bad at all. This implies that more blocks are good, so dividing the matrix up into more, smaller blocks is good because you get better load balancing. This characterization is general: with many, small amounts of work to do—or, in the jargon, fine **granularity** of parallelism—you can get good load balancing.

But wait a minute. We just got through finding out that small blocks are bad. They increase serialization overhead and lose cache efficiency. There is a problem here.

In most cases there is no perfect solution to this problem. You just have to find a hunk of work that is big enough to overcome serialization and cache effects, yet small enough not to suffer dramatically from load-balancing problems. Such intermediate sizes quite often exist. When they don't, the problem is simply not efficiently parallelizeable, at least not in the form being investigated; often other formulations will work.

In this specific case, however, there's a way around the problem. It's different enough from our prior approaches that it might be called another formulation.

Take a look at Figure 8-21, which looks more closely at the last stage of doing the fifth diagonal. When the first four blocks of that diagonal are done, there are other blocks that can be computed without violating any of the requirements, since the blocks above and to the left of them are complete. That means there's no intrinsic reason why those three underutilized processors have to just hang around waiting—there are other blocks available to be done. The difficulty is that the blocks to be done are in the next diagonal, and the way we've written the program, nothing on a diagonal can be started until the prior diagonal is completely finished: The **forall** statement, the source of the parallelism, operates only on one diagonal at a time.

Figure 8-21   Why Are Those Processors Waiting?

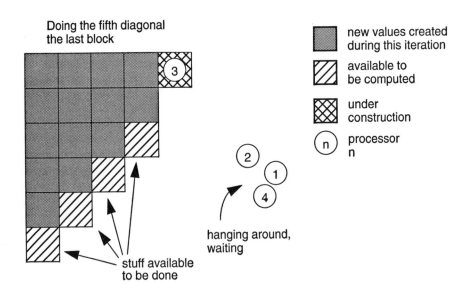

In Search of Clusters ✳

There is no straightforward way that I know of to fix this within the bounds of a **forall** statement. But there is a way to fix it. It involves what is probably the most quintessentially shared-memory approach to parallelism: Keeping in memory a shared, global queue containing items of work to be done. Each of the processors repeatedly goes to the queue, pulls off an item of work to be done, performs it, and goes back to the queue. When the queue is empty, we're finished. What keeps the queue replenished is that putting something on the queue is often part of "doing the work" taken off the queue.

What we want to do in our case is put a block on the queue whenever the blocks above and to its left have been done, no matter what diagonal it's on. Figure 8-22 shows the control needed to perform this. Much detail has been left out, most notably initializing the **block** data structures and resetting their **left_done** and **top_done** flags before each main iteration. Locks on the block data structures are required because a race in setting the flags might otherwise result in a block being enqueued twice. The queue itself can be an ordinary circular queue, with a lock protecting it. (There exist techniques for enqueueing and dequeueing items from a global queue with little or no serialization; see [AG94]. They are seldom used in practice for a number of reasons, including innate complexity and the number of times they require processor serialization.)

8.4.11   Concerning Global Queues

To say that global queues are very widely used is to be guilty of vast understatement. They are the basic mechanism by which work is distributed among the processors in every SMP operating system: When a job is eligible for execution, it is placed on the queue; some processor eventually pulls it off and executes it. It is also used in the same manner in many database systems, again on chunks of work—usually partial transactions. Other global queues are used to hold jobs that are inactive for some reason—waiting for I/O, waiting for a lock, whatever; when the I/O completes or the lock is acquired, the job is moved to another queue where it will get picked up for continued execution.

The technique is so pervasive that it would not be much of an exaggeration to say that the global queue is *the* SMP programming model. It isn't stretching the point too far to claim that every use of **forall** in the previous examples was effectively a global queue: A bunch of work in shared memory was identified, and all the processors just had at it from the pile.

Global queues are easily used in SMPs and without a doubt are marvellous for automatically balancing the load among processors. This stands in sharp contrast to message-passing systems, which, as we'll see, have nowhere particularly good to put a global queue, accessible by all.

However, as the number of processors grows, global queues break down in the sense that they are a potential source of inefficiency. This is true in two ways. First and fairly obviously, they can induce serialization delays; if the units of work aren't large enough, the processors can spend much of their time waiting on the global queue's lock, limiting the utility of additional processors, as indicated in Figure 8-9 on page 205. Second, they can really

Figure 8-22   Processing a Global Queue

```
/* Prime the while loop below by getting an initial block from the queue */
block = get_from_queue() ;

while (block != NULL)            /* quit when queue is empty */

    perform(block) ;             /* stuff block full of averages */

    /* mark the block to right, and put it on the queue if it's ready */
    acquire ( block.right->block.block_lock ) ;
    block.right->left_done = TRUE;
    if block.right->top_done then put_on_queue ( block.right ) ;
    release ( block.right->block.block_lock ) ;

    /* mark the block below, and put on the queue if it's ready */
    acquire ( block.below->block_lock ) ;
    block.below->top_done = TRUE;
    if block.below->left_done then put_on_queue ( block.below ) ;
    release ( block.below->block_lock ) ;

    /* get the next block to do, if any */
    block = get_from_queue() ;
end /* of while loop */;
```

```
PROCECURES, ETC.:

get_from_queue() returns a pointer to a block of work currently on the queue, or
        null if the queue is empty.

put_on_queue (block_ptr) puts the block of work that is its argument on the
queue.

perform(block_ptr) does an averaging operation on the block that is its argument,
        including updating the global max_change variable.

Each block is a data structure containing:
        indices and spans identifying the section of the array to be averaged.
        left_done and top_done, two booleans that are true if the blocks to the left
              and above this one have been completed.
        right and below, pointers to the blocks to the right and below this one. (Blocks
              at the edges point to a null block that put_on_queue() ignores.)
```

hurt cache locality. That requires a bit more explanation; it can occur for two more reasons.

In the first place, consider the queue itself: control pointers, data, and lock. It is seldom if ever accessed by the same processor twice in a row. As a result, the cache lines holding the queue are real road warriors, forever bouncing among the caches. But the amount of data involved is usually small, and therefore this is not very likely to be a problem—except, again, for systems with unusually large cache cross-interrogation times that effectively bend the SMP model.

The second reason is more likely to cause trouble. When a processor puts a unit of work on a global queue, it has essentially randomized the location where the work will be done next. Any of the processors could pick it up. This is fine if, having picked up a piece of work, a processor settles down and grinds on it for a while. We've been careful to use a large block of computation in our problem; can everybody do that? Hardly. Our example is a straightforward compute-bound process, without significant I/O. Database transactions, for example, often perform tiny squirts of work amid a thicket of I/O requests before they settle down to work, if they ever do. On such work, the randomization among processors done by a global queue eliminates nearly all chance of getting a head of steam up inside a cache; the application data is continually whipped about the caches; this was discussed as a reason why shared caches are often, counterintuitively, a good idea for commercial workloads ("Commercial Processing: Cross-Interrogation and Shared Caches" on page 156). Even in our own problem, if an operating system time-slices one of our nice big blocks, all that cached data will probably get cross-interrogated over to somewhere else.

Such difficulties, together with "straightforward" battles with serialization or Amdahl's law, have traditionally limited SMP systems to modest numbers of processors. At four or six processors (eight stretches it) many of the cache effects mentioned can simply be ignored. Beyond that, programmers must acknowledge that not all memory is created equal—recently used stuff is "more equal" than the rest—and include in their scheduling schemes something called **processor affinity:** making it more likely that an interrupted chunk of work is picked up by the processor that worked on it last. Processor affinity can be obtained by using multiple queues, one per processor, with each processor checking its own queue first before looking elsewhere for work. This works, but makes it more difficult to get the properties that arose easily with a global queue: load balancing, fairness, priority of execution, allocations, and so on. As was the case with the scaling of SMP hardware, there is no intrinsic reason this cannot be done—it's just expensive, and difficult.

8.4.12   *Not the End, Again*

At this point we have just about beaten this problem into submission for SMPs. That is not to say that there isn't more we could do.

For example, notice that there's still some loss of parallelism at the start and end of each iteration. At those points, there just aren't enough blocks to be processed—ultimately, just the single ones in the corners. This could be attacked, too, by overlapping sequential iterations: Start a new iteration, in the upper left, while the current iteration in the lower right is finishing up. Trying to do that would make it a challenge to keep **max_change** under control; and we'd have to convince ourselves that extra fractional iteration is all right to include in the answer or do something else about it. This technique could be extended to N simultaneous iterations, a different one running simultaneously on each diagonal.

But enough already. Let's move on.

8.5   Message-Passing

When we started doing our problem using shared memory, we began with the flow of control in the application and asked what was being done often enough to merit parallelizing. The location of the data wasn't an issue; it was just right there, in the shared memory.

Not so with message-passing. In fact, the key element of this model is not that messages are passed; it is the fact that messages *must* be passed because the data isn't in one place, but rather distributed among multiple, separate machines, each with their own private storage. Nonlocal data cannot be accessed without the active participation of another processor. Exactly how it is distributed is the primary issue. Many years ago, when distributed processing was in its infancy and the Internet (then ARPANET) was just getting off the ground, someone commented to me "Distributed processing, fooey. Tell me where the data is, and I'll tell you where the processing *must be.*"[7] That was a very true statement and captures much of what message-based programming is really all about.

Our journey through message-passing will be much briefer than the one through shared memory (both you and I are sighing with relief). For one thing, issues of different kinds of relaxation are already covered; they're obviously the same. More importantly for this book, many of the issues that

---

7. I wish I could remember who, but I can't. I was in graduate school at the time—it was a *long* time ago—so the quote was probably, more accurately, "Distributed processing, *foo.*"

In Search of Clusters   ✳

arose in the shared-memory context are general issues of overt parallelism, and there is no point to covering them a second time. Some of those parallelism issues have different immediate causes, but they come down to the same thing. Races, for example, can occur when an indeterminate order of message arrival changes the results of the computation; deadlocks typically involve a processor waiting to receive a message that never arrives; serialization is still serialization, although waiting on one processor now becomes really obvious, not a matter of analyzing lock waiting times. Locks, on the other hand, don't exist as such. And there's no such thing as a global queue; load balancing is explicit, a function of how the data is distributed, except for truly boulder-sized granularity of parallelism. The reason is that it takes much longer to transmit the data required from node to node: tens or hundreds of megabits per second are typical communication speeds, rather than gigabytes per second within SMPs.

One thing that explicitly will not be discussed is the interconnection topology—which machines are directly connected to which, with what message routing. This used to be the favorite topic of the parallel processing genre, an obsession Gordon Bell has called "topomania" [Bel92a]. He hopes we're all over that, and I agree wholeheartedly. It will be assumed that a message can be squirted to any other processor; if the interconnect system can't do that, it's time to buy another. (Or, time to put an appropriate software wrapper around the interconnect, a wrapper that makes that interconnect look functionally adequate.) For relatively few machines in clusters, connected by standard interconnection mechanisms, universal connectivity is in any event the correct assumption.

One final item, concerning notation: Since each computing entity in a message-passing system is more than a processor (it at least has memory and something to send messages, too), it's rather silly to call it a "processor." We'll call it a "node," which is more or less standard terminology.

8.5.1   Jacobi/Seidel/Chaotic "Mixed" Relaxation

Possibly the most straightforward data distribution that can be used is illustrated in Figure 8-23. We've simply taken the array, split it into equal-size rectangular blocks, and put a block in each processor. The overall plan of execution is then:

1. Every node exchanges "edge values" with its four neighbors: above, below, left, and right; these are the values at the periphery of the array blocks owned by each.

2. Using the received edge values as if they were boundary conditions, each node does a normal serial (Gauss-Seidel) averaging calculation on its own data.

Figure 8-23   Message-Passing, Mixed Iteration Strategy

Node 1	Node 2	Node 3	Node 4
Node 5	Node 6	Node 7	Node 8
Node 9	Node 10	Node 11	Node 12
Node 13	Node 14	Node 15	Node 16

Each node

1. Exchanges edge values with its neighbors:

2. Averages its portion of the array, using exchanged values as boundaries

3. Helps compute global max_change; if it's good_enough, everyone quits.

3. If everybody's **max_change** is **good_enough**, quit; otherwise, do it all again.

This leads to a style of iteration that mixes Gauss-Jacobi with Gauss-Seidel and, because it's a mixture, comes under the "chaotic" rubric. Recall: Jacobi bases new averages entirely on old values, Seidel uses a very specific mixture, and chaotic is, well, chaotic. The iteration style has elements of Seidel because each machine uses Seidel internally, but it treats the data from neighboring machines as if it were constant, that is, uses the old values. That's like Jacobi. This mixture is certainly no worse than the chaos we started out with in the shared-memory case; unlike that case, it is in fact already eminently usable.

Step 2 is obviously straightforward; it's the same thing the serial program did and won't be discussed further. While discussing the other steps, we'll refer to each node's block of the array as if it were the entire array **v[]**, with NxN elements.

To exchange edge values, we must get some identifier for the nodes to the right, left, and so on, of the one we're on. Many message-based programming packages provide this directly, as part of a facility laying out nodes in any-dimensional Cartesian grids (examples: [Hem91, Kol91, Mes94, Wal93]). So, for that identification that we'll just use an opaque procedure. The actual sending we'll do as four data-shifting operations: to the right, left, up, and down. The start of the code, shifting values left, might look something like this:

```
get_neighbors( &left, &right, &above, &below ) ; /* Set  node ids*/
send( right, v[N-1,*] ) ;    /* Send rightmost column computed here */
receive ( v[1,*] ) ;         /* Receive left's rightmost column into my boundary */
```

Time to worry about deadlocks (deadly embraces) again.

The reason we worry is that we haven't yet specified exactly how **send(to_who, message)** works. In particular, when is it finished? Does it simply pick up the message, ship it out in the direction of **right**, and, having consigned the bits to the howling ether, wash its hands, say "all done," and return? Or does it wait until it gets some word from Mr. **right**, saying the message was successfully **receive()**d on the other side? The former is called **nonblocking** message-passing, the latter **blocking**. Many message-passing systems offer both.

Blocking communication is easier to use because if something goes wrong, it either gets fixed then, invisibly, inside the **send()**, or you find out right there and can tell which procedure call caused the problem. Nonblocking can be faster, but if there's an error in transmission, you'll find out about it in some other piece of code, long after the **send()** has finished. The error needn't be something having to do with hardware, by the way; it could be an application-induced deadlock (deadly embrace).

Suppose the **send(right,...)** above is blocking. Then, everybody is inside **send()**, waiting for the **receive()** that will complete the blocking **send()**. But since everybody's in **send()**, nobody can reach a **receive()** and the application waits forever. We could deal with this by using nonblocking communication, but there are two ways around it that stay synchronous.

> ➤ Checkerboard it. Label even/odd nodes red and black. All the reds send while the blacks receive, then all the blacks send while the reds receive, like this:
>
> ```
> get_neighbors( &left, &right, &above, &below ) ;  /*Set node ids */
> if I_am_odd() then
>     send( right, v[N-1,*] ) ;   /* Send to right*/
>     receive ( v[1,*] ) ;        /* Receive from left; matches send() below*/
> else /* I must be even */
>     receive ( v[1,*] ) ;        /* Receive from left; matches send() above*/
>     send( right, v[N-1,*] ) ;   /* Send to right*/
> ```

> ➤ Use a combined primitive. This is not exactly an unusual thing we're doing here, so several packages that support message-passing provide it as a primitive operation. For example, the newly proposed standard for message-passing, MPI [Wal93], contains a

sendrecv() procedure. This procedure incorporates both a send and a receive, guarantees a lack of deadlock, and might even be implemented to use some special hardware by the system vendors. That would turn this fragment of our program into something like[8] the following:

```
get_neighbors( &left, &right, &above, &below ) ;
sendrecv( right, v[N-1,*],/* Send to right */
          left, v[1,*] ) ;  /* Receive from left */
```

We actually don't run into any deadlock problems here, because we don't have periodic boundary conditions. Therefore, we don't shift data off the right and into the far left, and thus avoid creating the cycle that's needed for a deadly embrace. For our case, the simplistic version of the code would look like this instead:

```
get_neighbors( &left, &right, &above, &below ) ; /* Set left, right, ... node ids*/

if I_am_not_rightmost() then send ( right, v[N-1,*] ) ; /* Send to right*/
if I_am_not_leftmost() then receive ( v[1,*] ) ; /* Receive from left */
```

This is deadlock-free, but at a price: serialization. Everybody does a **send()** except the rightmost, which does a **receive()**; that lets the next-to-rightmost's **send()** complete, so it does a **receive()**; that lets the next one loose, and so on. The operation ripples from right to left, serially, so if the logical grid of nodes is W wide, it takes W steps. The checkerboard method takes two steps, no matter how big W is. This might not matter much in smallish clusters, where W might not be much bigger than two.

All right, we've now successfully exchanged our edge values; shifting data in the other directions, left, up, and down, is obviously similar to the right-shift case. Next the program does an iteration of averaging, in the course of which each node computes its local **max_change**. How do we form the global maximum and let everybody know whether it's time to stop?

Since we're still not doing anything very uncommon, the simplest way is to exploit what is now a common facility of many programming packages, called collective communication. These are group communication facilities that every node is expected to join into.[9] A very common one is reduction, as

---

8. This is not the exact MPI syntax. There are several other arguments to all the MPI communication primitives, all well motivated, which make things more complicated than appropriate here.

9. Well, not necessarily every node. It's common to provide some form of "node group" and have every node in the group participate. This is one of the otherwise-irrelevant things alluded to in a prior footnote, where I said I was leaving out some things in MPI.

in **reduce(in_v, out_v, op, root)**. Reduction takes an input value, **in_v**, from each node and a function **op**, and does **op(in_v₁,in_v₂)**; then **reduce()** takes that result and combines it with **in_v₃**: **op(prior_result,in_v₃)**; then combines that with **in_v₄**, and so on for all the nodes. It deposits the ultimately combined ("reduced") result of this in the variable **out_v**, but only at the node named **root**. With an **op** of **max()**, which is usually provided as a primitive, this is the basis for exactly what we want:

> reduce(max_change, global_max_change, MAX, 1) ; /* find global max */
>
> broadcast(global_max_change, 1) ; /* tell everybody what it is */
>
> if global_max_change < good_enough then quit; /* stop if it's good_enough */

Putting the above fragment after the averaging loop will compute the maximum, putting it in node 1. Then, use of another common collective communication procedure, **broadcast()**, tells everyone what that global maximum was. Finally, everybody looks at the maximum and decides whether it's time to quit or time for another iteration.

These are very common primitives. If they're not available, however, a typical technique is to use a binary tree to do the reduction and the same tree to do the broadcast. (This is the source of the term "root" used above.) The use of such a tree for reduction is illustrated in Figure 8-24. It is one of those things that has terrifically simple implementation that depends in detail on the properties of binary numbers. A hint if you try programming it yourself, since I'm not going to do it here: Multiply a loop index by 2 every time around the loop.

Figure 8-24   A Binary Tree for Reduction (and Broadcast)

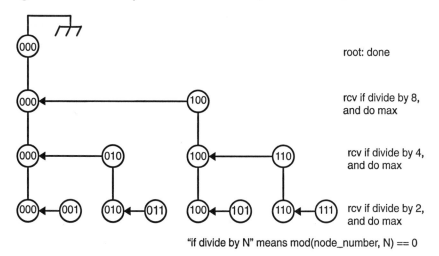

"if divide by N" means mod(node_number, N) == 0

8.5.2 Implicit Synchronization and Alternation Schemes

When we did the SMP implementation, we were driven to alternation schemes because of a lack of consistency: The program gave a different answer every time it was run on the same input data. That problem doesn't arise here, because a node cannot be given data surreptitiously. Nobody's invisibly messing with somebody else's cache; each receipt of data is an active act, requiring execution of a **receive()** operation. This implicitly synchronizes all the nodes, so none can go running off doing something without coordination. As a result, our basic, original program will always give the same answer when it is given the same input data.

So, we don't have the same motivation for using alternation schemes that existed in the shared-memory case. However, they might still be desirable because their properties are well known, unlike the properties of the rather *ad hoc* "mixed" iteration used. Better the devil you know, even if it is known to be a devil.

The use of alternation schemes poses no big challenge in the framework of the base program. To do whole-array alternation, for example, the principal thing that must be done is to change the individual node-averaging loops to read from one array and write into another. Then, when edge values are exchanged, the values from neighbors are placed in the array that will be "old" in the next iteration. Nothing otherwise changes.

The red/black methods are handled similarly but the amount of data sent between nodes is halved on each interchange: Only newly computed values need be sent, and on each half-iteration only half the edge values are changed. The checkerboard version is somewhat easier to do, because equal quantities of data are then exchanged on all four sides. The "striped" version may have no new data to send vertically on alternate half-iterations.

Of course, throughout all this we are still not getting the same answers as the original serial program. A way must be found to do true Gauss-Seidel iteration.

8.5.3 Wavefronts and Multiple Waves

Once again, we'll approach this by using a wavefront (or hyperplane) method, and will reuse the data distribution pattern already presented. Figure 8-25 shows the execution pattern. Whenever a node completes its portion, it sends updated edge data to the nodes below and on its right; when a node receives both messages, it starts.

The global **max_change** calculation can be piggybacked on the main data communication: Each node sends a **max_change** with each slab of edge data and uses the larger of the two received as its initial value, rather than 0, when computing its own local **max_change**. Then the **max_change** of the lower-right node is the global **max_change**, which can be broadcast to let everyone figure out whether to stop.

This is actually simpler than the original mixed-iteration program. High-level code for it appears in Figure 8-26 and is explained below.

The only node through both **receive()** statements at the start is the one in the upper left; it does an iteration, then sends data and **max_change** to the nodes to its right and left. Then it reaches the **barrier()**. This is another collective communication routine, possibly the most basic. It's a kind of inverse lock, whose function is to synchronize everyone: Nobody exits the **barrier()** procedure until everybody has entered it; then everybody exits it at the same time. When the top left node reaches the **barrier()**, it just stops for a while.

When the top left node executed its **send()** statements, it allowed the nodes below and to its right to complete their **receive()** statements. Both of them do work, send data down and to their right, and wait at the **barrier()** along with the top left node.

Figure 8-25   First Try at Message-Passing the Wavefront

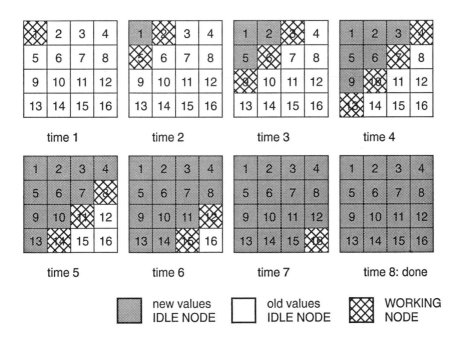

This keeps going on until the last node, with more and more nodes piling up at the barrier, until the one in the bottom right hits it. Now everybody's signed in, so they all continue. The universal **max_change** value from the lower right is then broadcast. Everybody checks to see if it is **good_enough** and, if so, quits. Otherwise the whole process starts again.

The message-based commencement of computation used here is reminiscent of the load-balancing technique used in the SMP version. Unfortunately, in this case it results in a truly horrific load-balancing problem. While Figure 8-25 looks at first glance just like the SMP case, look again at the legend. In SMP execution, there were a total of four processors; each processor was recycled—used on multiple diagonals. Here, we have 16 nodes, and no node is ever used more than once. Only the nodes marked as "working" are active—the others are idle. At most 4 out of 16 nodes are active simultaneously. This could be called a serialization problem, rather than a load-balancing problem; either way, it's bad.

One way around this is to pursue the suggestion at the very end of the SMP section: Run multiple wavefronts simultaneously. This promised to be a coordination nightmare with shared memory; in this context, it's very natural. As soon as a node finishes an iteration and ships off its edge values, it

Figure 8-26   First-Try Message-Passing Wavefront Program

```
get_node_ids( &right, &below, &lower_right_node ) ; /* Find out who's who. */
do forever;
    m_c1 = m_c2 = 0;              /* Make sure they are initialized if I'm top left. */
    if I_am_not_top_row() then
        receive ( v[*,1], m_c1 ) ;   /* Get top boundary & max_change from above */
    if I_am_not_left_column() then
        receive ( v[1,*], m_c2 ) ;   /* Get left boundary & max_change from left */
    max_change = max( m_c1, m_c2 ) ; /* Initial value for my max_change */
    /* Run an iteration of the averages, returning new max_change value. */
    max_change = do_useful_work ( max_change ) ;
    send ( below, v[*,N-1], max_change ) ;/* Give new bottom values to node below */
    send ( right, v[N-1,*], max_change ) ;  /* Give new right values to node at right */
    /* Wait for everybody to finish, then get global_max_change
        (or send it, if I happen to be lower_right_node). */
    barrier() ;
    broadcast ( max_change, global_max_change, lower_right_node ) ;
    if global_max_change < good_enough then leave do_forever;
end /* of do forever */;
```

simply immediately starts on the next one. The global **max_change** calculation flowing through the processors is completely unchanged.

In fact, the program for multiwave wavefront is exactly the same as the one in Figure 8-26, with one exception: While data first passes through the array—until the lower-right node has run for the first time—everybody skips the **barrier()**, **broadcast()**, and termination check and instead returns to the head of the loop unconditionally. For example, while the second two nodes are running for the first time, the upper left one doesn't wait. It computes its second iteration and is ready to send new values at (approximately) the same time the second two are ready to receive them again.

This has the effect of "priming the pump" of the logical array of nodes. After the lower right node has run the first time, and every time it runs following that, there is a new valid global **max_change** to be distributed and checked. So from that point on, everybody waits at the **barrier()** for a much shorter time, gets and checks the global **max_change**, and continues or not.

So, simultaneously running multiple waves is not such a big deal in message-passing and uses all the processors continuously. It doesn't give exactly the same answer as the original; when everything stops, the values distributed in the array are from a mixture of different iterations, not all from one iteration. But it does practice Gauss-Seidel relaxation and therefore is mathematically acceptable.

8.5.4   Wavefronts in Strips

There is a way, and in fact there are probably many ways, to obtain better load balancing without resorting to multiple simultaneous wavefronts. It involves using a different way to distribute the data among the nodes— which should come as no surprise; that is, as has been emphasized, what message-passing programming is really all about. Instead of dividing the array up into blocks like before, let's divide it up into horizontal strips, with one strip per processor. We're also going to divide each strip into blocks; this is illustrated in Figure 8-27 for the case of dividing the array among four processors, with eight blocks in each strip.

Processing now proceeds from left to right across each strip, by blocks. Node 1 does the block labelled 1 in the figure. As soon as that block's done, node 1 sends the bottom-edge values from that block to node 2. Then both can start doing the blocks labelled 2. When done, they both send their newly computed block edge data down; this gets node 3 into the act. Once node 4 gets into the act, all four nodes crank away until block 8 is done; then one by one they shut down. When block 11 is finished, **max_change** (which has been

Figure 8-27   Another Data Distribution

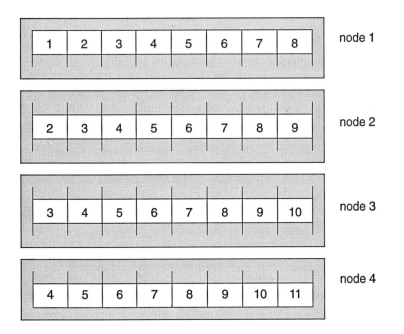

piggybacked on other data transmissions) for the whole array has been computed; it's broadcast, tested, and another iteration starts, or we're done.

Compared to the multiple wavefront version, this is a little disappointing in its load balancing; only some nodes are used at the beginning and end of each iteration. However, this version, without multiple wavefronts, is nearly as good as the SMP solution before we resorted to a global queue; its use of nodes looks as efficient as that version's use of processors.

But, at least for small problems that's an illusion. We haven't yet discussed the overheads involved yet and the resultant size of the blocks needed.

8.5.5   *Communication Overhead In Message-Passing*

In an SMP, all we need be concerned about regarding the size of the blocks is cache utilization. By making the blocks as small as feasible without hurting caching, we can split the array into many small blocks and obtain good load balancing.

In message-passing, cache utilization on each node is still important; doing less than the most efficient job of using a node amounts to parallelizing an inferior algorithm. For that reason, it is wise to use "cache blocking" in the computation used within the nodes. However, the blocks shown in Figure 8-27 (for example) must be very significantly larger than the blocks required for cache efficiency. The reason is the speed of communication between nodes, compared to communication between processors in an SMP. This has two aspects: bandwidth, the amount of data per second send; and latency, the time before the first bit of data is received.

On widely deployed, standard, nonproprietary media such as Ethernet, peak bandwidth is 10 Mbits/second. The bus or other facilities within an SMP typically operate in the range of high hundreds of Mbytes/second. Taking 500 Mbytes/second as typical (though low), the speed ratio is a factor of 400. That is bad. But as pointed out in Chapter 3, newer communications standards will raise that bandwidth to the point where it can, in some circumstances, even exceed the interprocessor system bus bandwidth of SMPs between the same number of processors. So, bandwidth is not, or at least will not be, a problem.

Latency is another matter altogether.

Communication between nodes, especially over standard, nonproprietary media using standard protocols, has fixed overheads that are currently on the order of milliseconds. For PVM, a popular message-passing package using the standard TCP/IP protocol, this has been measured at 1.2 milliseconds between 40–50 MIPS workstations when no data is sent (this was independent of the communication medium, Ethernet or FDDI) [SGDM94]. Similar latencies are reported for intermachine communication within distributed operating systems, such as Amoeba and Sprite [DOKT91], and in systems using special, non-IP protocols over ATM [HM], so this is not a fluke.

An SMP sending a cache line by cross-interrogation between processors can take, on a very bad day, 20 cycles—and at 10 nanoseconds/cycle, this is becomes 200 nanoseconds, a *factor of 2400* different from 1.2 milliseconds. This is Extremely Bad.

What is worse, it is software *overhead*, not hardware latency: The nodes' processors must actively compute for around a millisecond to figure out what must be done and move the data to where it must be for the I/O device to pick it up. This has to be done independently of communication time used to actually send something; bandwidth doesn't help. Since it's processor time expended, that time is intrinsically not available to do the "real" work on the problem.

All this means that to achieve 90% efficiency the nodes have to compute for 9 milliseconds before sending a single message. That's what our second version requires per block. Suppose we're running on systems able to do 50

MFLOPS average on our problem (reasonable, but perhaps a little slow). Since each run through a block with N values on a side requires $5N^2$ floating-point operations, we need a block that measures 950 elements on a side to get 90% efficiency. That compares with the range of 30 to 300 for good cache efficiency in an SMP; a factor of 3 to 30 larger.

Unfortunately, you seldom get away with just one message. The first version of our program had two messages (two sends, each matched with two receives), a barrier, and a broadcast for each block of "real" computation done in the node.[10] The latter internally involve multiple messages; the number depends on the number of nodes. Again for PVM [SGDM94], with eight nodes it's 15 milliseconds for a minimal-data broadcast and about 30 milliseconds for a barrier. Now, 90% efficiency requires 400 milliseconds of work, or nearly 6800 elements on a side—over 48 million elements. This is a factor of 20 to 200 worse than an SMP. It obviously is going to require use only on very big matrices. Furthermore, it doesn't change even if multiple wavefronts are used at the same time; doing that doesn't alter the efficiency. What this means is that our original versions are useless except on problems with enormous amounts of data.

This whole discussion has to do with what is called, in the parallel computing jargon, **grain size**: a computation with a large grain size does a lot between synchronization points, and one with a small grain size does a little. The overhead involved in sending messages forces a large grain size on message-passing systems that use standard communications channels and protocols. This means they're no good for small problems: a block size of 6800, with our 8x8 blocking, means a matrix with 54,000 values on each side!

Combining this with megabit rates of currently deployed LANs, one can readily wonder how anything gets done on LAN-connected clusters. It obviously depends on what's being done, and how. Batch systems, for example, effectively do have enormous granularity; the same is true of the multi-job parallel class mentioned in Chapter 7. Grand Challenge problems, under PVM, can attain 80–90% efficiency [SGDM94]. Grand Challenge problems are *big*, and aptly named. So even this is not insuperable under various circumstances—some occurring in widespread everyday use (batch and multi-job parallel), and others when you're taking the afternoon off to do the equivalent of build a Renaissance Cathedral or a Great Pyramid.

Will this overhead get better? Well, whether it *will* or not in general applications, it has been demonstrated that it definitely *can* get better. Systems using proprietary interconnection hardware and nonstandard protocols can

---

10. The second version also requires a barrier and a broadcast, but only one for every complete iteration through the array, after computing all blocks.

get message latency down to the few microsecond range (the IBM SP2) or lower (Cray T3D), and they may move the overhead computation out to a separate processor, so it can be overlapped with problem computation (the Intel Paragon). Those are highly massive parallel systems using message-passing; if they're to use thousands of processors, they had better keep the grain size down or they'll be useful only for problems so large that words, to say nothing of reality, fail to encompass them.

So it's possible. Will it happen? One would hope that the advent of the newer, faster communications media would make such system overhead stand out like the most gargantuan of sore thumbs, so much so that something would have to be done about it. With 1 millisecond latency, it will be hard to tell the difference between 10-megabit Ethernet and 1-Gbit ATM or FCS when transferring data using the now-common block size of 4Kbytes— no matter how big the total data transferred is. I wonder, however, whether that problem will be "fixed" only for special-purpose data transfer such as multimedia.

As long as communication is handled through the system structures conceived for I/O, there will be a problem; those were designed with, at best, disk latencies in mind—20–30 milliseconds. So, for example, they don't mind synchronizing by using a hardware interrupt on the processor, which in a modern pipelined superscalar system is about as reasonable as letting someone know you're in a room by hitting them on the head with a 2x4 block of wood.

8.6   Both at Once

At this point we'll leave our problem, which we've certainly twisted and pummeled out of all recognition at this point.

But before going, consider a final possibility: A collection of SMPs connected by message-passing—a cluster of SMPs. This seems like it's just squaring the technical complexity and adding the social difficulty that experts on SMPs and experts in message-passing are seldom on speaking terms with each other (this will be discussed shortly).

Consider, however, that from past work one might already have (or be able to get) an already parallelized, SMP version of a program. Now recall that in message-passing versions all had a section labelled, in effect, "do the node's work here." It is not unreasonable to believe that "the node's work" could be done using an SMP within the node. A message-passing "wrapper" surrounding that then allows the use of multiple SMPs together, in a cluster. This is actually the situation with many important commercial subsystems, as will be discussed in the next chapter.

On the other hand, if one is starting from scratch, the effort to make either version work will militate against putting large quantities of work into the other. Then, it is notable that the message-passing code can be made to work within an SMP; a block of shared memory, appropriately carved up into queues, can take the place of intermachine wires. On the other hand, the shared-memory code will be difficult if not impossible—probably a significant rewrite, at least—to run in a message-passing environment. But the message-passing version won't use the shared-memory system at its full potential...

I draw no final conclusion from this. A major point of this chapter, which should be clear by now, is that shared-memory and message-passing programming are just plain different. There are no magic wands that turn one into the other. That is part of what different programming models are all about.

8.7   SIMD and All That

Speaking of different programming models, shared memory and message-passing are certainly not the only ones. This was pointed out at the start of this chapter, where a summary of some of the others was promised. Here it is. This section provides what is in effect a dictionary of programming models. Since several are best known as elements of an (always limited) taxonomy, where appropriate the taxonomy will also be briefly described.

8.7.1   SIMD, MIMD, and SPMD

Unquestionably the most famous taxonomy of computational or programming models was published in 1972 by Michael Flynn [Fly72], who picked two characteristics of computers and tried all four of the possible combinations. Two stuck in everybody's mind, but the other two are still there. Here are the four.

> **SISD: Single Instruction, Single Data.** This is a conventional, single-processor Von Neumann-style computer. There is one instruction stream ("single instruction") and one data stream ("single data"). This term is almost never used; it didn't stick.

> **MIMD: Multiple Instruction, Multiple Data.** This is a broad class of machines that includes all the types that are the subject of this book. There are multiple processors independently executing instruction streams ("multiple instruction") and each has its own, separate stream of data ("multiple data"). SMPs and clusters are members of this class, as are many other types. This is one of the

two terms that stuck; it is very frequently used. For example, the proposed MPI message-passing standard is described as a way to program "MIMD distributed memory concurrent computers."

➤ **SIMD: Single Instruction, Multiple Data.** This is a class of machines that rises and falls in fashion; most recently it's out, perhaps permanently. In this class, there is a master controller (executing the "single instruction" stream) that figuratively stands in the middle of a large roomful of slaves and shouts ADD! Everybody adds, each adding a different pair of data values ("multiple data"). If one does matrix arithmetic for a living, this type of organization sounds reasonably appealing. ILLIAC IV was of this type. It was a rectangular array of arithmetic units, each with local storage, presided over by a central controller. Early offerings of the Thinking Machines Corporation were of this type, although their last offering abandoned it for the flexibility of MIMD. Vector facilities, typified by the traditional Cray offerings, are effectively more flexible but less parallel variants of SIMD; they perform operations between whole columns of numbers with a single instruction. The inflexibility of having every computing element always do the same thing makes this organization much harder to bend to general use than MIMD, although special-purpose systems often use it. This is particularly true in areas like image processing and signal processing. It's a great way to put a large amount of arithmetic processing in a small box, but it cannot readily use the power of standard microprocessors. This term also stuck; it's commonly used.

➤ **MISD: Multiple Instruction, Single Data.** It's a little hard to imagine how to do multiple things simultaneously to a single data item, so even Flynn was hard-pressed to give a convincing example of this category. Pipelined systems through which data flows may qualify. This term, representing a vacuous set, didn't stick and is never used.

More than a decade after Flynn's publication, I coined a related term as a conscious extension of Flynn's taxonomy: **SPMD,** for **Single Program, Multiple Data.** The intent was to concoct a term that described the way in which virtually all multiple-processor operating system code, and virtually all application code, was in practice being written: There is one program, and every processor executes it. The processors may take different paths through the program because they evaluate conditional statements (including locks) differently, but everybody's executing the same program. Both SMPs and message-passing systems typically use SPMD; every program in this chapter is SPMD, and every subsystem discussed in the next chapter is SPMD.

The term is now fairly widely used, usually without attribution; its first publication was [DGNP88].

The **SPPS (Serial Program, Parallel (Sub-) System)** term introduced in this book is another obvious spinoff from Flynn's taxonomy.

By the way, even after well over a decade the jury is out on how you pronounce these. Mim-dee? Sim-dee? Em eye em dee? Ess eye em dee? Take your pick. In the usual tradition of parallel processing, there's no consensus. I suspect I'm not alone in being inconsistent, using sim-dee and ess eye em dee (for example) interchangeably.

8.7.2   UMA, NUMA, and NORMA

A taxonomy that is popular with those who design operating systems was devised by David Black, then at Carnegie-Mellon University working on operating systems (surprise). It is based on one dimension of difference between machines: accessibility of memory.

> ➤ **UMA: Uniform Memory Access.** Every processor has equal access, using normal loads and stores, to all of memory. This is the standard SMP organization.

> ➤ **NUMA: Non-Uniform Memory Access.** Every processor has access to all of memory using normal loads and stores. However, there is a noticeably different, usually very noticeably different, delay depending on what parts of memory are accessed. DASH and some of the ways SCI can be used create NUMA organizations; they were discussed in "Distributed Directories" on page 150.

> ➤ **NORMA: NO Remote Memory Access.** Processors cannot access other processors' memories by normal loads and stores, but instead must communicate by other means. For all practical purposes, this is another term for message-passing systems.

The distinction between the two forms of shared-memory organization, NUMA and UMA, is particularly important because it points out that one cannot program NUMA machines the way one programs UMA machines. Thus, the later development of DASH and many SCI organizations is implicitly acknowledged as needing different programming than the common, garden-variety SMP support that is commonly available. The development of this taxonomy seems to have legitimized NUMA systems, at least in the eyes of hardware developers.

8.7.3 Distributed Virtual Memory and COMA (ALLCACHE)

There are those for whom it is an article of faith that parallel programming using shared memory is inherently simpler than parallel programming using messages. This is nowhere so clear as among the developers of **distributed virtual memory** (otherwise known as shared virtual memory, or distributed shared virtual memory, or shared distributed...), who universally begin every paper by saying, with little or no explicit justification, that they're doing this because shared-memory programming is easier. What they're doing is extending the standard notions of virtual memory—allowing a program to think it's using more memory than really exists by transparently putting currently unused parts on disk—across multiple machines.

In everyday virtual memory, when a program tries to access data that it thinks is in memory but isn't, the operating system is automatically called. It clears some space, brings in the necessary data from disk (in fixed-size units called "pages"), and restarts the program where it left off. Distributed virtual memory is the same, except that the page of data may be obtained from another machine, which may, shared-memory fashion, also be using it.

So this is just like moving lines between caches for cache coherence, except that each "line" is the size of a page, typically multiple kilobytes long; and instead of nanoseconds, by the time one goes through the operating system and communications to retrieve the page, the delay is at least multiple milliseconds. These differences—a factor of around 100 in "line size," and a factor of 10^6 in time—mean that to write an efficient parallel program one must be exquisitely aware of that "line size" and where one's data lies within it. False sharing is otherwise going to be rampant, and the attendant "thrashing" of pages between machines will bring efficiency as close to zero as desirable.

This makes a rather substantial difference in how programs must be organized if they are to run efficiently. Programs written to an SMP programming model, where the hardware tries very hard to make even the length of a cache line invisible, will not run efficiently under distributed shared memory except by accident. This doesn't mean that as a programming model it's bad or even hard to use; just that it's different, and not the same as what is in practice "shared memory": the SMP.

It is quite possible to use the techniques of distributed virtual memory to simplify the task of migrating processes from one cluster node to another; this has, in fact, been done [PW85]. However, using distributed memory this way is not the same thing as writing programs using a distributed virtual memory programming model.

A related notion was dubbed **COMA, Cache-Only Memory Architecture,** by a NUMA-inspired group, and is referred to as **ALLCACHE** by its developer, Kendall Square Research [Rot92]. This is rather like distributed shared memory, except for two things: All movement of data is done by hardware, not software, bringing typical "miss times" down into the microseconds and below; and there is no "main memory," only multiple levels of caches with ever-larger line sizes. Whether the hardware actually helps has been studied [SJG92]; that one study came to the conclusion that it did not—you could, in effect, do just as well with DASH-like structures and software to migrate pages to where they were used—but the conclusion is controversial.

Since the one company that sold a product based on COMA has failed—not necessarily for any reasons having to do with the merit of its technology—the future of this technique is at best uncertain; the technology might diffuse to other companies, or it might be abandoned.

8.7.4   Dataflow and Reduction

And now for something completely different: **dataflow** and **reduction** programming models. Neither of these has processors in the conventional sense. Neither even has a program counter, and they might not have a conventional memory. Instead, computation is performed as soon as the data required is available (dataflow) or when its results are needed (reduction). Dataflow has therefore also been called data-driven computation, and reduction called demand-driven [TBH82]. Both have the common characteristic that, unlike conventional programming models, one does not and indeed cannot say exactly *how* to do something; one can only *declare what* is to be done, and leave it up to the language and/or hardware to figure out the details of "how." The specifications (declarations) one makes leave plenty of scope for the language processors or hardware to perform operations in parallel, without explicitly parallel programming of any sort. While languages for dataflow look more-or-less conventional, typical functional programming languages often look like nothing you've ever seen unless you have made the acquaintance of abstract algebra.

A discussion of these programming models that is anywhere near adequate is far beyond the scope of this book. Although prototypes of dataflow-based hardware have been constructed [e.g., GKW85], a practical production machine or programming language based on these principles has yet to emerge, although it does continue to influence some more conventional architectural work [e.g., A$^+$91]. For further information see [AG94, Hwa93], which contain thorough discussions and references to the rich literature on these subjects, or [Vee86], a dataflow survey.

It is, however, fairly common to use the dataflow notion of scheduling a chunk of work as soon as all the requisite data is available. It was used earlier in this chapter, when a global queue in shared memory was employed to overcome load-balancing problems: blocks of the array were enqueued as soon as they could be processed. It was also used in the message-passing wavefront methods. Strictly speaking, this is **macro dataflow**, the use of dataflow concepts on large chunks of work rather than items the size of single instructions. As indicated in the discussion of global queues, it is effectively used in every operating system and database scheduler; they employ global queues, and put work on them as soon as the work is eligible for processing.

8.7.5   Linda

In a category all by itself is the **Linda** system [CG89]. This is a software system that effectively implements in any system—including message-based ones—a global queue. But not just any global queue. Linda implements a relational-database-like **tuple space**: Any process(or) can drop a "tuple," a linear list of data of varying data types, into the tuple space by using a **put()** operation; any other processor can, by using straightforward pattern-matching syntax in a **get()** operation, retrieve tuples and work on them. Simultaneous execution of multiple **put()** and **get()** operations by many processors or nodes is taken care of within the **put/get** software itself.

The simplicity of using just two operations, **get()** and **put()**, to do parallelism is appealing. The practicality of doing so, measured in terms of the popularity of Linda compared with message-passing, is definitely not clear—although there are circumstances where paired **put()** and **get()** operations known to be run on different machines can, at preprocessing or compile time, be automatically turned into a straightforward pass of a message.

8.7.6   General Comments on Other Programming Models

All the less-universal programming models suffer from a chicken-and-egg problem. Substantial applications and subsystems will not be created using them until practical production systems have been deployed that implement them, and there is little point to constructing such systems until there is a sufficient mass of applications and subsystems written to use them.

This is true no matter what their intrinsic merit might be. Distributed virtual memory, for example, may offer a very practical way to program message-based hardware. But programs written to the SMP programming model, with the characteristic global queue, will (except by lucky accident) thrash horribly when run in a distributed virtual memory system. Therefore, rewriting is necessary to use distributed virtual memory. But the current rewriting that's being done to applications and subsystems targets the SMP and message-passing models. Who's writing major applications and subsystems using distributed virtual memory? Nobody. The same is true of dataflow, NUMA, and all the others.

This situation has been called the "critical mass" problem: Without a minimum critical mass of already installed systems, application developers won't be attracted. On the other hand, without the applications, you can't sell that many systems.

The importance of critical mass is often lost in the research and/or university contexts that engender programming models. With a few exceptions, each generation of graduate students can't figure out the previous generation's code and is inclined to rewrite it anyway. That may be as it should be. Everybody can't be inhibited by short-term practicality; new ideas have to arise somewhere. In the market, however, the critical mass issue places an immense inertial drag on the use of programming models that are not nearly universally accepted. The only way around this dilemma is application portability, and changing the programming model is the antithesis of portability; this is further discussed below.

8.8   Importance

Having covered a number of programming models and demonstrated some of the pitfalls and intricacies of parallel programming, it's time to return to the question of why this stuff is important.

Programming models are vitally important for two reasons: First, since some are easier to use than others, they have an effect on how difficult it is to write a program in the first place. Second is the issue of portability; as indicated at the start of this chapter, a program written using one model can be extremely difficult to move to a computer system implementing another model.

8.8.1   Ease of Use

The ease-of-use question is very controversial.

Recall the analogy that a programming model is like the rules of a game, while programs are particular plays or game strategies. Using that analogy: Imagine getting a bunch of basketball fans and football fans to agree about which game is the more difficult to play. If you like less violence, try bridge players and chess players. (On second thought, maybe that wouldn't be less violent.)

The resulting melee is mirrored, usually at a more civilized level of discourse, in ease-of-use debates between proponents of various programming models. Agreement has certainly not been attained, and its prospects are at best unlikely. In particular, holy wars have raged over whether shared memory is or is not an easier way to write parallel programs than message-passing—the paradigmatic programming-model distinction.

At present, all that can be said is that any programming model *may* be equally easy to use in the following sense: If one starts with *both* (a) a blank sheet of paper, that is, one is writing an application from scratch; *and* (b) a mind attuned to the particular programming model involved; *then* it is probably as easy to write an application in one programming model as in another.

I do not expect shared-memory proponents, in particular, to agree with that statement; I know, because I used to be one of them. They are likely to say that their way is easier to use because it is closer to the uniprocessor model that everybody knows. But the message-passing bigots will counterclaim that the shared-memory bigots have had their minds hopelessly polluted by programming in FORTRAN, C, BASIC, COBOL, or whatever. If they would only just get used to thinking another way, they would see the light and discover that the discipline of message-passing ends up making the problem easier.

This would seem to fly in the face of some other evidence, however. Distributed computing uses message-passing, and we are all in the process of finding out just how hard distributed computing is: very. The promises of client-server computing are turning out to be hard to fulfill.

But the fact that distributed computing uses message passing does not mean that message-passing is distributed computing. In addition to its use of message-passing, distributed computing is characterized by heterogeneous systems; communication that has high overhead, low security, and low reliability; and a consequent need for robust operation in the face of failure. As was mentioned back in Chapter 5, the use of hardware with these characteristics, while enormously convenient, complicates life very considerably for the programmer of cluster or parallel functions.

An example of this added complexity appears in the discussion of parallel processing grain size in this chapter. The most straightforward message-passing solution to our problem simply does not work with normal standard communication overhead because it is too inefficient. This was true even in a version enhanced with techniques beyond what shared memory used—multiple wavefronts, which happen to be easily incorporated into message-passing. Having to find *a very large grain* message-passing solution is significantly harder than just finding *a* message-passing solution; much more ingenuity is required [Bel92b].

In short, distributed computing involves embedding into one's program the ability to tolerate very bad message-passing systems. Message-passing using fast, reliable, secure hardware and low-overhead software should not be damned by association with distributed systems.

Given this distinction between message-passing parallelism and distributed processing, I am at present inclined to agree with the message-passers that their approach can be as easy to use as shared memory. Aside from some experience, there is reasoning behind this. There seems to be some connection, albeit probably superficial, between object-oriented programming and message-passing models. These are not the same, any more than procedure calls and remote procedure calls (RPCs)—discussed in the next chapter—are the same, and for much the same reasons. (Among other things, you can't pass pointers in a message, and OO systems just dote on pointers.) However, they are similar enough in overall structure to invite comparisons of the learning process.

It is well documented that successful use of object-oriented methodologies requires a phase of reeducation that involves "unlearning" old ways of thought, following which the practitioners are better off than they were before. It is not unreasonable to believe that a similar situation exists for message-passing. (The message-passers were actually saying this well before Object Orientation was picked up by the software community.)

Such reeducation is neither simple nor free. But very significant education and experience is required to pursue any parallel programming at all—definitely including shared-memory parallel programming; recall all the pitfalls we stumbled into when doing the example in shared memory. An "unlearning" phase is certainly an addition to the retraining required.

Is that addition a significant additional burden compared with the total that must be learned?

I consider that last question unanswerable, at least at present, and so conclude that under the two conditions mentioned above, all that can be said is that shared memory and message-passing *may* be equally bad.

But, and this is a very significant "but," SMPs have a very significant market presence; there are many more memory-sharers out there than there are message-passers. So, you're vastly more likely to find shared-memory programs already written and programmers already able to write programs using the shared-memory model.

8.8.2 Portability

The "blank sheet of paper" qualification on ease of use was extremely significant. There is rather less controversy about how hard it is to *move* a program written in one programming model to another, the primary difficulty that motivates this whole chapter.

Let's start by inspection. Was the code for the message-passing version of our example anything like the code for the shared-memory version? No. They were simply nothing alike. We didn't try to translate one into the other; for message-passing we re-thought the problem. Were the thought processes, the mental models of how the system was operating, even similar? No. One concentrated on how threads of control interacted with each other (shared memory), and the other concentrated on how data was distributed and passed around; in fact, message-passing programming or variations on it have been called "data parallel" programming [FHK+90].

Why does this happen? Consider the game analogy again, recalling that programs are like plays or strategies. This time, consider a play that works well in, for example, (American) football. Imagine trying to apply it to basketball. Doing so may be possible, but it certainly isn't going to happen without a lot of reinterpretation and reorganization at a very abstract level, stripping the play down to its essential philosophical core. The underlying organizations of the two sports are simply too different.

Translation within one game is, by comparison, straightforward: A soccer strategy expressed in Portuguese, for example, can be translated into Italian rather straightforwardly. Some subtlties may be initially lost in translation, but for all practical purposes they can be expressed by using appropriately vigorous gestures.

The implicit translation provided by traditional high-level languages and system standards is like the single-game language translation example above. (Vigorous gestures don't work, however, unless perhaps they're directed at the compiler writer.) This translation works well as long as one is moving from one vendor's implementation of a programming model to another vendor's implementation of that same programming model.

A program written in programming model A, however, may well simply not work at all when run on a computer system that efficiently supports only model B. If it does work, it will most often work so inefficiently that it might as well not work.

System software standards do not help because the different programming models use different standards. For example, standard UNIX SVR4 (System V Release 4) **shared segments** are often used to create a shared-memory environment, but they do not work at all between processors that are not coupled in an SMP-like manner—that is, systems that don't implement the SMP programming model. In the other direction, UNIX BSD 4.2 **sockets** (or SVR4 **streams**) are standards used for communication between machines that don't share memory. They will work within an SMP, but they impose a stiff overhead penalty that is totally unnecessary in the SMP environment and will significantly decrease performance.

Traditional high-level languages do not help for two reasons. First of all, they are being used to call the standard facilities. A procedure call creating a **socket** is not going to produce a **shared segment** just because you compiled it on an SMP—there are **sockets** on SMPs, too, so a **socket** is a **socket** is what you get.

The second reason high-level languages do not help is that the algorithms used and the way they are expressed will in many cases change radically when one moves from one programming model to another. For example, consider the techniques used to find the maximum error in the sample problem used in this chapter. For the straightforward shared-memory SMP case, locking a global location and updating it was appropriate, with a bit of fairly straightforward loop chunking to lower the serialization overhead. In message-passing, equally straightforward, but different, techniques were used: a packaged **reduce()** or piggybacking a local maximum on another message. Compilation is not going to translate chunked loops into piggybacking; they're different programs.

Can't automatically parallelizing compilers, the AMO systems mentioned in the previous chapter, help? Yes, but at the current state of the art they can't switch programming models in the sense meant here—including appropriate algorithmic change—and it's reasonable to question whether that situation will ever change without having to say "A Miracle Occurs."

What current automatically parallelizing compilers (APCs) can do, and it is extremely valuable, is take a program that has been written in serial form and turn it into the corresponding parallel program: a program that runs in parallel, and has the same overall structure and algorithms as the original serial code. The programmer is freed from debugging parallelism; this is a huge benefit since it eliminates worrying about races and deadlocks and transient, nonrepeatable errors; if they occur, it's a compiler error.

This kind of shortcut could have been used in the examples above, more or less by coding the **forall** loops as simple **for** loops; if we had made some error that invalidated parallelizing those loops, the compiler wouldn't have turned the loops parallel, thus avoiding runtime errors. Some of the worst versions presented in this chapter, like the original one with multitudinous race conditions on the **v[]** array, would never even be produced by any self-respecting (and correct) compiler; it would refuse to parallelize the loop or, if adequately sophisticated would jump directly to the wavefront method—which was originally developed as a general automatic loop-parallelizing technique. We would still have had to write the various programs in different ways to produce the later versions, like the one with a global queue, or one using multiple wavefronts.

In addition, there are versions of languages, such as "data-parallel" High-Performance Fortran [Ste93], in which the compiler can be given declarations of how data is distributed for message-passing, plus serial code; from that, message-passing parallel programs can be automatically generated. But the original serial code must still be written in a manner that executes well on the target architecture—and that means it's different for machines supporting different programming models.

APCs can actually help more than that; they can help manually restructure programs, either for better performance when using one programming model, or for moving between programming models. Since they analyze the program in great detail, they can point out internal dependencies of one datum on another that inhibit parallelism; letting the programmer know about that is an aid to restructuring. Some provide that capability already.

But this is still not automatically moving a program from one programming model to another.

Can that ever be done? Well, the definition given at the start of this chapter effectively precludes it by saying that a programming model is inherently above the level of traditional high-level languages. The qualifier "traditional" was used because some as-yet-undeveloped, even-higher-level language might provide the cross-model portability, perhaps by allowing programs to be expressed in a more general programming model that spans all the others. However, this is not even on the horizon at present. Should it occur, it will probably have a hard time because it will be a new *language*, not just a new compiler of an already deployed language, and the language will have to get past the pervasive, all-but-deadly inertia of the "critical mass" problem discussed earlier.

What can really help, where it is applicable, is the SPPS technique: Don't write applications in parallel at all, period. Let somebody else, a specialist, do it. Let different implementations of a subsystem, for different programming models, worry about all the parallelism. Databases do this, as will be discussed in more detail in the next chapter. Facilities like Fermilab's CPS (see "Fermilab" on page 21) do this, too. These systems only do it, of course, for database applications and for applications fitting the model of CPS. But in the areas where they apply, they are a tremendous help.

Even with SPPS, though, there's a possible pitfall. For databases in particular, the applications written under them can explicitly or implicitly use, for example, shared memory. Commonly used programming techniques closely associated with distributed programming do this (threads). Then, even though the database operations are immune from programming model changes, the applications are not.

So we finally reach the conclusion that there's no way around making a choice, and that choice is not a simple one.

A final point, which has been noted before. One of the two common models does have an obvious edge: You can at least make message-passing programs run on shared memory machines, whereas shared-memory programs won't run, or will run with devastatingly horrible inefficiency, on other machine forms like message-passing or NUMA. Message-passing is, in fact, a kind of lowest common denominator—it will run on nearly anything (possibly not on dataflow and reduction machines, but that hardly matters).

Message-passing programs can also be made to run with "reasonable" efficiency if they are written in terms of a higher-level, standard API like MPI or PVM, rather than, for example, directly in terms of system software communications primitives like **sockets** or **streams**. The implementation of the higher-level facilities can change dramatically beneath the surface to directly invoke shared-memory capabilities when those are available; hen they are not, the implementation can revert to the higher-overhead inter-machine communication. However, this will at best result in a program that runs as if it were on an extremely well-endowed message-passing machine. It still will not be optimized for shared-memory execution, and so may fall far short of what the hardware is actually capable of. In practice, it may be good enough.

CHAPTER 9

Commercial Programming Models

Never underestimate the inertia of software.

The previous chapter discussed the types of programming models realistically available and the ways in which programs are written using them, giving an example from the technical computing realm. The next question is: Where and how is such programming used in commercial computing? This is a crucial question, because the existing multiple millions of lines of commercial software may not be right—in fact, they may be nowhere *near* "right," in any aesthetic or technical sense of the word—but they for sure are not going to get rewritten any time soon. This fact alone has kept (and will keep) many computer hardware vendors in a rather lucrative business for long periods of time.

To answer this question, we must extend the usual processor-centric notion of "programming model" to include input/output facilities, because several of the cases to be discussed differ most prominently in the way they treat input/output. In addition, we will use a somewhat more fine-grained distinction between programming models; there are, for example, at least two different ways in which shared-memory SMP programming is implemented, and here we need to distinguish between them.

This chapter will also justify the raw assertion of the last chapter that the shared-memory (SMP) and message-passing models are, with traditional uniprocessors, the only programming models worthy of practical consideration at the present time. The origin of the previously alleged connection between distributed computing and SMPs is explained here, too.

That said, take a look at Table 9-1. That table summarizes the programming models in use by a number of database vendors, other commercial contexts, and several technical/numerical areas. The remainder of this chapter consists entirely of an explanation of that table. Once again, as was the case with caches, the immense body of work on database and transaction-processing systems will be short-changed here. For more background, consult a text such as [KS86].

Also keep in mind throughout this discussion that moving from one of these programming models to another is an arduous task.

Table 9-1   An Inventory of Programming Models

| Type | User | Small N | Large N | |
			Processor-Memory	Input / Output
Commercial	Oracle	SMP with shared segments	global lock *SMP	global disk; other I/O local
	Ingres	SMP with threads	global lock *SMP	global file system; other I/O local
	Sybase	SMP with shared segments	RPC *SMP	local
	Informix	SMP with threads	RPC *SMP	local
	DB2/6000 Parallel Edition	SMP with threads	DCE RPC *SMP	local
	commercial batch	UNIX interprocess communication	UNIX interprocess communication	global (desirable, not always available)
Technical	Grand Challenge	none; Small N is uninteresting.	message passing	little I/O (except graphics)
	seismic	SMP with threads	message passing	global (desirable)
	engineering analysis	SMP with threads	none (no Large N)	none (no Large N)
	computational chemistry	SMP with threads	message passing	little I/O (except graphics)

9.1 Small N vs. Large N _____

The programming models currently in use depend strongly on the size of the parallel system: **Small N** refers to the model implemented and preferred for a small number of active processors or nodes, usually processors; **Large N** refers to the model preferred for a larger number of active processors or nodes, usually nodes.

The boundary between Small N and Large N differs depending on the application or subsystem involved, and is somewhat vague. In general, Small N means "typical small SMP size," that is, four to six processors, and Large N means bigger than that. What, then, about big SMPs? In many cases, the Large-N software solutions (programming models) are used inside them. This is true for some databases, for example; several of the database vendors listed have stated that they would use their Large-N solution inside large SMPs, even though the Large-N techniques did not require the use of shared memory. This sounds strange; wouldn't it result in a loss of efficiency? Compared to the alternative it doesn't, because the Small-N versions run out of scalability and efficiency sooner and more precipitously.

There are, however, cases in which the challenge of extending SMP-based, Small-N solutions to larger numbers of processors is being taken up. This is discussed in more detail later in this chapter.

9.2 Small-N Programming Models_____

Each programming model actually has two parts: on the one hand, how it treats processors and memory; and on the other hand, how it treats I/O. Since all the Small-N models treat I/O identically—specifically, they all use the global I/O model—Small-N I/O models were not separately listed in Table 9-1, and won't be discussed in this section. The global I/O these models use is described later, under "Large-N I/O Programming Models."

9.2.1 Threads

Suppose one were programming a server system to do something for its client machines that involved server I/O. The simplest example of this is the familiar file server, but databases and other more complex operations fit this description also. The course of execution might look like that shown below in Figure 9-1: The server receives a client request, does some computation that figures out exactly what I/O to which file, disk, or device is appropriate, and calls on the local server operating system to do that I/O operation. Since external devices are usually rather lethargic, a fairly long delay (milliseconds) ensues; then the I/O operation completes and returns to the server program. Finally, the answer is passed back to the client, and another request can be accepted.

The code to do this would, in outline, look something like this:

```
do forever
    receive_request ( client_data );
    pull_apart ( client_data, client, io_data );
    do_io ( io_data, result );
    return_data ( client, result );
end /* of do forever */;
```

The operation called **pull_apart()** separates out the pieces embedded in the **client_data** to find out who the client is (**client**) and what I/O operation to do (**io_data**).

The wait for I/O to be completed is the chief element limiting how fast the server can handle requests. This will be true even if multiple disks are attached, with client data spread among them, since only one I/O operation, and therefore only one disk, is used by this server program at a time. The operating system itself need not impose any such limitation and usually does not; it can overlap processing of multiple I/O requests and might even

Figure 9-1   Single-Thread I/O Server Operation

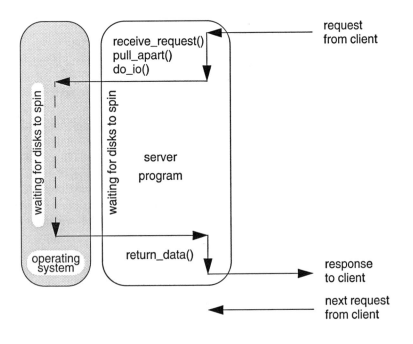

In Search of Clusters ✳

reorder I/O to each disk so disk seek times are optimized, reducing the total time to do all the operations. These commonly available abilities do not matter, though, because the server program never does more than one I/O operation at a time.

Obviously, we'd like to do something about this. The solution of choice in distributed computing is to use **multiple threads of execution** within the server code, along with asynchronous I/O operations. The latter initiate I/O operations, but do not wait for them to finish; instead, they return right away to the user program. Completion is signalled by an interrupt when the operation actually completes.

9.2.2   User-Mode Threads

The notion of multiple threads of execution is actually a programming language construct. Related terms and concepts include *coroutine* (the oldest use of the notion), *procedure activation*, and *generalized label*; there are others. Very closely related concepts appeared in languages for Artificial Intelligence that incorporate backtracking, such as Prolog and the long-ago (early 1970s) Planner and Conniver languages.

The basic idea behind all of this is nothing more complicated than a bookmark. With a bookmark, you can stop reading, put the book down, go do something else, and later pick up the book again and restart where you left off.

In a program, the thread/coroutine/activation/label equivalent of a bookmark is an execution context. It is a complete record of what a processor is currently doing: the next location to execute (program counter), the contents of all relevant registers, and the current language stack of called procedures, temporary data, and so on.

There is always an execution context. Manipulating that context—changing registers, allocating and altering variables, and so on—is what an active program does. The unique thing about multithreaded operation, however, is that there can be more than one of them. This is just as if you were reading a book and got bored, so you put in a bookmark and put the book down; then you picked up another book, read it for a while, and put it down with a *different* bookmark. With multiple bookmarks, you can restart reading any of the books whenever you like. Picking up a new book is like creating a new thread; putting in the bookmark and putting it down is like bundling up the execution context into a data structure and tucking it away somewhere.

This doesn't sound particularly abstruse. But here comes the good part.

The wacky, weird and wonderful thing about multithreaded systems is that by reactivating a context, you can go *back into* a procedure *from which you've already exited*. When you come back, you find everything just like you left it: your old variables have the same values, do-loop indices are the same, and if you return from the procedure (another time!) you return to the place you were called from, which has its old local variables and so on. All this was packed up in the context and put into suspended animation.

This isn't done willy-nilly, of course. You only return to a point that you've previously marked, and you can only have one point marked in a thread.[1]

Let's see how this is used in practice.

Suppose we rewrite that server loop as follows:

```
do forever
    receive_request ( client_data );
    create_thread ( do_client_stuff, client_data );
end /* of do forever */;
```

The **create_thread()** procedure makes a new thread, starting it off executing the procedure **do_client_stuff()** with the argument **client_data**. In other words, **create_thread()** just calls **do_client_stuff()** like a normal procedure, but it interjects creation of a thread at the start of the procedure invocation. **do_client_stuff()** is where we put all the work, more or less like before:

```
do_client_stuff ( client_data );
    pull_apart ( client_data, client, io_data );      /* figure out what's to do */
    until_io_done = async_do_io ( io_data, result );  /* start up the I/O */
    suspend_me ( until_io_done );                      /* Stop here, */
    return_data ( client, result );                    /* ...but start again here. */
    suicide();                                         /* Done. Good-bye, all. */
end /* of do_client_stuff procedure */;
```

async_do_io() does the same I/O request as before, but asynchronously. It doesn't wait for completion but instead merely initiates the I/O, and returns something—called **until_io_done**—that can identify that particular piece of I/O when it's completed.

The thread magic is in **suspend_me()**. It actually *returns* from **do_client_stuff()** back into **create_thread()**. This drops you back into the main loop! That main loop then continues executing, just as if **do_client_stuff()** had

---

1. The AI languages weren't such party poopers—they let you have lots of places in the same program at which execution could be resumed.

returned, which it has, and proceeds to call **receive_request()** to get the next client request.

But **suspend_me()** is no ordinary return. An ordinary return would "pop the stack" and effectively destroy all the information about where the program was within **do_client_stuff()**. **suspend_me()** uses the fact that this is in a multithreaded environment to save that information; it tucks away the context (where the program is in **do_client_stuff()**) on a list, together with the information in **until_io_done**.

As indicated, since we've returned to the main loop, that loop simply continues: It cycles back to **receive_request()** and will receive another request from another client if one's been sent. When that happens, the loop will call **create_thread()** to start another thread; that thread will initiate I/O and **suspend()** itself, returning into the main loop again. The main loop then cycles up to get another request, which starts up and **suspend()**s yet another thread; then another, and another...

In the meantime, the disks have been churning away. Finally they start rolling in the data and interrupt the main program. This interrupt initiates the other half of the thread magic.

The interrupt handler looks at why the system got whacked upside the head by an interrupt and passes that data to the thread manager, which compares the reason for the interrupt to the values of **until_io_done** it's got tucked away. When it finds a value that matches, it reinstates that thread's context and restarts it.

Presto, you're back inside **do_client_stuff()**, right after the **suspend()** and about to execute the **return_data()**.

The values of local variables are restored, so when **return_data(client,result)** is done, the right **client** and the right **result** are used. There are, of course, lots of different **client** and **result** variables existing at any time—specifically, there's one set for each suspended thread. The right ones are always used— they're the ones in a thread's context. (The **client** and **result** variables really should have been declared in the **do_client_stuff()** procedure. If they're declared outside, then, by normal language variable scope rules, there is just one copy of each, shared by all the threads; this is not what we want. I just didn't want to complicate the example, which isn't written in any formal language, anyway.)

After the result has been sent back to the client, the work this thread was created to do is finished. So it commits **suicide()**, returning the thread data structures to free storage and, in the process, returning to the thread manager. This is the true "final exit" of a thread. The thread manager then picks something else to do.

The net result of all these shenanigans is shown in Figure 9-2: Many more clients are serviced in the same interval. All this amounts to is a use of the classic technique of overlapping I/O with computation, and can increase throughput by a large factor. Exactly how much depends on the amount of computation done by the server program, how fast client requests can be received, and so on, but increasing throughput by a factor of 10 to 100 is certainly in the realm of possibility.

Such increases in speed are not to be trifled with; client-server support packages really like threads. They are included, for example, in the OSF's DCE (Distributed Computing Environment) and are directly built into facilities for doing remote procedure calls, which are the client-server control structure of choice in a majority of contexts.

Figure 9-2   Multithread I/O Server Operation

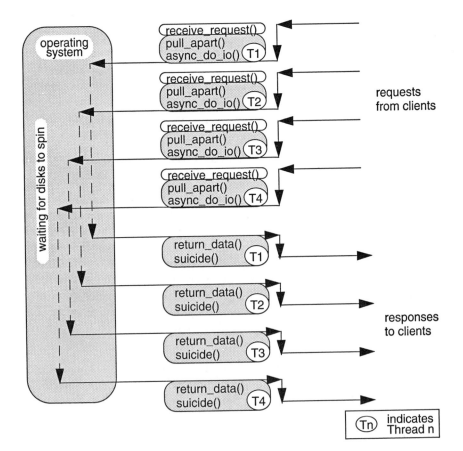

In Search of Clusters ✳

Even such large performance gains, however, are not the only reason for enthusiasm about multithreading. The fact that the local variables are automatically allocated and unique to each thread makes it very useful to have a separate thread for each client request, even if performance is not an issue. It simplifies the code, which otherwise would have to deal with storage allocation and deallocation on a request-by-request basis, explicitly programming the relationship between requests and their allocated data. Instead of doing all that, one simply spins off a thread per request and declares local variables; the system automatically associates the variables' data with the request, because the data is part of the thread's context. Anything that significantly simplifies programming is highly desirable, and threads do that for server programs.

This simplification is particularly notable when remote procedure calls, themselves a simplification, are used. Remote procedure calls will be discussed later.

Not all the data a thread accesses need be, nor should it be, completely local to the thread. As parenthetically mentioned earlier, data that's not locally declared is shared by multiple threads, so common resources and information can readily be shared.

Of course, should one do that, one should be careful, shouldn't one, when updating shared data? An interrupt could occur at any time, resulting in a switch to another thread, which might then access some partly updated shared data... Uh-oh.

Remember races? Locks? Unrepeatable results? Deadlocks and deadly embraces? Yes, they're all here when thread-shared data is used. There is only one processor acting at any time, so this is multi*programming*, not multi*processing*, but the same difficulties exist. As was stated back near the start of Chapter 8, multiprogramming and multiprocessing have a lot of things in common.

But hey, as long as we're partly pregnant, why not...

9.2.3   SMP with Threads

...use different processors to execute the different threads and get some computational speedup?

Indeed. There is a natural affinity—some might even say an unholy alliance—between threads, hence client-server distributed computing on the one hand; and shared-memory programming on the other.

They are very close to being the same programming model. While there are indeed differences, those differences can (with care) be encapsulated inside locking, scheduling, and synchronization routines. For example, it is totally useless to spin in a tight loop, waiting for a lock to free up, when you're multiprogramming. No other processor is ever going to reset the lock; you must switch to another thread, because only another thread can possibly reset the lock. Conversely, you don't have to be careful about sequential consistency, since only one processor is involved. But otherwise there's quite a large overlap of techniques.

But so far, in our discussion of threads, only one processor has been involved; it's been strictly a discussion of context saving and restoration within a language running on a single processor. The way multiple processors get into the act is through the good graces of the operating system. In fact, the term "thread" was most widely popularized by its use in the well-known Mach operating system [BRS+85, Ras86], which became the basis of the OSF/1 system from the Open Software Foundation. Mach dissected the traditional UNIX notion of "process" into (a) an address space, (b) one or more threads of control executing inside that address space, and (c) a bunch of other stuff that need not concern us here.

The reason the operating system has to get in the act is that it owns the processors. There must be something in there that's recognized by the operating system if the OS is going to assign a processor to it. For multithreading systems, that something is called a **kernel thread**; it is essentially just like the threads we've talked about until now, which in contrast are **user-mode threads**. The big difference is that the "bottom" of the language stack of a kernel thread, and a chunk of its context, resides in and is presided over by the operating system, which can apply a real separate hardware processor to it. Kernel threads are created by a system call, of course, usually syntactically-sugared through a subroutine package such as an IEEE standard UNIX **pthreads** package, or OSF's DCE threads package (which actually implements an early draft of the IEEE standard). When a kernel thread commits **suicide()**, it's a system call that deallocates a processor-dispatchable thing from within the operating system kernel.

Kernel threads are what is meant by the notation "SMP with threads" in Table 9-1 on page 260. They are used as in the above user-mode thread discussion in the commercial subsystems and applications. As for the technical applications, well, now you have some idea what goes on inside that innocent-looking **forall** construct used in Chapter 8.

"SMP with threads" was used in the table only to indicate the use of kernel threads. Virtually all the commercial subsystems use user-mode threads, often with their own unique support code, for the program structure benefits described above; and some use both. Others just use user-mode threads; for example, Sybase has its own user-mode threads for program structure and uses a different technique (described below) for multiprocessor speedup.

Why use both user-mode and kernel threads? Overhead.

A pure user-mode thread is, or at least can be, a very svelte, fast construct. Not a single system call need be involved in either creating or switching between them; a bare minimum thread switch can involve very little more overhead than a subroutine call (although figuring out which thread to switch to adds to that cost). If one is aiming at supporting thousands of clients, with at least one thread per client, such low-overhead operation is very important.

Kernel threads, on the other hand, require trips to the operating system to create and destroy. Also, there's little point to having many, many more kernel-mode threads than there are processors; all that does is hand thread scheduling over to the operating system, which will do the best it can but really has no idea what the program is trying to accomplish. However, you'd like to have many, many threads for software structuring.

As a result, in many if not most cases, a user-mode thread package multiplexes a smaller number of kernel threads among a larger number of user-mode threads. This adds to the complexity and hence the overhead of the user-mode threads but is a good tradeoff between program structure and overhead.

Historically, "SMP with threads" is less common in the Open Systems area because it has not been standardized in UNIX; the IEEE standard is still only in a draft form while this is being written. "SMP with shared segments" (below) was standardized many years ago with the System V release of UNIX. The equivalent of kernel-mode threads has existed in proprietary operating systems for a long time. In MVS, for example, jobs (like UNIX processes) can have within them multiple tasks; these are like kernel-mode threads.

9.2.4   SMP with Shared Segments

What do you do when you haven't got threads? Try shared segments; they work out just fine.[2]

---

2. And what have you got when you get through a lock? / I'm not certain, but I know it's mine. / Oh, I get by with a little help from my cache / gonna try with a little help from that stash. This time, *Pace* The Beatles. I may have to learn to control myself more.

That's what the "SMP with Shared Segments" category in Table 9-1 on page 260 is all about. It can be considered a stone-age version of kernel threads for UNIX. Never underestimate the inertia of software, but what the heck, it can be made to work fairly well. The way it operates is described below.

First, you use the standard UNIX **fork()** and **exec()** calls to create a whole new UNIX process. The system works a while, and there it is, complete with address space, file pointers, paging space, and the rest of the kitchen sink. Now you use UNIX System V system calls to create another address space, with a name: "Joe." Joe is tacked onto your address space, so the process just created can load and store into that region of (virtual) memory.

Now create some more processes. After a suitable pause, there they are, N address spaces, lots of paging space allocated, and so on. Each of those processes, unlike the first one, does not create yet another address space; instead, they politely ask the system "link me to Joe, please" and lo, it is accomplished. The result is illustrated in Figure 9-3: several processes, each with some private memory, but all sharing Joe in the normal, shared-memory, SMP fashion.

Since each process is known to the operating system as an active entity, it will (as the Gods of scheduling and dispatching decree) be assigned a processor; so we can get computational speedup. The usual way to use this is to run with absolutely the minimum possible private area, placing everything in the shared segment that one can: A database's "cache" of disk-resident data, for example, goes in the shared segment so every processor can get at it. Also, the structures for managing user-mode threads usually go there, too; that way, the processors (one per process) can be used at will to run any user-mode thread for good load balancing. The ubiquitous global queue of work items to do goes there, too. And so on.

There's really very little wrong with this technique, and it was the only portable way of getting computational speedup out of an SMP UNIX system prior to the standardization of kernel threads; software inertia being what it is, this technique is still commonly used. The process-creation overhead occurs only once, at start-up, unless an application or subsystem dynamically adjusts the number of processors requested during its operation. Since few presently feel the need to do this, little is lost, aside from the kernel data structures and other appurtenances that processes require but threads do not.

Depending on the particular support system used, the shared segment technique may also be found in a number of technical areas despite what appears in Table 9-1 on page 260.

Figure 9-3   Shared Memory Using a Shared Segment

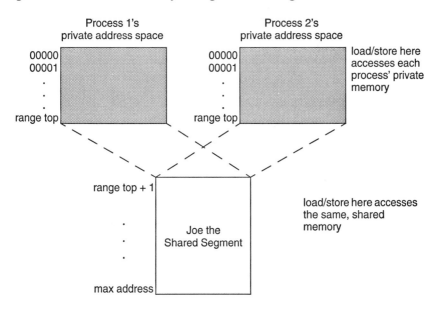

9.2.5   UNIX *Interprocess*

Commercial batch processing in UNIX typically involves multiple job steps that are programmed as completely separate UNIX processes. To the degree that they communicate at all, they use standard UNIX primitives for communication and synchronization: pipes, semaphores, sockets, files, and so on. That's why this is called the **UNIX Interprocess** model in Table 9-1 on page 260. System V shared segments are also a standard UNIX interprocess communication facility, but using that facility produces a program structure different enough to warrant calling it a different model.

9.3   Large-N I/O Programming Models _____

Since the I/O Model for Small-N systems was left for the Large-N discussion, it seems only reasonable to begin the Large-N discussion by skipping a column in the table and starting with I/O.

Two general I/O programming models are in use: global and local, and a variation or two on each. They are described in the sections following.

There is, however, a great degree of coupling between the use of Large-N I/O models and Large-N processor/memory models. In addition, cross-dressing of I/O programming models—putting software on one kind of hardware that makes it look like another—is significantly easier and more practical than processor/memory cross-dressing. The reason is that I/O data rates are lower, and techniques for overlapping I/O and processing are well understood and deployed.

The net effect of all of this is to turn the separate discussions of each into a somewhat dry recitation until the combinations are compared. This is done in the section titled "Shared Disk or not Shared Disk?" on page 277, which directly addresses the controversy involved—one that's at least as big as shared memory vs. message-passing. Hang on, we'll get there.

9.3.1   Global I/O

In the **global I/O** model, all devices and files are equally usable and equally visible to any program running anywhere in the system. Furthermore, the same name is used to refer to a device or file no matter where in the system that reference is done. In the jargon: There is a single global name space for devices, and similarly a single global name space for files. The kernel or other subsystems accept those global names as the target of I/O operations.

This is, as was mentioned, the I/O model used for all the Small-N programming models. This is not surprising, since the Small-N models are basically variations on the shared-memory SMP programming model, and the "symmetric" in symmetric multi-processor implies hardware support for global I/O (among other things).

There are variations on global I/O. In particular, some subsystems (primarily Oracle's database system) require global device I/O, specifically UNIX "raw" mode disk I/O; no other devices or capabilities need be global. Others (Ingres' database system) require global file I/O and nothing more. Needless to say, it is possible to provide one without providing the other. Or vice versa.

It's worth noting that the two databases requiring global I/O were originally written to exploit the DEC VAXCluster back when that was what Digital's Open VMS Cluster was called. This provided global disk I/O via the Star Coupler, as was described in Chapter 2. None of the more recent cluster/parallel database designs have this requirement; it is very much out of fashion. Commercial batch and technical applications do require global I/O, however—although "require" for the technical case is probably too strong a term. It is certainly desirable, but in many cases its lack can be programmed around.

Use of a global I/O model requires the same kinds of programming considerations present in share- memory operation. Locks are required, for example, so that multiple processors don't attempt to give commands to the same disk at the same time with the usual disastrous results. This is why the deadly embrace discussion in the previous chapter referred to "resources," not just memory. Oracle's use of shared disks is interesting in this connection. Each separate node has a very large—multiple megabytes to gigabytes—in-memory database cache of disk data. This, naturally, leads to cache coherence issues, which are solved using techniques rather like those used for processor cache coherence. This is further discussed later in "Global Locks" and "Shared Disk or not Shared Disk?".

Distributed facilities effectively provide part of the effect of global I/O to application programs. Distributed file systems, for example, provide global file I/O for that part of the file system that is held on a server: As far as the application is concerned, it is doing normal, local I/O, using regular old operating system calls, with a perfectly normal file name. Remote queueing systems for printers perform a similar function, allowing system calls that put a file on a queue to do so as if it were local, but with global effect; with appropriate conventions a large group of machines/nodes can use the same names for a physically distributed collection of printers. This is a one-by-one conversion process, however; other devices—scanners, tape libraries, and so on—are not typically globalized.

9.3.2   Local I/O

In the **local I/O** model, each node of the system has its own local name space for devices attached to that node. A node cannot do I/O to a device attached to another node—at least, not using normal operating system I/O operations. The same is true of files: There is a local file system, and that's all a node can access.

This, obviously, is not all there is to it; an application or subsystem running across a group of nodes must somehow access devices and data on other nodes. The way this is done is by pulling the necessary function up into the program: A program on node A sends a message to a program on node B requesting that the B program do something, for it, such as accessing a disk attached to B or twiddling some other device. If what is requested is a plain I/O operation, such as reading a "raw" disk sector and sending the data back, this process is called **I/O shipping**. If what is requested is a higher-level function, requesting some processing be done on the data and only the results be sent back, the process is instead called **function shipping**. These terms arose in the distributed database community, which has had great fun over the years debating which is better and/or easier and/or more efficient under what workloads.

Note, however, that it was the program that did those operations. The programming model under which that program was written was still local I/O. I/O shipping done within the operating system can give the appearance of the global I/O model to user programs.

9.4   Large-N Processor-Memory Models _____

There are three Large-N programming models in use: messages, remote procedure calls, and global locking. In addition, each of these can be present with a variation: the SMP-node variation. This is noted by ***SMP** in the table. The SMP variation will be discussed after the basic models.

9.4.1   Message-Passing

The programming model indicated by **message-passing** in Table 9-1 on page 260 refers to the pure form of the message-passing model described in the previous chapter. It involves the use of multiple disjoint address spaces, each with a only a single thread of control active at a given time. In other words, multiple, traditional UNIX processes are used, although multiple user-mode threads might be used for program organization. (The *SMP variation is noted in the table only when the nodes can use SMPs for speedup.)

9.4.2   Remote Procedure Calls (RPC and DCE RPC)

The **remote procedure call (RPC)** programming model is a higher-level model usually built on top of the message-passing model. The intent is to simplify message-passing by allowing a program to invoke a function on another node much the same way as a procedure call is done: The program specifies the name of the operation and the arguments, and off it goes; sometime later, execution resumes with the requested operation carried out and the results returned in some of the provided argument slots, just like a procedure call [And91].

There are, however, differences from a normal procedure call.

> ➤ The name of the procedure called cannot be given in the normal syntax for a procedure, resolved by a compiler and linker. Cross-node agreement is required, with names declared specially; usually, a preprocessor is provided to make it easier to use such names, and to make things implied by the other differences more palatable.

> ➤ There is no shared memory between the caller and the callee, so pointers to addresses cannot be used as arguments, nor can the argument data itself contain pointers. This makes passing data struc-

tures difficult, to say the least. Structures must be "flattened" into simple concatenations of pure data before they can be either sent out or received back.

> It takes a lot longer. RPC operation over LANs is measured in milliseconds, whereas a procedure call is done in microseconds or even nanoseconds. Nobody is likely to confuse an RPC with a procedure call when there is a factor of a thousand to a million involved in performance. Part of the reason for the difference is that the arguments must be "marshalled": all packed into a simple string of data, with descriptors, that can be sent to another machine; on the other end, they must be "unmarshalled," pulled apart again. This is at least a semi-interpretive process, usually involving data copying, and simply takes time. The other reasons are the usual overhead in using I/O-attached communications gear: operating system invocation, the interaction of the operating system with a protocol stack, and so on.

RPC follows the procedural semantics of suspending the caller until the operation is complete. This appears to make attaining speedup, even given the overhead, a mite difficult. However, RPCs are usually used in the context of multithreading or other forms of multiprogramming; suspending the thread that did the RPC does not necessarily stop all local computation, just one thread's. In addition, forms of RPC that are "asynchronous" also exist. The asynchrony involved is the same as that in asynchronous I/O: The RPC is invoked, but the caller does not wait for completion; rather it continues and is later informed when the operation completes. This is occasionally debated as something that destroys the whole concept of a remote *procedure* call, and furthermore the same effect can be obtained by multithreading; nevertheless it's often offered and used.

The notation **DCE RPC** is used in Table 9-1 on page 260 for those cases where the specific RPC support being used is that provided by the OSF's Distributed Computing Environment.

9.4.3   Global Locks

In two of the cases—the Oracle and Ingres Large-N programming models— the primary communication between nodes is via global I/O and **global locks.** These are locks guaranteed to be atomic across an entire system. Little other explicitly internode communication takes place, since data is transferred between the nodes implicitly, using global I/O, after it has been appropriately locked. This is the mechanism by which these systems perform database cache management across multiple nodes.

Global locks are not, however, the simple locks we used back in Chapter 8, with a simple **acquire()** and **release()** interface. They are complex structures, which separate read locking from write locking; allow multiple simultaneous readers; provide for "promoting" a reader to a writer; allow locking any arbitrary thing, indicated by an arbitrary character string as the lock "name." Perhaps most interesting, they often keep sufficient track of things that in the event of a failure, all the data owned (locked) by a failed node can be identified and released for use by others.

This model, like RPC, is typically implemented in software using the message-passing model. A node sends a lock request as a message to a lock manager residing somewhere among the nodes of the system; this message may require the lock manager to send a request to the current holder of a lock, asking that it be "demoted" to read or completely released so that someone else can write. The lock manager can be centralized on one node, which produces a bottleneck, or in Very Large N situations—and in this case, Very Large can be as small as 8—distributed across multiple nodes, each holding a subset of the lock data. Obviously, in the last case, you need some way to find out who has the lock; typically, a hash function applied to the lock name is used.

There is obviously significant overhead involved in this if standard message-passing techniques are used, which is why the IBM Sysplex, which also has global locks, uses the Sysplex Coupling Facility to provide a hardware assisted, centralized locking facility (along with other functions). The Digital (Encore) Memory Channel provides a similar hardware function for locking and transmission of modest amounts of data. Of course, providing a special-purpose hardware "stunt box" that does not generalize to arbitrarily large numbers of nodes is often deprecated by the distributed/parallel community because such boxes seldom scale to large node counts; but we're worrying here about humble clusters, not Grand Challenges.

9.4.4 The SMP Variation (*SMP)

All of the database subsystems adapted for Large-N processing can simultaneously use two levels of programming model: The nodes of the Large-N model can be symmetric multiprocessors, so the Small-N model is used on nodes and joined by the Large-N model. This is indicated by the notation ***SMP** in the table.

This characteristic is not shared by any of the technical computing areas, as was discussed back in Chapter 8. The programmers and writers of automatically-parallelizing compilers for technical applications, who usually have many different programs to deal with *en masse*, tend to throw up their hands at the notion of effectively dealing with two levels of programming model simultaneously, which is what the *SMP variation implies: one between the processors of an SMP, and another between the nodes that are SMPs. They can, of course, use message-passing between the processors of SMPs as well as between nodes that are SMPs, but that's nearly as bad because the two types of message-passing—inter-SMP and intra-SMP—have vastly different costs.

Database vendors, on the other hand, have only one program to deal with (although it's a *great big* program…). So, they manually do what's required to deal with two levels simultaneously.

9.5   Shared Disk or not Shared Disk?_____

Global I/O vs. local I/O is, within the database community at least, at least as controversial a topic as the shared-memory vs. message-passing imbroglio continues to be within computationally oriented parallel programming. This is to be expected, since it's the same issue, just at a different level of the storage hierarchy: Should one use physically shared disks, which can be directly accessed by all the nodes, or should only one node "own" each disk? It should be noted here that the issue is whether sharing should be part of normal operation. Multiple physical connections to disks are required to provide the availability that is a major benefit of clustering, and local I/O systems usually have that; but in local I/O, the "other" connection is used only in the exceptional circumstance of failure, at which time ownership of a disk switches from one node to another.

On the shared side, we have Oracle Parallel Server, Ingres' distributed version, and IBM's IMS DB and VSAM; on the local side, we have Sybase (and NCR's) Navigation Server, Informix' Dynamic Scalable Architecture, IBM's DB2/6000 Parallel Edition, and last but certainly not least, Tandem. The winner so far in market share among open systems appears to be Oracle, if for no other reason than that they've been selling systems for years longer than the others; even so, Tandem and IBM IMS (which are not "open systems") are not to be trifled with, and the universal choice for new implementations has been local I/O. The rest are still, at this writing, in various stages of Greek-letter testing trying to get things to work robustly.

Before getting into who can claim what and how, let's describe how the three chief variations work: True physically shared disk, I/O shipping, and function shipping. The discussion will deal with issues other than just database systems, since the same issues arise in cluster file systems.

9.5.1 Physically Shared Disks

The key issue with physically shared disks is that, just as with shared memory, nodes cannot simply whack away at the disks without some control being placed on what they're doing, where they're doing it, and when they do it. Races and all those evil things can occur, so some form of control—meaning locking—is required.

In addition, we've got caching to worry about again. Both file systems and databases cache data from disk in primary memory, for the same reason that caches are used in processors: Real workloads exhibit locality of reference to stored data, not just data in main memory, so caching the data in primary memory often eliminates the need for a slow reference to the spinning brown stuff.

Processor cache coherence and the shared-memory programming model use separate techniques to deal with the coherence and logical problems of sharing; coherence is done in hardware, and the logical problems are dealt with primarily in software. Shared disk systems, on the other hand, typically use global locks as a combined solution to both types of problem.

Suppose, for example, node Able wants to write into a block on a shared disk. Node Betty has recently written into that block, so it's in Betty's main-memory database cache. Somehow Betty has to be told to give it up. That's the job of the lock manager. The lock manager could reside in Able or Betty, but to reduce the confusion we'll assume it resides in a third node: Carlos.

The sequence of operations required is shown in Figure 9-4.

1. Able sends a write lock request for the block to the lock manager, Carlos.

2. Carlos looks up the block in his table of locks, sees that Betty has it, and sends Betty a request to give up the block.

3. Betty gives up the block by first writing it back onto the disk, which she's allowed to do because she currently owns the write lock. Having done that, she deallocates that block from her primary memory, and then sends Carlos an "unlock" message. (If Able had just wanted to read, Betty could have kept the block in her cache with a read lock on it; since Able is writing, that copy would be wrong.)

4. Carlos gets Betty's unlock, notes an ownership change from Betty to Able in the table of locks, and sends Able a "lock granted" message.

5. Able now reads the block from disk and proceeds to scribble all over it to his heart's content.

In Search of Clusters ✳

Figure 9-4   Writing to a Shared Disk

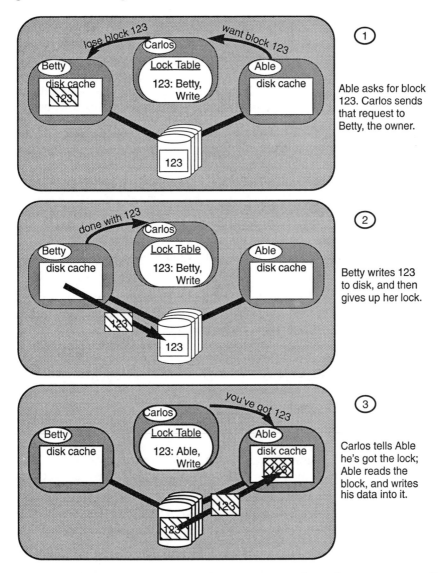

① Able asks for block 123. Carlos sends that request to Betty, the owner.

② Betty writes 123 to disk, and then gives up her lock.

③ Carlos tells Able he's got the lock; Able reads the block, and writes his data into it.

The similarities between this and processor cache coherence protocols should be blindingly obvious. In fact, the actions of Carlos are very like those of a cache coherence scheme using a centralized directory, carried out in ultraslow motion. One big difference is that transfer of data is through the disk: Betty writes, then Able reads it. This is like writing processor-cache data to main memory, and then reading it back again. Why do that? Why not just send the data direct from Betty to Able?

Well, I keep hearing people threaten to do it, but it never seems to happen. One reason is that, unlike the processor case, there have been few deployed high-speed inter-node buses and switches. In contrast, centralized directories (and snooping caches) for processor cache coherence use high-speed internal switches and buses to flush the data around. Even though it would save waiting for two disk latencies, LAN communication overhead is such that the change would barely be worth it; perhaps when faster communication is generally deployed, the situation will change. However, there are other issues involved; they are discussed more fully in "Further Comparisons" on page 283.

9.5.2   I/O Shipping

Even if disks are not physically shared, they can be logically shared. That's what I/O shipping is: shared-memory cross-dressing for physically unshared disks.

A typical sequence of events for obtaining a disk block by I/O shipping is shown in Figure 9-5. Node Able is getting a block from Node Betty this time, and Carlos isn't involved. The sequence is this:

1. A program on Able issues a request to read a block, number 123 again. This proceeds through Able's operating system to the device driver (although it could be elsewhere), which looks in a table and discovers that block 123 isn't on a disk attached to Able. It's attached to Betty. So the device driver sends a request over to Betty.

2. On Betty's side, the request again goes into a device driver, Betty's this time, which sees that the block requested is on a local disk, gets it, and sends it back to Able.

3. Able's device driver picks up the data just as if it had been read from disk and presents it to the requesting program.

Well, that was a whole lot simpler than the first case.

But wait a minute. What about the locks, data integrity, and all that? Who checks to see if somebody else is scribbling away in it like mad in another copy of that block?

The answer is that I/O shipping doesn't handle that. It only ships I/O. The coordination must be done at a higher level—meaning, in the program that requested block 123 in the first place. In effect, I/O shipping treats Betty as if it were a particularly intelligent disk controller, attached using a LAN and a TCP/IP protocol rather than by a conventional disk adapter and SCSI bus.

In other words: I/O shipping is simply an emulation of a multi-tailed disk, using software and interprocessor communication rather than a direct physical attachment. It is more "scalable" than multi-tailed disk, because interprocessor communication allows many, many nodes to be connected no matter what limitations the disk devices themselves may have; the disk drives only need be attached to one computer.

Figure 9-5   I/O Shipping

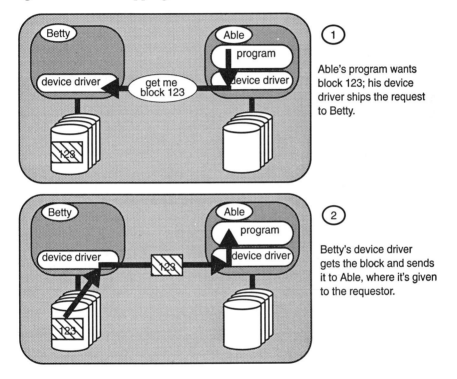

1

Able's program wants block 123; his device driver ships the request to Betty.

2

Betty's device driver gets the block and sends it to Able, where it's given to the requestor.

I/O shipping has actually been used by Oracle in place of physically shared disks in an implementation that runs on an NCube highly parallel computer. It is also used in Oracle's implementation on the IBM Scalable Parallel systems [LC94], and will probably be used by Oracle to effectively simulate shared disk on any number of other similar systems. When I/O shipping is used this way, a number of the nodes are designated as I/O controllers, and internode communication is used to send requests to them. In addition, for the NCube implementation a very carefully designed, highly-distributed lock manager was also implemented, and used in its usual fashion to control access to the disk blocks.[3] A locking protocol like that of Figure 9-4 was used, but instead of just reading the data from disk, the protocol of Figure 9-5 was then used to transfer the data.

There is one potentially significant difference between I/O shipping and physically shared disks, however. The "owner" of a disk can maintain its own cache, in its own primary memory, of the data on its disks. That cache is not directly subject to coherence issues, because the owner is the only node that can write to the disk. So, instead of reading the data from disk in step 2, the data might well be sent directly from the in-memory cache; when this happens, it is likely to save enough time to overcome any communications overhead that might arise.

On the other hand, high-performance disk controllers have their own caches; so in the physically shared disk case, the data might well be read from the controller cache. This also saves a mountain of time—rotation latency is 20–30 milliseconds at best—and transfer rates in disk subsystems are 3 or more Mbytes per second, not the 10–16 Mbits per second of current typical LANs.

Yet on the third hand, the intensely faster intermachine communication that is arriving dwarfs the data rate to single disks; the amount of memory in a node is usually significantly larger than that on an adapter; the algorithms used for caching can at least potentially be better tuned to the application; and this cheap general-purpose memory can replace a fancy, expensive disk controller with cache. Now, if that communication overhead could only get down to a rational level…

Didn't I mention before that this was controversial?

9.5.3 Function Shipping

The final technique draws its name from the database area, but in a more general context can be seen to be common in distributed computing. **Function shipping**, as it is called, is somewhat similar to I/O shipping. But instead of simply requesting I/O, the requestor asks that a significant piece of work be done and only the results be shipped back.

The typical example involves an SQL database **select** statement: **select**, applied to a relational database table, returns another table consisting of

---

3. I have been told by an Oracle representative involved in that lock manager design, tailored to work well with several hundred processing nodes, that creating that highly-tuned, highly-distributed lock manager was the hardest, most painstaking programming he had ever been involved in. Massive parallelism has its drawbacks.

only the rows of the original table that match some criterion. For example, one might ship to another node, owning a table of employees, a request to **select** out of that table all the employees who are in department 77; or out of a list of credit card receipts, the ones for airline tickets.

A common application of function shipping in the database arena involves the parallelization of queries. As in message-passing, the data involved are first distributed among the nodes involved; for example, a big table of credit card receipts might be partitioned into many tables of approximately equal size, uniformly distributed across the disks of all the nodes of the system. Then, when a query comes in asking who bought airline tickets, the **select** function is shipped out to all the nodes of the system. Each one operates on its own partition and returns the subset of the data requested.

The same kind of thing can be and is done with shared disk systems, but without the logical requirement that the tables be prepartitioned; each node is simply assigned a chunk of the table, much as chunking is used in a **forall** loop, and goes at it. (However, this requires qualification; see "Further Comparisons" below.)

Function shipping is, as a programming model, very close to RPC, so that's what is typically used to implement it—by IBM's DB2/6000 Parallel Edition, Informix' DSA, and Sybase's Navigation Server. Tandem also uses partitioned tables and function shipping.

In a sense, it's also what every distributed file system does (just to pick one common distributed example): A symbolic file name and offset is shipped over, the function of finding that symbolically addressed data is done, and the result shipped back. In that sense, function shipping is extremely common.

9.5.4   Further Comparisons

A number of other points can be raised about the shared vs. non-shared disk issue.

In a physically shared disk system, all the nodes have direct access, through their I/O systems, to all the disks of interest (there may be private disks local to each node, but that won't concern us here).

This means the disks themselves must be "multi-tailed," meaning they can accept commands and data from more than one source. Unfortunately, conventional mass market SCSI, SCSI-2 and SCSI Fast/Wide disk interfaces don't do this very well, even though they can be physically connected to multiple nodes. The problem is in switching from one master to another when multiple nodes are actively using the disks, not in "failing over" in the event of a failure. So, score one for local I/O: You need proprietary disk technology to make shared disks work well.

Furthermore, disk multi-tailing facilities are usually limited to two- or four-way sharing, limiting the size of the systems that can be constructed. Score two for local I/O, particularly since one reason for clustering is I/O connectivity: using more machines for more I/O slots, allowing the attachment of more disks. If all the systems in a cluster must physically attach to all the disks, there is no increase in I/O connectivity over a single system.

However, remember Fibre Channel Standard (FCS), discussed back in Chapter 3? An ANSI standard, proposed to ISO, with gigabit rates, many-way switching (16, 64, more), a reach of kilometers, and it carries the IPI-3 standard disk protocol. Sun has already announced a SPARCcluster series that shares disks using this medium [Sun94a]. As FCS or other similar technologies are more fully deployed they can be used to physically share a large number of disks among a large number of nodes. This can completely eliminate the I/O connectivity bottleneck of physically shared disks. So can proprietary facilities like the IBM ESCON Director, another switching system, or the Digital Star Coupler.

From a marketing viewpoint, shared disk is easy to explain. Instead of one computer processing the workload, N computers do. See those cables right there? That's how they all access all the data! Local I/O systems require further explanation just to reach the point where customers understand how all the machines can get to everything.

The shared disk advocates typically point to issues like load balancing and convenience as being in their favor: You just put all the data out on the disks, and whoever needs to get at it, gets it. In comparison, the local I/O folks have to partition the data ahead of time, spreading it out among disks according to the anticipated query workload. Some have elaborate front-end tools to help this process. Sybase's Navigation Server, for example, has a tool that take the anticipated types of queries as input, determines a good partition for that on the basis of analytical models or simulation, and outputs an pile of shell scripts that will perform the partitioning for you.

However, simply dropping data in any old way on the disks of a shared disk system does not necessarily lead to good performance. It's seldom useful to parallelize a query, for example, if all the tables being used are on the same disk; that disk's bandwidth will be the bottleneck. At least some partitioning is necessary, just as it was necessary to have multiple memory banks with interleaving when putting together an SMP.

Another difficulty with sharing arises from the database equivalent of cache cross-interrogation. This can lead to trouble if some of the database records are "hot"—frequently accessed by many different nodes. In that particular case, intelligent local caching of I/O data can help, and function shipping can be a significant gain: If everybody's function on the "hot" item is queued up, it's entirely possible that significant performance gains from processor cache locality of reference can result.

There's another issue here, too, that brings in an issue completely different from the discussion that's been going on so far. It concerns the key ability of a database or transaction system to actually perform **transactions**—internally consistent alterations to data that either completely, consistently happen, or do not happen at all—no matter what hardware, and most software, failures occur (see [KS86], for example, for how transaction semantics can be implemented). With shared disks or I/O shipping, the special processing necessary to ensure transactional semantics can be done on a single node: All the data and all the control over the disks is implicitly gathered into a single place. With function shipping, however, even a simple transaction cannot usually be done on a single node; several nodes, all doing part of the work, must cooperate. Performing operations as true transactions, even though the operations are spread across multiple nodes, is by no means impossible. The technique called **two-phase commit** is probably the most common way to accomplish that feat. Here's a horribly simplified description: A controlling node first makes sure everybody is "prepared" to commit the transaction (phase 1), and if everybody agrees then all are told to move from the "prepared" state to the fully "committed" state (phase 2). This method works. It also requires significantly more processing at each node and, perhaps more importantly, significantly more internode communication to accomplish it. Function-shipping systems must incur this additional overhead on many, if not most, transactions; the gathering process used in the shared systems avoids it.

Of course, if the sharing systems are used to do parallelism inside a single large operation, they, too, do things simultaneously on multiple nodes and must use two-phase commit or an equivalent protocol. And the trade-off of shipping function may reduce the total communication enough that even with two-phase commit, there's little if any additional overhead. Overall, the function-shippers do appear to have a definite disadvantage in attaining high throughput on many small transactions, particularly if internode communication is subject to large overheads.

So, what is the ultimate direction? In the short run, the relative simplicity of the shared-disk systems and the heavy overhead involved in internode communication make physically shared disk systems hard to beat when data updates must be done. In the longer term, as internode communication rates rise and overhead hopefully declines, the system that can effectively exploit the cheapest hardware will win out. That implies that it will become a battle of I/O shipping vs. function shipping. For example, Tandem already has fast, proprietary communication, and its function shipping produced the amazing TPC-C record referred to in Chapter 2, which Tandem expects to see stand for at least a year.

On the other hand, I've spoken with at least one ex-administrator of a system that uses partitioned data who has done everything but swear on a stack of Bibles to never again have anything to do with data partitioning as long as he lives. Whether this is a personal idiosyncracy, a comment on the tools available, or an indication of the intrinsic difficulty involved—I do not know. But it does give one pause.

9.6 Small N vs. Large N in Commercial Subsystems_____

It was mentioned earlier that in some cases, the Large-N solutions mentioned would be run inside large SMP systems. This is the primary reason why the terms "Small N" and "Large N" were used rather than "SMP" and "clustered" for the two categories of models.

That anyone would propose doing this—and more than one database developer, not marketeer, has proposed this to me—appears strange. (The marketeers all glibly say that you just keep adding SMP processors and grow, grow, grow.)

The reason is interesting. The developers do not blame the hardware. Very possibly they could, but they don't. They blame the structure of their own programs, which in many cases prohibit scaling above around six processors in an SMP.

What has happened is that the SMP programming model has been taken too literally, without consideration for caches. A global queue is typically used, and as the number of processors increases, the locality of reference for each processor goes down—since who gets to do a task is effectively randomized by the use of the global queue.

All this is not a new concept; its possibility was discussed back in Chapter 8. The important thing is that it is actually happening, in practice, on large, economically important, commercial subsystems.

The next question obviously is: What are database vendors going to do with the large SMP systems currently being sold or in plan by major open systems vendors? Sequent, for example, goes up to 32-way, Sun Microsystems has a 20-way, HP has announced 12-way, and so on. In some cases, what the database vendors do just doesn't matter. The application running under the database system just scales wonderfully: Each transaction grinds away for so long that there's plenty of time for the caches to get fully loaded up and cooking at full speed. But in many cases—the TPC-A benchmark, for example, and to a lesser extent the TPC-C benchmark (see Chapter 12)—what the database vendors do matters a great deal.

Since few if any database vendors were in any sense prepared for large SMP systems, the systems seem to have been developed on the philosophy that "If we build it, they will come." They are coming, as it turns out, from two directions.

The first direction is the surprising one indicated above: Run the Large-N solution inside the SMP. On a 12-way SMP, for example, a database vendor might run 3 copies of their Small-N system, connecting them with a copy of their Large-N system. Each of the Small-N systems is completely independent of the others; they just send messages, perhaps just locking messages using an optimized-for-SMP locking implementation, to each other. Cache coherence between those copies, except as needed to make the messages and locks work, is unnecessary; there is virtually no cross-interrogation between the groups of processors that individually run a copy of the database system. (Assigning each copy to a group of processors sharing a level 2 cache could result in tremendous efficiencies.) Each of the Small-N copies uses 4 processors, so all 12 processors are used. Several database vendors anticipate that this "Large-N over Small-N" arrangement will run substantially better than attempting to use the Small-N solution for many processors in an SMP. Furthermore, it will require no structural changes to their code. This includes accounting for the additional overhead involved in coordinating multiple copies of the Small-N solutions, such as global locking and two-phase commit protocols.

The Large-N over Small-N technique also means that their software doesn't need large-way SMP hardware. In fact, the SMP hardware and operating system gets in the way. The I/O performed by each copy of the Small-N version, for example, could be completely separate and their systems would work perfectly well. In an SMP, each Small-N I/O stream is not separate; both in hardware and in software, the independent copies will interfere with each other unnecessarily. All the hardware and software commonalities of SMPs give no benefit to the database subsystem in this scenario. The database could just as well be running on a cluster of relatively small-way SMPs—in fact, it could be argued that a cluster of smaller SMPs is the ideal hardware architecture for this type of system. If only the communication latency could be brought into a rational range.

The second direction from which "they are coming" is this: Bite the bullet and actually implement the painstaking internal structural changes required to extend the Small-N solution to larger degrees of parallelism in a shared-memory, SMP environment. The kinds of things that need to be done are along the lines of those mentioned in Chapter 8: having separate local work queues per processor, aging from the local queue to global queue for global load balancing, and so on. Some database vendors have already started this process, and by the time this book sees print the results will undoubtedly will be in beta test if not beyond, to general availability. How successful they will be is an open question at this time.

Single System Image

If there is a single unifying element to the concept of "cluster," it is the notion of a **single system image (SSI)**. A single system image is the illusion, created by software or hardware, that a collection of computing elements is a single computing resource.

Despite my initial denials when defining a cluster, this definition of SSI definitely is part of the definition of a cluster. A collection of connected machines is not a cluster unless it is used as a single computing resource, so single system image is what makes a cluster a cluster.

Many discussions of single system image focus on something not mentioned in the SSI definition given above, namely system administration. System administration is actually just one aspect—although a critical one for practical cluster use—of the more general issue. It is not the only aspect of a cluster that should ideally exhibit a single system image, and it is certainly not the sole defining characteristic of single system image.

Some examples: The cluster batch job submission facilities described in Chapter 2 effectively provide a single system image *from the point of view of the user* submitting a job. The database systems running across clusters, described in Chapter 2 and Chapter 9, effectively provide a single system image *for their applications* and often for their own administration. The cache coherence schemes used in SMPs described in Chapter 6, particularly those spanning multiple machines such as SCI and DASH, effectively provide in hardware a single system image *of memory, for all programs.*

The availability of the batch submission and database single system images, which are obviously independent of each other, is the basis of much of the current utility of clusters. Flaws in currently available single system images for administration—unity of the system *from the point of view of an administrator*—constitute one of the greatest difficulties that currently inhibit the use of clusters.

Once it has been pointed out, the fact that there are multiple single system images floating around appears obvious. The next question is: Are all those images completely independent, randomly generated things, or is there some order limiting, and suggesting, what is possible?

A key that provides structure to the universe of single system images lies in noting the following two points:

1. every single system image has a **boundary**; and
2. single system support can exist at different **levels** within a system, one able to be built on another.

Why this happens and what it means is the subject of the rest of this chapter.

10.1 Single-System-Image Boundaries _____

Consider a reasonably designed batch submission system for a cluster, such as any of the ones listed back in Chapter 2, in Table 2-2 on page 38. A user submits a job to the batch system, and so to the cluster as a whole, not to any specific element of the cluster. The batch system runs it on one of the machines of the cluster—the user does not necessarily know which one, just that it's in the cluster somewhere—and returns the results. During execution, the user can submit queries about the job or cancel it by asking the batch system—not by referring to a machine on which it may be queued. As far as that user is concerned, the cluster as a whole is one thing, a single, job-queueing system. That is a single system image.

But suppose the user issues some command—for example, the UNIX **ping** command that "bounces" a message off another machine to see if it's alive and talking to the communication network. That command (at least in exposed clusters) will distinguish the various cluster machines; each has its own name, and each individually may be functional or not. In general, if the user performs any operations that aren't part of the batch system's suite, the illusion of a single system is undone: The user is outside of the SSI boundary, and the many machines again appear as many machines, not as a single facility.

A way to visualize an SSI boundary is illustrated in Figure 10-1: When you're inside the SSI boundary, the cluster as a whole looks like—exhibits the image of—one big machine; in this case, the machine illustrated is a supercomputer. But if you do anything outside that boundary, the cluster again appears to be just a bunch of connected computers.

Different SSI-creating applications can provide different images of the same cluster. Consider using two, for example a database system and a batch submission system (Figure 10-2). As you move from one to the other, you're moving from inside one SSI boundary to inside another. In both cases, by definition, you see a single system image. However, their (single system) images—plural—are different, as illustrated.

This difference in appearance is inevitable and obviously desirable. Batch and database systems (for example) are different things; they have different functions, and different commands. If they looked the same, why have them both? Their single system images are just plain different.

But there are common elements that SSI applications can, and should, share. For example, it is in many cases a wholly unnecessary irritant to require users to have different identifiers and passwords for different applications

Figure 10-1 An Application's Single System Image Boundary

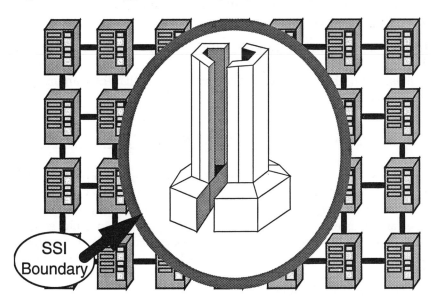

Figure 10-2   Two Applications' Single-System-Image Boundaries

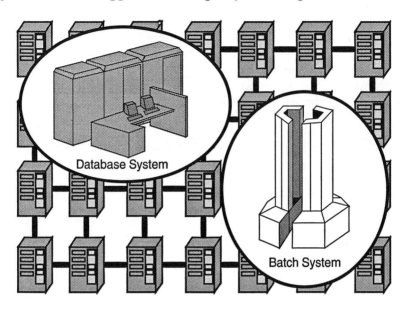

Database System

Batch System

and to go through different, separate, authentication rituals when moving from one application or subsystem to another. In other cases, the issue isn't merely a question of irritation, but of function: For example, two SSI applications may require access to the same data; the function they are supposed to provide will not exist if they use different, incompatible ways to obtain a single system image of that data.

So, the supporting structures and facilities must themselves exhibit a single system image if they're to be useful to SSI applications; but that support is not, in itself, a usable application. The implication is that there are multiple levels of single-system-image support.

10.2 Single-System-Image Levels_____

The notion of "levels" of single system image is the computer science notion of levels of abstraction. A house, for example, is at a higher level of abstraction than walls, ceilings, and floors; those in turn are at a higher level than lumber and plasterboard. It is certainly not impossible to build a house directly from lumber and plasterboard (and nails, and so on); in fact, this is common practice. But construction is vastly simplified if prefabricated walls, ceiling, and floors are used—in other words, if a level is built using the level of abstraction below.

Types of single system images can similarly be recognized as belonging to different levels in a hierarchy of levels of abstraction. Table 10-1 shows the three groups of levels that will be used in the discussion here: the application/subsystem levels; the operating system kernel levels; and the hardware levels. (The table headings will be used later.)

By basing applications on common support structures (lower levels of SSI support), it is possible both to save effort and to avoid the kinds of gratuitous incompatibilities mentioned in the previous section. What this means is that the lower levels of support provide common SSI semantics to applications. In general, the lower the level, the more pervasive and deep the common SSI semantics becomes. Different applications can still choose to present those semantics to users in different ways, but that is an issue outside the bounds of this discussion.

It is easier to obtain an SSI by using the levels below it, but two points must be emphasized: First, "easier" does not mean "free"; in general, work must still be done to obtain the single system image desired for a program that exploits the multinode nature of a cluster. A purely serial program may indeed get a kind of SSI for "free." Second, skipping levels in our construction technique is certainly possible and, under some circumstances, preferable or necessary. We'll see examples of all of this as our discussion covers each of the three major levels in turn, illustrating how each can be further subdivided.

Table 10-1   Outline of the Levels of Single System Image

Level and Name	Examples	Boundary	Importance
APPLICATION AND SUBSYSTEM LEVELS			
OPERATING SYSTEM KERNEL LEVELS			
HARDWARE LEVELS			

There are undoubtedly other choices of levels into which single system images can be divided and different ways to subdivide the levels used. The one presented here appears to be a useful one, but it's probably not unique.

10.3 The Application and Subsystem Levels ___

The application and subsystem levels are the highest levels at which a single system image can exist. They include the ultimate level—the application level, the one that a user sees. However, there are other levels. The collection of these levels, in order, is appears in Table 10-2; each is described below.

10.3.1 The Application Level

The application level is the highest and in a sense the most important level because it is what the user sees. One common example, a batch job submission system, has already been covered. Another example is the electronic forms applications that form part of the office applications of several companies, including Digital and IBM.

These systems typically run across multiple machines, so that a form filled out on one machine is routed to the appropriate personages whose approval is implicitly sought by the original filer—whether or not the filer knows who they are (or why they've got to approve a request). A user can typically submit a query for a form that's entered the system, finding out who's seen and approved it, and who has to be nudged to get the thing out of his or her electronic in-basket. During the query, the user need have no idea which of a collection of machines the form, or the data about it, actually resides on; the application has created a single system image potentially spanning a large enterprise.

This level is in a real sense the most important because it is the only level an end user ever sees. It is therefore the only thing for which any anybody will ever hear a "market requirement." The only purpose of all the other levels is to make it easier for developers to create top-level applications exhibiting a single system image to the user.

The term "end user" is perhaps misleading, since by it I simply mean anyone who uses an application. In particular, if the application involved happens to be system management, the "end user" is the system administrator. And this, by the way, is where system management comes into the picture; it's the one application suite that every computer necessarily has. There will be more discussion of this subject later.

Table 10-2   The Application and Subsystem Levels of SSI

Level and Name		Examples	Boundary	Importance
A 4	application	cluster batch systems, system management, electronic forms	an application	what a user wants and needs
A 3	subsystem	distributed DB, OSF DME, Lotus Notes, MPI, PVM	a subsystem	SSI for all applications of the subsystem
A 2	file system	Sun NFS, OSF DFS, NetWare, and so on	shared portion of the file system	implicitly supports many applications, subsystems
A 1	toolkit	OSF DCE, Sun ONC+, Apollo Domain	each toolkit facility: users, service names, time, membership, ...	best level of support for heterogeneous systems

KERNEL (OPERATING SYSTEM) LEVELS

HARDWARE LEVELS

10.3.2   The Subsystem Level

The next important level of SSI support is that of subsystems. (The term "middleware" has become popular in referring to what is meant here by "subsystems.") These are programs not an integral part of the operating system that provide desirable or necessary services to other, application, programs. Database and On-line Transaction Processing systems are the typical examples of subsystems, but communication and other subsystems are common. OSF's DME, a subsystem for administrative applications, is another example.

One of the more valuable services a subsystem can provide to an application is a single system image. If it is provided, application programs written to use that subsystem will automatically see a single system image, without any effort on their own part. As illustrated in Figure 10-3, the applications ride within the single system image created by the subsystem.

The single system image boundary in this case is the API (Application Program Interface) of the subsystem: As long as an application uses only facilities provided though the subsystem's API, that application will see a single system image—assuming, of course, that the subsystem has provided a complete SSI over its entire API interface. Step outside the boundary—for example, by bypassing the subsystem's facilities and directly using an operating system call because it's faster or more convenient—and again the illusion is undone.

Several examples of databases providing an SSI over a cluster have been given in Chapter 2; virtually every vendor of an "open systems" database provides this as a feature (or will provide it soon), as do several vendors of proprietary database systems. The kinds of clusters these SSI databases can run on varies, but all provide the ability to span multiple machines. Applica-

Figure 10-3 Applications of a Subsystem Using Its Single System Image

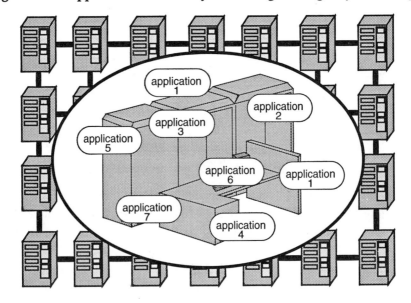

tion programs neither know or care about that as long as they operate through the database API.

Another example of this type of subsystem is Lotus Notes [OHE94], the groupware subsystem that facilitates mail, conferencing, electronic form submission systems, and similar applications. Applications written under this system are distributed across multiple workstations in a client-server fashion, and multiple servers communicate to form a web of connections in which any change to Lotus Notes' databases is visible to any user of the system at that user's workstation. As far as users of the many client machines are concerned, there is just one copy of each collection of data. The important thing at this level is that the applications did not have to work to bring that about—it was inherited by virtue of being an application residing in the Notes subsystem. Were the application to somehow access data outside the Lotus Notes framework, this inheritance would no longer work: The many machines in the web, including the ones Notes runs on, would again appear as multiple machines and not a unified resource.

As mentioned previously, probably to the point that the reader is bored with the emphasis, this is an important layer; it provides crucial enablement for commercial use of clusters by supporting the SPPS model of application execution. It could be implemented without significant lower-level SSI support, but no examples the author is aware of do that.

While subsystems are important and are often the primary workload run on a system, it is must be realized that they still have a single-system-image boundary, and there are important things outside that boundary that must be done. If one needs to do anything outside a database—such as, for example, add a new disk to one of the machines, check error logs, and so on—one is outside the boundary and does not see a single system image. (That example was used because workers in the database area seem particularly prone to forgetting that anything exists outside the bounds of the database.) That the examples here come from system management is significant; that's the application, as will be mentioned, that must be run on every system.

10.3.3 The File System Layer

The file system layer is familiar to many because of its ubiquity. Distributed file systems such as Sun's NFS [S+85], CMU's AFS [San90], OSF's DFS [Ope93], and Novell's NetWare are well known, and many users believe they have a perfectly adequate single system image because they have a distributed file system. This belief provokes arguments with other folks who believe single system image is single system image system management. The position taken here is that the file-system side is correct—if you restrict your vision, looking only within the SSI boundary of the distributed file system. Of course, the administration side is correct, too, if you look only within the SSI boundary of administration.

The SSI boundary induced by a distributed file system is the portion of the file system (usually a subtree or subtrees) that is shared with others. File operations performed within that boundary exhibit a single system image in the following sense: They are visible to anyone who has access to those files, without any further action than normal open/close/read/write calls to the operating system. This implicit support for many unchanged applications makes this level of the SSI support hierarchy also valuable.

Once again, of course, it is possible for an application to step outside that SSI boundary. If one accesses files *not* in the shared portion of the file system, the fact that the files reside on different machines becomes excruciatingly visible.

The position of the file-system layer in this support hierarchy is somewhat problematical. The file system API is part of the kernel API, a lower layer that is discussed later, and distributed file systems are generally installed as part of the kernel or a kernel extension. I've placed the file-system layer where it is, however, since every known instance of a distributed file system is supported by the toolkit layer that certainly comes next, and subsumption into the kernel is actually a later occurrence, an optimization of earlier implementations outside the kernel, an organization that is still going strong in the PC world.

10.3.4 The Toolkit Layer

The name for this layer is problematical.

On the one hand, I've called it the "Toolkit Layer" because it consists of a variety of tools and toolkits designed to support higher layers: naming services, communication services such as remote procedure calls, lock and other synchronization services, grouping services such as group membership and group multicast, and so on *ad bizarrum*. Examples include Sun's ONC+ [Ram93], OSF's DCE [Ope93], IBM's HACMP/6000 programming support [IBMa], IDS ISIS [Bir95, BJ87], the elderly and innovative Apollo Domain system [Pek92], and others. As with the subsystem layer, as long as an application or subsystem uses the API of such a system, there is the image of a single system; go outside that API and the illusion is undone.

On the other hand, it could easily have been called something like the "Over-Kernel" layer to reflect a very important characteristic: This is the level at which the greatest breadth and depth of SSI support is possible without significant modification to an operating system kernel itself. This is an important implementation distinction because it's necessary to provide intersystem portability; in addition, distinctively, that in turn implies that this level is the best that can be achieved for heterogeneous clustered systems containing different operating systems (and possibly different hardware).

Achieving breadth of SSI support is important, for a reason first mentioned under "Single-System-Image Levels" above. The broader the common semantic base on which applications are built, the more feasible it is for them to avoid a confusing proliferation of different types of single system images. That is why integrated, comprehensive toolkits that provide a consistent broad framework, such as OSF's DCE, are important.

At this stage it is worthwhile to pause and consider the kind of "overall" single system image that can be provided at this, the best possible heterogeneous level. That situation is illustrated in Figure 10-4.[1] Each SSI-enabled application has its own single system image, as semantically common with the other applications as feasible. However, each also has its own SSI boundary, and there are definitely cracks between the applications into which users fall if they fail to use, or do not have, the SSI version of an application.

Unless literally every application and command is (re)implemented to use the toolkit SSI facilities, and those facilities are broadened to include all possible things every application needs to use, the SSI illusion cannot be complete. Is it possible to achieve completeness? This is a debatable question.

Building an SSI directly into important subsystems, with semantics provided by a general tool layer, provides that SSI in great measure without burdening the programmer. Examples where this works well are distributed file systems and SSI-enabled database systems; neither simple commands like **dir** or **ls** nor a debit transaction need change in their programming to inherit an appropriate SSI. These capabilities could, perhaps, be extended to all facilities and to all applications.

However, the author knows of nobody actually proposing literally distributing *every* element of a system in an over-kernel manner. This would be a never-ending job. Instead, what is proposed and implemented are the facilities required to support specific important applications and subsystems, not wall-to-wall total coverage. Halfway measures, leaving cracks in the overall SSI, are both common and inevitable.

For example, consider X Windows. Use of this facility gives all graphics applications a distributed structure, but this is not the same as a single system image. Actually making an application run somewhere else while dis-

---

1. Figure also called "Author goes nuts with clip art."

Figure 10-4   Achievable Over-Kernel "Overall" Single System Image

playing on one's home display requires arcane (to a user) creation of strange files with odd names and contents. This is not just another user-hostile UNIX interface; from the viewpoint used here, it is revealed as a crack in the single system image because the names of each source of graphics must be explicitly listed.

Similarly, under UNIX it is impossible at the over-kernel level to attain a complete SSI in the file system. The reason is that the file system contains more than files; the **/dev** directory provides access to the devices attached to a machine. Conventions can produce a near-equivalent to complete file-system SSI, but near-equivalents are continually subject to errors and mistakes.

10.4 The Operating System Kernel Levels ____

The next levels of single system support lie at the edge of the operating system or within the operating system kernel itself. They deal with providing the unifying illusion at the boundary of the operating system and with how that illusion can be implemented within the operating system. The levels involved here are shown in Table 10-3 and discussed below.

Table 10-3   The Operating System Kernel Levels of SSI

Level and Name		Examples	Boundary	Importance
		APPLICATION AND SUBSYSTEM LEVELS		
K 4	kernel (operating system)	Locus, TCF, OSF/1 AD TNC, Sprite, Amoeba	each name space: files, processes, pipes, devices, and so on	kernel support for applications, administration, subsystems
K 3	kernel interfaces	UNIX (Sun) vnode, Locus (IBM) vproc	types of kernel objects: files, processes, and so on	modularizes SSI code within kernel
K 2	virtual memory	none supporting operating system kernels	each distributed virtual memory space	may simplify implementation of kernel objects
K 1	microkernel	Mach, Chorus, OSF/1 AD, Amoeba	each service outside the microkernel	implicit SSI for all system services
		HARDWARE LEVELS		

10.4.1   The Kernel API Layer

Dissatisfaction with cracks in the single system illusion, the inability to ever completely finish the entire job, to support everything and do it right—these are significant motivations for moving to the next lower layer, that of the operating system kernel itself. The operating systems Amoeba, Sprite, QNX, Locus, AIX TCF, and OSF/1 AD TNC are examples of systems providing this level of SSI support. ("AD" and "TNC" stand for "Advanced Development" and "Transparent Network Computing"; the latter is a separate technology from Locus Computer Corp.)

As rather feebly illustrated in Figure 10-5, supporting SSI at this level means that a consistent, coherent single system image is seen on every system call made by every program running on the system: application, subsystem, and tool. Furthermore, this SSI is enforced by hardware facilities, not convention: No program can access anything outside its address space without using through a system call, and requirement that forces it through the system code maintaining the SSI. The way in which this is manifested is primarily that all the names used for every facility throughout the system—files, processes, devices, pipes—are guaranteed to be unique system-wide identifiers that allow users to gain access to all the types of "thing" the system defines, without specifying where any of it is.

In addition, the implied subsumption of several kernel capabilities into the single system image produces a requirement that the kernel do some things that over-kernel support seldom does. Load balancing and the migration of jobs from one node to another are two examples of this.

Effects

From the point of view of a user or administrator, there is a dramatic difference between the best that over-kernel systems can do, on the one hand, and a true kernel-level SSI, on the other. Perhaps an analogy is the best way to get at this difference.

Figure 10-5 Kernel-Level Single System Image

In Search of Clusters ✳

Consider trying to actually get something completed on a multiple computer system as being like trying to cross a river. You *really* don't want to fall in; getting swept away will at least cost you time that may ultimately prove calamitous. All the various individually distributed tools of the over-kernel layer are like a collection of stepping stones that can be used to walk across. They may be flat, dry, with good traction, and even linked in some underlying basalt. But there are still cracks between them. When crossing, you're never quite secure; you always have to be careful where you place your feet.

A kernel-level single system image, on the other hand, is a bridge across those troubled waters, one with solid guardrails (they're hardware-enforced). "Objectively," meaning using a reductionist one-on-one individual feature comparison, that bridge might not provide one tiny shred of additional function; it might even provide less—for example, its maximum allowable load might be less than that allowed by the stepping stones.

Nevertheless, like a bridge over troubled waters, it eases your mind.[2] You don't have to think about where you put your feet (which commands you use) because there are no cracks, and if you lose your balance, you'll just bump against the guardrail and not fall in. People who are naturally highly coordinated, with an excellent sense of balance, and physically quick probably won't notice the difference. The rest of us poor slobs will prefer to take the bridge.

There happens to be a reflecting pond in the center of the IBM Austin campus that has, across it, a delightful-looking set of broad, flat, regular stepping stones that provide a quite usable and direct path across the pond from one of the buildings to another. I've walked across them many times. Between the stones, there are cracks where the water is visible. They're small cracks, narrower than men's shoes, and help form an overall effect that is visually and architecturally charming. But I have to say that I am always watching where I put my feet when I use that route. It's not a huge burden. But it's one more thing to worry about, and that is something we can all do without.

Sources

What, technically, is the source of this mind-easing benefit?

A primary factor, which directly follows from having a kernel-level SSI, is that SPPS processing is by default enabled for everything run on a clusters—just as it is enabled for traditional SMP-supporting operating systems.

---

2. Tell me you didn't see that one coming. *Pace* Paul Simon again.

- ➤ Separate jobs (in UNIX, **processes**) are "automatically" placed on separate nodes as appropriate, just as they are "automatically" placed on separate processors in an SMP—and this happens for standard, unaltered, serial uniprocessor programs; it is built into the (serial) system primitives they use to create and manipulate jobs.

- ➤ Operations that are split into multiple processes using standard, uniprocessor, serial communications facilities (in UNIX: **pipes**, **sockets**, **signals**, and so on) can, as they do on an SMP, exhibit speedup by being run on multiple nodes simultaneously.

- ➤ Individual jobs may run with increased efficiency because system-provided parallelism can off-load system operations—for example, I/O—onto nodes other than the one on which the user program is running. (This again is equivalent to common SMP operating system function.)

This factor makes a cluster of machines remarkably more useful. Programs do not have to be written in a new form, do not have to use a "distributed" version of operations that is different from the operating system's version, do not have to wait until the standards for the new, distributed form have been negotiated: The existing, standard operating system interfaces are *preserved*, reinterpreted for a cluster environment; new ones are not necessary.

Of course this reinterpretation is precisely what SMP operating systems do also, and it is why SMPs are as widely used, and as usable, as they are. The system-level, SPPS parallelism that is broadly enabled by this level of single system image is often the primary, and in many cases only, way that parallelism is exploited by SMP installations.

If individual programs are to internally run in parallel, the way databases and other economically important, high-use subsystems do, they must of course be rewritten under a kernel-level SSI—just as they must be rewritten for an SMP. To target an SMP, they must be rewritten for an SMP shared-memory programming model—threads, shared segments, or syntactic sugarings of those constructs such as **forall**; to target a cluster, they must be rewritten to a message-passing programming model.

For a cluster supported at this level of single system image, that does not mean programs must be rewritten to be what is commonly called "distributed" environments today; it may be significantly easier. Current distributed programs must in general deal with a complete lack of single system image among the machines they use, as well as high-overhead, low-bandwidth communication; current parallel programs on highly parallel message-passing machines must deal with a paucity of operating system services. The writing of message-passing programs in an environment that has both high performance communication and broad SSI system services should be significantly easier, as has been discussed previously. And there's the issue of stepping stones vs. bridges again, which can be very significant. The mere use of a message-passing programming model, without the other extraneous complications, definitely does not guarantee excessive difficulty in comparison to the difficulties of shared-memory parallel programming; demonstrating that was why I dragged you through Chapter 8.

Cost

All of this function is not achieved for free. Substantial, skilled, expensive software effort must be put into creating this grand illusion of a single system. Furthermore, much if not a majority of the work is actually outside the kernel; and that work doesn't deal with intellectually amusing computer-science topics like unifying name spaces. Instead, it deals with the grubby details of getting the commands and libraries of an operating system to work.

In many cases commands and libraries just work without modification. Debuggers, for example, (mostly) port without change because kernel-level SSI maintains, across nodes, the same process tree and interfaces to processes—even remote ones—that is provided on uniprocessors. In other cases, however, utilities must be modified to do their job correctly on an SSI cluster. As many of these modifications are in the system management arena, examples are given later in that discussion.

Command, library, and utility modification constitutes the real bulk of the work required to implement kernel-level SSI support, because, for UNIX at least, that's the location of the bulk of the code by an overwhelmingly large margin. This is not bad; it means the UNIX "tools" philosophy works. It's also true that a many of the tools "just work" without modification. But even the remainder is large; so there's much work to do, and it all must be done before the kernel-level SSI support hits the street. Systems lacking a full range of command and library support at introduction are crippled.

The command and library modifications required, by the way, are by and large the same elements that must be rewritten—although in some cases less completely—to deal with multiple processors of an SMP.

Evaluation

Is it worth it?

At present, the vote of the general computing community appears to be much more in favor of over-kernel facilities than kernel-level SSI. Many more people are engaged in creating over-kernel facilities than in creating kernel-level SSI systems.

One reason for this choice is the proliferation and influence of distributed systems, which, as opposed to clusters, must handle heterogeneity among the operating systems of the nodes. It's just a bit hard for a kernel-level SSI operating system to be heterogeneous—in fact, it's a contradiction in terms. The effect of this on systems with a kernel-API single system image is discussed later, in Chapter 12, "Why We Need the Concept of 'Cluster'"; in the author's opinion, the effect has been profoundly negative.

There is, however, another reason why kernel-level SSI has not caught on, a reason that has nothing to do with the ultimate desirability of kernel-level vs. over-kernel SSI; it has to do with incremental funding and reward.

Over-kernel SSI facilities can be implemented one at a time, with visible gain from each increment. When an application works, it can be shipped; the revenue from that can be used to fund the next application, and so on. Kernel-level SSI, on the other hand, is a kind of "big bang theory" of SSI: You do it all, you do it completely, you do it once; and you don't have one single blasted thing you can sell until everything's done. This is a heavy economic decision to undertake, and the industry as a whole has so far voted with its feet for the venture that was less economically risky.

Another very significant factor has been that the industry as a whole has had no idea whatsoever what a cluster is, how significant it can be, or even, really, the benefits can accrue from a kernel-level single system image. Also, microkernel structures make enough of a difference to possibly change the trend and provide an incremental pathway, as will be discussed.

10.4.2   The Level of the Kernel Interfaces

Just as various underlayers in the Application and Subsystem layers supported SSI applications, an SSI at the Kernel API layer can be supported by several layers of constructs that reside inside the operating system kernel. Here we are in the realm of operating system structuring, tools used by kernel-level system programmers. A variety of techniques, not all necessarily mutually compatible, are possible.

The level of the kernel interfaces is one at which particular collections of objects used by the kernel independently acquire what amounts to a single system image: All of them, no matter where they are, are manipulated through the same programming interface. Of necessity, these are each specific to a particular operating system kernel.

One example of such an SSI construct is the UNIX **vnode** interface. With this in place, the existence of a distributed file system (or indeed any number of different file systems) is modularized away from the remainder of the kernel. By use of the **vnode** API, a single system image of the file system is essentially maintained. Outside that API the illusion is, of course, shattered.

Another example, modelled after **vnode**, is the **vproc** interface. As **vnode** does for files, **vproc** allows internal kernel code to manipulate a process no matter where it is without getting involved in the details of how the distribution is accomplished.

The purpose of such constructs is modularity. Without them, implementation of a kernel-level SSI can pervade a kernel, involving a very large number of very small changes to a very great fraction of the modules comprising the operating system. Such modifications are ugly and miserable to debug and maintain compared to a a few changes to a few modules, and the addition of one large-ish, separate module.

The **vproc** interface, in particular, was developed by Locus Computing Corp. and IBM as part of a proposal made to OSF for an SSI kernel. (OSF decided they were buying tools, not kernels, at the time; they did DCE instead.) Prior implementations of the Locus-derived kernel-level SSI, embodied in the UCLA Locus operating system and the IBM TCF product, were of the pervasive, ugly persuasion. **vproc** modularizes another piece of the puzzle quite well; too bad name-space resolution in the kernel isn't the only thing that a kernel-level SSI requires.

10.4.3   *The Distributed Virtual Memory Level*

There are levels within the level of the kernel interfaces, as there are for other levels. At one of the lower ones resides distributed virtual memory. This sublevel produces the effect of a single system image for the memory of the system under circumstances where the hardware does not support it directly. While distributed virtual memory can be surfaced all the way to application programs as a means of parallel (or distributed) programming, one of the hopes of some of its adherents is that it could be used to simplify the implementation of a single system image at the kernel level.

As indicated previously, however (page 249), distributed virtual memory is a distinct, different programming model that requires the programs using it to be significantly modified for efficient operation. In this case, that requirement applies to programs within the kernel itself. Using distributed virtual memory techniques selectively on user processes, however, as opposed to its own separate programming model, is certainly a feasible way to simplify the task of migrating processes between nodes for various purposes, including load balancing.

10.4.4 The Microkernel Level

Operating systems based on the microkernel concept have a structure that is particularly well suited to supporting kernel-level single system image across message-passing clusters. This is inherent in the structure that a microkernel imparts to an operating system, plus one additional "feature."

The notion of a microkernel is to provide, in the operating system kernel, only the absolute minimum set of facilities required in any operating system: process creation, the bases of virtual memory management, primitive I/O, and, very importantly, interprocess communication. That set of facilities is chosen to be just minimally sufficient, in the sense that the facilities can't be made from each other and all other required operating system function can be created using them.

The rest of the required operating system functions are provided by service programs that are written, and run, outside the kernel. These provide the services of file systems, trees of process structures, particular algorithms and techniques for virtual memory management, and so on. The true application processes communicate with those service providers, and the service providers with each other, using microkernel-provided communication; that communication comes in the form of message passing.

Thus, if an application process wants to create or open a file, it sends a message to the file system service; if it wants to create another process with the UNIX-like semantics of a hierarchy of processes, it sends a message to the UNIX-process service; and so on. This is a client-server paradigm within an operating system.

Obviously, when you're sending messages there must be a way to identify the service to which you're sending a message. This is another of the required minimum facilities the microkernel provides.

Well, All You Have To Do Is Just make the message-passing work between machines—implying that the identifiers form a cross-machine single system image—and presto change-o, you've got a kernel-level single system image. Every application automatically talks to the (one) file system server on all the machines, the (one) UNIX-process server, the (one) external communications server, and so on, automatically unifying every one of the traditional operating system facilities implemented under the microkernel.

Microkernel systems such as Chorus [A⁺92], Amoeba [Tan92], QNX [Hil93], Mach [Tan92, BRS⁺85, Ras86] and OSF/1 AD [WLH93] provide such cross-machine message-passing. The identifiers are unified in Chorus through Universal Identifiers (UIs), and in Mach through what's called NORMA IPC

(IPC = Inter-Process Communication; for NORMA, see page 248), and QNX through what's called FLEET.

When you've enabled cross-machine message passing you've got a very workable single system image. Unfortunately, you very probably also have a massive serial bottleneck. Or rather, a collection of them. Every application reading from a file, for example, has to go through the file server even if the files are on different machines; every application creating a UNIX process has to get (at least) a UNIX process **id** from the UNIX-process server; even more ludicrous, every application requiring virtual memory would have to go through a single server on every page fault. As a result, it's still necessary to parallelize the servers, distributing them through the machine; this is, for example, the "TNC" part of OSF/1 AD TNC.

I did say *"may"* have a bottleneck, right? The above is utterly true, no "may" involved, for massively parallel systems. What if you've just got a li'l 'ol cluster of four or so machines? Some things still have to be done as part of release 1.0; a centralized bottleneck in a virtual memory system, for example, will cripple anything. Nevertheless, you no longer have to do everything all at once. The work of parallelizing different servers can be prioritized—and shipped incrementally, just as over-kernel applications can be shipped and might just begin returning incremental revenue. Or, machines in a cluster that are specialized for file serving might be the only ones running the (parallelized) file server. While there's still no such thing as a free lunch, the incremental shipping of function may at least break the log-jam of funding a kernel-level SSI as a "big bang."

All of the above discussion of microkernel benefits is relevant only if micro-kernel-structured systems are good for server systems, with their high system and I/O demands. I am not going to open up that topic here, but rest assured that it is not a point with which everyone agrees.

10.5 Hardware Levels

To round out this discussion, it should be noted that there is no reason for single-system-image support to come to a halt even with the lowest levels of software. Levels of hardware-supported single system image are shown in Table 10-4.

Memory-coupled clusters, such as could be created using the techniques of DASH and SCI, provide a single system image of the various memories in the different cluster nodes.

At the very bottom level we of course have the SMP, which provides hardware-level SSI support not only for memory, but also for I/O within a system. Perhaps such lowest-layer hardware support is one of the reasons why

Table 10-4   The Hardware Levels of SSI

Level and Name	Examples	Boundary	Importance
		APPLICATION AND SUBSYSTEM LEVELS	
		OPERATING SYSTEM KERNEL LEVELS	
H 2	memory	SCI, DASH	memory space	better communication, synchronization
H 1	memory and I/O	SCI, SMP techniques	memory and I/O device space	lower overhead cluster I/O

SMP software exhibiting an SSI is common, whereas more general cluster-based kernel-level SSI is not. On the other hand, perhaps that support is common because an SMP is totally useless without it, whereas clusters can limp along.

10.6 SSI and System Management _____

Having divorced system management from the notion of single system image, it is necessary to indicate where it fits in. The functions involved in system management are many; the general areas involved and some examples are listed in Table 10-5. Notice that these functions do not include load balancing or other direct performance issues; here we are discussing management only.

System management is, in the SSI formulation used here, a suite of applications. Furthermore, it is the one application suite that every system must provide. No matter what else is done with a computer system—OLTP, number-crunching, multimedia gropeware, whatever—system management must always be done. It is the one universal application.

It is also a large, messy, tedious, and generally ugly task whose minimization is earnestly desired by everybody. On top of that, it is pure overhead: It does not directly contribute to the functions for which the system was purchased.

All the above implies that of all applications that could be SSI-enabled for clusters, system management is the most desirable. Nobody wants to multiply a large, already-messy task by the number of nodes in a system. Some would go so far as to say that without SSI-enabled system management, there is no single system image at all. I do not, because there are useful applications and subsystems (for example, batch systems, databases, OLTP) that provide major SSI function in the absence of SSI system management.

There are significant differences in system management depending on whether it is done in the context of a non-SSI kernel (the toolkit layer) or in the context of an SSI kernel API. Those two cases will be discussed separately.

Table 10-5   Aspects of System Management (Not Exhaustive!)

Resource Management	Subsystem Management	Network Management	Security Administration	Problem Management
Installation Install Update Merge Uninstall Device Configuration Users Accounting . . .	Subsystem Configuration Control Start Stop Status Subsystems Spooler TCP/IP SNA NFS	Alerts SNMP NetView . . .	C2 functions Authentication Users . . .	Alerts Diagnostics Error Report Logging . . .

10.6.1   Over-kernel SSI System Management

SSI constructed by using over-kernel facilities, such as is supposed to be supported by OSF DME, HP OpenView, IBM NetView, and Sun NIS+, is a kind of meta-application suite. It provides a framework that glues together individual machines' independent system management functions, collecting data from them and controlling them. The individual machines' system management facilities must still be present and, in general, must be modified to communicate with the framework and be consistent with it.

This organization is wholly consistent with the origins of this type of support in distributed computing, where heterogeneity is a fact of life. It would be impossible to create one system management program suite that directly managed all manufacturers' systems; many system management functions are there to deal with specifics of the operating system and the hardware that differ from vendor to vendor.

The distributed origin of over-kernel facilities causes the functions provided to be overkill for clusters (they are also insufficient in some ways, which will be noted later). The task these facilities set for themselves is much harder than the management of clusters, because clusters are single, not multiple, computing resources and so their nodes should be managed uniformly.

As an example, consider software distribution. An elaborate mechanism is defined for the OSF DME (Distributed Management Environment) that allows an installer to take into account which systems have licences for the software to be installed and which do not, as well as the update level of each system. All of this is specified in a way that handles problems of very large scale; in particular, data and storage structures are used that are capable of handling thousands of distributed system nodes. The resultant subsystem allows the construction of sophisticated software distribution applications; it is not a solution of itself.

Virtually all of this complexity is unnecessary with clusters. Problems of scale for around ten machines, kept as similar as feasible, do not require such sophistication. The software environment on each node can, for most clusters, be identical, since it is a single computing resource and any job could be run on any node; in fact, the issue with clusters is often how one manages to make and keep that environment identical.

The DME facilities could be used to construct a distribution system appropriate for a cluster. There are two difficulties with this approach. In the first place it is both inelegant and inefficient, exposing the user (system administrator) to complexities that are completely unnecessary in this context. In the second place, what happens to clusters that, as they assuredly will be, are connected in distributed systems? Distributed systems are big enough already, but are more or less limited in size to the number of desks at which people sit. If clusters proliferate, the number of nodes will grow substantially. It is a vast simplification of the overall problem to be able to consider each cluster as a single node relative to the distributed system, a node that uses the equivalent of a single-system "install" problem to install each item of software once, for the entire clustered machine. The hierarchy of system management control implied here could be constructed with over-kernel DME(-like) facilities; but once again it exposes the user (administrator) to unnecessary complexities.

On the other hand, distributed computing is extremely widespread, and whatever else a system administrator does, he or she will do system management of distributed systems. The tools provided will already be familiar, and the complexities of heterogeneity will already be mastered. Management of clusters may well be considered, in this context, an already-solved problem.

Except, of course, that the above paragraph is hypothetical. The solutions to this problem are potential only; the grand unification of DME has not yet been deployed and is in fact getting competition from vendors' individual solutions, which are expanding to control systems made by other vendors. It will take quite a while to achieve universal coverage.

10.6.2 Kernel-level SSI System Management

System management for systems providing an SSI at the kernel level is a very different proposition from the over-kernel case. Rather than being a meta-application suite, it must be the same as the system management functions of a traditional single system.

The reason is that many of the functions of system management involve changes to data used by the operating system: descriptions of devices, tables of users, priorities, and so on. There is exactly one operating system in a kernel SSI system, so there is exactly one copy of all this information[3], and exactly one application to manipulate it. Managing a kernel-level SSI system is precisely like managing a single machine.

This is precisely the most desirable solution for clusters: Manage them as if they were single, giant computers. In a distributed context, it still is the desired solution. The (single) system management functions of a kernel-level SSI system can interact with the distributed management framework, when it exists, exactly the way any other individual system would. It is "one" system and acts like that in the framework.

The development cost of this solution is essentially the same as the development cost of the system management facilities required for any substantially changed operating system. How great it is depends on where one is starting; in particular, systems already supporting SMP architectures are closer to what is needed than systems that do not do so, since they are already modified to account for the existence of multiple processors.

---

3. This is a simplification that depends on the hardware and software implementation. Among other things, configuration data held in machines' nonvolatile memory will clearly be replicated at each node; so will other items.

Many of the required functions just port without change, taking advantage of the kernel-level SSI provided by the system. For example, a printer management subsystem, which on UNIX controls queue daemons and the like, will work fine and automatically take advantage of multiple nodes in a kernel-level SSI cluster. This follows from kernel-level SSI's maintenance of the uniprocessor image of process trees and I/O devices, and from an assumption of at least primitive automatic load balancing.

Other functions require modifications consistent with SMP support. The UNIX **ps** command, for example, tells a user facts about their own (and others') processes. It must have not just the usual modifications for different kernel data but in addition must allow users to find out whether their processes are on multiple machines—along with, presumably, yet another option allowing that data to be either displayed or not.

More serious than modifications to **ps** are the implications of a cluster having multiple physical I/O subsystems, one for each node in the cluster. This means that there must be an additional identifier associated with each I/O device, something that says which I/O subsystem it's physically attached to. Devising such an identifier is easy; it's sure to be directly derived from whatever is used to name a cluster node. However, the use of that identifier must now permeate all device manipulation programs, at least to some degree, right up to the user level interface. In a UNIX context, one might be able to avoid some of the complexity, kludging something together by using some strange encoding within the major and minor device number fields. However, systems using an interactive, iconized, graphical user interface to ease system management should grow some graphical representation that allows visual grouping of devices according to the node they're plugged into. (Making it work with multi-tailed disks is be an interesting problem.)

All this work would, of course, be unnecessary if good distributed system management were universal. So would any and all enhancements to the management of single machines. I don't see that work stopping yet.

On the other hand, while the computer-science-theoretical issues of name spaces and parallelizing ("distributing") operating system functions are getting some play in the research community, I don't see anybody lining up to do the same for system management.

Part 4:

Systems

11

Symmetric Multiprocessors vs. Clusters

This chapter *does not* state that symmetric multiprocessors do not scale.

What it does state is almost as easy to understand.

➢ Both the hardware *and* the software costs of dramatically scaling an SMP up in size increase quite rapidly as the size of the system increases.

➢ The hardware cost of similarly scaling a cluster does not rise nearly as rapidly, and the software cost probably does not, either.

➢ Clusters have inherent advantages in some areas not related to performance scaling, such as system availability and low entry cost.

➢ The advantages of clusters may be moot if necessary software functions do not (yet) exist in cluster-parallelized form, forcing larger per-installation software investment.

I've highlighted the first statement above, and led off with an only slightly misleading summary, because experience has proven that there's a drastic tendency to oversimplify the discussion about to begin, very often turning it into "Mine scales, yours doesn't." "Does to!" "Does not!" This is true whether the discussion is technology- or marketing-oriented.

For example, while this book was being written a colleague engaged in market support approached me. He knew I'd been writing the book and wanted some technical ammunition for a cluster over a large SMP in a marketing situation. The conversation went something like this:

"Do you have anything technical," he asked, apparently meaning magical, "written down that I can use to prove they should buy a cluster to support a really big system?"

"Look, it's really not all that simple." Typical technical answer, right? "Maybe they shouldn't. If it were simple, I wouldn't be writing a whole book about it. And the book's not finished."

"But I really need something now. We're meeting with them tomorrow." (They're always meeting with them tomorrow.)

"Well, I've already written a discussion of the things SMPs have to do to scale, and how that affects their scaling. I'll print out a copy and give it to you."

That was an earlier version of Chapter 6 about SMPs, which at the time contained some of the discussion now appearing in this chapter. Several days later I saw him in the hall.

"Hey," I said, "how did the meeting with that customer go?"

"Great! Oh, that was a really good chapter. I enjoyed reading it. Feel like I learned a lot."

"Thanks. I'm glad it was helpful. What did you tell the customer?"

"Oh, you have to boil these things down. We told him SMPs don't scale."

Aarrgghh!

That is not just the outraged cry of an offended technical weenie. There is a practical problem with this. It leads to the "everybody's a liar" technology-merchant syndrome, which is closely related to the more well-known "everybody's a cheat" rug-merchant syndrome. In the latter, the first Byzantine rug merchant who a customer approaches in a bazaar says "Don't buy from anybody else. They're all cheats." Whether it's true or not, this at first seems like a pragmatically useful thing for the merchant to say,[1] but it's useful only if the customer doesn't talk to any other rug merchants. Visiting all ten of rug merchants in the bazaar reveals that everybody says the same

---

1. Of course, if untrue this statement is immoral, but I wouldn't want to have to count the number of ways there are to wriggle a weather-beaten conscience out from under that. "It's better for him to buy from me anyway, for other reasons." "I have a wife and kids to support." And so on.

thing, so every merchant has 9 out of 10 people saying he or she's a cheat. It doesn't take the customer too terribly long to conclude that everybody's a cheat—after all, nearly everybody said so—and treat them all accordingly.

"Everybody's a liar" works similarly. If the issues are boiled down too much, like "SMPs don't scale," or, on the other side, "Clusters aren't an industry-standard solution," you leave open the possibility that a competitor will say "But we go to 30 processors" or "But we adhere to the following four thousand industry standards." These counterstatements actually have little to do with the questions asked. That doesn't matter. What a customer, who has better things to do than learn the technology, will see is two "experts" contradicting each other and will likely conclude that everybody's a liar. Replying later—"Well, under some circumstances they can scale, but not yours" or "But not all standards are important"—even though true, implicitly admits that the original statement was a lie. "But I was just *simplifying* things for you" is a feeble counter. It's clearly better to gain credibility from the outset, and doing so can cut the legs out from under oversimplifiers before they open their mouths. If you don't want to plod through every detail, buy another copy of this book and give it to your customer. Make that many copies, and give them to all your customers. Let them start collections. Great, big collections. If you give them enough copies, they might even read some of it in their spare time. Yes, I'm shameless.

Among the technical community, things also tend to get simplified. However, it often happens for a different reason.

There are "dog people" who can barely tolerate sharing a planet with cats, and "cat people" who express equivalent sentiments about dogs. Similarly, there are technical "cluster people" who, having invested immense mental and physical resources to advancing the cause of cluster products and technology, consider SMPs the work of the Devil; and technical "SMP people" who, having similarly invested in SMPs, consider clusters deviant, unnatural abominations whose existence should not be tolerated.

Specialization and the attendant mental and career investment is usually necessary. Also, the always-limited funding available for development and purchases (customers make career and financial investments in these things, too) often forces an attitude of "if you're not with me, you're against me because you're stealing my resources." Since each species has plenty of both good and bad points, discussions between their polar adherents, while amusing to watch for a while (sort of like professional wrestling), seldom conclude satisfactorily (unlike professional wrestling).

This is the chapter in which I try to play the unwashed technical agnostic, attempting to summarize the issues on both sides. I am certain that the result will satisfy neither camp; in particular, the SMP folk will, not without justification, consider me biased. After all, what's the title of this book?

To those of you who have slogged all the way through all the previous chapters, congratulations! And thank you for the implied compliment. Unfortunately, you'll find that this chapter contains some redundancy, as well as an unconscionable number of references to what has come before, but I fear it's justified. I know from past experience (see "History" in the Preface) that there are people who will pick up this book and immediately read this chapter first, without paying any attention to what came before.

11.1   What's Being Compared? _____

It was pointed out in Chapter 5 that cluster hardware organizations can vary all over the map. How can we compare SMPs with something so nebulous? The comparisons, as it happens, are based on just a few characteristics, shared by nearly all forms of cluster. Specifically:

> ➤ **Local Memory.** Each machine in the cluster has its own local memory. Communication with the other machines is less efficient than access to a machine's own memory. There may be memory that's shared in the sense that multiple machines can reference it by addresses. If the memory is not all shared, the local memory referred to here is the unshared, private part. If, on the other hand, all the memory is accessible by all processors, it's assumed that there is a local-remote distinction wherein remote access is less efficient.

> ➤ **Local I/O.** Each machine has its own attached I/O. Access to another machine's I/O is less efficient than access to a machine's own I/O. There may be shared disk, access to which is less efficient than access to private disk; this inefficiency may be due, for example, to the protocols involved.

In contrast, an SMP can be crisply defined as was done in Chapter 6. It's a computer with multiple processors and only multiple processors, no multiple memories or multiple I/O systems, and every processor has equal (therefore complete) capabilities. "One memory" implies cache coherence and uniform access time to all of memory.

These two cases do not cover all the possible overtly parallel computer organizations. In particular, confusion may arise over the memory or memories are organized. Systems that share memory, but have nonuniform access noticeable enough to affect programming (NUMA systems) are not SMPs as treated here, because they violate the assumptions of the SMP programming model (Chapter 8). Neither are computers that have no, or partial, cache coherence or strange difficulties with ordering of operations; same reason. These may be clusters. Or they may be tributes to the imagination and/or persistence of their inventors. In any event, they're not treated here.

Even though most comparisons are covered by the above, the many possible variations on cluster hardware organizations may still cause variations in the details of the discussion below. While not every nubbin can be examined in detail, most of the larger effects will be noted.

A final, general, preliminary comment: Despite the fact that clusters have been sold for several decades, the countervailing fact that they aren't considered a recognized discipline (Chapter 1) has prevented that experience from being adequately digested by the broad computer technical community in the open literature. The situation is just as if there were little experience in the use of clusters, even though that's actually not true. The result, nevertheless, is that in several cases the comparison below is limited by lack of knowledge.

Curiously, this happens most often in situations where clusters are at a disadvantage.

11.2   Conventional Wisdom

While performance is not the only issue involved in comparing cluster and SMP, it is certainly an important issue. Other issues, such as reliability, are discussed later.

The conventional wisdom about the relative performance of SMPs and clusters is qualitatively represented in Figure 11-1. Notice that the graph in that figure contains no numbers whatsoever (that, and the fact that its content goes up and to the right, makes it a perfect marketing chart). It is, in fact, exceedingly difficult to get any two individuals to agree on any of the key numbers on the horizontal axis. I have even had people nitpick the detailed shapes of the curves, despite the fact that it's only claimed to be qualitative. That nitpicking is why, for example, the curves exhibit only the faintest actual drop from their peak as the number of processors is increased. God Forbid it should look like the performance can decline noticeably when you *add* processors. For either SMPs or clusters. (P.S.: It can.)

Despite all of this, the curves' *general* shape does appear to capture the intuitive beliefs of a fair number of practitioners of the aggregate computing art. The specific features capturing those beliefs are the vertical gap between the curves on the left-hand side and the continuing rise of the cluster curve. The

Figure 11-1   SMP vs. Cluster: A Marketing Graph With Two Humps

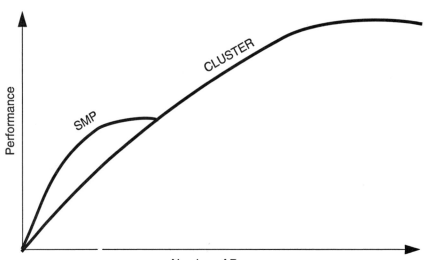

reasons why these features are generally believed will be lightly touched on here and discussed in more detail in later sections.

The vertical gap indicates that for systems containing relatively few processors, SMP systems produce the best performance: they get more out of each processor. They have a general advantage in easier load balancing. As long as the number of processors is modest, that load balancing, along with the intrinsically "tight" low-latency communication SMPs provide, more than adequately compensate for problems that may arise in memory bandwidth, I/O bandwidth, and the like. Clusters lag because of their generally greater overhead for internode communication, which leads to greater difficulty in load balancing, queueing effects, and I/O directed through "other" nodes.

As the number of nodes increases, however, the scaling challenges described in detail in Chapter 6, "Symmetric Multiprocessors", come into play: SMP designs must expend more and more energy and cost to provide adequate memory and I/O bandwidth, contention becomes an issue, and load balancing has to deal with more and more esoteric phenomena.

Since clusters remain intrinsically balanced in their memory and I/O capabilities—when you add a node, you add a memory subsystem and an I/O subsystem—they keep on increasing in performance beyond the largest point at which SMPs can cope. They do not keep using their processors as inefficiently as they did with few nodes. They get worse. However, they don't get worse as precipitously as SMPs do, and as a result they eventually pull ahead and provide greater available performance than SMPs.

One result of relationship this is that SMPs offer better cost-performance than clusters as long as one is within their applicable performance range. They simply utilize their processors better, so where they can be applied, they will be superior. The range of SMPs does not, however, extend as far as clusters' range.

This is actually a trivially true statement, since the nodes of clusters can themselves be SMPs. So take your biggest SMP, and add another to make a cluster. You're bound to get *something* out of the additional machine—more than the biggest SMP alone.

All of this begs a very important question: Performance doing what? What are the characteristics of the application workload? This issue was considered in some detail in Chapter 7. There is a very broad range of applications, overlapping the range used for SMPs almost entirely, that utilize clusters at sizes greater than SMPs can attain. These include applications running in the highly parallel SPPS mode—Serial Programs, Parallel (Sub-) Systems—which require no user-level, complex parallel reprogramming whatsoever and are the primary use of overt parallelism.

The statement above did say "almost" entirely overlapping in application range. There are applications that work well on SMPs but simply die, horribly, on clusters because they cannot be performed with an adequately large grain size (Chapter 8) because of our current problems with intermachine communication overhead. Bandwidth of standard, open communications, on the other hand, can already be larger between N machines than on the internal bus within an SMP with the same number N of processors (Chapter 3, Chapter 6).

What about the other issues: Is availability important? Time to market? The usability of clusters compared to the standard, complete single system image of SMPs? (Answer: not as good.)

"All generalizations are false, including this one."[2] That's part of the reason why SMP vs. cluster remains, and probably will remain, a controversial issue for some time to come. It's also why a simple explanation does not completely suffice, so a more detailed discussion follows.

---

2. Alexander Chase, "Perspectives," 1966.

11.3 SMP and Other Scaling_____

A key issue raised by Figure 11-1 is just where the higher intersection point is: How big do you have to get before clusters take over? What this question really means is: How big can you usefully make an SMP? Do SMPs scale?

Well, how many processors can you stick on one of these things? Do you believe that sales rep, probably glistening with 100%-commission snake oil, when he says you can just plug in more processors, no matter how many, no matter what the workload, and performance keeps going up? Then what about the statement that you can find in myriad papers and books on parallel processing, repeated mantra-like beyond the point of boredom at technical conferences and workshops on parallel processing, or used to be, anyway, before commercial large-ish SMPs starting coming out: *S M Ps don't scale. | Four to six is it. | My machine scales beautifully, but <repeat>*[3]. At least they aren't on commission (most of them, anyway)—but: If that's true, what are companies like Hewlett-Packard, IBM, Sun Microsystems, Pyramid, Encore, and Sequent doing marketing SMPs that can have 8 to 32 processors each? A factor of 32 in performance growth sounds fairly scalable to me, and even 8 isn't particularly shabby. Those are reputable companies. They can't all be lying, for heaven's sake. Well, OK, maybe one might try; it's a competitive business. But *all* of them?

So, do SMPs scale? The answer is yes... and no. (Of course.) Since there's obviously a bit of controversy involved here, you shouldn't expect every expert on the subject to agree with the answer presented here.

As is usual in this kind of thing, the real issue is semantic: What do you mean, "scale"?

As Gordon Bell has pointed out [Bel92b] in an article favoring SMP scaling, there are many different ways in which a computer can scale: generation scalability, the ability to use successive generations of ever-faster processors intact; problem scalability, the ability to attack ever-larger problems; and size scalability, the ability to grow larger. We're primarily concerned here with size scalability, with some problem scalability thrown in. Even just size scalability, however, is sufficiently illdefined that it's not explicitly defined in textbooks (necessarily noncontroversial). Here is one definition.

From a computer-scientific point of view, a system that scales has four properties.

_____

3. Best used as accompaniment to a Conga line.

1. **It can be really, really big.** If you can't reach over 100 processors, you're not in the club. Thousands of processors are more common claims, if not achievements. Making really big computers is the basic issue; the other properties are just there to make sure there's some practicality and purpose to doing so.

2. **You make it big by replication** of some basic elements. Wheeling out the old box, and wheeling in a completely different one, is cheating.

3. **Really big ones don't have exorbitant cost.** The key word here is "exorbitant." Obviously making a machine twice as big will at least double the cost, assuming quantity discounts of some kind aren't in effect. However, making a scalable machine twice as big shouldn't, for example, cause some key component to get four times as expensive (nothing should go up as the square of the size—N^2—or faster; increasing at $N \log(N)$ is considered acceptable, since otherwise communication gets rather hard).

4. **Really big ones are (nearly) as efficient as small ones.** If you don't get something out of making a big computer, there's no point to the exercise. This quality has two competing variations on the ground rules for "as efficient."

   - In the first, more traditional, variation, the size of the work must stay the same as the machine grows: On a bigger machine, the same work should run faster. In the second, more recently expounded *problem size scaling* view, the problem size grows along with the machine: Double the size of the machine, and you should do twice as much work in the same amount of time.

   - The problem-size scalers say the reason for a bigger machine is to run bigger problems; running the same old thing faster is irrelevant. The traditionalists say the problem-size scalers are cheating, because many of the mathematical problems used as examples increase their work faster than the problem size (matrix dimension, for instance), so when scaled up they strain the machine less in crucial aspects like communication and synchronization.

No matter what side you take on the problem-size debate, this is a reasonably strict definition. Unfortunately, it really doesn't have much to do with what sales personnel, company public-relations flacks, and most customers of SMPs mean by the term "scale."

Proponents of marginal systems have predictably devalued the term "scale" for marketing purposes. They are likely to claim that a system scales if you can plug in more processors. Period. All that proves is that the cost scales up as more processors are purchased. It may do absolutely no good, or do some good only when running some deranged workload—and never mind exactly how much good. The word "linear" is often thrown in, apparently because it sounds technical. Speed can't, for example, double when a second processor is added unless someone's figured out how to eliminate all inter-machine synchronization overhead (I won't bother listing all the chapters mentioning that). The only other possible meaning of "linear," a straight line on a graph, is satisfied if adding each processor adds the same amount of performance. Any amount. 0.0001%, for example.

Pressed, marginalizers will retreat into phrases like "it doesn't scale on *every* workload," or even "how *well* it scales can vary." This neatly obfuscates terms like "most cases," since in defining them you end up with ratios of infinities: even the most deranged case can have an uncountable number of variations.

By no means are all vendors like this, but there's nothing to stop anyone from using the word this way, and it's happened enough that the term "scale" means little or nothing when appearing in a press release or product information flyer. That is, unless it has been explicitly defined, preferably with reference to a standard benchmark so you can tell under exactly what conditions the system scales. This devaluation of "scale"[4] is one reason why standard benchmarks are extremely important (but see "Benchmarks" in Chapter 11 regarding cluster benchmarks).

Between the extremes of strictness and meaninglessness lie most users of computers.

Customers would like a system that can grow with minimal disruption and cost to cover two contingencies: anticipated growth of their business, and uncertainties in estimating exactly how much computing power they need for new applications or procedures. Plugging in a few more processors is tremendously simpler and cheaper than tediously reprogramming a system to be more efficient. With a purchased application, the reprogramming option may not even exist. So, the customer issue is headroom. This issue is closer to the problem-size scalers than the traditionalists, but doesn't really care about actual efficiency unless it interferes with growth.

How do SMPs do with respect to the only real definition, the one customers want?

---

4. To say nothing of the devaluation of every other word describing a good quality of anything. It's almost enough to make one call for the word police. Benchmark police will have to do.

It is almost certainly possible, given a sufficiently large amount of effort, resources, and ingenuity, to build an SMP in which a very, very large number of processors can be efficiently used. By very, very large, I mean *big* by current standards—certainly a much larger number of processors than any SMP currently on the market, possibly by a factor of two. Thousands of processors is probably beyond reach, but ignoring that aspect of "scale" isn't bothersome for practical purposes. A hundred? Quite possibly. This estimate assumes, of course, that you don't break the SMP programming model. If you do, all bets are off, the sky's the limit, and have I got a bridge to sell you.

Assuming appropriately tuned system software and a suitable workload— an extremely big and rather tenuous assumption—such a machine would scale, in the sense that plugging in more and more processors would result in more and more performance.

There is, however, still a problem. The base cost of a few-processor system, and the incremental cost of adding a processor, gets larger as the maximum usable number of processors goes up. Figure 11-2 illustrates what this

Figure 11-2   The Cost of SMP Scaling

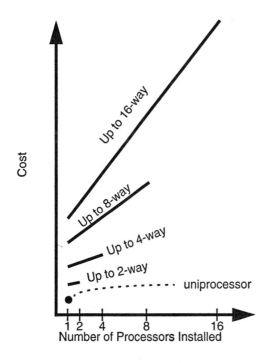

Assumption:

Except for their maximum scaling, all 5 system designs are identical and use all of their processors with equal efficiency.

means. It plots the cost of five hypothetical SMP systems against the number of processors installed in them. The five systems are assumed to be identical, including the efficiency with which their processors can be used, except for the maximum usable number of processors each supports: 1, 2, 4, 8, and 16. (The 1-processor system isn't an SMP, of course; it's a uniprocessor.)

Supporting a larger maximum number of processors injects more fixed cost into the system, so the 1-processor version of the 16-way costs more than a 1-processor version of the 8-way, and so on. That fact sets the differing heights of the leftmost point of each line. The support structure that must be included with each processor becomes more costly when a larger maximum number of processors is to be supported. This makes the slope of the 16-way's cost line larger than that of the 8-way, and so on.

In addition, the problem gets worse as processor speed goes up. With reference to Figure 11-2, the leftmost points of the lines spread further apart and the slopes diverge even faster.

It would be nice to be able to inject some hard data into that qualitative graph, since the quantitative issues are crucial. Who cares if the base cost goes up if it goes up only 1% when moving from a 2-way to a 32-way maximum system?

Unfortunately, this quantification is impossible. Accurate cost data is always closely held, company-confidential information, particularly when it's accurately assembled, and costs estimated in academia never take all factors (negative and positive) into account. Prices are public, but their relationship to cost varies not only from company to company but within a single company's product line. In particular, there is usually less profit margin built into the price of smaller systems. There's also the difference between list price or street price, which can vary not only geographically but by market segment; engineering or scientific users typically demand, and receive, much deeper discounts than do commercial users (who often care less because they intend to make a huge amount of money using the systems, anyway). All these factors make prices at best an extremely fuzzy indicator of cost.

Nevertheless, and under these circumstances justifiably not naming names: There is at least one open-systems based, UNIX-oriented SMP on the market, the product of a successful vendor, designed to scale to at least 16 processors, whose base list price is nearly 100 times the base list price of several uniprocessors that are very comparable in uniprocessor performance, technology, general market, and so on. A factor of 100 is sufficient to pierce the fuzz surrounding this comparison and indicate that the differences are huge. Figure 11-2 is, if anything, qualitatively understating the case.

Why is scaling SMPs up (in the dictionary sense of "scale") so expensive? If doubling the maximum number of processors more than doubles the price, and it does, perhaps we should be looking at other ways of getting a bit more lowly parallelism—like clusters.

Some of the reasons for a larger base cost are blindingly obvious. If you're going to fit more processors into a box, you need a bigger box. You also need larger basic circuit boards (motherboards or backplanes), a larger power supply, and more fans to carry away more waste heat. You also have increased shipping costs because all of those things make it heavier, and you quite possibly have to invest more of your field force's time in setup because the whole thing is physically more unwieldy. Did I mention increased insurance premiums because it does more damage when dropped on someone's foot?

Such things add up to a very significant difference in cost, but hardly of the magnitude suggested by the price difference mentioned. They also don't readily explain why the incremental cost of adding a processor should be larger. This is where the memory contention, memory coherence, and sequential consistency discussed in Chapter 6 start coming in.

That chapter did not demonstrate, nor could it, that SMPs don't scale in a usable, marketable, customer-oriented sense. It couldn't because it's not true. You can build big machines in which many processors can be effectively used. What it did attempt to demonstrate is that there are intrinsic costs to building large SMPs that are disproportionate to the size of the system. Compared with smaller SMPs, larger ones must have:

➤ larger caches

➤ longer cache lines

➤ more memory banks

➤ more expensive switches

➤ bigger, faster buses

➤ more complex coherence protocols

➤ shared caches

➤ more expensive serial consistency facilities

Moreover, these are not artifacts. They are necessary responses to the required SMP programming model and the resulting Von Neumann bottleneck. Attempts to circumvent them, such as DASH and SCI, suffer when applied to common commercial workloads that perhaps take the SMP model a bit too seriously.

Each of these techniques is expensive and exerts a multiplier effect on the cost of the system. They are all in addition to the "blindingly obvious" cost increases mentioned above. The net result is that scaled-up SMPs are intrinsically less cost-effective than small ones, and the difference is quite significant.

That conclusion is based on hardware alone. The cost of increasing the parallel efficiency of software must also be included. As implied in Chapter 8 and discussed explicitly for databases in Chapter 9, stringent measures must be taken in the key parallelized applications, subsystems, and operating systems, the programs that enable SPPS operation, to obtain parallel efficiency in large SMP systems. Locks must be even finer, granularity even smaller, and cache locality taken explicitly into account—which starts to bend, if not break, the so-convenient SMP programming model. Imposing such measures is also an increasingly expensive undertaking as the number of processors increases.

The net of this scaling discussion is that SMPs have limits to their ability to scale, but the limit is not a crisp, sudden, solid, brick wall. It is, rather, like an increasingly steep slope; the incline never reaches a point of pure vertical impossibility, but progress becomes increasingly difficult.

A lot of this discussion, however, is based on the assumption that the machines involved will strictly adhere to the SMP programming model. There are solutions that are SMP-like, and scale better by breaking away from that model (SCI, DASH, distributed virtual memory, and so on). But these are different programming models. This runs up against the "critical mass" problem (Chapter 8). Software has to change to use them, particularly lucrative commercial subsystems. It won't until they're there. But you can't get them there until they change. Moreover, the trend is to mass-market, inexpensive, portable programs that aren't going to change to fit your wonderful hardware; you can bribe a few people to port to it, but this quickly becomes a losing proposition. The only opening other than SMP is the one that comes in out of the distributed processing arena, the message-passing model. Clusters.

Before drawing any conclusions from all this, as if I haven't already, let's directly compare SMPs not with themselves, but with clusters, and consider some things other than performance.

11.4   SMP-Cluster Performance Comparisons_

Table 11-1 summarizes the primary issues involved in comparing cluster and SMP performance. Each issue is discussed individually in the sections that follow.

This section in particular may appear to be anti-SMP. That is not the intention. The situation is simply that for many basic hardware "feed and speed" issues, it is rather straightforward to point out challenges that SMP systems must overcome and clusters just don't have in the first place. Clusters face other different challenges, like adequacy of system administration and a smaller repertoire of applications and subsystems; it doesn't do much good to have a wonderfully hardware-efficient system that won't run the application you want.

11.4.1 Memory Bandwidth

The *bete noir* of SMP system design is memory bandwidth, which becomes increasingly difficult to provide. For SMPs, this one has already been beaten to death. How do clusters fare?

Table 11-1   Performance Comparisons of SMPs and Clusters

Characteristic	Symmetric Multiprocessor	Cluster
memory bandwidth	to avoid limiting performance, must become increasingly expensive	scales automatically with cluster size
memory contention	to avoid limiting performance, must become increasingly expensive	does not exist between nodes
I/O bandwidth	to avoid limiting performance, must become increasingly expensive	scales with cluster size, but inter-node communication requires 2X increase for I/O-intensive workloads if clusters are connected through their nodes' I/O
load balancing	increasingly expensive, but routine use of global queues provides good results if grain size large	degradation due to the need to have separate queues per node
overhead for "other node" I/O	does not exist; no degradation	effects not well understood; may or may not be significant; large internode bandwidth requirements again for I/O-intensive workloads

Clusters just do not have this problem. Every time you add a node, you add not only a processor (or a whole SMP) but also a memory subsystem to support that processor. This keeps the whole in balance in a very straightforward fashion.

11.4.2   Memory Contention

SMPs' other *bete noir*, or perhaps it's just a *bete gris*, is memory contention. This has been beaten to death, too, as have the complicating factors of memory coherence. Clusters?

Since the separate nodes of clusters do not access the same memory, they exhibit no memory contention in this form. That was straightforward, too. But there are other complications.

The degree to which contention takes place in an SMP depends heavily on the software workload. It can be argued that if an SMP were programmed like a cluster—specifically, carefully programmed to avoid interprocessor sharing and data access of all kinds, since that has lower efficiency—it would exhibit no more contention than the cluster does. It was pointed out that database vendors, to support the heroic SMPs that are out there, are doing just that (Chapter 9). But, in fact, no SMPs are programmed *exactly* like clusters are programmed. For example, the database vendors who are talking about running cluster code on big SMPs (page 286) still get their I/O and system functions funneled through an SMP operating system. Furthermore, when cluster-like programming is used, some of the things provided through the SMP model would be at least reduced if not lost: load balancing, running previously-created applications and subsystems that use the shared-memory programming model, and so on.

Those wondering about the effects of different cluster structures may well wonder if clusters connected by using memory-coupling techniques can exhibit contention overhead, too. 'Course they do. Many of the system formations possible using SCI (or DASH) as a coupling technique, for example, will look like SMPs, or look like clusters, depending on how one chooses to program them. If such systems are programmed like an SMP, their added internode latency will cause the contention overhead to be excruciating. This is a case where an SMP (-like) system will—or at least should—be programmed like a cluster so that contention effects are minimized.

Since contention depends on software, the degree to which it affects performance depends (very strongly!) on the design of the operating system, subsystems, and applications being run.The commonly nasty cases are heritage commercial subsystems, of the type that engender the shared-cache SMP systems discussed in Chapter 6.

11.4.3   I/O Bandwidth

Let's now cease assuming that we are dealing solely with CPU-bound applications whose performance is limited only by pure processing speed. If one increases the processing power of a system by a factor of N, one should also increase its available I/O bandwidth by the same factor. Otherwise the desired increase in throughput or turnaround time will be limited by the I/O system.

This situation is very similar to that of memory bandwidth. SMPs are limited by intrinsically having a fixed-size I/O system that either limits them, or, if designed to avoid limitations, adds the cost of overdesign when the processor slots aren't fully populated. However, this is an easier hurdle to cross than the memory issues. Since most I/O devices (but not the newer communications links) have a relatively low data rate, large machines look more like they're leaking data as a mist of fine droplets—the death of a thousand cuts rather than the gushing of a single artery. It's usually, but not always, easier to add a bunch of cuts than to find a new artery.

Clusters sing the same old tune they did for memory: You add an additional I/O subsystem every time a new node is added, so they intrinsically stay in balance.

In this case, however, it's possible to point to difficulties with clusters that SMPs do not have: additional internode communication requirements. The bandwidth between cluster nodes, for I/O-intensive workloads, must equal the total useful I/O bandwidth of any other node if performance is not to be degraded. See Chapter 5. So, if inter-node communication is I/O-attached in a cluster, the required I/O bandwidth requirement of each node is doubled.

Getting the communications bandwidth needed to achieve this doubling does not appear to be a problem. The data firehoses now becoming available for internode communication—FCS, ATM, SCI—can handle this requirement (Chapter 3). But hardware I/O subsystems, to say nothing of the software, are going to have their hands full handing that communication at full bandwidth. And, of course, current communication latencies must be improved.

Of course, if clusters are used to run multiple, serial, computationally intensive, tasks that have minimal I/O requirements, this extra communication is not required. Whence the current utility of assembled and preassembled clusters.

11.4.4   Load Balancing

Load balancing refers to distributing work across the nodes of any system in an attempt to keep all nodes equally busy. As was discussed in Chapter 8, load balancing is not a trivial operation on SMP systems. Nevertheless, it is routinely performed in what is usually judged to be an adequate manner; examples were given in Chapter 8 and Chapter 9. The existence of a common global pool of memory and I/O resources is a significant, if not crucial aid in accomplishing load balancing.

There is not much experience with clusters in this area. Nevertheless, as the example in Chapter 8 indicated, it can safely be said that clusters have a much harder time at it. There is no good place to keep a global queue of tasks; other, less satisfactory techniques must be used. If a global pool is maintained, the additional overhead of communication between cluster nodes comes into play. It is much easier on a cluster than on an SMP for a global queue to become a serial bottleneck, and even on an SMP it is common to have trouble with it.

Even if there is no problem finding out what jobs are to be done, the additional internode communication overhead of clusters is a negative factor. Compared to an SMP, a cluster requires the use of more processing power and time to migrate a job from one node to another. This overhead limits a cluster more than an SMP in how well it can balance the load. This may change, however, as the faster communications facilities become more widely deployed.

11.4.5   "Other Node" I/O

In balancing the computational load across a cluster, one will often wind up with a job on one node requiring data that resides in the I/O subsystem of another node. Getting jobs to execute on the "right" node with respect to their resource needs is a substantial problem with clusters, and one that assuredly will not always be solved with respect to data location.

It is entirely possible for an I/O request at one node of a cluster to be satisfied by real I/O done on another node. This is done all the time today with distributed file systems, for example. However, there is clearly noticeable overhead involved; and as discussed back in Chapter 4, if a distributed file system is actually used, the disk I/O of the entire cluster is limited to the capacity of the communication to the file server—clearly a serial bottleneck and much lower than the capacity of just about any single machine's I/O systems.

However, as also mentioned in Chapter 4, it is possible for a cluster to use an internal peer-to-peer I/O system. The shared disk file system of Open VMS Clusters is one example, while the "I/O shipping" or "function shipping" of databases is another.

SMP systems, once again, simply don't have this source of overhead. Accessing the common I/O facilities does involve overhead, such as data structure locking and attendant contention, but the magnitude of this overhead is quite possibly lower than it is in a cluster.

11.4.6 Scalability

SMP scalability, like a few other topics, has already been covered in perfectly adequate detail (translation: beaten to death). What about clusters?

The limits to scaling cluster systems are not well understood. Load balancing, queueing, I/O, and "Other Node" I/O effects undoubtedly limit them. Nevertheless, production cluster systems exist that are very much larger than any proposed true SMP. Furthermore, as was mentioned above cluster nodes can themselves be SMPs. So, make a two-machine cluster of the largest SMP available, and you've got scalability above that possible with an SMP.

11.5 Other Comparisons _____

Performance is not everything. In many cases, it is not even the first bar over which a product must pass. How SMPs and clusters compare in other areas is summarized in Table 11-2, and discussed in this section.

11.5.1 Memory Utilization

Clusters are somewhat poorer at utilizing a given aggregate quantity of memory than are SMPs. This is true in two ways.

First, each node in a cluster must contain an independent copy of at least the kernel of an operating system, whereas a single copy is shared by all the nodes of an SMP. This is not as large a difference as one might initially think, because the actual space used by an operating system kernel is in large part determined by data structures whose size is proportional to the system resources and load. For example, tables for memory management are in many cases proportional to the total real memory available and to the amount of memory allocated for all active jobs. For comparison purposes, one should assume that the aggregate, job-required memory size and job load is the same on an SMP and a cluster. Then, the aggregate table size

Table 11-2   Other Comparisons of SMPs and Clusters

Characteristic	Symmetric Multiprocessor	Cluster
memory utilization	"optimal" due to existence of single memory pool	suboptimal because of boundaries between nodes' memories, but probably not a large effect
application and subsystem support	common using industry-standard techniques, e.g., threads	not as common as SMPs, but rapidly increasing
high availability	difficult to achieve: shared data structures, global power boundaries; few if any implementations exist	easier to achieve: data structures and power are naturally separate; many implementations exist
programming model	SMP shared memory; will not work on clusters	message passing; works with greatly reduced efficiency on SMP

added up across all cluster nodes will be in the same range as the total allocated in an SMP's memory. Nevertheless, there are unique items, such as the code itself, base table structures, standard per-machine daemon processes, and so on, that must be replicated. So clusters are at a disadvantage in this regard, but it is seldom a major disadvantage, and in most cases it is insignificant.

The second memory utilization issue arises because the aggregate memory of a cluster is divided into chunks, one at each cluster node. While it may be possible to access foreign nodes' memory with certain cluster organizations, the overhead is larger than in an SMP. This means that there are job mixes that can run on SMPs that cannot run as efficiently on a cluster. Assume, for example, that the aggregate memory in both a two-node cluster and a two-node SMP is 100 Mbytes: 100 Mbytes in the SMP, and two 50 Mbyte memories in the cluster. The SMP can simultaneously run two jobs with memory requirements of 30 Mbytes and 70 Mbytes respectively. The cluster cannot run the 70 Mbyte job without degradation anywhere, since no one node's memory is larger than 50 Mbytes.

This difference may possibly be alleviated by the use of distributed virtual memory techniques applied between cluster nodes, letting one node swap pages back and forth from the other, effectively using it as a fast disk cache (something like this was proposed as an alternative to the ALLCACHE system of KSR). With the very fast communication potentially possible between nodes, this technique might work quite well. Again there's a disadvantage for clusters, but it's not clear that it's a very big one.

11.5.2 Application and Subsystem Support

Another point that must be reckoned with is how well subsystems and applications can make use of the system.

SMP hardware is effectively an industry standard. Threads and other techniques, covered in Chapter 9, are common, and, by whatever means, support is nearly ubiquitous.

Although there is significant and growing activity in this arena for clusters, as documented in Chapter 2 and Chapter 9, it is frail in comparison. Support is growing among open system database vendors, and several hardware and software vendors offer administration, batch, and login facilities. This is an area of much activity.

Nevertheless, the facilities available for support of general use of clusters have nowhere near the universal availability of such facilities for SMP systems.

11.5.3 High Availability

Availability is an area in which clusters have natural, inherent advantages.

Consider, for example, a processor failure that occurs during an I/O operation, and suppose the processor simply goes catatonic, that is, stops in its tracks—the most common case. The other processors are not directly affected; they continue to go about their business normally. The afflicted processor was probably (by Murphy's Law) deep into the manipulation of esoteric data structures that are far within the operating system kernel and when it stops will leave them in a disheveled state: Locks may be set that the processor will never reset, data structures may be in an inconsistent state with pointers aiming who knows where, and so on. All of this will be true of both an SMP and a cluster system, but the effects are different.

In the SMP system, the other processors all share the same kernel data structures; they must, since that is the way they keep themselves from stepping all over each other's feet while accessing shared resources such as the I/O subsystem. Therefore, sooner or later, other processors will encounter the deranged data structures. They may sit forever, waiting to acquire a lock that the dead processor will never release; or they may follow a lunatic pointer into oblivion; or they might even notice that things aren't kosher— and issue the dreaded kernel panic and stop. The net result is that the damaged processor eventually brings the whole system down. This can be summarized as: Processors in an SMP exhibit sympathy sickness.

In a cluster, on the other hand, each machine has its own, private set of data structures for managing its own, private I/O operations in its own, private I/O subsystem. Another node's problems do not affect it; it can keep on going more or less indefinitely. The relatively simple inclusion of a hardware and software "heartbeat monitor" can enable it to detect when a sibling is dead and initiate appropriate action, such as a forced power-on reset. That will often fix the problem, since most failures these days are software, not hardware. (The "processor failure" above was more likely a software failure causing the processor to enter into an infinite loop of some sort.) If it actually was hardware, well, it is easy for the machines in a cluster to be on separate power boundaries and probably separate power supplies. This arrangement allows one node to be powered down without affecting the others, so maintenance can be done with the rest of the system still operating. Few SMP systems put processors on separate power boundaries.

This is not to say that SMPs cannot be made more highly available. It is possible to write code that detects processor failures and "cleans up" after a malfunctioning processor, and it is possible to put SMP processors on separate power boundaries. It has, in fact, been done for years in the mainframe arena. The only problem is that this is an excruciatingly difficult trick to pull off. For example, far more code must be devoted to error detection and backout from a failed function than is devoted to doing the function in the first place.

That expense is the primary reason why no open-system SMP vendor has equivalent availability function built into its hardware and software. It's just so much cheaper, nowadays, to provide a whole separate computer onto which processing "fails over" when the primary machine dies. Every open-system vendor now provides that, either on its own or through a third party (mentioned in "Availability Clusters" on page 43). Surprise! They're all two-node clusters. And every customer immediately wants to use both nodes at once...

But don't let anybody tell you that their SMP is "highly available" just because it has more than one processor. What is usually meant by that such availability claims is that the system can re-boot and come back with a dead processor configured out. While a usable facility, it is far from "high availability" by anybody's definition, especially since most failures are in software these days. (Well, after you count loss of power, anyway.) (And failures of fans.)

There is an interesting, and somewhat unfortunate, linkage between inherently lower availability and cache coherence. The example of an SMP given above, with the other processors exhibiting sympathy sickness, effectively assumed that while the processor had gone bye-bye its cache was still operational. This is probably an unwarranted assumption. If the cache is also *hors de combat*, then other processors will immediately begin seeing the incorrect values in memory that cache coherence masks. The effect is the same: sympathy sickness. This effect, however, is likely to spread the disease faster.

This problem afflicts scalable coherence schemes, like SCI and DASH. It obviously affects them if they're programmed like SMPs; the cases discussed above apply directly. It will be true even if they are programmed for the most part like clusters, but use their shared-memory capability to do message-passing. SCI, for example, threads a coherence chain through multiple nodes. Nodes may appear on the chain because they participated in a linkage sometime in the past, not only because they're involved in immediate operation (cache randomness again). If any node on that chain is inoperative, attempts to manipulate the chain as a whole will fail, as will manipulations that happen to affect it because of position (like casting out a line from a working node). DASH gets in similar trouble; it just doesn't happen as sequentially. So, while these methods may possibly lead to clusters with much lower-overhead communication than through an I/O system, they sacrifice one of the key characteristics of clusters.

11.5.4   Programming Model

The largest nonperformance difference between SMPs and clusters is that they naturally support different programming models. This difference is the one that underlies differences in system availability and the number of applications and subsystems that run on one or the other. Two chapters were devoted to this issue, so little will be repeated here. However, again it must be mentioned that SMP shared-memory programs will not run on clusters, whereas message-passing programs will run on SMPs, albeit at significantly reduced efficiency. And message passing should not be maligned because of difficulties with distributed processing; distributed processing systems are necessarily very bad message-passing systems.

11.6   Conclusions? _____

Who wins? There's obviously no TKO; this bout must be decided on points.

SMPs, for reasons that are both historical and inherent, have very significant advantages over clusters in the areas of software and usability: single-system administration, load balancing, middleware support, and so on. At the same time, clusters have a number of basic hardware "speed-and-feed" advantages over SMPs: memory bandwidth, lack of memory contention,

I/O bandwidth, availability, and are positioned to immediately benefit from the new, fast communication technology as it arrives. This is a hard one to call in general.

For large systems, however, that argument has been hopefully made strongly enough that very large SMPs are disproportionately costly.

That conclusion by no means indicates that building large SMPs is immoral, illegal, fattening, or even mildly stupid. Customers often enough want the biggest machines they can fit under a single system image, and the industry standard for that is currently the SMP. If customers want something, building it can't be wrong. The market for large machines and therefore the engineering effort is primarily performance driven, and only secondarily cost driven. That is why even disproportionately costly solutions make sense.

This conclusion about SMPs also does not impugn the solutions that have been developed to SMP challenges. The collection of tools and techniques that have been developed are without question technically admirable. Multihundred pin buses, for example, running at over a gigabyte a second, with bursty traffic, and moreover manufacturable in quantity, are fantastic achievements indeed.

It does, however, mean that large SMPs are potentially vulnerable in their market position. If large SMPs are disproportionately costly, small ones are, conversely, disproportionately inexpensive.

More: As the other shoe of mass-market microprocessor performance inexorably drops, the integration levels, volume production, and lower-cost sales channels of this other market paradigm are going to make little SMPs as cheap as dirt relative to heroically large SMPs. That market will never produce large, cheap SMPs. It's a market that's allergic to heroic hardware because it's primarily driven by cost and client machine needs, not performance and server machine needs. But the individual processors—just a few per system—are still going to be very, very fast.

Once upon a time, as these things go, mainframes were also disproportionately costly. Were the reasons similar? Probably not; it's hard to tell, and the reasons really don't matter. If cheap, small, potent SMPs can be coupled to produce customer-required performance levels, and, moreover can be coupled in ways requiring less heroic measures than building large SMPs—then no more is required. History will repeat itself in short order. The workloads the cheap solution covers (Chapter 7) overlay SMP uses too much. The disproportionately cheaper solution will triumph as inevitably as workstation-class machines have triumphed, for the moment, over the old minicomputer and mainframe markets.

Those unheroic, workaday, cheaply coupled guys are clusters.

Why We Need the Concept of "Cluster"

The preceding chapters have been concerned with defining and elaborating on the concept of a cluster of computers, along with the comparisons and issues raised by that concept. All this has hopefully been interesting and useful.

But before those discussions, the introduction indicated that even more was involved—that we *needed* the concept of a cluster, distinct from general parallel or distributed systems. Lacking that concept as a normal part of our thinking, a number of bad things are happening without our intention or notice.

1. Benchmarks are not giving us the information that we expect.

2. Research and product development directions are misguided.

3. Conceptual issues are confused, to the detriment of a variety of areas.

4. Products are being pursued that are maladapted to the market.

This is the chapter that backs up those assertions, explaining exactly how, and in what sense each of them is meant.

12.1 Benchmarks _____

Ideally, standardized benchmarks should provide purchasers and developers of computer systems with many different types of information. They should let you:

> compare systems of similar architecture—for example, a collection of SMPs;

> compare systems of differing architectures—for example, SMPs, vs. uniprocessors, vs. clusters;

> identify the parts of systems whose enhancement will yield the biggest benefit—for example, a developer might analyze benchmark execution to determine whether total performance is enhanced more by increasing the cache size or by increasing the CPU speed;

> choose an initial list of candidate systems for implementing a particular application, in two senses: first, by narrowing the performance range to the approximate level required; and second, by determining the interest of a vendor in that type of application, as indicated by the vendor's willingness to go through the often expensive process of running a related benchmark. The cut on performance can only be approximate, of course, because no benchmark's characteristics exactly match the real application that is to be run.

No benchmark is perfect. Otherwise, there wouldn't be so many of them, each emphasizing different aspects of system performance. That's the reason for the qualification mentioned at the end of the above list: All a benchmark measures is how fast the benchmark runs, not how fast your application will run—even though that's what everybody wants to use it for.

Unfortunately, some of the most common benchmarks in use for commercial processing do not recognize the difference between distributed systems and clusters: They lack the concept of a cluster. As a result, their ability to provide every one of the benefits listed above is, for clusters, significantly compromised.

12.1.1   The TPC Benchmarks

The most widely used and quoted benchmarks in commercial data processing are those of the Transaction Processing Performance Council (TPC). The TPC is a consortium of 44 leading hardware and software companies worldwide; it was founded in 1988 to define transaction processing and database tests. The council's TPC Benchmarks A, B, and C (TPC-A, TPC-B, and TPC-C) are far and away the most popular standard benchmark for determining performance and price/performance in a commercial context [Tra93a, Tra93b, Tra93c].

For all practical purposes, these are *the* industry benchmarks for on-line transaction processing; there is no other game in town. Since on-line transaction processing is a very large market, these benchmarks are widely used even though they are large, expensive, and require a very significant investment in equipment and time to run. The cost of the system that had to be assembled to perform the TPC-A benchmark on a Compaq server, for example, was over one million dollars, even though the base price for the system benchmarked was less then $20,000. Publication of the benchmarked system's price every time the performance is mentioned is one of TPC requirements.

These benchmarks are also quite carefully defined and controlled. Compliance with the definitions is independently audited for each system whose results are published.

The various TPC benchmarks are based on different commercial scenarios. TPC-A and -B are modelled on a branch banking debit/credit scenario and are currently the most widely quoted; TPC-A is interactive, whereas TPC-B is a batch version of the same thing. The more recently defined—and even more expensive to run—TPC-C benchmark is modelled after a warehouse order entry and fulfillment facility. As this is written, it is the intention of the TPC to phase out TPC-A and -B by the end of 1995 in favor of TPC-C as a more realistic overall indicator of commercial performance. A new benchmark, TPC-D [Tra94], is now being developed to provide performance information in a decision-support scenario.

12.1.2   Parallel Execution

When any of these benchmarks is run on a symmetric multiprocessor, the benchmark's workload is distributed among processors the way one might intuitively expect, as illustrated in Figure 12-1. No distinction is made between a uniprocessor and an SMP. A single input stream of transactions to be performed is simply presented to the machine. Exactly how that stream is presented, whether through front-end machines or via terminals, or whether a client-server variation is used, is the subject of very detailed specifications that have nothing to do with this discussion.

The issue we're concerned with is this: It is up to the operating system, database system, and possibly transaction monitor (if used) to divide the work among the processors to obtain the best possible throughput. This is, at least, what I'd expect—that the effectiveness of a parallel system's distribution of work is one of the things implicitly measured by the benchmark.

Figure 12-1   TPC Workload Distribution in an SMP

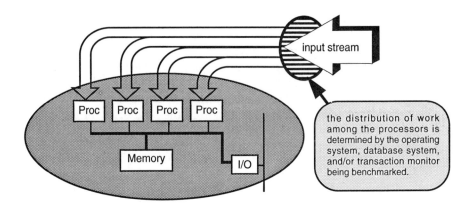

All of these benchmarks explicitly include consideration of distributed computing. For TPC-A and -B, distributed branch banking is modelled by splitting the input into separate streams. Each stream represents a transaction workload for a separate machine serving one or several branches, so 85% of each stream's the work load is *completely local*: it is *defined by the benchmark specification* to require no data outside the machine on which it impinges. The other 15% is uniformly distributed among the machines being benchmarked.

This "85/15 rule," as it is colloquially referred to by benchmark mavens, very appropriately models branch banking. Most teller transactions, at least 85% in the benchmarks, deal only with accounts at that branch; but some, less than 15% in the benchmarks, deal with accounts at other branches. The reason for the qualifiers "at least" and "less than" is that the nonlocal fraction is uniformly distributed across *all* the machines, including the local one. This means that some of those 15% come back to the local branch and/or machine. For example: If two branches are involved, each will get 7.5% (15%/2) of the uniformly distributed transactions in addition to its base 85%. Thus a total of 92.5% of each machine's work is purely local, requiring no communication, synchronization, or interaction at all with the computer at the other branch.

This scenario of distributed processing is also applied to clusters, even if the clustered machines are rather geographically localized—meaning all the machines are in the same machine room or even the same rack. Figure 12-2 illustrates this for a two-machine cluster.

This is the way every published TPC benchmark result for a cluster should be interpreted. It is the accepted, audited interpretation of the TPC-A and -B

**Figure 12-2   TPC-A, -B Workload Distribution In a Two-Machine
Cluster**

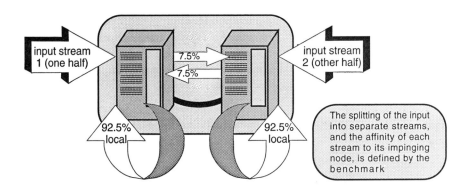

input stream
1 (one half)

7.5%

7.5%

input stream
2 (other half)

92.5%
local

92.5%
local

The splitting of the input
into separate streams,
and the affinity of each
stream to its impinging
node, is defined by the
benchmark

benchmarks[1]and is performed in this manner by every vendor of clustered systems. Distributed systems are defined to be evaluated in the way described, and clusters, as is usual, are lumped in with distributed systems while SMPs are not. The concept of a cluster, as distinct from a distributed system, is missing.

It was mentioned above that the TPC-A and -B benchmarks were being phased out. What about the newer TPC-C benchmark? The situation is similar, but slightly more complex. TPC-A and -B have only one type of transaction. TPC-C has several different types, and each is distributed according to different rules. In TPC-C, the transaction type defined to be (at least one of the) the most voluminous, the Payment transaction, is governed by an 85/15 rule. The other transaction types also have locality rules: 99/1, or even 100/0. Unlike TPC-A and -B, however, TPC-C does contain operations (table inserts) that intrinsically require communication beyond that implied by these locality rules. The degree to which that affects the amount of intermachine communication depends heavily on the implementation of the database system that is benchmarked. There is insufficient experience with this benchmark to gauge the general effect of these table inserts. Counterbalancing the situation with the inserts is the fact that TPC-C contains some very long-running transactions, which will require little if any communication during their execution. This is believed to be more representative of most

1. Specifically, it is the interpretation of section 5.3.4 plus Example 2 of Clause 10 in the *TPC Benchmark A Standard Specification, Revision 1.2*; and section 5.3.5 plus Example 2 of Clause 10 in the *TPC Benchmark B Standard Specification, Revision 1.2*. Both were cited above; see the references for details.

commercial practice than the TPC-A and -B situations, which have only very short transactions.

The net of all these "buts" and "excepts" is that there is very likely at least as much locality built into TPC-C as into the others, and probably significantly more. Such locality is a characteristic one very reasonably expects in geographically dispersed, truly distributed systems, for a very straightforward reason: The geographical distribution of the physical warehouses implies that their customers will tend to be local, as was the case with branch banking.

As was the case with TPC-A and TPC-B, applying these rules of locality to geographically compact clusters is the accepted, audited interpretation of the benchmark definition, and every published TPC-C result should be interpreted as conforming to those rules.[2] This is why the discussion of Tandem's record TPC-C result on page 33 emphasized that it was benchmarked as a 7-node cluster, even though each of those nodes, a 16-cell loosely-coupled multiprocessor in Tandem's terminology, could technically have been considered a 16-way cluster of itself.

12.1.3   Difficulties

If someone intends to use a cluster for on-line transaction processing with multiple input streams that have significant locality, this benchmark definition, and its cluster interpretation, is very reasonable. If that is not the intended use, this benchmark is not suitable. This is just like any other benchmark: If it matches the intended use, the benchmark is appropriate; if it doesn't, it's not.

Nevertheless, the characteristics of the TPC benchmarks as applied to clusters cause difficulties.

The first problem is that TPC benchmark results for SMPs and clusters are measured using the same unit. For example, a system's performance is specified as so many "tps-A" (transactions per second, TPC Benchmark A) whether it is a uniprocessor, an SMP, or a cluster. The use of the same unit, to say nothing of the same benchmark name, encourages everyone to compare the tps-A of a cluster with the tps-A of an SMP, as if they measured the same thing. Even if the TPC were to shout the difference from the housetops, people would still compare them just because they've got the same name. For a uniprocessor and an SMP, they are the same. For a cluster, clearly they are not.

---

2. Specifically, the rules stated in sections 2.4.1.5, 2.5.1.2, 2.6.1.2, 2.7.1, and 2.8.1 of the *TPC Benchmark C Standard Specification* referenced above.

This name confusion alone limits the ability of these benchmarks to perform one of the four functions mentioned at the start of this section, namely perform meaningful comparisons between different architectures. Such comparisons breaks down particularly in the area of scaling: how performance increases (or doesn't) as one adds additional, parallel, processing capability. The predefined locality present in the benchmark causes clusters to demonstrate rather good scaling characteristics: Their tps-A (or tps-B, or tpm-C) ratings usually increase quite nicely as more cluster nodes are added, even if internal cluster communication facilities are relatively meager. SMPs, which do not enjoy this predefined locality, have a much harder time scaling their performance on these benchmarks.

Unlike clusters, whose internal communication is bounded by the 15% limit, SMPs must contend with interprocessor communication that keeps increasing as the number of processors rises. As a result, the measurements published for SMP systems are more robust than they are for clusters, meaning: The SMP results tend less than the cluster results to predict lower performance than one will achieve in practice. In practice, you can encounter a worse workload distribution than is used for a cluster; but you cannot encounter one worse than the SMP benchmark uses.

This disparity betwèen SMPs and clusters affects another item in the list of things benchmarks should be good for: choosing a candidate list of systems appropriate to a particular application. Often neither sales personnel nor customers understand the difference between the SMP and cluster benchmarks. Actually, my experience is that this is an understatement. In the last few years, I've met with over a hundred customers and potential customers for open server systems, and a good fraction of that many sales representatives. I have yet to find *one* of them who understood this difference before it was explained.

The results of this confusion? Customers include clusters in their initial list of choices on the basis of the published standard benchmarks. Then, when they run their own benchmarks, everybody is dumbfounded over why the system isn't performing as well as anticipated. (This is the point at which I receive an often frantic phone call from the field.) Time and money has been wasted. Even more of both is wasted if the cluster is installed solely on the basis of the standard benchmark, without benchmarking the customer's application—absolutely never recommended, but it happens often enough—and shortly thereafter the machine is thrown out, accompanied by suitable invectives, because it doesn't perform adequately. These situations are far from universal; more cluster installations are successful than not. However, customers do encounter these problems on a regular basis, and as a result end up convinced that clusters simply don't work or require inhumanly complex data and input partitioning efforts to work adequately. Sales representatives wind up with similar opinions, reducing the number of customers to whom clusters are even suggested.

So far, the discussion has deliberately avoided a key question: Is the benchmark as defined appropriate for clusters? Another way of stating that is: Does the benchmark adequately predict the performance of clustered systems as they will typically be used? My experience has been indicated above. None of the *cluster* situations I've personally observed had multiple input streams with the kind of locality exhibited by the benchmark. Distributed situations are, of course, another issue; locality is usually quite apparent there. Several years ago I heard of, but did not personally investigate, one cluster installation that did exhibit such locality; it involved a cluster of mainframes.

It's therefore my personal opinion that for clusters, as opposed to distributed systems, the vast majority of customers (to say nothing of the hapless sales and other field personnel) would be better served by a benchmark that can be compared to the uniprocessor/SMP case without being misleading. This could be accomplished in at least two ways: If locality is considered normal, one could incorporate it into the SMP as well as the cluster benchmark. If locality is not considered normal, eliminate it from the cluster benchmark. Or, if it's impossible to decide whether locality is normal, have two benchmark variations—one with and one without locality—and publish separately labelled results.

All this presumes, of course, that one recognizes that a cluster is not the same thing as a distributed system.

Let's assume that a "0/100 rule" (no locality) is closer to "typical" customer use—a hard thing to define; everyone thinks they're typical—than the "85/15 rule" used in the benchmark. Under that assumption, the current benchmark's ability to provide the other benefits one can expect from standardized benchmarks is also compromised.

Comparison between machines of the same architecture—between clusters—is compromised because of the small amount of internal, intermachine communication engendered by the 85/15 rule. This low level of communication means that after one has installed minimal communication, additional communication facilities will not improve benchmark performance. Machine A, with minimal communication and faster processor complexes, might well benchmark faster than Machine B, with much better communication but slightly slower processors. This result would certainly not be bad if the 85/15 rule corresponded to "typical" use; in fact, it would then be the answer one would want the benchmark to give. But if 0/100 is closer to actual use, one will never find out that Machine B might well be better.

Improving the breed, pinpointing areas that yield the most cost-effective performance improvements, is the final area where these benchmarks are compromised if the 85/15 rule is not representative of most situations. In parallel systems of all stripes, including clusters, the important issues are always communication, synchronization, and load balancing, with administration hanging in there as the very important but grubby practical issue that nobody ever wants to work on. The TPC benchmarks are not intended to deal with administration (as I said, nobody wants to work on it). But the 85/15 rule does most of the load balancing for the system; and the internal communication and synchronization required under the 85/15 rule are sufficiently minor that clusters could probably be connected by wet string and still benefit from faster processors, not better communication.

In fact, this rule leads to the silly result illustrated in Figure 12-3: Suppose you take three collections of identical processors, with eight processors in each collection. One collection you make into a cluster of uniprocessors connected to each other using shared disks and Ethernet (even if it's not wet). Another collection you make into a single large SMP, internally connected by a great, big, fast bus. The third you make into a cluster of moderate, say four-way, SMPs. Assume everything else is as similar as possible: everyone has at least enough memory, large caches, the same aggregate I/O bandwidth and I/O initiation rate (harder for the SMP, but assume it anyway), the same number of disk drives, and so on. Benchmark them using the TPC benchmark rules. Ignore cost (but the clusters are probably cheaper). Because of the 85/15 rule, the cluster of uniprocessors will win by a large margin, and the cluster of SMPs will come in second. Every time.

Figure 12-3   Handicapping a TPC Race

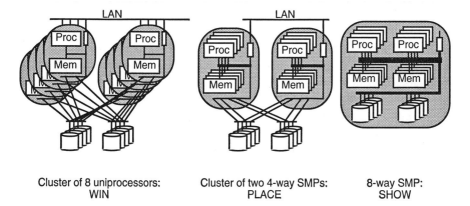

Cluster of 8 uniprocessors:
WIN

Cluster of two 4-way SMPs:
PLACE

8-way SMP:
SHOW

The reason this result is silly is because it says that Ethernet (10 Mbits/second) plus disk bandwidth (a few Mbytes/second, with milliseconds of rotational latency) is a *better* communication medium than multi-hundred-megabyte/second or even gigabyte/second internal busses connecting the same number of identical processors.

12.1.4   Why Am I Doing This?

This section, by far the longest of this chapter, has been devoted to showing in some detail why clusters might not give as good performance on commercial workloads as we have been lead to believe. This probably seems like an odd thing for a proponent of clusters to do. It may quite possibly lead to fewer of the current crop of clusters being sold.

Even if the standard benchmark results for clusters aren't directly comparable to those of uniprocessors and SMPs, pretending they are can still get you in the door, and anybody with any exposure to marketing knows how valuable that is. Once you're in, even if performance isn't, well, quite as good as was anticipated, it will still be possible to emphasize some of the many other factors present in any purchasing decision: high availability, lower cost, support, scalability (with appropriate tap-dancing around performance), financing, customer relationship, delivery schedule, and so on. These things make a large difference, and a customer might very well be happier with the whole package that can be offered with a cluster than with, for example, an SMP system lacking the other goodies. But an initial performance cut is like single-issue politics: No matter what else you have to offer, you don't get in the door and don't even get a chance to bring up the other issues.

But truth will out, in the long run truth in advertising is best, and the good guys always win in the end. Right? OK, I had long hair and a beard (actually, a goatee) in the 60s too, but along with everybody else I've grown a 90s reality bump and it's uncomfortable with that.

The real problem is not that clusters might not be as good as the current crop of numbers indicates. The problem is that word "might." To design systems you have to have a workload against which to evaluate them. For commercial systems, the TPC benchmarks are it. Nobody I know of looks seriously at much else when designing systems for commercial data processing. This is not entirely bad. They could do much worse, especially for uniprocessors and SMPs; the TPC benchmarks definitely have cache, memory, and I/O characteristics that appear to be at least roughly appropriate for commercial data processing. Besides, you have to publish the benchmark numbers eventually anyway; might as well know what they are likely to be. So, they get used, and since there are always limited resources very little else gets looked at. Result: Nobody knows the degree to which artifacts like the 85/15 rule are affecting system designs. We can't understand clusters without breaking this mold. While it holds, we don't know what we're doing.

A short story:

Once upon a time there were two system designs, call them A and B, and only enough money to pursue one. Happens all the time. Design B—not mine, by the way; I was an onlooker, and for a number of reasons irrelevant to the current discussion I didn't like it—I've called "B" because it was a very Bad Boy. Not only was it politically unpopular, it also egregiously violated several of the more religiously held technical dogmata concerning how parallel systems should be built. But wow, did it have a whale of a lot of internal communication and fast synchronization. Its internal communication was exceeded only by the stubbornness of its advocates, without which it never would have lasted as long as it did. (Also happens all the time.)

Design A, on the other hand, followed the path of righteousness. Politically and techno-aesthetically correct, it boasted fairly good internal communication with the usual overhead entailed by righteous communication. This would merely be a typical story of product development politics, since Design A did of course win (for a number of complicated reasons having little if anything to do with the point of this story), except for one thing.

In the course of the struggle, some performance modelling was carried out, based on benchmarks very much like those of the TPC. Unlike other such modelling, this version had the ability to vary the local/global ratio. At the TPC-standard 85/15 value, assuming the same processors and support gear all 'round, you couldn't tell the difference in performance between A and B. At 0/100, under the same assumptions, the Bad Boy won Big. In fact, it won big enough to represent almost an entire generation of microprocessor development, worth millions of dollars.

Is that what we're throwing away?

Does anybody really know?

By the way, that modelling was officially judged irrelevant to the decision between the designs. Why? It was declared that the modelling showed the designs to have identical performance in customer situations officially sanctioned as "typical."

12.2 Development Directions _____

There really is more than one reason why we need the concept of clusters. I will now stop droning on about benchmarks and discuss more of those reasons.

The next reason on the list is the issue of development direction. Without the notion of a cluster as a target for development, a home for various products and projects, there are hardware and software efforts that are expending unnecessary effort trying to be something they are not; they are also not getting the recognition and success they deserve for doing things that are natural to them. This section will concern itself with just one example of this, the development of kernel-level, single-system-image (kernel-level SSI) operating systems.

Kernel-level SSI systems such as Locus TNC [Thi91], Amoeba [Tan92], Sprite [O⁺88], and QNX [Hil93] have been developed in the distributed computing milieu.³ They had to be developed there; traditionally there is no other place for them. Usually they are positioned as alternatives to over-kernel toolkits like DCE [Ope93, CP93]; again, there is no other place for them. But such systems are not the best fit to the requirements of distributed computing for at least three reasons.

The first reason is that distributed computing places a very high value on the coupling of heterogeneous systems, specifically including machines running differing operating systems and having different hardware data formats. This is a very important issue in distributed computing; much of the distributed computing market lies in creating order out of an existing chaos of previously purchased workstations. Pursuing this goal is abundantly right and proper for distributed systems, but kernel-level SSI systems have a hard time of it. Portability across operating systems is a contradiction in terms, since they are the operating system; how can they not replace what's there? Denigration city. (Locus TNC is an extension of an operating system personality under a microkernel, which is not quite the same thing but is close enough.) Dealing with different hardware data formats is certainly possible, but the degree of coupling such systems entail causes this to be a much larger performance burden than afflicts the looser coupling of over-kernel toolkits. Despite such problems, heterogeneity has been pursued by kernel-level SSI developers because it is of great value in distributed computing—and, lacking clusters, there is no other place for these systems.

The second reason kernel-level SSI systems are disadvantaged derives from the need to accommodate local autonomy. This is highly desired within distributed computing: This is my workstation, with the software tools and hardware widgets I paid for, but please update all the standard stuff for me, but I didn't mean *that* stuff—I don't use it and I need the space for some-

---

3. Amoeba actually targets what amounts to a cluster; good for them. QNX targets embedded control situations, which is a different milieu altogether. They are all, however, published and evaluated against the standards of distributed computing.

thing else; oh, and this whole department all wants it like this except for Joe, and the dummies in Accounts Receivable across the hall want something totally different. Like hardware heterogeneity, local autonomy probably can be done within kernel-level SSI systems; Turing machines are indeed universal. But it is against the grain; it's not what they naturally do, which is make everybody exactly the same; so it is awkward and expensive. That they find it harder counts against these systems. It's irrelevant that this is most often precisely what's desired in clusters.

The third reason concerns a a less well advertised characteristic of the distributed computing environment: high-speed variation. In any sufficiently large collection of workstations, somebody's always turning their machines on or off (to say nothing of spilling coffee on them), messing with the communications links, and so on. Therefore, machines are always popping in and out of visibility and whole collections may be isolated for some periods. With respect to kernel-level SSI systems, Turing was still right, doggone him; techniques have been developed that allow those systems to cope with this variation (see [Thi91]), and their developers are probably, justifiably, quite proud of them. It's an enormous mental and probably physical effort to make that work.

From the standpoint of clusters, that effort could have been saved. How often is communication within a single room (or rack) going to be interrupted, much less split into autonomous survivable groups, or one machine go down while the others stay up? It's not that such events will never happen, but an order of magnitude or two difference in how often they happen can make an enormous difference in the complexity of the programming needed to respond to them. Even after accomplishing coping with this temporal irregularity, the developers get little recognition for their efforts, because the techniques devised depend heavily on a kernel-level SSI context. Therefore it's dismissed as not being terribly relevant. It's indeed not relevant—to distributed computing.

As a result of difficulties like those mentioned above, kernel-level SSI systems have not attained any great degree of popularity. Unlike over-kernel toolkits, they are mismatched to the market they are trying to serve. They do continue to be pursued; good researchers are nothing if not persistent.

Yet in their pervasive, well-defined, and cleanly delineated single system image, kernel-level SSI systems have significant advantages that over-kernel toolkits lack—when considered in the context of clusters. It is difficult to conceive of dynamic load balancing with process migration, for example, outside of the context of such systems; in the canonical fully heterogeneous, widely distributed system with provision for local autonomy such load balancing is against the grain—a task so difficult it is not worth doing outside of special cases. Kernel-level SSI systems' all-encompassing, single-system administration for clusters has been mentioned earlier as an area where these systems provide a tremendous advantage; yet because it results in OS-specific administration of multiple machines, it is anathema to traditional heterogeneous distributed computing, which must supply a common denominator. It's regarded as a problem rather than the major benefit it can be—for a cluster. Without the concept of a cluster, these benefits are hard to appreciate.

Kernel-level SSI systems may yet flourish, as they have not so far. But they will not flourish as *distributed* operating systems, as they are more commonly known. Rather, they may flourish as excellent *cluster* operating systems. The route may not be direct; OSF/1 AD TNC on the Intel Paragon and the Convex Exemplar operating system are recognizable as a successful route to system-level support for massive parallelism. That, of course, involves tuning and concentration on not quite the right set of issues for cluster support—a point returned to in "The Lure of Large Numbers" later in this chapter.

12.3 Confusion of Issues _____

Another reason why we need the concept of a cluster is to enhance diversity. By adding any new system concept to our repertoire, comparing and contrasting it with existing ones can clarify issues that otherwise remain confused.

For example, consider Chapter 10 on the subject of single system image. This has been an area of significant confusion, replete with meaningless adjectives like "seamless," and thoroughly confused with the separate issue of system management. The discussion in that chapter arguably brings to this subject some order and structure that was not previously present. It certainly applies not just to clusters but also to other forms of computing.

Could this clarification have taken place without consideration of clusters? Possibly. But it did not. Consideration of clusters brought it into the high relief necessary to resolve some of the muddle.

Are there other areas that consideration of clusters might clarify? Perhaps, but it is hard to tell until the job has been done. One I hope might become more clear is communication. It's certainly confusing to me that it takes more effort and overhead to communicate between "intelligent" devices—programmable computers—than between one "intelligent" device and a dumb one, like a disk drive. But I fear that this may be too much to hope for. Communication has been a subject crossing the distributed and parallel boundaries for a long time, and little has come of that cross-fertilization. On the other hand, so has the notion of single system image.

12.4 The Lure of Large Numbers _____

If you hang around marketing people long enough, some of their thought processes inevitably rub off whether you like it or not. A flake that's rubbed off on me, a rather elementary aspect of the area, is represented by what's called a generic market volume pyramid, shown in Figure 12-4.[4] This illustrates how many of any kind of widget will be sold, based solely on its size and/or price. Whether one is selling cars, potato chips, or computers, you sell a whole lot of little ones, fewer medium-sized ones, and rather few really, really big ones. The differences in market volume can be dramatic.

Figure 12-4 The Generic Market Volume Pyramid

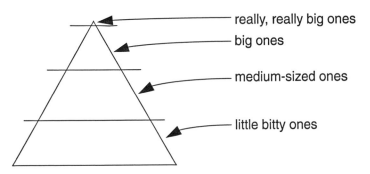

really, really big ones

big ones

medium-sized ones

little bitty ones

Here is one way to segment the computer market in that manner. The bottom segment is the "client" personal computer market: machines used by individuals, one person to a machine. That is a market of millions of units per year; enormous revenue, but thin profit margins. Next up are the PC servers. These have, to use a very rough number, less than a tenth the sales volume of PCs; but each server is a larger machine, with larger revenue, that is not quite as price-sensitive because users buy fewer of them and need not be as penny-wise about each. Above that lie larger, more complex system servers and multiuser systems capable of handling large, active databases and heavier computational loads. Other slices can be made, and rather intense discussions occur over how many slices there are and where they reside (and in which industry, geographic area, and for all I know what ranges of customer hair length), but for this discussion we're interested in the peak: That's where the massively parallel machines have their target.

---

4. This is the only marketing diagram I have ever seen that does not go up and to the right.

The point of the pyramid diagram is to make it blindingly obvious that few of those big machines are going to get sold.

This is well known and understood by the people who build and market massively parallel machines. They expect to sell only a few, if any, of their machines fully populated with the largest possible number of processing nodes. They also expect to sell many more that are less fully packed. That's what happens. But that's not the issue. The issue is the fact that their design target is the biggest feasible machine.

When you have targeted a design to highly massive proportions, scaling it down does not produce the best fit to the requirements of the market for smaller machines: systems that scale *up* to very large numbers of parallel nodes do not scale *down* to few nodes in an appropriate way. This has already been exhaustively discussed for the case of SMPs. It is equally true for massively parallel systems, for reasons that are entirely analogous to the heroic SMP case, but different in some technical details.

For example, the blindingly obvious issues apply directly. Massively parallel machines can participate in industry economies of scale by using processor and support chips in common with lower regions of the pyramid. But of necessity, since they target large numbers, they have to use bigger boxes. And bigger frames, power supplies, shipping costs, and so on, just as was mentioned for heroic SMPs back in "SMP and Other Scaling" in Chapter 11. Paradoxically, they require smaller-than-standard packages, too; since the point is to pack many processors into a small floor space, the repackaging performed on workstations (or PCs) results in units that are nonstandard because they contain less memory, less disk capacity, and fewer I/O slots than are considered adequate for stand-alone systems. Just as was the case with large SMPs, all of those things cannot participate in the much larger volumes available lower in the volume pyramid.

The less-populated versions of massively parallel machines, therefore, can't match in cost what's possible by simply sticking together a few of the higher-market-volume units without changing their packaging at all—quite feasible when the number of units stuck together is in the range of eight or so. The high-end designs have been warped to the needs of the lure of large numbers.

The large SMP situation had an additional technical problem with caches and memories, as was dissected in gruesome detail earlier. There's an analog in the massively parallel world: communication networks. There are problems in the design of very large, very fast communication networks, problems that are sufficiently technically interesting to have occupied many researchers for decades and generated an immense technical literature which demonstrates that some quite nonobvious effects can occur (for example, there's what is referred to as the " 'hot spot' controversy" in [AG94], initiated by the myself and Alan Norton [PN85]: unbalance communication by 0.1% with 1000 nodes and everything goes to pot). Also, the sheer design problems of wire routing for large machines pose quite interesting problems for packaging.

None of this says that large machines cannot be built. They can. And the issues involved are technically challenging and interesting to deal with. If the small (but exorbitantly publicized) population of customers for those machines can afford them, so be it; there's no reason not to satisfy those customers and make some money in the bargain. However, the depopulated versions, the versions one would hope to sell in larger numbers, are, like big SMPs vulnerable in their market position compared with systems *designed* to the more modest, higher market volume, segments.

There is a similar story to tell for software. The issues and problems of large numbers exert a strong lure there, too. They're interesting, challenging, and justifiably cause practitioners to feel that they're working on something of immense significance. They may well be.

But those large number problems lure effort away from the mundane, boring, grubby, practical issues—like, making the machine as easily administered as an SMP. They also inject synchronization and control overhead that is unnecessary for smaller numbers, a practice that unnecessarily reduces efficiency when used in more modest ranges. This lure appears to be affecting the kernel-level SSI developers, too.

But the market volume pyramid says something about this. It says that the effort is being expended for a market segment that is small. And the processor speed increases that continue to occur indicate that market segment will become ever smaller over time.

The lure of large numbers is, therefore, deluding many vendors and an unconscionable number of researchers and teachers into ignoring the real mass of customers who need smaller systems and more ease of use—the old system administration story again, from which one is easily distracted by intrinsically interesting large number effects. The middle layers of the pyramid need clusters, but the lure of large numbers keeps people working on systems that cannot scale down to produce good cluster products.

Without even the notion that there is a respectable conceptual target—the cluster—there is no antidote to this lure.

That has been the point of this chapter. We need the concept of cluster.

Conclusion

Attempts to use overtly parallel processing have previously been crippled by wimpy microprocessors, slothful communication, and the need to rebuild painfully complex parallel software from scratch on each attempt.

The result of this situation has been the completely justifiable conviction that overt parallelism simply was not worth the trouble unless it provided enormous gains in performance or function. With a performance focus came a fixation on massive parallelism; with a functional focus came a fixation on massively distributed processing.

The sole exception to this has been the symmetric multiprocessor (SMP), which has nearly always used the most powerful possible processors and the fastest possible communication. As a result, its practical use requires the parallel programming of only a handful of key system and subsystem programs. All other software, the broad and deep mainstream, can remain serial; it need not cope with the Byzantine intricacies of parallelism on top of the already back breaking complexity that is its primary limitation. Fixations on massiveness have been unnecessary for symmetric multiprocessors.

Nevertheless there is a demonstrable need for server computing facilities with greater performance, cheaper entry configurations, and higher availability than modestly scaled SMPs of four or so processors. SMPs can, technically, achieve those goals, but in doing so, they become disproportionately expensive.

Three things have happened to alter this situation. Microprocessors are now fast enough, are becoming ever faster at a tremendous rate, and tremendously fast ones are on the threshold of becoming tremendously inexpensive. Communication rates over standardized media are increasing dramatically, to the point where they can exceed the communication within an SMP. The foundations of reusable message-based software support have been laid on an initial framework derived from distributed processing—a usable framework, though actually more difficult to use than this case requires.

These factors make *clusters* of computers—groups of whole, standard computers each used as a single, unified resource—an adequate way to meet the needs of server systems now and a dramatically less-expensive way to do so in the near future.

The future holds this promise because the technology trends producing the cluster conquest are not abating. They will continue for good and sufficient reasons having nothing to do with clustering. The dramatic differences in price that once differentiated "open systems" from proprietary mainframes and minicomputers will play out again on a field of clusters and heroically large SMPs.

Clusters have not yet, however, captured the imagination of the computer industry. In part, this has been because the faster standard communication is neither widely deployed nor adequately usable, restricting nonproprietary versions of clusters to the relatively, indisputably lower-profit technical sections of the computer market. That will soon change. It's also partly because clusters aren't as flashy a topic as the Biggest, Baddest Computer Ever Made.

This lack of public enthusiasm also exists because the very concept of a cluster—with its emphasis on using serial, not parallel, user programming and its focus on single system image rather than remote distributed access to function—has at least until now been lacking recognition as a vital subparadigm of parallel and distributed computing.

Clusters exist now and will become ever more widely used. But the route forward can be unnecessarily painful, or it can be made easier by attention to some of the gaps that must be filled to make clusters more useful more quickly. The remaining few sections of this book reemphasize where those gaps are, and say a little about filling them.

But let there be no doubt: The gaps will be closed, and clusters will become common. The only question is who will be the first, among both computer vendors and customers, to profit from the result.

13.1 Cluster Operating Systems

The one most crucial element clusters lack is a complete illusion of a single machine—a single system image—as good as that presented by uniprocessors or SMPs, particularly with respect to the one universal application suite, system administration and management.

This single system image already exists to an good extent in several proprietary cluster solutions, and needs little enhancement for simple "availability" clusters. However, the general use of multi-machine, open-system clusters is being lead by sites with enough technical expertise to pull together the required tools with chewing gum, baling wire, and assorted Shell Scripts from Hell. They are not the general case.

Cluster batch systems and cluster-usable database and OLTP systems already exist or are being enhanced anyway. These are vital and underlie much current cluster use because they enable serial programs, without the added complexity of parallelism, to use clusters profitably: the Single Program, Parallel (Sub-) System, SPPS, technique. They do not solve administration problems outside of their limited, albeit important, domain.

So-called "distributed" operating systems, just a little to the side of the main distributed programming bandwagon, provide an excellent solution framework through a kernel-level single system image. However, none are as yet fully industrial-strength products, particularly in the area of system administration.

This is the primary gap that must be closed. There are no theoretical roadblocks to doing so, although an elegant and modular way to structure all the requisite function in an operating system remains to be found. The use of microkernel structuring appears to help greatly, but does not encompass the whole problem. Pragmatically, however, this can be accomplished now, with sufficient effort. Someone simply needs to make the investment and provide the function on highly cost-effective hardware platforms.

13.2 Communication Overhead

The aggregate bandwidth now or soon to be available between systems on standard communication is rivalling, and can be said to exceed, the internal bandwidth available *inside* symmetric multiprocessors.

If this were an aggregate among very large numbers of machines, it would not be news. There's tremendous aggregate amount of bandwidth, if you add it all up, among all the personal computers on earth that have modems. Now, however, the aggregate comparison that can be done is between the same number of nodes as there are in a current large SMP.

That is amazing. It turns any number of system assumptions inside-out. It could dramatically liberate message-based parallel programming from its large-grain-size ghetto and increase the utility of clusters tremendously.

Unfortunately, it may end up useless except for special cases. There are two reasons for this.

First, normal hardware and software system I/O architecture is simply not equipped to deal with these data firehoses. This may change from "natural causes" as system designers learn to deal with other fast devices, such as parallel disk arrays and image-oriented graphics, but in any event it will be a struggle and may not be wholly successful.

The other reason is overhead produced by the perversely immiscible (until now, at least) combination of operating system structure and communication protocol structure needed to get bits into and out of a computer. In many cases, this overhead is apparently caused not by either the system or by the protocol, but by a mismatch in the way they interface with each other. Even if current protocols are improved significantly, for the bandwidths now possible their sights are not yet set at even the proper order of magnitude for the new communications media. If the bandwidth available exceeds internal SMP bandwidth, the latency target should be in that region, too. Perhaps being within a factor of ten—say, below a microsecond of overhead—is not too much to ask? And this must be usable latency from a user program to a user program, not "advertising" latency available only inside the operating system kernel. It's a tall order.

Such a reduction in latency appears manifestly impossible when the external protocol is so complex that a fast microprocessor must be placed on every adapter card to assemble and reassemble packets, as is the case with ATM and FCS. The latency situation may not end up proving to be quite as bad as that makes it seem, but the starting point is not good. There may be ways to fix this without falling into other traps, like the way large-scale cache coherence entails availability problems, but such solutions are certainly neither deployed nor even on the horizon.

The real danger here is that all that bandwidth may end up impossible to use outside of flashy, easily demonstrated and advertised, special-purpose multimedia applications engendered by elements of the computer industry that lust after the glitz of Hollywood and really flashy in-store demos. This could result in special-purpose, otherwise unusable protocols and hardware that bypasses the computer proper—it's too slow!—and merely slap data directly onto a display.

Were that to come about, it would be a tragedy.

13.3 Standards

There are no standards that apply distinctly to clusters. Since the concept of a cluster hasn't existed, that's really not too terribly surprising. But as a result, there really is no such thing as an "open" cluster, just collections of "open" distributed machines that happen to be physically located unusually close to each other, and occasionally—horror of horrors, to the distributed world—actually share access to disks.

There are things that could very usefully be standardized. Right now, for example, every vendor of a cluster-oriented batch system, availability system, parallel programming package, database system, or OLTP system reimplements a collection of common functions. These include cluster membership, event multicast, occasionally cross-system locking, and other basic facilities. Few of these implementations are particularly large, but they are often, to put it mildly, tricky to implement; in addition, few have complete functionality—not all functions are needed for every product—and few are fully robust, able to take advantage of clusters' intrinsic availability characteristics. They are also unnecessarily inefficient, because to be portable they have to use only standard, least common denominator capabilities.

Without standards, this situation cannot change. Database vendors, for example, are not going to use a system vendor's package; they don't want to be locked into that vendor's systems. The system vendors, contrariwise, can't afford to do a special implementation of every database vendors' support layers; they don't want to lock their system into one database vendor.

Standards are, if you will pardon the pun, the key to unlocking this stalemate.

Beyond such general cluster-support packages, or perhaps more properly beneath them, new, higher-than-current-level standards for intermachine communication may provide another key, this one to getting around the communication latency and overhead problem discussed in the prior section.

Commercial parallel efforts, such as those for parallel databases, must now constrain themselves to write in terms of standard facilities such as **sockets** or **streams**, because they cannot afford to invest in a nonportable implementation. However, that locks them into very specific system structures and protocols designed for another era. The technical computing community, on the other hand, is now well into the process of bypassing that hurdle by defining a standard higher-level Message-Passing Interface (MPI) [Wal93, Mes94] that is independent of any specific system interface and bids fair to be adopted by a large number of parallel computer vendors. The efficiencies potentially, and in some cases demonstrably, attainable by vendor-specific implementations at that level are spectacular relative to the normal modes of communication: microseconds of overhead, compared with milliseconds.

The MPI interface does not at present address all the needs of commercial users; that wasn't its intent. Availability issues, in particular, were deliberately not addressed, and neither were remote procedure calls. MPI does, however, suggest itself as a very solid start towards a more universally usable communication standard, one that system vendors could strongly optimize to allow highly efficient use of ever-more macho interconnects, setting the hardware jocks free again to invent even more wondrous switches. How fast can you build something to multicast to a specific set of processes spread across a group of computers? (First, you had better ask the system programmers what to do when those processes are swapped out.)

13.4 Software Pricing

Suppose you've purchased a cluster. You have four cluster nodes, each node a four-processor SMP. You did so because it provides more performance than a sixteen processor SMP and higher availability, all for a lower price.

How many copies of the operating system did you purchase?

Oops.

How about the compiler? The communication subsystem? The database, the application, ...?

What was that about "a lower price" than a sixteen processor SMP?

Software licenses for a sixteen processor SMP cost more than licenses for the corresponding uniprocessor, but the price rise is much less than proportional to the number of processors. For example, a license for a sixteen processor SMP costs substantially less than four times the cost of a license for a four-way SMP. As long as the cluster is considered a group of separate machines, however, each machine must bear the burden of its own software license. So, as a cluster owner, you are paying four times the cost of a four-way SMP license--substantially more than the SMP software cost. Software costs commonly exceed hardware costs, so the total cluster cost can easily exceed that of a roughly equivalent (but usually inferior) SMP.

The price break for SMPs is partly based on the fact that SMP performance is far from proportional to the number of processors. That's been discussed at length, and it's not surprising; it's true, as a general rule, of every parallel system. However, it's also true of clusters. Why don't they get the same price break?

Well, for one thing the concept of a cluster doesn't exist. It's rather hard to price something that most people don't believe in.

Another reason clusters don't get the same price break is the potential for abuse. Are those four workstations part of a cluster, therefore eligible for a cluster pricing, or are they separate computers? How do you tell? Are they in the same room? (Does that matter? Recall campus-wide clusters.)

As was mentioned in Chapter 2, preassembled vendor-constructed clusters occasionally get around this by assigning a single serial number to the cluster as a whole. Then software licenses can simply follow serial numbers, and cluster software licensing can scale up with nodes as slowly as SMP licensing scales with processors. This arrangement is by no means automatic. It exists only because of negotiation with each software vendor by each hardware vendor--negotiation that starts right at home with the hardware vendor's own software shop, trying to get a reasonable price for the operating system. Talking to a software vendor who hasn't yet been "softened up" to clusters will almost always elicit the knee-jerk reaction of requiring a fully-priced, separate license per machine.

The serial number dodge doesn't help user-assembled clusters. Their nodes were bought as separate computers, and that's that.

This problem has an analog in distributed systems that share a single centrally-administered copy of a program. It's not yet fully solved there, and as usual clusters add their own bit of complication not addressed by the distributed case.

Until this software pricing problem is solved, the real cost advantages of cluster hardware may be moot. It will be solved, however, because the current situation is unstable. Once one software vendor moves its pricing policy, others will be forced to follow suit or endure being uncompetitively priced on the most cost-effective hardware platforms in the computer industry.

13.5 Coda: The End of Parallel Computer Architecture

Finally, a thought that arises from an entirely different direction.

Discussing the political and economic ramifications of the events surrounding and following the end the Cold War, Francis Fukuyama writes in *The End of History and the Last Man*:

> The apparent number of choices that countries face in determining how they will organize themselves politically and economically has been *diminishing* over time. Of the different types of regimes that have emerged in the course of human history, from monarchies and aristocracies, to religious theocracies, to the fascist and communist dictatorships of this century, the only form of government that has survived intact to the end of the twentieth century has been [...] democracy. [Fuk92, p. 45; italics in the original]

The issues Fukuyama is discussing obviously overreach this book's technical topics so broadly that no connection between their causes, even extremely indirect, is defensible to the slightest degree. Nevertheless, there are striking similarities in computer architecture to the situation he describes.

Specifically, deliberately constructing a direct paraphrase:

> Is it not the case that the apparent number of choices that people face in determining how they will organize overt parallelism has been *diminishing* over time? Of the different types of overtly parallel computer organizations that have emerged, from SIMD to vector supercomputers, from associative arrays to dataflow, from reduction machines to MIMD-SIMD combinations, from hierarchies to webs to pyramids, the only forms of overtly parallel computer organization that have survived intact to the mid-90s have been symmetric multiprocessors, clusters, and clusters' flamboyant sisters, the massively parallel multicomputers.

There may yet be scope for new, wild, weird and wonderful covert parallelism. Internal processor organizations can still incorporate any number of possible schemes for covert parallelism, from the sublime to the unusually bizarre. Nor is there a barrier to flamboyant intermachine communication systems. There is also nothing inhibiting thought experiments in parallel architecture that are at least interesting, if not able to shed dramatic light on other aspects of computer science.

But the external, software-visible architecture of practical, marketable, overtly parallel computer systems is another matter. On the one hand, there is the mass-market economics of integrated circuit manufacture, driven by stupendous and ever-increasing requirements for investment in production facilities; it is also driven by the smaller, but not negligible and also increasing individual chip development costs. On the other hand, there are the license-counting economics, perpetual development crisis, and awesome inertia of software. Those two hands have a death grip on overt parallelism because they combine to create a critical mass problem—if it doesn't exist already, you can't sell it—so ever-increasingly severe that it is impossible to conceive of a situation where the basic unit of overt computer parallelism is not a standard, Von Neumann architecture machine, communicating with other such machines via messages.

This conclusion is not one that can be reached lightly, and it is, perhaps, rather sad to contemplate. It may be the price of increasing maturity. Fukuyama also says of democracy that we've reached this point after utter exhaustion, exhaustion caused by experimenting with all the other possibilities, using two world wars in our experimental procedure. The same could again be directly paraphrased—with market shake-outs substituting for world wars—for the case of overt parallelism.

It's not impossible that this may also be true of *covert* parallelism, as manifested in different processor instruction-set architectures. As was noted in the chapter about symmetric multiprocessors, processors are getting faster more quickly than are memories. Once a processor is fast enough to continuously saturate a memory system, what difference does its internal architecture make? For computer performance in a wide and increasingly broad class of applications, "It's the memory, stupid!" The ability to saturate the memory system does depend on the processor architecture, but not on many if any of the characteristics currently hyped in the RISC / CISC / VLIW wars now in progress.

The general loss of freedom being discussed here may not be inevitable. I'd like it not to be. But I do not at present see any practical way around it.

Whether it is true or not, and whatever changes the future rings into the computer industry, I am certain of one thing:

We will not have to search for clusters any more.

They will be commonplace.

Annotated
Bibliography

Over the last three-plus decades, parallel processing has accumulated a technical and popularized bibliography of cosmic proportions, and distributed processing, while perhaps a bit younger, is rapidly catching up. As a result of that, there are lots of references here. Furthermore, the entries in this bibliography span a very wide range of types. They go from press releases that appeared during the final phases of writing, through heavily mathematico-logical treatises, graduate and undergraduate textbooks, all the way to semipopular cartoon-illustrated guides to the wonderlands of distributed computing (actually, quite good guides). Those who might want to pursue some of these topics more deeply might end up sorely disappointed without some indication of what they're in for.

Therefore, I've annotated each of the entries that appear here. The annotations are by no means a complete capsule reviews of every entry, although my opinions will not be found to be in short supply; nor is there an interwoven collection of cross-references that disentangles a cross-coupled web of literature. I've tried to give some idea of what to expect were you were to get hold of these reference materials.

[AB86]   James Archibald and Jean-Loup Baer. Cache coherence protocols: Evaluation using a multiprocessor simulation model. *ACM Transactions on Computer Systems*, 4(4):273–296, November 1986. Describes in a consistent way the bus-based protocols most popular at the time it was written (Dragon, Firefly, Illinois, and so on) and compares their performance against a consistent set of workloads. Comes to the conclusion that the most complicated wins.

[AG94]   George S. Almasi and Allan Gottlieb. *Highly Parallel Computing, 2d edition.* The Benjamin Cummings Publishing Company, Inc., 390 Bridge Parkway, Redwood City, CA , 1994. Good, broad, highly readable coverage of many of the aspects of traditional areas of highly parallel computing, both hardware and software. Lots of sidebars and a number of interesting anecdotes and asides in addition to good coverage of the technical bases.

[AGZ94]   R. C. Agarwal, F. G. Gustavson, and M. Zubair. Improving performance of linear algebra algorithms for dense matrices, using algorithmic prefetch. *IBM Journal of Research and Development*, 38(3):265–275, May 1994. A demonstration of how to improve the performance of an RS/6000 Model 590 on dense-matrix linear algebra. The authors went from about 36 to about 44 MFLOPS by doing loads of data prior to when they were needed, just to overlap the cache fill time.

[AH90]   Sarita V. Adve and Mark D. Hill. Weak ordering-a new definition. In *Proceedings of the 17th Annual International Symposium on Computer Architecture*, pp 2–11. IEEE, June 1990. This description of weak ordering of interprocessor instruction execution is the one most referenced in later years. I think that's because hardware guys think software guys understand and/or accept this definition—at least, that was the point of the presentation as made here, to make a definition that was comprehensible in software terms.

[Amd67]   G. Amdahl. Validity of the single-processor approach to achieving large-scale computer capabilities. In *Proceedings of the AFIPS Conference*, pages 483–485, 1967. The original Amdahl's Law reference, stating that a

In Search of Clusters ✳

parallel machine can only speed things up to a limit governed by how much serial execution must still be done.

[And91]   Gregory R. Andrews. *Concurrent Programming: Principles and Practice*. Benjamin/Cummings Publishing Company, Inc., Redwood City, CA, 1991. Excellent reference on all the issues involved in writing parallel programs: Shared variables, RPCs, message-passing, monitors, heartbeats, and so on. Very significant emphasis on proving that such programs work, which is extremely appropriate but makes for nontrivial reading.

[AR94]   Thomas B. Alexander, Kenneth G. Robertson, Deal T. Lindsay, Donald L. Rogers, John R. Obermeyer, John R. Keller, Keith Y. Oka, and Marlin M. Jones II. Corporate business servers: an alternative to mainframes for business computing. *Hewlett-Packard Journal*, pp. 8-33, June 1994. A description of the Hewlett-Packard T500 series of SMPs.

[A⁺91]   Anant Agarawal et al. The mit alewife machine. In *Proceedings of Workshop on Scalable Shared Memory Multiprocessors*, Boston, MA, 1991. Kluwer Academic Publishers. Dataflow concepts live on in the new proposal for a highly parallel machine. (The Alewife Brook parkway is in one of the towns making up the Boston metroplex.)

[A⁺92]   L. Albinson et al. UNIX on a loosely coupled architecture: The chorus/mix approach. *Future Generations Computer Systems*, 8(1-3):67–81, July 1992. Description of the Chorus microkernel system, and how it can be used to distribute Unix semantics across multiple machines.

[BBDS94]   David H. Bailey, Eric Barszcz, Leomardo Dagum, and Horst D. Simon. NAS parallel benchmark results 3-94. Technical report, NASA Ames Research Center, Moffett Field, CA, March 1994. Evaluation of various machines on parallel jobs. Includes redefinition of some of the benchmarks to avoid unintended implementation methods. Shows workstations very competitive with current Crays.

[BBK+68]   George H. Barnes, Richard M. Brown, Maso Kato, David J. Kuck, Daniel L. Slotnick, and Richard A. Stokes. The illiac iv computer. *IEEE Transactions on Computers*, C-17(8):746–757, 1968. The original paper on the ILLIAC IV computer, one of the first efforts, if not the first effort, in multipurpose massively parallel computing.

[BDG+91]   A. Beguilin, J. Dongarra, G. A. Geist, R. Manchek, and V. S. Sunderam. A users' guide to pvm parallel virtual machine. Technical Report # ORNL/TM-11826, Oak Ridge National Laboratory, July 1991. Detailed users' guide to PVM, the most popular system for parallel programming of clusters. A requisite document if you want to use PVM.

[Bel92a]   Gordon Bell. An insider's views on the technology and evolution of parallel computing. In *Software for Parallel Computers*, R. H. Perrott, ed, pp 11–26. Chapman & Hall, 2-6 Boundary Row, London, 1992. Quite interesting reading. Atypically readable, typically curmudgeonish look by Gordon Bell at how parallel machines have evolved over time, what's proven practical, and what's really not.

[Bel92b]   Gordon Bell. Ultracomputers: A teraFLOP before its time. *Communications of the ACM*, 35(8):26–47, 1992. Trying to reach a teraFLOP too soon has produced machines that scale in only one sense—the amount of money you can pay for them. Better to wait, since it will only be a few years for the technology to naturally reach the point where these performance levels are achievable with reasonable ecomony. Many useful insights in a paper that is unfortunately not as well organized as it might be.

[Ber94]   Josh Berstin. Sybase for hacmp/6000: An architected approach to clustered systems. *AIXpert*, pp 46–52, May 1994. One of a series of articles on cluster database systems in that issue of AIXpert. Describes how Sybase is approaching the problem for clusters, as opposed to NCR's approach (which is sold as Sybase Data Navigator).

In Search of Clusters ✳

[BGvN62]   A. W. Burke, H. H. Goldstine, and J. von Neumann. Preliminary discussions of the logical design of an electronic computing instrument, part ii. *Datamation*, 8:36–41, October 1962. A later reprint of some of the design notes written during the birth of what is now known as the Von Neumann architecture computer.

[Bir95]   K. P. Birman. Replication and fault-tolerance in the isis system. *Operating Systems Review*, 19(5), December 1995. Discussion of the reliable multicast protocol technology used as the basis for the ISIS system at Cornell, later commercialized by ISIS Distributed Systems (IDS). Also appears in the Proceedings of the Tenth ACM Symposium on Operating System Principles.

[BJ87]   K. P. Birman and T. A. Joseph. Reliable communication in the presence of failures. *ACM Transactions on Computer Systems*, 6(1):47–76, February 1987. Detailed discussion of how one can have a reliable multicast by using a special protocol, when media and nodes are unreliable. This is the core technology of the ISIS distributed system support, developed at Cornell and later commercialized by ISIS Distributed Systems (IDS).

[BJS88]   F. Baskett, T. Jermoluk, and D. Solomon. The 4d-mp graphics superworkstation. In *Proceedings of Spring Compcon '88*, pages 468–471, 1988. Description of the Silicon Graphics SMP workstations used as nodes (they call them clusters) in the Stanford DASH system.

[BL92]   R. Butler and E. Lusk. Users' guide to the p4 programming system. Technical Report ANL-92/17, Argonne National Laboratory, 1992. Detailed users' guide to a popular portable system for parallel programming, used for clusters as well as other machines. Developed at Argonne Lab.

[BMR91]   Sandra Johnson Baylor, Kevin P. McAuliffe, and Bharat Deepu Rathi. An evaluation of cache coherence protocols for micprocessor-based multiprocessors. In *Proceedings of the International Symposium on Shared Memory Multiprocessing*, pages 230–241, April 1991. Looks at data-sharing aspects of several scientific programs by simulation, comparing several hardware-based and a software-based coherence protocol. Less than 3% of references turn out to be shared, which is a very interesting and extremely useful result. But watch out if the cache line size gets too big; you get false sharing galore.

[Boo83]   Daniel J. Boorstein. *The Discoverers*. Random House, New York, 1983. A really extraordinary book. Extremely interesting, nontechnical(!) history of many important basic technologies, such as printing, geography, music, and so on.

[Bou92]   J.-Y Le Boudec. The asynchronous transfer mode: A tutorial. *Computer Network and ISDN System*, 24:279–309, February 1992. An introduction to ATM. Fairly readable.

[BRS$^+$85] R. Baron, R. Rashid, E. Seigel, A. Tevanian, and M. Young. Mach-1: An operating environment for large-scale multiprocessor applications. *IEEE Software*, 2:65–67, July 1985. Description of the Mach microkernel operating system, developed at Carnegie-Mellon University. Clearly the most influential microkernel system ever developed, and the origin of the term "microkernel."

[BW89]   J. L. Baer and W. H. Wang. Multilevel cache hierarchies: Organizations, protocols and performance. *Journal of Parallel and Distributed Computing*, (6):451–476, 1989. Technical description of several multilevel caching schemes, with their performance analysis.

[CF93]   Alan L. Cox and Robert J. Fowler. Adaptive cache coherency for detecting migratory shared data. In *Proceedings of the 20th Annual International Symposium on Computer Architecture*, pages 98–108. IEEE, May 1993. Description of a snoopy, bus-based cache coherence protocol that dynamically switches between updating and expunging lines in other caches on write. Also, a good root for a tree of cache coherence references.

[CG89]   N. Carriero and David Gelernter. Linda in context. *Communications of the ACM*, 32(4):444–458, April 1989. A description of Linda, a system for parallel programming of clusters that takes a unique approach to communication and program organization that some people like a lot. Linda began life as a project by Gelernter at AT&T Bell Laboratories, an attempt to make use of a typically nonstandard, clusterish parallel machine dreamed up by engineers who had no idea how hard it might be to program. Later expanded as a major Yale research project (Gelernter and Carriero are Yale faculty), then became the primary product of a spinoff company, Scientific Computing Associates.

[CGST94]   H. Jonathan Chao, Dipak Ghosal, Debanjan Saha, and Satish K. Tripathi. Ip on atm local area networks. *IEEE Communications Magazine*, pages 52–59, August 1994. The various techniques a number of people are using, including the ATM Forum, to provide standard LAN (IP) communications protocols over ATM's nonbroadcast medium. Includes a description of the standard LAN techniques of bridging and routing.

[Chr94]   Gregg A. Christman. Informix-online's dynamic scalable architecture. *AIXpert*, pages 32–36, May 1994. One of a series of articles on cluster database systems in that issue of AIXpert. Describes how Informix is approaching the problem. This is written and published before this product was shipped or even officially announced. Indicates that they're attempting to conquer SMP, NUMA, and NORMA parallelism all with one program structure. It'll be great if it works.

[Col92]   William W. Collier. *Reasoning About Parallel Architectures*. Prentice Hall, Inc., Englewood Cliffs, NJ 07632, 1992. An intense, detailed, mathematical treatise dissecting issues such as sequential consistency, organized around ways of telling whether computer architecture A exactly equals computer architecture B—which is another way of saying that a program running on machine A will do exactly the same thing when run on machine B, a rather useful thing to know. Extremely useful if you really want to get interprocessor consistency right. Not for those lacking a mathematical bent.

[Cos94]   Terry Costlow. Sci gaining acceptance as scalable link. *Electronic Engineering Times*, (787), March 7, 1994. Overview of progress to the publication date on implementations of SCI.

[CP93]   Daniel Cerutti and Donna Pierson. *Distributed Computing Environments*. McGraw-Hill, Inc., New York, 1993. A collection of generally rather good and readable papers that discuss many of the issues involved in distributed computing. The papers are tied together by introductions written by the editors. Very complete coverage of issues and trends, and all papers maintain a high standard of readability.

[CY93]   Christopher Cheng and Leo Yuan. Electrical design of the xdbus using low voltage swing cmos (gtl) in the sparccenter 2000 server. In *Symposium Record of Hot Interconnects '93*, pages 1.3.1–1.3.4. Stanford University, August 1993. Sun Microsystems paper on how they built a bus to support 20 SuperSPARC processors. Unlike other papers at this workshop, this one is a complete written paper rather than a collection of presentation transparencies.

[DGNP88]   Frederica Darema, David A. George, V. Alan Norton, and Gregory F. Pfister. A single-program-multiple-data computational model for epex fortran. *Parallel Computing*, 7:11–24, 1988. Original definition and first use of the term SPMD to describe the programming model that is effectively used everywhere on both shared-memory and message-passing machines.

[Dig93]   Digital Equipment Corporation, Maynard, MA. *Open-VMS Clusters Handbook*, 1993. Document # EC-H2207-93 Rel. #79/93 06 43 60.0. Introduction to the various forms and capabilities of Open VMS Clusters. Really quite readable; other vendors should copy the style and format of this series of small books.

[Dig94]   Digital Equipment Corporation, Maynard, MA. *Digital's Unix Clusters Lead Industry in High Availability Commercial Solutions*, October 4, 1994. Announcement at 1994 UNIX Expo, mentioning both 18-second failover time for DECSafe high-availability and the Memory Channel work with Encore.

[Dij65]   Edsgar W. Dijkstra. Solution of a problem in concurrent programming control. *Communications of the ACM*, 8(9):569, 1965. The original, and most famous, mutual exclusion algorithm. Like most classics, short: a one-page paper. Expect to spend several hours figuring out why it works.

[DOKT91]   Fred Douglis, John K. Ousterhout, M. Frans Kaashoek, and Andrew S. Tannenbaum. A comparison of two distributed systems: Amoeba and sprite. *Computing Systems*, 4(4):353–383, Fall 1991. Very interesting comparison along a number of different axes: Assumed system structure (glass-house vs. campus-wide cluster), microkernel vs. macrokernel, UNIX base vs. written from scratch, and so on.

[Dol95]   Dolphin Interconnect Solutions, 5301 Great America Parkway, Suite 320, Santa Clara, CA. *SBus-1 Product Overview*, 1995. Product flyer for Dolphin's SBus card that provides an SCI-based link between machines for clustering.

[Edd94]   Guy Eddon. *RPC For NT: Building Remote Procedure Calls for Windows NT Networks*. Prentice Hall, Englewood Cliffs, NJ, 1994. An entire book about all the ways to create and use RPCs, sparing no detail, to simplify life when doing client/server computing using Microsofts Windows NT system.

[Edi91]   Edinburgh Parallel Computing Centre, University of Edinburgh. *Chimp Concepts*, June 1991. Overview of Edinburgh's parallel message-passing system, one of the systems whose concepts had a significant influence on the MPI emerging standard.

[EGKS90]   Suzanne Englert, Jim Gray, Terrye Kocher, and Praful Shah. A benchmark of nonstop sql release 2 demonstrating near-linear speedup and scaleup on large databases. In *Proceedings of the 1990 ACM SIGMETRICS Conference*, pages 245–246, New York, 1990. ACM. Demonstration of increased speed and increased scaling as you add nodes to a Tandem system.

[Exe87]   Executive Office of the President, Office of Science and Technology Policy. *A Research and Development Strategy for High Performance Computing*, November 1987. The official, government-approved definition and list of Grand Challenge problems.

[EY92]   David John Evans and Nadia Y. Yousif. Asynchronous parallel algorithms for linear equations. In *Parallel Processing in Computational Mechanics*, Hojjat Adeli, editor, pp 69–130. Marcel Dekker, Inc., 270 Madison Ave., New York, 1992. Discussion and comparison of a wide variety of ways of solving linear and differential equations in parallel, with emphasis on shared memory techniques. Shows chaotic relaxation (called "pure asynchronous" here) is best in many cases.

[FBH+92]   D. Frye, Ray Bryant, H. Ho, R. Lawrence, and M. Snir. An external user interface for scalable parallel systems. Technical report, International Business Machines Corp., Armonk, NY, May 1992. Description of the EUI message-passing subroutine library developed for the IBM Scalable Parallel series of machines. EUI stands for End User Interface, a name thought up by folks in the IBM Research Division, giving you some idea who they thought the "End" users were.

[Fec94]   Giles Fecteau. Db2 parallel edition. *AIXpert*, pages 24–30, May 1994. One of a series of articles on cluster database systems in that issue of AIXpert. Describes how IBM DB2/6000 is approaching the problem of parallel/cluster database processing, using function shipping.

[FHK+90]   G. Fox, S. Hiranandani, K. Kennedy, C. Koebel, U. Kremer, C. Tseng, and M. Wu. Fortran d language specification. Technical Report # TR90-41, Department of Computer Science, Rice University, December 1990. A complete specification of FORTRAN D, which was the predecessor to High Performance FORTRAN. The D stands for Data-parallel, as opposed to Control-parallel.

[FJL+88]   Geoffrey C. Fox, Mark A. Johnson, Gregory A Lyzenga, Steve W. Otto, John K. Aalmon, and David W. Walker. *Solving Problems on Concurrent Processors, Volume I: General Techniques and Regular Problems*. Prentice Hall, Englewood Cliffs, NJ, 1988. An excellent introduction to techniques for message-based parallelism on regular scientific and technical problems. Many of the methods described arose from the Concurrent Computation Program at California Institute of Technology, originator of the original hypercube machines.

[Fly72]   Michael J. Flynn. Some computer organizations and their effectiveness. *IEEE Transactions on Computers*, pages 948–960, September 1972. The original paper defining the programming models MIMD, SIMD, SISD, MISD.

[Fuk92]   Francis Fukuyama. *The End of History and the Last Man*. The Free Press, A Division of Macmillan, Inc., New York, 1992. With the collapse of authoritarian regimes, is there an endpoint to history-directed change in human affairs—with liberal democracies and capitalism the final, ultimate socio-political system? What kind of people inhabit such an end-result world? Is it stable?

[Gal93]   Mike Galles. The challenge interconnect: Design of a 1.2 gb/s coherent multiprocessor bus. In *Symposium Record of Hot Interconnects '93*, pages 1.1.1–1.1.7. Stanford University, August 1993. Silicon Graphics' paper on how they built a system bus to support 36 MIPS R4400 processors. Unfortunately, the proceedings contains only the presentation transparencies, not a complete paper. Much information is nevertheless contained here.

[GKW85]   J. R. Gurd, C. C. Kirkham, and I. Watson. The manchester prototype dataflow computer. *Communications of the ACM*, 28(1):34–52, January 1985. Description of one of the few live, working dataflow machine ever constructed; done at the University of Manchester. This work was quite influential and often cited in dataflow literature.

[GLL$^+$90]   Kourosh Gharachorloo, Daniel Lenoski, James Laudon, Phillip Gibbons, Anoop Gupta, and John Hennessy. Memory consistency and event ordering in scalable shared-memory multiprocessors. In *Proceedings of the 17th Annual International Symposium on Computer Architecture*, pages 15–25. IEEE, June 1990. Description of release consistency, the inter-processor memory access ordering used in the Stanford DASH project.

[GS93]   G. A. Geist and V. S. Sunderam. The evolution of the pvm concurrent computing system. In *Proceedings of the 26th IEEE Compcon Symposium*, pages 471–478, San Francisco, February 1993. A description of the most popular system for parallel programming of clusters.

PVM is a highly portable system making message-passing programming easier. Supports heterogeneous, as well as homogeneous, collections of machines. Highly portable freeware.

[Gus92]   David Gustavson. The scalable coherent interface and related standards projects. *IEEE Micro*, 12(1):10–12, February 1992. Very readable description of the SCI interconnect and the issues it addresses, written by one of the primary proponents and principal parents of this technology.

[Hal94]   Tom R. Halfhill. 80x86 wars. *Byte*, 19(6):74–88, June 1994. How all the "other" 80x86-architecture vendors-Cyrix, AMD, IBM—are now going to start doing their own designs, not waiting for Intel do something new and then copying it.

[HC85]   Robert W. Horst and Timothy C. K. Chou. An architecture for high volume transaction processing. In *Proceedings of the 12th International Symposium on Computer Architecture*, pages 240–245, Boston, MA, 1985. IEEE. Description of Tandem's cluster and/or parallel database system architecture, used in the Tandem Cyclone and later products.

[Hem91]   R. Hempel. The anl/gmd macros (parmacs) in fortran for portable parallel programming using the message passing model - user's guide and reference manual. Technical report, GMD, Postfach 1316, D-5205 Sankt Augustin 1, Germany, November 1991. Detailed users' guide to the the PARMACS system for portable message-passing parallel programming of clusters.

[Hil93]   Dan Hildebrand. An architectural overview of qnx. In *Proceedings of the Usenix Workshop on Micro-Kernels and Other Kernel Architectures*, April 1993. QNX is a micro-kernel designed for real-time and embedded applications that has been successfully used in many cluster-like products, as well as extended downward to PDAs. This paper outlines its architecture and compares its performance to a traditional macrokernel (SVR5). Paper available by ftp from quics.qnx.com /pub/papers and ftp.cse.ucsc.edu /pub/qux. The proceedings where it appeared are ISBN 1-880446-42-1.

[HKM94]   Chengchang Hwang, Eric P. Kasten, and Philip K. McKinley. Design and implementation of multicast operations for atm-based high performance computing. In *Proceedings of Supercomputing '94*, November 1994. How to do collective communication operations for parallel processing over an ATM-based LAN.

[HM]   Chengchang Hwang and Philip K. McKinley. Communication issues in parallel computing across atm networks. *IEEE Parallel and Distributed Technology*, to appear. Overview of ATM and parallelism, then results of doing experiments in broadcast, reduction,and so on, over an ATM-based LAN. It still takes a minimum of a millisecond to get anything out of a computer.

[HM89]   A. Hac and H. B. Mutlu. Synchronous optical network and broadband isdn protocols. *IEEE Computer*, 11:26–34, November 1989. Introduction to ATM at a mildly technical level. Broadband ISDN is ATM, for all practical purposes.

[HP90]   John L. Hennessy and David A. Patterson. *Computer Architecture A Quantitative Approach*. Morgan Kaufmann Publishers, Inc., San Mateo, CA, 1990. Excellent textbook on computer architecture, with special emphasis on quantitative measurements, RISC vs. CISC, and caches. Currently clearly the best textbook on the subject. Too bad it stops short of SMPs, but it's pretty big already.

[Hwa93]   Kai Hwang. *Advanced Computer Architecture: Parallelism, Scalability, Programmability*. McGraw-Hill, Inc., New York, 1993. Broad coverage of many of the aspects of parallel processing. Includes descriptions of SMPs and cache coherence issues, which is rare. Aggressively technical and formal.

[IBMa]   IBM Corporation, Armonk, NY. *High Availability Cluster Multi-Processing/6000 System Overview*. Document # SC23-2408-02. Description of the IBM HACMP/6000 system for clustering RISC System/6000 workstations and servers.

[IBMb]   IBM Corporation, Armonk, NY. *Introduction to JES3*. Document # GC28-0607-2. Not-too-basic introduction to IBM's JES3, a system for distributing work across a cluster of mainframes.

✳ *Annotated Bibliography*   381

[IBMc]   IBM Corporation, Armonk NY. *LoadLeveller General Information Manual*. Document # GH26-7227. General description of IBM's LoadLeveller product, a technical computing batch facility originally developed for the IBM Scalable Parallel (SP) series but also running on a variety of vendors' workstations.

[IBMd]   IBM Corporation, Armonk, NY. *Sysplex Hardware and Software Migration*. Document # GC28-1210-00. All the things to worry about, hardware and software, if you are considering clustering IBM mainframes together in an IBM Sysplex.

[IBMe]   IBM Corporation, Armonk, NY. *Sysplex Overview*. Document # GC28-1208-00. Well written. Basic introduction to parallel processing (and data sharing) targetting readers familiar with large-scale commercial computing. Good description of the basic IBM Sysplex (mainframe cluster) hardware facilities, but insufficient depth for real technical satisfaction.

[IBM94]   IBM Corporation, Armonk, NY. *IBM Delivers New Versions of its PowerPC RISC Microprocessors*, October 10, 1994. Press release announcing availability and pricing for 100 MHz PowerPC 601 and 604, and 66/80 MHz PowerPC 603 microprocessors.

[Ins93]   Institute of Electrical & Electronic Engineers, New York. *IEEE Standard for Scalable Coherent Interface (SCI)*, August 1993. IEEE Std 1596-1992. The official definition of SCI. Required reading for anyone attempting to implement or really understand it. Hideously detailed, as one would expect from a standards document.

[Int94]   International Data Corporation (IDC). *Cost of Unix Midrange Systems*, 1994. A study of all the costs of ownership of a midrange commercial UNIX system; not just the hardware, but software, maintenance, staffing, and so on. Uniquely, it was done by studying not artificial configurations but actual, "live" sites—hundreds in both the US and Europe.

[Joh91]   Mike Johnson. *Superscalar Microprocessor Design*. Prentice Hall, Englewood Cliffs, NJ, 1991. Excellent, quantitative, detailed technical discussion of the issues involved in superscalar processor design, done with a consistently maintained "everything in moderation or it will cost too much" viewpoint. Very good appendix on why RISC is intrinsically better than CISC, and how hard it is to use RISC-y techniques on a CISC machine. However, the author has apparently changed his position on how bad CISC is, given recent comments on the HP/Intel alliance. He's entitled; time passes and more thought ensues.

[KEW⁺85]   R. H. Katz, S. J. Eggers, D. A. Wood, C. L. Perkins, and R. G. Sheldon. Implementing a cache consistency protocol. In *Proceedings of the 12th Annual International Symposium on Computer Architecture*, pages 2–11. IEEE, June 1985. The Berkeley cache coherence protocol, one of several popular bus-based snoopy protocols.

[KLS86]   Nancy P. Kronenberg, Henry M. Levy, and William D. Strecker. Vaxclusters: A closely-coupled distributed system. *ACM Transactions on Computer Systems*, 4(3):130–146, May 1986. Description of the highly successful Digital VAXCluster hardware and software architecture. One of the more successful and popular clustered systems. Now called Open VMS Cluster.

[KLSM87]   Nancy P. Kronenberg, Henry M. Levy, William D. Strecker, and Richard J. Merewood. The vaxcluster concept: An overview of a distributed system. *Digital Technical Journal*, 4:7–21, September 1987. Keynote paper in an issue of the Digital Technical Journal that has several papers devoted to the VAXCluster (now called the Open VMS Cluster).

[Kol91]   Adam Kolawa. The express programming environment. *Workshop on Heterogeneous Network-Based Concurrent Computing*, October 1991. A description of Parasoft's Express product for message-passing on clusters and massively parallel machines. It began life as a very successful programming system for the CalTech cosmic cube, then migrated to a spinoff company, Parasoft.

[KS86]   Henry F. Korth and Abraham Silberschatz. *Database Systems Concepts*. McGraw-Hill, Inc., New York, 1986. A standard textbook on database systems, covering many of the topics of interest in general but not (in this version, anyway) adequately dealing with newer parallel models of database execution.

[KSS+91]   H. T. Kung, R. Sansom, P. Steenkiste, M. Arnould, F. J. Bitz, F. Christianson, E. C. Cooper, O. Menzilciogly, D. Ombres, and B. Zill. Network-based multicomputers: An emerging parallel architecture. In *Proceedings of Supercomputing '91*, pages 664–673. IEEE CS Press, 1991. Clusters can do grand challenge problems, particularly when connected by ATM and highly intelligent adapters.

[Lam]   Leslie Lamport. The parallel execution of do loops. *Communications of the ACM*, 17(2):83–93. Derivation of the notion of a hyperplane of array computations that can be done in parallel when ordinary indexed loops are parallelized. Referred to in this book as the wavefront method.

[Lam79]   Leslie Lamport. How to make a multiprocessor computer that correctly executes multiprocess programs. *IEEE Transactions on Computers*, C-28(9):690–691, September 1979. The original definition of sequential consistency. This two page paper—actually, a short note—is rigorously referenced by everybody who ever says anything about interprocessor instruction ordering, all the way up to 1994.

[LC94]   Sandra Lee and Annie Chen. Oracle parallel technology empowers aix systems. *AIXpert*, pages 37–42, May 1994. One of a series of articles on cluster database systems in that issue of AIXpert. Describes how Oracle is approaching the problem, with description of Oracle Parallel Server implementation for the IBM SP2 highly parallel system.

[LLG+92]   Daniel Lenoski, James Laudon, Kourosh Gharachorloo, Wolf-Dietrich Weber, Anoop Gupta, John Hennessy, Mark Horowitz, and Monica S. Lam. The stanford dash multiprocessor. *Computer*, pages 63–79, March 1992. Introduction to DASH, a Stanford University CS project in coupling multiple conventional SMPs into one great big coherent-memory NUMA SMP.

[LLJ+92]   Daniel Lenoski, James Laudon, Truman Joe, Luis Stevens, Anoop Gupta, and John Hennessy. The dash prototype: Implementation and performance. In *Proceedings of the Annual Symposium on Computer Architec-

ture, pages 92–103, April 1992. How the Stanford University DASH (in this case, capitalized) project is implemented, how much hardware it takes and how long memory accesses take. Pictures of circuit boards as well as technical data.

[LLJ⁺93]   Daniel Lenoski, James Laudon, Truman Joe, David Na-hahira, Luis Stevens, Anoop Gupta, and John Hennessy. The dash prototype: Logic overhead and performance. *IEEE Transactions on Parallel and Distributed Systems*, 4(1):41–61, January 1993. Stanford University DASH implementation in detail with lots of measurements of various shared-memory applications rewritten to run on the completed prototype.

[Llo92]   I. Lloyd. Oracle parallel server architecture. In *Proceedings of Super-Computing Europe 92*, pages 5–7, 1992. Description of Oracle's parallel database, the Oracle Parallel Server product. Unlike everybody else's approach, it uses the much-maligned, old-fashioned shared disk technique, which everybody else's paper feels obliged to trash. But Oracle Parallel Server is out there in many installations, working, while they're still in beta (as this is written).

[LO87]   Ewing Lusk and Ross Overbeek. *Portable Programs for Parallel Computers*. Holt, Rinehart and Winston, Inc., 1987. Many examples of portable parallel programming, focused on programming using the P4 system developed at Argonne National Laboratory, home location of the authors.

[Man93]   M. Morris Mano. *Computer System Architecture Third Edition*. Prentice Hall, Englewood Cliffs, NJ, 1993. Revered and heavily used textbook on computer architecture. Getting a bit dated in its emphases. I would prefer Hennessey and Patterson now.

[Mar94]   John Markoff. Bigger, faster hardly matters. *Austin American-Statesman (also NY Times)*, C1, C5, August 8, 1994. Newspaper article about the death of supercomputers, pointing out how they are dying with shrinking defense spending. Confuses Thinking Machines with a traditional supercomputer vendor, but otherwise makes good points.

[Mes94]   *MPI: A Message-Passing Interface Standard (Version 1),* May 1994. Message-Passing Interface Forum, available from the University of Tennessee, Knoxville, Tennessee. Multihundred-page, highly detailed, standard definition for the newly proposed standard for message-passing, created by an international *ad hoc* group called the Message Passing Interface Forum. This is the first version (not a draft) of the specification from which vendors will build their implementations of MPI.

[OHE94]   Robert Orfali, Dan Harkey, and Jeri Edwards. *Essential Client/Server Survival Guide.* Van Nostrand Reinhold, 115 Fifth Ave., New York, 1994. Join Zog the Martian on a fun-filled trip through the jungles and swamps of client-server computing. Stacks, NOSs, SQL, transactions, groupware, Lotus Notes, distributed system management and other assorted topics treated in a usefully light-hearted way. A very large amount of useful information is contained herein, and a spoonful of sugar helps the medicine go down.

[Ope93]   The Open Software Foundation. *Introduction to OSF DCE,* 1993. Prentice Hall, Englewood Cliffs, NJ. General high-level but technical introduction covering all of DCE's features and capabilities, with a glossary and a listing of all other DCE documentation.

[O+88]   John K. Ousterhout et al. The sprite network operating system. *Computer,* 21(2):23–26, February 1988. Description of the Sprite operating system developed at Stanford. This is a macrokernel system that distributes UNIX semantics across multiple workstations. Interesting file system caching at the workstation enhances response time significantly.

[PBG+85]   G. F. Pfister, W. C. Brantley, D. A. George, S. L. Harvey, W. J. Kleinfelder, K. P. McAuliffe, E. A. Melton, V. A. Norton, and J. Weiss. The research parallel processor prototype (rp3): Introduction and architecture. In *Proceedings of the 1985 International Conference on Parallel Processing,* pages 764–771, August 1985. Description of one of the typical highly parallel processing projects that sprang up in reaction to the Japanese Fifth Generation projects: Up to 512 processors, with a particularly interesting memory organization. (Well, I thought so anyway.)

[Pek92]   M. Fernin Pekergin. Parallel computing optimization in the apollo domain network. *IEEE Transactions on Software Engineering*, 18(5):296–303, April 1992. Description of the Apollo Domain distributed computing support system, one of the most influential, original distributed computing environments. Influenced Hewlett-Packard's work in this area.

[Pfi86]   Gregory F. Pfister. The ibm yorktown simulation engine. *Proceedings of the IEEE*, 74(6):11–24, June 1986. Description of a special-purpose, highly parallel computer for the simulation of computers. The machine architecture of that system is yet another brainchild of John Cocke, who invented the concept of RISC computer architecture.

[PN85]   Gregory F. Pfister and V. Alan Norton. "hot spot" contention and combining in multistage interconnection networks. *IEEE Transactions on Computers*, C-34(10):943–948, 1985. How to get in a huge pile of trouble if your intermachine communication is even 1% away from uniformly distributed.

[PP84]   Mark S. Papamaroos and Janak H. Patel. A low-overhead coherence solution for multiprocessors with private cache memories. In *Proceedings of the 11th Annual International Symposium on Computer Architecture*, pages 348–354. IEEE, June 1984. Original paper on the MESI cache coherence protocol (although it's not called that in this paper). This is the bus based cache coherence protocol that is one of the most commonly used.

[PW85]   Gerald Popek and B. J. Walker. *The LOCUS Distributed System Architecture*. MIT Press, Cambridge, MA, 1985. A description of the original, non-microkernel Locus system developed at UCLA. Provides a detailed description of how UNIX operating system semantics can be distributed across multiple machines.

[QD94]   Gregory Quick and Kelley Damore. Workstation arena feels growing heat of pentium. *Computer Reseller News*, page 1 & 317, July 25, 1994. Article about how Intel is specifically targeting the technical workstation market.

Now that Pentium has caught up sufficiently in floating-point performance, system designers are embedding 3-D graphics capabilities as the other thing needed to crack this arena.

[Ram]   Rambus Inc., 2465 Latham Street, Mountain View, CA USA. *Rambus Architectural Overview.* Rambus is a new kind of memory channel and DRAM memory chip interface that allows higher-performance memory access in general. This report and related information are available by ftp from rambus.com, in the /pub/doc/rambus directory.

[Ram93]   Rick Ramsey. *All About Administering NIS+.* Prentice Hall, Englewood Cliffs, NJ, 1993. NIS+ is Sun Microsystems' facility for easing the administration of distributed workstations. This book's title describes its contents well—a readable, administrator-oriented description of everything you ever wanted to know about how to use NIS+ to administer systems.

[Ras86]   R. F. Rashid. Threads of a new system. *Unix Review*, 4:37–49, August 1986. Description of the Mach microkernel operating system, developed at Carnegie-Mellon University, written by one of its primary architects. Mach is very possibly the most influential microkernel system ever developed, and the origin of the popularization of the term "microkernel."

[Ray86]   M. Raynal. *Algorithms for Mutual Exclusion.* MIT Press, Cambridge, MA, 1986. More ways to keep processors out of each other's shorts than you ever imagined could possibly exist.

[Rot92]   James Rothnie. Overview of the ksr1 computer system. Technical Research Report TR92020001, Kendall Square Research Corporation, Cambridge, MA, March 1992. Description of the KSR1 "ALLCACHE" machine architecture, a highly-parallel system with a unique approach to organizing memory: Everything's a cache; there are no absolute memory locations; the cache lines just get bigger and bigger. Company now defunct, apparently primarily for financial reasons, so this may be hard to get hold of directly.

[San90]   Mahadev Santayaraman. Scalable, secure, and highly available distributed file access. *Computer*, 23(5):9–21, May 1990. Description of the Andrew File System (AFS), a distributed file system developed at CMU to serve thousandss of users simultaneously. The Distributed File System (DFS) of the Open Software Foundation (OSF) Distributed Computing Environment (DCE) is based on AFS.

[SGDM94]   V. S. Sunderam, G. A. Geist, J. Dongarra, and R. Manchek. The pvm concurrent computing system: Evolution, experiences, and trends. Technical report, Oak Ridge National Laboratory, to appear. Good overview, performance data, and examples of use for PVM, the very popular portable parallel programming system.

[Sha91]   Jay Shah. *VAXclusters*. McGraw-Hill, Inc., New York, NY, 1991. A detailed description of how to work with, and on, Digital Equipment Corp.'s VAXClusters. Predates the change to Open VMS Clusters. Describes in minute detail how to configure and use the system.

[SJG92]   Per Stenstron, Truman Joe, and Anoop Gupta. Comparative performance evaluation of cache-coherent numa and coma architectures. In *Proceedings of the 19th International Symposium on Computer Architecture*, 1992. Compares NUMA, with page migration in software, to the KSR system (COMA), which moves all data around by using hardware. Comes to the conclusion that all that hardware doesn't help much, if at all. In my opinion, it's unclear that a fair comparison has been made; judge for yourself.

[SSCK93]   M. Swanson, L. Stoller, T. Critchlow, and R. Kessler. The design of the schizophrenic workstation system. In *Proceedings of the USENIX Mach Symposium*, April 1993. In terms of this book, these folks are building a campus-wide cluster system and have noticed in great detail that it must have multiple personalities.

[Ste93]   Guy L. Steele Jr. High performance fortran: Status report. *ACM SIGPLAN Notices*, 28(1):1–4, 1993. Current (11/93) status and readable, short description of High

Performance Fortran, extensions to FORTRAN making it not intrinsically impossible to automatically compile it to run in parallel on message-passing systems.

[S⁺85]   Ralph Sandberg et al. Design and implementation of the sun network file system. In *Proceedings of the Summer Usenix Conference*, pages 119–130, 1985. The original description of the original, *de facto* standard for UNIX, NFS distributed file system.

[Sun94a]   Sun Microsystems, Inc., Mountain View, CA. *New Sun Parallel Database Servers Deliver Leading Performance and Availability for Mission-Critical Applications*, October 1994. Announcement of the availability of the new SPARCcluster 1000 PDB and 2000 PDB systems, two- to (eventually) eight-way high-availability clusters. Initially these systems will run Oracle Parallel Server; eventually, they will run Sybase and Informix' parallel offerings.

[Sun94b]   Sun Microsystems, Inc., Mountain View, CA. *SPARC-cluster 1 Product Overview*, October 1994. General description, features, and specifications of Sun's cluster dedicated to providing NFS performance and higher availability. Little detail on how things like load balancing are actually accomplished.

[Tana]   Tandem Computers Incorporated. *NonStop Himalaya Range*. Document # CD0194-0993, order number 102603. Overview of Tandem's Himalaya series of computers, their top of the line at this time.

[Tanb]   Tandem Computers Incorporated. *TorusNet Interprocessor Connections*. Document # CD0194-0194. Overview of Tandem's Himalaya series of computers, with emphasis on the TorusNet interconnection topology.

[Tan92]   Andrew S. Tannenbaum. *Modern Operating Systems*. Prentice Hall, Englewood Cliffs, NJ, 1992. Really good book on operating systems. Reads like a novel. Basic issues, plus descriptions of classical UNIX, DOS, Mach, others, and a primary reference for Amoeba distributed OS.

[TBH82]   Philip C. Treleaven, David R. Brownbridge, and Richard P. Hopkins. Data-driven and demand-driven computer architecture. *Computing Surveys*, 14(1):93–

143, March 1982. Description and comparison of the dataflow and reduction programming (computational) models, two highly nonstandard ways to do computing that have been intensely popular in academic computer science programming theory circles.

[Thi91]   Greg Thiel. Locus operating system, a transparent system. *Computer Communications*, 14(6):336–346, July-August 1991. Description of Locus, a system developed at UCLA that distributes single-system UNIX semantics across multiple machines. The version described here did not localize the changes required, but rather made a huge number of small changes to a huge number of code modules. Brrr.

[Tra93a]   Transaction Processing Performance Council (TPC). *TPC Benchmark A Standard Specification, Revision 1.2*, March 1993. The Transaction Processing Performance Council, 777 North First St., Suite 600, San Jose, CA 95112, e-mail: shanley@cup.portal.com. The official definition of the TPC-A interactive-use benchmark. The TPC benchmarks are probably the most important commercial transaction processing benchmarks there are. It is the intention that this benchmark be phased out in favor of TPC-C.

[Tra93b]   Transaction Processing Performance Council (TPC). *TPC Benchmark B Standard Specification, Revision 1.2*, March 1993. The Transaction Processing Performance Council, 777 North First St., Suite 600, San Jose, CA 95112, e-mail: shanley@cup.portal.com. The official definition of the TPC-B batch-mode benchmark. The TPC benchmarks are probably the most important commercial transaction processing benchmarks there are. It is the intention that this benchmark be phased out in favor of TPC-C.

[Tra93c]   Transaction Processing Performance Council (TPC), *TPC Benchmark C Standard Specification, Revision 2.0*, October 1993. The Transaction Processing Performance Council, 777 N. First St., Suite 600, San Jose, CA 95112, e-mail: shanley@cup.portal.com. The official definition of the TPC-C benchmark, which contains a mixture of transaction types. The TPC benchmarks are probably the most important commercial transaction processing benchmarks there are. This is intended to be the successor to TPC-A and TPC-B.

[Tra94]   Transaction Processing Performance Council (TPC), François Raab, editor. *TPC Benchmark D Standard Specification, Working Draft 7.0 for Company & Public Review*, May 1994. The Transaction Processing Performance Council, 777 N. First St., Suite 600, San Jose, CA 95112, e-mail: shanley@cup.portal.com. Preliminary version of the definition of the TPC D benchmark, which is not yet final. It is intended to be a benchmark for decision-support, as opposed to transaction-processing operation. The TPC benchmarks are probably the most important commercial transaction processing benchmarks there are.

[TS87]   Charles P. Thacker and Lawrence C. Stewart. Firefly: A multiprocessor workstation. In *Proceedings of the Second International Conference on Architectural Support for Programming Languages and Operating Systems*, pages 164–172. ACM, June 1987. The Firefly cache coherence protocol, another popular, bus-based, snoopy cache coherence protocol developed at the now-defunct DEC Western Research Laboratory.

[vDR94]   Ronald van Driel and Daan Reuhman. The x station: A high-end workstation in disguise. *HP.Omni*, pages 22–25, August 1994. Description of the cluster used at Philips National Laboratory; users connect from X stations to the cluster nodes via ethernet switches. Locally developed software is used for login (xldb) and batch load balancing (SQS), as well as for cluster system administration (SOS).

[Vee86]   Arthur H. Veen. Dataflow machine architecture. *Computing Surveys*, 18(4):365–396, December 1986. One of the more recent surveys of all the various types of dataflow machines that have been proposed and built, including some chip-level parts available for purchase.

[Wal93]   David W. Walker. The design of a standard message passing interface for distributed memory concurrent computers. Technical Report ORNL/TM-12512. Oak Ridge National Laboratory, Oak Ridge, TN, 37831, October 1993. Compact, readable, general description of the currently-emerging standard interface for message-passing systems.

[WLH93]   Bruce J. Walker, Joel Lilienkamp, and Joe Hopfield. *Open Single System Image Software for the Multicomputer or MPP (Massively Parallel Processor).* Locus Computing Corporation, 9800 La Cienega Blvd., Ingelwood CA 90301-4400, 1993. Description of how Locus was applied to a UNIX personality server under the OSF/1 AD microkernel to achieve application transparency for the Intel Scientific Computing Corp.'s Paragon massively parallel machine.

[WP89]   B. Walker and J. Popek. Distributed unix transparency: Goals, benefits, and the tcf example. In *Winter 1989 Uniforum Conference Proceedings*, 1989. Description of the Locus distributed operating system, with the example of how it was embedded in UNIX-equivalents for the IBM S/370 and PS/2 as the Transparent Computing Facility (TCF). A very useful idea that did not sell well for a variety of reasons.

[ZR93]   Syrus Zial and Cheryl Ranson. Summit: A 1 giga-byte per second multiprocessor system bus. In *Symposium Record of Hot Interconnects '93*, pages 1.2.1–1.2.9. Stanford University, August 1993. Hewlett-Packard paper on how they built a system bus supporting 16 HP PA processors, type unspecified. Remarkable for its electrical engineering: inputs switch on the leading edge of the wavefront of the electrical signal. Unfortunately, the proceedings contains only the presentation transparencies, not a complete paper; much information is nevertheless contained here.

In Search of Clusters ✳

Index

distributed system 50, 69, 306, 339, 344, 352, 360
  anonymity of nodes 75
  client-server 76
  cluster as a node 77
  distinction from cluster 92
  file system 76, 273, 298
  heterogeneity 312, 352
  high-speed variation 353
  load balancing 78
  local autonomy 352
  name server 79
  node individualization 82
  node size 82
  number of nodes 82
  performance metric 81
  physical locations of nodes 75
  security 82
  three-tiered hierarchy 80
  tools 50, 51, 69, 76
distributed virtual memory layer of SSI 307
distributed virtual memory programming model 103, 249, 252, 307, 330, 336
diversity-loving people 88
DME 51, 296, 311, 312, 313
dog people 319
dogs 72
  obedience training 74
  pack 73
Dongarra, Jack 120
DQS 37
DRAM 114, 116, 117, 122, 130, 133, 152
  cost vs. SRAM 117
  nibble mode 123
  page mode 123
dropping the other shoe 59
DSA, Informix 38
dubbing machines as clusters 91, 92
Dynamic Random Access Memory, see DRAM
Dynamic Scalable Architecture, see Informix DSA

E

economic model 61
effort of parallelism justified 179
enclosed cluster 90–93, 95
Encore 30, 324
  reflective memory 100
enhanced standard litany 49, 93
  scavenging 91
enhanced Sysplex, see IBM Sysplex
equation, LaPlace 192
ES/9000 58
ESCON 34
  Directors 34
Ethernet 245
EUI 40
everybody's a liar marketing syndrome 318
execution context 263
Exemplar, Convex 69
expense of SRAM vs. DRAM 117
explicit parallel programming 182
exponential backoff 164
exposed cluster 90–93, 95
Express 39

F

failover for high availability 32, 43
false sharing 138, 249
Farm, the 20, 21, 24, 103
fast(er) memory 116
fault-tolerance in hardware 44
FCS 26, 36, 37, 46, 50, 63, 77, 92, 99, 245, 284, 333, 362
  enclosed cluster (privacy) 92
  Fibre Channel Initiative 64
FDDI 26, 29, 37, 99, 243
FermiLab 24
Fermilab 22, 24, 154
Fibre Channel Initiative 64
Fibre Channel Standard, see FCS
Fifth Generation Project 7
file server 77, 103, 261
file system 76, 176, 273, 298

HP 4, 13, 26, 43, 54, 122, 286, 324
  HP/UX operating system 42, 101,
    153
  OpenView 311
  T500 147
hyperplane scheme 220

I

I dub thee a cluster 91
I/O
  attachment of communication 98,
    99
  bandwidth 322, 333
  batch 176
  noncoherent in uniprocessor 167
  programming model 271
    global 271, 272, 277
    local 271, 273, 277
  shipping 77, 103, 273, 280, 281, 282,
    335
  SMPs 166
  see also communication
I/O-intensive workloads 103
  batch 104, 176
  OLTP 106
  query processing 105
IBM 4, 9, 13, 43, 54, 58, 183, 307, 324
  DB2 34
  DB2/6000 Parallel Edition 31, 38,
    77, 277
  ESCON Director 37
  The Farm 20, 21, 24, 103
  HACMP/6000 46, 79
  IMS 58, 277
  JES 34
  LoadLeveller 37, 38, 95
  MVS 269
  MVS/ESA 58
  NetView 311
  OS/2 153
  OS/2 for PowerPC 113
  POWER/4 100
  PowerPC 59
  RISC System/6000 54, 120, 148

Scalable Parallel systems 26, 74,
    245, 281
  stock price 54
  Stretch 7090 113
  Sysplex 34–36, 51, 99, 276
  Sysplex Coupling Facility 34, 37
  Sysplex Timer 34
  TCF 42, 95
  TPF 58
IEEE Futurebus 66
ILLIAC IV 7, 48, 247
IMS 34, 58, 277
inconsistent results 208
incremental growth 48
inertia of software 252, 259, 367
inferior algorithm use 5, 218
Informix 36
  DSA 31, 38, 277, 283
Ingres 31, 277
  global I/O programming
    model 272
input/output, see I/O
instruction, loads and stores 115
instructions executed out of
    order 162
Intel 4, 9, 59, 122
  P6 59, 60
  Paragon 42, 74, 245, 354
  Pentium 60
interactive workload 177
  login 177
interchangeable nodes 75
interconnect 63
  bandwidth compared with
    SMP 66
interconnection topology 233
interinstruction dependency 162
interleaving of memory 134
intermittent error 201, 208
International Business Machines
    Corporation, see IBM
internode bandwidth 105
internode security 82
IP address failover 79
iteration
  chaotic 234

About the Author

Dr. Gregory Pfister has been attempting to make parallel computer systems useful since 1969, when he noticed that nobody actually made good use of some hardware he had designed. This bothered him sufficiently to send him from computer hardware to software, and he has been oscillating between the two ever since. He is currently an IBM Senior Technical Staff Member in the IBM RISC System/6000 Division in Austin, Texas, working in the area of server system strategy. Born in Detroit, MI through a fluke of his father's World War II posting, he was soon moved to Long Island, NY, where he grew up. He received his S.B., S.M., and Ph.D. from MIT in 1967, 1969, and 1974, respectively. He has taught Computer Science as an Instructor at MIT and an Assistant Professor at the University of California at Berkeley; and he has worked in IBM development, research and corporate headquarters on computer graphics, parallel programming, highly parallel computer architectures, and clustered systems. In IBM Research he was Principal Scientist of the RP3 project, a research effort in highly parallel computing. He has been elected to Eta Kappa Nu, Tau Beta Pi, Sigma Xi, and Senior Membership in the Institute of Electrical and Electronic Engineers (IEEE), and has been a Distinguished Visitor of the IEEE Computer Society. He has six patents and an IBM Corporate Technical Recognition Award. His numerous published papers include two that received "best paper" awards at major technical conferences.